Children's Interests/Mothers' Rights

Children's Interests/ Mothers' Rights

The Shaping of America's

Child Care Policy

Sonya Michel

Yale University Press

New Haven and London

Publication of this work has been supported by a grant from the Oliver M. Dickerson Fund. The Fund was established by Mr. Dickerson (Ph.D., Illinois, 1906) to enable the publication of selected works in American history, designated by the executive committee of the Department of History of the University of Illinois at Urbana-Champaign.

Printed in the United States of America.

Library of Congress Cataloging-in-Publication Data

Michel, Sonya, 1942–
    Children's interests/mothers' rights : the shaping of America's child care policy / Sonya Michel.
      p. cm.
    Includes bibliographical references and index.
    ISBN 0-300-05951-5 (cloth : alk. paper)
    ISBN 0-300-08551-6 (pbk. : alk. paper)
    1. Child care—Government policy—United States—History.
  2. Child care services—United States—History. I. Title.
HQ778.63.M52   1999
362.71′2′0973—dc21   98-34830
                                       CIP

A catalogue record for this book is available from the British Library.

The paper in this book meets the guidelines for permanence and durability of the Committee on Production Guidelines for Book Longevity of the Council on Library Resources.

10 9 8 7 6 5 4 3 2

For my children
Joshua
Colin
Nadja

"Wait just a moment, Nettie, till mamma finishes this page," said Ruth, dipping her pen again into the old stone inkstand.
—Fanny Fern, *Ruth Hall*

Contents

Abbreviations

ABCC	Act for Better Child Care
ADC	Aid to Dependent Children
ADNNYC	Association of Day Nurseries of New York City
AFDC	Aid to Families with Dependent Children
ANA	American Nurses' Association
CB	U.S. Children's Bureau
CCDA	Comprehensive Child Development Act of 1971
CCDBG	Child Care and Development Block Grant of 1980
CCPA	Child Care Parents Association
CCPP	Child Care and Protection Program
CETA	Comprehensive Employment and Training Act
COS	Charity Organization Society
CWA	Congress of Women's Auxiliaries of the CIO
CWLA	Child Welfare League of America
DCC	Day Care Council of New York City
EMIC	Emergency Maternal and Infant Care
ENS	Emergency Nursery Schools
ESS	Extended School Services

FAP	Family Assistance Plan
FERA	Federal Emergency Relief Administration
FIDCR	Federal Inter-Agency Day Care Requirements
FWA	Federal Works Administration
GFWC	General Federation of Women's Clubs
HEW	U.S. Department of Health, Education, and Welfare
ICC	Inter-City Council for the Day Care of Children
ISS	Infant School Society
JPA	Juvenile Protective Agency of Chicago
NAACP	National Association for the Advancement of Colored People
NAC	National Advisory Committee on Emergency Nursery Schools
NACW	National Association of Colored Women
NADN	National Association of Day Nurseries
NANE	National Association for Nursery Education
NCCC	National Conference on Charities and Corrections
NCDCC	National Committee on the Day Care of Children
NCM	National Congress of Mothers
NCPE	National Council of Parent Education
NFDN	National Federation of Day Nurseries
NMC	National Manpower Council
NWP	National Woman's Party
OBRA	Omnibus Budget Reconciliation Act of 1981
OE	U.S. Office of Education
PCSW	President's Commission on the Status of Women
PRWOA	Personal Responsibility and Work Opportunity Act of 1996
SPCC	Society for the Prevention of Cruelty to Children
SSA	Social Security Administration
UPA	United Parents' Association
WB	U.S. Women's Bureau
WCTU	Women's Christian Temperance Union
WHC	White House Conference
WIN	Work Incentive Program
WPA	Works Progress Administration

Prologue

American mothers have invented many ways to care for their children while they work. Native Americans strapped newborns to cradle boards or carried them in woven slings. Colonial women placed small children in standing stools or go-gins to prevent them from falling into the fireplace. Pioneers on the midwestern plains laid infants in wooden boxes fastened to the beams of their plows. Southern dirt farmers tethered their runabouts to pegs driven into the soil at the edges of their fields. White Southern planters' wives watched African American boys and girls playing in the kitchen yard while their mothers toiled in the cotton fields. African American mothers sang white babies to sleep while their own little ones comforted themselves. Migrant laborers shaded infants in baby tents set in the midst of beet fields. Cannery workers put children to work beside them stringing beans and shelling peas. Shellfish processors sent toddlers to play on the docks, warning them not to go near the water.

Mothers have left children alone in cradles and cribs, and have locked them in tenement flats and cars parked in factory lots. They have taken them to parents, grandparents, co-madres, play mothers, neighbors, and strangers. They have sent them out to play with little mothers—siblings sometimes only a year or two older. They have enrolled them in summer camps and recreation programs, taken them to baby farms, given them up to orphanages and foster homes, and surrendered them for indenture. They have taken them to family day care providers and left them at home with babysitters, nannies, and nursemaids, some of them undocumented workers.

Mothers have taken infants and toddlers and preschoolers to places called Miss Moon's Nursery School, Floretta Wright's Kindergarten, Yehevath Beth Yehudah, St. Mark's Community Nursery, Guardian Angel, The Home for Little Wanderers, Cadillac Pre-School Cooperative Play Group, Casa Maria, Doctors' Wives' Cooperative Nursery, Wee Care, Tot Lot, Tot-Orium, Purple Circle, Tabernacle Day Nursery, Little Lamb, Kinder Cassel, Kiddie Kampus, Park-A-Tot, Little Bar None, The Little Red Schoolhouse of Hollywood, The Learning Tree, Modern Play, Community Pride, The Caring Place, Imagination Station, Mother's Morning Out, Kinder Care, Wheezles and Sneezles, Lilliputian, La Petite Academy . . .

Mothers have dropped off youngsters dressed in tatters, with smudged cheeks and stringy hair, and picked them up garbed in starched smocks, rosy-cheeked, smelling of soap. Children have been turned away because they had fevers or runny noses or lice; mothers have left their jobs in the middle of the day to pick up children with ear infections, chicken pox, temper tantrums. They have parted from offspring who were howling, whimpering, whispering in the corner with friends, and found them later giggling, hungry, cranky, half-asleep. They have walked out feeling guilty, sad, anxious, fearful, with their hearts in their mouths, without a care in the world.

Mothers have left babies dozing in carriages outside movie palaces, at department store day nurseries, and at parking services in bowling alleys and shopping malls. Some mothers have placed their children in the care of others and have never come back.

Children's Interests/Mothers' Rights

Introduction: Child Care and Social Citizenship for Women

In the United States today, most mothers of preschool and school-age children are gainfully employed.[1] Yet the nation has no comprehensive system of child care. Unlike many other democratic market societies, it has failed to develop universal, state-sponsored child care provisions.[2] Children from poor and low-income families are currently eligible for a limited number of federally subsidized child care slots, whereas middle- and upper-income families can take advantage of indirect support in the form of tax write-offs or pretax rebates for child care expenses. One purpose of this book is to discover why the United States has this peculiar distinction. That is, why, despite a long history of mothers entering the workforce accompanied by an equally long history of public concern over the welfare of children, does universal child care, organized and supported by the government, remain an elusive social good in the United States?

In societies where universal child care has been established, it tends to neutralize the discriminatory effect of motherhood on women, enabling them to pursue education and training and enter the labor force on a (relatively) equal footing with men, whether or not they have children.[3] Access to child care affords women a degree of economic independence that in turn empowers them within households and families or gives them the option of setting up households on their own.[4] It also assures them that their children are receiving adequate care, protection, and developmental encouragement.

For women in such societies, child care might be said to constitute part of what political theorist T. H. Marshall called "social citizenship." Marshall introduced this term in his famous 1950 essay "Citizenship and Social Class."[5] In market-based democracies, he pointed out, wage earning is essential if individuals are to avail themselves of their full political and civil rights; those who have only restricted access to economic participation are implicitly denied a portion of their rights as citizens. In her gloss of Marshall, political theorist Carole Pateman explains, "Citizens thrown into poverty lack both the means for self-respect and the means to be recognized by fellow citizens as of equal worth to themselves, a recognition basic to democracy. Poverty-stricken individuals are not and—unless the outcome of participation in the market is offset in some way, cannot be—full citizens."[6] The purpose of the modern welfare state is, in Marshall's view, to compensate for the inequalities of the market by providing the resources for social participation.[7]

Marshall did not have women in mind when he traced the evolution of modern citizenship and the emergence of the welfare state; his economically disenfranchised citizen, though "genderless," was implicitly figured as male. Thus Marshall did not consider the sorts of resources a *female* worker might need to achieve equality.[8] As Pateman and other feminist theorists have argued, the key to women's disadvantaged position in liberal polities and market economies lies in their cultural and social assignment to the family, specifically to the role of mother.[9]

Whether or not women actually become mothers, "compulsory motherhood," to vary a phrase by poet Adrienne Rich,[10] affects the way they are perceived and channeled within the employment market. Women either are or will become mothers (neither single women nor lesbians are exempt from this expectation any longer), and once they have children, they will, presumably, take primary responsibility for nurturing and rearing them. Unless adequate alternatives for a mother's care can be provided (for few women want to abandon the role entirely), women who are mothers cannot embark on educational or training programs or look for jobs, much less compete equally with men, even those who are fathers. To ensure equal citizenship, social rights for women must, therefore, take into account their assignment to motherhood.[11]

The issue of working mothers has turned up only rarely on the American political agenda, usually during periods of national crisis.[12] And when it has appeared, the discussion has been more likely to turn on children's need for care than on mothers' need to earn. Child welfare experts, government officials, and even day care advocates, have all expressed the concern that employment takes mothers out of the home, depriving children of care. Within this discourse, the presence of mothers in the workforce is presented not as a normal feature of advanced market economies but as a "social problem"; thus children's interests are implicitly positioned in opposition to women's rights.

Mothers have seen the matter of employment differently. Many have regarded financial support of their children as an essential part of their self-definition as parents.[13] To them, children's interests and mothers' rights are not irreconcilable but synonymous—and universal child care is essential to both.[14] Because wage-earning mothers have seldom mobilized as a group, however, children's advocates have readily assumed positions of relative authority, and it was their message that became hegemonic.

Historian Mary Frances Berry has argued that this deeply ingrained preference for "mother care" has prevented Americans from accepting the idea of public provision of child care.[15] I do not disagree with her, but in this book I show that this preference was not, as she implies, somehow endemic to Americans. Rather, it was reproduced, over and over again, as countless experts on childhood confronted the "problem" of what to do with the children of working women. Some accused mothers of child neglect, reporting them to authorities and in extreme cases threatening to remove their children. Others offered concrete help in the form of some type of child care, but under strictly limited conditions that fell short of establishing the basis for a permanent system of state-supported child care. Ironically, many of these experts were women; thus the failure of child care policy should not be attributed solely to a "male conspiracy" to keep women out of the labor force but also to a politics of maternalism which accepted the notion that mothers properly belonged at home with their children.[16]

Although the history of child care in America is one of rights withheld, it is also one of working mothers' efforts to find care for their children when formal or institutional services were unavailable. Using what I call "maternal invention," they constructed child care provisions from whatever resources were available. Sometimes they appropriated institutions intended for other purposes, such as orphanages or summer camps. At other times they relied on neighbors, hired caregivers or older siblings, or, as a last resort, left children alone at home or in the streets outside factories. Throughout this book, I attempt to recover and describe the myriad forms that child care has taken over many decades.

Because American child care has come in many forms, we must define it as broadly as possible in order to capture its full history. Simply put, it is the care of children by someone other than their parents, whether in an institution or in some sort of informal or domestic arrangement inside or outside the home. Over the years, child care has been called by many names. "Day care," the term used currently, came into vogue in the 1930s. I use the more generic "child care," but even this term cannot evoke the many institutions, programs, and private schemes that parents have used to care for their children while they worked.

The absence of public child care has not kept mothers out of the labor force, but it has meant that they were often compelled to take up employment under less than optimal conditions. By the same token, the very existence of child care has not, as many critics feared, driven mothers into the workforce, but it has helped to determine the types of occupations they entered, the kinds of work-places they found congenial, and their experiences as workers. The perennial shortage of child care in urban areas prompted many women to engage in industrial work that they could do in their homes,[17] whereas rural and migrant mothers turned to agricultural labor because of the possibility of bringing small children along with them.[18] Many issues—their anxiety or contentment concerning the arrangements they had made for their children, the proximity of the child care, the hours it was available—were on women's minds as they went to their jobs, influencing their performance in the workplace and shaping their identities and self-perceptions as mothers, wage-earners, and citizens.

Child care has changed over time. In the nineteenth and early twentieth centuries, there were infant schools, crèches, and finally those workhorses of Victorian philanthropy, day nurseries. This type of assistance was limited, however, by the small capacity, niggling requirements, and moralistic tone that characterized most nurseries. Many working-class mothers preferred to avoid running a daily gauntlet of starch and Scripture simply to obtain care for their offspring. To provide a true resource for working mothers—to be counted upon as a social right for every woman (just as public education has come to be considered a right for every citizen)—child care would have to rest on the broader financial and ideological shoulders of government. During the Progressive Era and especially during the New Deal, many of the social provisions that had originated in the nineteenth-century private sector became public responsibilities, first of the states and then of the federal government. These included assistance to the poor; care for orphans, the mentally ill, and the disabled; workmen's compensation; and old-age insurance.[19] Child care, however, did not become a permanent part of this expanding welfare state. During the Depression, some WPA-sponsored nursery schools were used as child care, but it was not until World War II that federally supported services became widely available, and those lasted only briefly. Efforts to retain these services in the postwar period met with spotty success.[20]

Starting in the mid-1950s, American child care began to take on a distinctive public-private pattern that has continued to the present. In 1954 Congress passed a child care tax deduction, which was converted into a tax credit in the 1970s and extended in the 1980s. These measures, presented as a means of enhancing "parent choice," mainly benefited middle- and upper-income families and spurred the growth of both voluntary and commercial services in the private sector. In the 1960s, federal funds for child care once more become available, but because they were linked to efforts to reduce dependency on welfare (by requiring mothers to find employment), eligibility was limited to poor and low-income families. This association between public child care and poverty reform—so redolent of nineteenth-century charity—precluded the possibility of developing a universal system despite repeated legislative efforts throughout the 1970s and 1980s. Instead, in 1988 and then again in 1996, the federal government expanded, and made more stringent, welfare policies that deployed public child care as a lever for mandatory work programs for poor mothers.

The history of American child care has multiple beginnings in both formal and informal arrangements. Philanthropic institutions first appeared in America as early as the 1790s, casual practices well before that. In taking up a subject like this, a historian could all too easily follow the trajectory of records through the voluntary organizations and government agencies that monopolized most of the financial support for child care and, through their official pronouncements, dominated discourses about child welfare and maternal employment for so many decades. Because wage-earning mothers rarely formed their own advocacy groups or set up regular programs, it is more difficult to gain access to their thinking or see what they accomplished. Often it is only by reconstructing what it was that elites *opposed* that we can discover what wage-earning mothers and their children actually *did*. Indeed, the history of child care is full of tensions between the daily practices of low-income, working-class, and minority families on the one hand, and white middle-class prescriptions for motherhood and social responsibility on the other. This history also reveals gaps between the intentions of planners and advocates and the actual administration of policy, as well as frequent subversions and appropriations by parents using policies and institutions for their own ends.

From the late eighteenth through the late nineteenth centuries, formal child care was carried out in benevolent institutions such as crèches and day nurseries, scattered across American cities. Until the 1890s, these operated more or less independently, although they shared a remarkably coherent sense of purpose, which was to prevent poor mothers from becoming "pauperized," or dependent upon relief, by helping them help themselves through wage earning. Notably, child care philanthropists did not endorse maternal employment in general—only in cases of family crisis. Whatever their ideology, the day nurseries of the nineteenth century were too few in number and their criteria for admission too restrictive to accommodate all the children who needed care. Instead, many wage-earning mothers relied on servants and kin, neighborhood networks, or independent child minders, sometimes disparagingly called "baby farmers." Some mothers, determining that their children were self-sufficient, left them to their own devices. It was practices such as these that reformers, including day nursery advocates, sought to correct. When leading child care philanthropists came together at the 1893 World's Columbian Exposition in Chicago, they launched a national movement to expand the number of day nurseries. But because of their elitist views, they never attempted to gain governmental support for universal provisions, and thus private child care services remained limited and stigmatized.

The history of child care in the twentieth century takes place on several terrains—within the voluntary sector and also at the level of local, state, and federal governments. Individual private institutions continued to operate both outside and within the interstices of the larger public structures, while wage-earning mothers went on making informal arrangements, both out of preference and to compensate for gaps in institutional provisions. As middle-class women began entering the workforce, they hired nursemaids or nannies, whereas for working-class children, child labor could serve double duty as child care. During the Depression and World War II, national need was perceived as sufficiently urgent to rationalize federal funding for nursery schools and then child care centers, but this patriotic consensus eroded in the postwar period, although maternal employment increased and the need for services continued, greater than ever.

It was not until the 1960s, with the establishment of President John F. Kennedy's Commission on the Status of Women and the birth of the women's movement, that Americans began to consider child care as a service not just for children or families in distress but for *women* in general. For a moment, the opposition between children's interests and mothers' rights dissipated; feminists in particular argued that the two should be seen as mutually inclusive. Since that time, women have made significant advances in the areas of civil and political rights (although these gains have not come easily and continue to be contested). But in the area of social rights, women remain stymied. Antifeminist backlash has represented child care and other aids to maternal employment as inimical to family life. Many contemporary advocates have, as a result, emphasized the links between child care and children's interests but avoided any association with women's rights out of a fear that it would only harm their cause.

Concern for family life seems to have gone by the wayside in the debates over welfare reform of the late 1980s and 1990s. Consensus formed rapidly around the idea that requiring poor mothers to enter the paid labor force would "end welfare as we know it." But the commitment to providing child care has been incommensurate; at one point House Speaker Newt Gingrich (Republican–Georgia) even proposed placing the children of poor single mothers in state-run orphanages—a cavalier rejection of both children's interests *and* mothers' rights.[21] The provisions for child care included in the Personal Responsibility and Work Opportunity Act of 1996 (PRWOA) are, according to most experts, woefully inadequate.

The history of child care in the United States partakes of several historiographies: those of women, families, children, labor, early childhood education, social welfare, and the welfare state. Yet in all these fields, there are curious disjunctures. Women's historians, for example, examine female participation in the labor force without asking how mothers dealt with their children while they were on the job. Historians of children and families detach child care from maternal employment and compartmentalize it (along with education and other aspects of children's lives outside the home) instead of conceptualizing both activities as an integral part of daily life. It is almost as though both mothers and children become different selves once they are outside the family—that their identities are somehow discontinuous. Yet both mothers' work and children's care outside (or inside) the home are intrinsically linked to each other and to the lived experience of families.

There is also a disjuncture between the history of child care and the history of education. Here gender bias, reinforced by age and class, comes into play, producing an intellectual hierarchy that favors higher education over early childhood education, colleges and universities over kindergartens and nursery schools. Even scholars of early childhood education tend to dismiss child care on the grounds that, until quite recently, it has been primarily "custodial," its practices far below the standards considered necessary for good development. Yet the tensions between early childhood education and child care, which persisted throughout the 1920s and 1930s, when both fields were seeking legitimation and authority, are instructive and require exploration.[22]

Yet another set of disjunctures lies in the history of social welfare and welfare-state development. Child care seldom appears in American social welfare history, but when it does, it is usually subsumed under the heading of "child welfare," a move that not only obscures its social and gender implications but reproduces the association between child care and poverty, thus losing its universal potential. Welfare history in general focuses on institutions, movements, ideologies, leaders, and professionals.[23] When applied to child care, this approach misses the non-institutional, informal arrangements that have constituted the bulk of child care for so many years, and it thus fails to acknowledge the role that working mothers have played in creating resources for themselves and their children. Social welfare historians, while acknowledging one of child care's goals—to serve children—overlook the other—to allow parents (usually mothers) to engage in nonparental activities such as education, vocational training, or, most often, gainful employment. However, the artificial division between social welfare history and women's history has prevented scholars from drawing connections between child care provision and mothers' economic and social status.

In the related field of American welfare-state development, child care has also remained a minor theme. One reason is that for many years child care shared the fate of other policies affecting women: it was ignored by scholars who did not take gender into account. These scholars defined "the welfare state" in terms of policies like workmen's compensation and old-age pensions, which were conceived as benefits for men, rather than mothers' pensions and maternal and infant health care, which served women. Several studies have now challenged these definitions and begun to analyze the establishment and administration of "woman-friendly" provisions, both separately and in conjunction with those targeted toward men, within a gendered framework.[24]

Historians and other social scientists concerned with gender and social policy have also introduced these concerns into the comparative study of welfare states, and here the history of American child care raises an interesting set of issues. The link between public provisions and poverty running throughout that history is characteristic of the "residual," "liberal," or "public-private" type of modern welfare state, of which the United States has been identified as a prime example.[25] In such states, it is assumed that citizens will provide for their own needs through employment; the government steps in only in the event of family breakdown or loss of employment. At the same time, through tax credits, subsidies, and other incentives to both individuals and businesses, the state encourages the development of child care and other services in the private sector, where access is controlled either through employment, in the case of employer-sponsored benefits, or through the market.[26] With regard to child care, the distribution of provisions through this system is highly uneven. Given occupational segregation, American women seldom earn enough to afford high-quality child care, nor does the market yield a steady supply of services. Yet, in keeping with the "residual" pattern, the federal government makes provision only for the very poorest families, currently, recipients of public assistance who are being shifted "from welfare to work."

Comparative analysis reveals that the United States has, at least since the 1980s, lagged behind other democratic market societies in the creation of universal child care as well as most of the other types of social programs that facilitate women's employment and enhance their socioeconomic status.[27] One might argue that, given the nature of the American welfare state, such an outcome is entirely predictable. But this reasoning begs several historical questions: How did such a state, and such a limited system of child care, develop? How much weight should be given to such factors as general attitudes toward state provision and the expansion of government, and how much to the specific values and assumptions surrounding appropriate gender roles and children's needs? And finally, to what extent is the American child care system not simply a *product* of the American welfare state but a *constituent* of it? This book addresses these issues.

As a comparative analysis suggests, the unique history of child care in the United States has significant implications for American women today. The warped and limited development of public provisions, culminating in the Personal Responsibility and Work Opportunity Act, has compelled most American wage-earning mothers to seek private alternatives. Some mothers of preschool children have turned to employer-supported services, while others make arrangements with relatives or neighbors, hire nannies or babysitters to care for children at home, or place them with family providers or in voluntary or for-profit child care centers. They may send older children to after-school programs run by public schools, voluntary agencies, or commercial enterprises.

The division between public and private (whether for-profit or voluntary) child care has prevented the population of wage-earning mothers (and, increasingly, fathers with primary responsibility for children) from forming a solid constituency to claim universal provisions. Parents are separated not only by firmly held preferences and patterns of utilization but also by cleavages of race, ethnicity, and class lying just below the surface of these expressed preferences.[28] Such divisions widened during the 1980s, as the Reagan administration reduced funding for public provisions while encouraging the development of private services through substantial tax breaks to employers, commercial providers, and individual taxpayers. The PRWOA increases federal support for child care but at the same time reinforces the link between public services and the poor. Moreover, members of Congress believe that they have resolved the child care issue for the nonce, effectively closing the door to federal subsidies for universal provisions in the foreseeable future.

Thus, on the cusp of the twenty-first century, U.S. child care policy appears to have returned to its nineteenth-century roots in poverty reform. Without state guarantees and subsidies for universal child care provisions, neither women's right to employment nor children's entitlement to a secure, nurturing, and developmentally sound environment—whether or not their mothers work outside the home—can be assured. And both are essential components of social citizenship for women.

Chapter 1 The Multiple
Origins of American Child Care

In child care circles, apocryphal stories abound concerning the "first day nursery" or the "first day care center." One account locates the origins of American child care in Philadelphia in 1863, another in New York City in 1854, a third in Troy, New York, in 1858.[1] These are rich but slippery historical documents because of their guileless blend of fantasy and fact, and like many stories of the origins of an organization or movement, they are self-serving. While offering some insight into the historical events they purport to describe, they more fully illuminate the subsequent phases of the history of child care during which they appeared.

Consider these two examples, one written during the Progressive Era, the other at the end of the post–World War II period. The first anecdote comes from an official history of day care compiled around 1909 by the Federation of Day Nurseries of New York City:

> In November 1863 at a time when the strain of war was great, there was started in a small house in a retired street of Philadelphia, the first Day Nursery in America. Its origin was the outcome of a visit to Paris, paid by Miss. Hanna Biddle. While there, being impressed by the charitable work

of "La Crèche" she conceived the idea of instituting something similar to it in Philadelphia. It had been her custom with others to visit the children [of the poor] in their homes, where they frequently found them locked into rooms alone, and occasionally they would only see them through a window in the hall. Miss. Biddle was profoundly touched by the lonely condition of these young children thus left unprotected during the day while their mothers were out working, the men at war—some never to return. Never was there a time when the need for such a charity was greater or more evident. Miss Biddle saw this, and was moved to pity for these forlorn children, either shut up in their rooms, or allowed to wander about the streets without suitable food, and completely demoralized. . . . Miss. Biddle thought of the Crèche she had seen in Paris, and felt, that this was the best way to brighten the lives of these children. She at once formed her plans for the amelioration of these conditions. She invited twelve ladies to cooperate with her in forming a Board of Managers.[2]

In 1960, Elinor Guggenheimer, president of the National Committee for the Day Care of Children, told this story at a national conference on day care in Washington, D.C.:

Back in 1854, Mrs. Cornelius Du Bois, young, attractive, well taken care of by an indulgent husband, was riding in her carriage through the streets of [the] Lower East Side of New York one afternoon. The carriage halted to avoid running into some children playing on the street, and as the noise of the wheels ceased she thought she heard the thin, high cry of—it could have been a puppy or a kitten—or perhaps a very young child. Despite the efforts of her coachman to dissuade her, she entered a dark and evil smelling room where there was one lumpy bed—and lying in a carton next to the bed was an infant—half starved, half dead. Mrs. Du Bois was a woman who cared and a woman who could be indignant. She discovered that in this part of the city there were many, many women who were forced to work in order to survive, and that their children were often left alone for the nightmare long working day. In what has become the most effective method of getting things done, she proceeded to go home and nag her husband and her friends—and her friends' husbands until they responded from sheer exhaustion. The result was the Infant and Child's Hospital—the first crèche or day care center in this country.[3]

Although these stories contradict one another, they also have something in common. They are infused with the combination of noblesse oblige, pity, and sense of women's particular responsibility for children that has come to be called "sentimental maternalism."[4] In both accounts, the shock of discovery moves upper-class women to action, each in her characteristic way. For Biddle, a single woman from a venerable and wealthy Philadelphia Quaker family who has already dedicated her life to public service, awareness of the children's plight dawns gradually, during the course of routine "friendly visiting." But it is the French crèche (which she has seen during a European tour evidently devoted to research as well as pleasure) that gives her the idea for a solution. Following the custom for women of her station, Biddle turns to her female network to help found and manage her charity. Du Bois, the seemingly indolent, pampered pet of a wife, also becomes activated while visiting a poor neighborhood, although her motives initially seem more voyeuristic than philanthropic.[5] She, too, uses a network of women, not to run the charity itself but to reach the wealthy men, including her own husband, who can support it.

Both Biddle and Du Bois seek to rescue poor children from starvation and loneliness by establishing institutions to care for them. Notable by their absence, however, are the parents of the children. In 1863, the fathers are presumably off at war; in the 1854 scenario, they are not mentioned at all. Both accounts concede that the mothers are forced to work in order to survive, but they also implicitly indict these women for leaving their children neglected and forlorn. With the formation of the charitable day nursery, a dyad is created between benefactress and child that, in effect, excludes the mother. The nursery will ostensibly benefit mothers as well as children. Yet, it is the day nursery reformer who first defines the child's plight as a social problem, devises the solution, and will mete out services in the future.

These two accounts, while tracing the origins of child care to the nineteenth century, display patterns that characterize the dynamics of the child care movement throughout its history. Both tell stories of individual acts of benevolence that create private philanthropies rather than political initiatives that result in public provision. Both focus on institutions organized by middle and upper-class women rather than on informal arrangements devised by wage-earning women themselves. And both are concerned primarily with the well-being of children—children's interests—rather than the prerogatives of women—women's rights.

Finally, both accounts reveal a great deal about the ongoing struggle for child care in the specific periods in which they were written. It is not surprising that an anecdote recounted in 1909 would stress the sense of maternalist noblesse oblige and the international influences that surrounded the origins of child care, for these were prominent features of women's reform efforts during the Progressive Era.[6] The author of this brief history was apparently seeking to link her organization, the National Federation of Day Nurseries, to the broader women's movement of her day.

Elinor Guggenheimer had a different purpose in recounting Mrs. Du Bois's personal campaign to create a day nursery in New York City. She wanted to demonstrate how "fanaticism" like Du Bois's (which she implicitly likened to her own approach) could eventually achieve results. As she described them, Du Bois's tactics of nagging and cajoling seem far less dignified and purposeful than Biddle's methods, but perhaps Guggenheimer felt that an audience of women tutored by *The Honeymooners* and *I Love Lucy* would feel empowered by Du Bois's success. What is striking about Guggenheimer's speech is that more than a century after the founding of the Infant and Child's Hospital, after decades of women's activism in both the public and private sectors, a leading advocate would still feel compelled to call for acts of individual heroism to strengthen the cause of child care.[7]

A SLIPPERY SUBJECT

Although these accounts are evocative, neither is accurate in a strict historical sense, for any attempt to fix the origins of American child care exactly is bound to be futile. Not only do such efforts come up against competing stories, but they must also grapple with the problem of defining a phenomenon that defies specification. Child care began in crèches, day nurseries, and day care centers; in institutions designed for other purposes, including nursery schools and kindergartens, orphanages, shelters, refuges, workhouses, and houses of industry; and as informal care by neighbors, relatives, and other children. Although we might be able to identify one particular day care institution as the first (according to *my* research, it was the nursery at the Philadelphia House of Industry, founded in 1798), in fact the practice of child care had multiple and staggered origins, going back to colonial America and before that to early modern Europe.[8]

In seventeenth- and early eighteenth-century America—that is, before the industrial revolution—white women were nominally responsible for their own children, at least up to about age six, but child rearing was not the exclusive or all-encompassing concern for mothers that it was to become from the late eighteenth century onward. Early American mothers combined child-rearing activities with dozens of other household chores, including production for family consumption, exchange, or the market. Following European custom, they swaddled infants to immobilize and protect them and simplify their care. As historian Karin Calvert notes, "the swaddled baby, like a little turtle in its shell, could be looked after by another, only slightly older child without too much fear of injury . . . [and] could be laid anywhere—on a bed, table, or shelf, on the ground in the field, or even hung from a peg for safekeeping."9 For toddlers, colonial Americans had several devices, including standing stools (fig. 1.1), hanging swings, walking stools (also called walking cages or go-carts), gogins, and cradle settees, all designed to hold small children and keep them out of harm's way (fig. 1.2).10 But it is evident from the frequency of childhood accidents—instances of children falling into wells or being burned by hot coals—that these devices were not foolproof and that household production sometimes took precedence over child care.11

For somewhat older children, New England mothers turned to local dame schools, which fulfilled child care functions as well as, if not better than, their putative educational aims. Begun as early as 1673 and fairly numerous by the late seventeenth century, dame schools could be rather makeshift arrangements. Widows or housewives often ran them in their own homes, looking after domestic responsibilities while offering rudimentary instruction in reading, writing, and arithmetic. Because fees were so low (usually only a few pence per week for each child), many teachers carried out other remunerative work at the same time.12 A mother of four who "kept school" in Northfield, Massachusetts, also sewed shirts for Native Americans at eight pence each and breeches for the colonial militia at one shilling six pence per pair.13 Another, who ran a school in her kitchen, spun flax while she sang hymns to her pupils.

The ages of the pupils varied. In Boston dame schools, children had to be between four and seven years old, but outside the city they could begin as early as two or even younger, "almost the only conditions being that they could stand up and keep their places."14 Sometimes even this requirement was waived; in her memoir of nineteenth-century life, Lucy Larcom recalled that at "Aunt Hannah's" establishment in Beverly, Massachusetts, "If a baby's head nodded, a little bed was made for it on a soft 'comforter' in the corner, where it had its nap out undisturbed."15

The quality of instruction was also uneven. One former student who attended dame schools in Boston around 1825 recalled that they were "very shabby. . . . They were kept, not taught, by elderly or middle-aged dames who dozed in their chairs, took snuff, drank tea, and often something stronger from a bottle stowed away in the cupboard."16 It is not surprising that New England girls, whose years in dame schools sometimes constituted their only formal education, had high rates of illiteracy. But according to Larcom, who began school at the age of two, dame schools were not really expected to educate: "The mothers of those large families had to resort to some means of keeping their little ones out of mischief, while they attended to their domestic duties. Not

Fig. 1.1. Wooden standing stools or baby tenders kept young children safe while other household members were busy with their daily tasks; toddlers learned to stand by pulling themselves up on the slats. This one provided a seat, but others gave the child no alternative but to remain standing. Old Sturbridge Village photo by Henry E. Peach.

much more than that sort of temporary guardianship was expected of the good dame who had us in charge."[17]

If no dame school was available or if a mother could not afford it, she might rely on community, kin, or servants for child care, or use older children to look after younger ones. No one would have questioned or criticized these women for shifting some of the responsibility for children to others, for throughout this period European American families valued women's productive labor at least as highly as their child-rearing functions and were willing to make tradeoffs for the benefit of the family's economy.

IDEOLOGY AND INDUSTRY

From the mid- to late eighteenth century, depending on the region, two factors transformed women's relationship to child care and domestic industry. One was economic: the growth of the market and the advent of the putting-out system[18] dramatically altered the structures of domestic manufacturing, making it more difficult for women to participate. The other was ideological: Americans began to place unprecedented emphasis on women's role in child rearing. Mutually reinforcing, these two factors discouraged mothers from working for wages and underscored their association with home and family.

The market grew throughout the eighteenth century, but it was not until after the American Revolution that merchant capitalism became a dominant

Fig. 1.2. From left to right: a swing
chair, a go-gin, a hollowed-out cylinder,
and a walking stool or go-cart. These
devices, like standing stools, were used to
hold children while adults were
otherwise occupied. All could be made
by the householder using simple
instructions. From J. C. Loudon,
*Encyclopedia of Cottage, Farm, and Villa
Architecture* (London: 1830), 351;
courtesy of the Rare Book Room,
University of Illinois at Urbana-
Champaign Library.

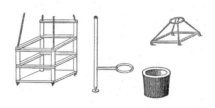

force. In agriculture, this had the effect of stimulating demand for such products as butter and cheese, which were now brought into urban areas and sold for
cash instead of being bartered locally.[19] Domestic production of such items as
shoes and textiles changed as independent artisans (usually the male heads of
producing households) came to rely on storekeepers to supply raw materials
and returned finished goods in exchange for cash or credit.[20]

For both women and men, the encroachment of the market, and particularly
the putting-out system, meant that they had less control over the nature and
pace of their own work. Men watched their proprietary sense of artisanship
eroding, while women lost the opportunity to combine market and domestic
labor as easily as they once had. In the early New England shoe industry, for
example, when the entire manufacturing process occurred within the household, women were able to contribute by working in their own kitchens, alternating shoe binding with homemaking tasks, including child care. But, historian Mary Blewett explains, as shoemakers strove to meet external quotas set by
merchant capitalists, the bulk of production shifted to "ten-footers," small
factories where the shoemaker and *his* apprentices worked together on almost
all phases of the manufacturing process. For the specific task of sewing uppers,
however, they still depended on women, who, in turn, had to maintain the pace
of the shop. As Blewett puts it, "The kitchen was transformed into a workplace
where external demands from the ten footer shaped both time and tasks."[21] If
the number of shoes to be bound was very large or the time very short, a mother
with small children and other household duties might not be able to keep up

and the task would have to be assigned to other workers. Women's rates of production—and their wage-earning ability—rose and fell with the number and ages of their children.[22]

The housewives whom Blewett examines seem to have had the option of turning down waged labor when it conflicted too greatly with their domestic responsibilities; perhaps they could afford to do so because their husbands, with the help of their apprentices, were prospering. The fact that women received far lower rates than men for their part in shoe production meant, ironically, that their wages would be less sorely missed.[23] Not all wage-earning mothers, however, had the option of abandoning waged work when the demands of child care became too great.

Late colonial and early Republican ideologies also encouraged mothers to eschew manufacturing. With the pre-Revolutionary growth of the market, according to historian Jeanne Boydston, the gap between the "economic" and "non-economic" spheres of society began to widen; women, of course, were identified closely with the second sphere. The Revolution temporarily renewed the value of women's contributions to the economy, but in the postwar period the decoupling of women and the formal cash economy resumed, accelerated by images of "Republican motherhood" and the "moral mother."[24] While the first image valorized child rearing as a vital contribution to the new nation, the second carved out a unique role for women as child rearers because of their innate spiritual qualities. Together, these prescriptions made it difficult for mothers to defend the use of surrogates, such as servants, to care for their children, except in extreme circumstances.[25]

The new domestic ideologies also obscured the fact that not all mothers were in a position to devote themselves fully to child rearing; many were also compelled to work at wage-earning tasks, either during times of crisis or on a more or less permanent basis. Those who were single, widowed, or deserted might be the sole breadwinners in their families, but even those with working husbands and/or children might not be able to get by on the family's collective income. These women had two choices: they could apply for poor relief from local authorities, either public or private, or they could seek waged employment. Either course had significant drawbacks in terms of their ability to keep and care for their children.

Over the course of the eighteenth century, poverty had become a permanent feature of the American landscape, and reformers noted that chief among its victims were women, particularly mothers of small children who had been left without male providers due to war, disease, or other circumstances beyond their control. From the earliest colonial days, local governments had provided for the poor, either by assigning paupers to specific townspeople, auctioning them off for keeping to the lowest bidder, or giving outdoor relief—monetary and material donations that would enable the poor to sustain themselves in their own homes. As the number of paupers grew, overseers of the poor deemed these arrangements impracticable, ineffective, and expensive, shifting instead to indoor relief—incarceration in a workhouse or almshouse. In applying for relief, mothers risked being separated from their children. At best they might be assigned to different boarding arrangements or institutions; at worst, children—some as young as five or six—might be "bound out" as indentured servants or workers.[26]

By the late eighteenth century, indenture had become a favorite cost-cutting measure among poverty officials. It not only freed institutions and guardians of the poor from further financial responsibility for a child but also fit reformers' belief that learning a useful trade would inoculate an individual against future pauperism. The shift in welfare practice also illustrated the malleability of definitions of children's interests—the slippage between calling for child protection on the one hand and condoning child labor on the other.[27]

If women turned to employment rather than poverty relief, other risks and inequities awaited them. Reformers implied that mothers who were willing to leave their children and go out to work were somehow "unnatural." The famous Philadelphia pamphleteer Mathew Carey claimed that many women could not do paid housework because "maternal tenderness" would not permit them to be separated from their children.[28] At the same time, however, he noted that wages for women were generally inadequate. Prerogatives of skill and custom limited the occupations open to women, and wages for "women's work" were far lower than for men's, seldom enough to support a family even at bare subsistence level.[29] "Crowding" kept wages down in the few occupations open to women. Carey estimated that in the Philadelphia area some 5,000–6,000 women depended on needlework for support—about one-third of them widows with small children. In one year's time, 1,100 women applied to the charitable Provident Society for work.[30] According to *The Ladies' Magazine* in 1830, "Many destitute widows are now suffering for the common necessaries of life, because they cannot obtain work, or a fair compensation for their work."[31]

Economic historian Claudia Goldin has found that women's earnings for agricultural employment were slightly less than 29 percent of men's in 1815, and in manufacturing, they ranged from about 30–37 percent of men's in 1820 to 44 percent in 1832 to 46–50 percent in 1850.[32] Thus if women could find regular jobs, they had to work for many hours just to come close to earning enough to support themselves and any dependents.[33] This meant being away from their children for long stints. If they had to resort to scavenging, begging, or street vending, this activity also took them out of the house and into the streets.[34] Even if mothers had factory outwork to complete at home, it paid so poorly that they could spare little time for their children if they were to earn an adequate wage.

It was in these situations that laboring women turned to "maternal invention." Many poor families shared quarters with one another, primarily to economize on rent but perhaps also to alleviate the burden of child care.[35] Otherwise, mothers left children with neighbors or "little mothers" (their own older children); sent youngsters out into the streets to peddle or scavenge; or, at worst, locked them up alone, in as protected an environment as possible. As Jeanne Boydston notes, "in the laboring poor and working classes, as in the middle class, women were primarily responsible for child care. Rarely were they able to accomplish this to the satisfaction of middle-class reformers—or perhaps to their own satisfaction."[36]

In the minds of laboring women, distinctions between work, play, and child care were blurred. They did not seem to conceptualize their own children, at least those who had outgrown infancy, as a fully distinct class of beings, either separate from or totally physically and emotionally dependent upon themselves. For this reason, they made informal arrangements for their children as best they could, but evidently it did not occur to them to try to structure collective solutions on their own or to turn to public or philanthropic bodies for help with child care.

"THE VERY FIRST"

Indeed, the earliest institutional child care came about at the behest not of working mothers but of charitable reformers. It took the form of a nursery created as part of the Philadelphia House of Industry, which was founded in 1798 by the Female Society for the Relief and Employment of the Poor. The House of Industry represented something of a departure from other charities of this period. Its founders, a group of female Quaker philanthropists, sought to counter the practice of family breakup—placing poor widows or other solo mothers in the almshouse and binding out their children or sending them to an orphanage—by offering such women the means to support themselves *and* keep their children with them.[37]

The nursery was an offshoot of a spinning room that the benevolent women had set up to provide employment for widows of victims of the 1793 yellow fever epidemic—women who, "unused to labor, were suddenly compelled to provide."[38] Prior to bringing these widows into the spinning room, the Quakers had treated them with the typical methods of "outdoor relief," visiting their poor sisters where they lived and distributing material goods and "given-out work"—spinning to be done at home. Observing that the women's industry was hampered by "the smallness of their rooms, want of fuel, and embarrassment of their children,"[39] the philanthropists decided to bring them under one roof, where they could be fed, warmed, and supervised more economically and efficiently—and where their children could be cared for separately.

This was not the first time philanthropists had set up a workroom for impoverished widows. In 1753 Boston's city fathers established a Linnen Manufactory House for this purpose, but it failed after about five years because productivity levels never rose to the point where the factory could be self-sustaining.[40] The Philadelphia workroom succeeded where the Boston one had failed because the women who managed it understood that their employees could not work productively if they had to care for their children at the same time. The once-genteel recipients of their charity, "unused to labor," had to be trained in proper work habits, which included surrendering their children to be cared for by others. "The Rules of the House," which were posted prominently and read aloud at least once a week, stated: "Those women who bring children shall leave them in the room appropriated to them, under charge of the Nurse, who will take good care of them. The children must not be admitted into the working room, neither shall the parents visit the nursery oftener than is necessary."[41]

As this document reveals, the Committee of Managers anticipated that the mothers might be apprehensive about giving over the care of their children to strangers and sought to reassure them, but at the same time the managers wanted to assert their own authority and instill discipline. Though mindful of their employees' maternal affection, they would not allow it to interfere with production; the mothers who came to their workroom had to give up the preindustrial practice of repeatedly interrupting their sewing or spinning to attend to the wants of their children and instead adopt the steady rhythm of the modern factory.[42]

The managers understood that in providing care for the children they had an opportunity as well as a responsibility. Unlike the male Overseers of the Poor in Philadelphia and elsewhere, these women did not believe that the best course for the families they were helping was to indenture children as quickly as possible.[43] Nor did they want to set children to labor in their own workrooms. Rather, they conceived of the children of the poor as they did their own offspring, not as "miniature adults" but as individuals passing through a distinct stage of life. All children required nurturance, protection, instruction, and time and space in which to develop fully before taking on the responsibilities of adulthood.[44]

The managers' understanding of children, while fundamentally democratic, was nonetheless inflected by class. All children were highly malleable, for either good or evil purposes, but the children of the poor were especially vulnerable to negative influences. Therefore it was crucial to reach them at an early stage and shape them properly. The nursery could be used to inculcate habits and virtues that would prevent them from following their parents down the path to poverty. One of the "Thoughts for the House" stated: "It is seen in children as in others that the more any bad way is indulged, the more it grows. The longer right training is delayed, the harder it will be to bring the child into right training. Begin early to implant, through Divine help, that which is good in the mind, and fruit may assuredly be hoped for in due season."[45]

At first, care of the children was given over to several elderly women who were deemed no longer "capable of laborious employment," but later a matron was hired expressly for this purpose, the elderly women probably finding it difficult to establish strict discipline among the children. There are few data on what occurred in the nursery; presumably, the caretakers or matrons attempted to catechize the children, keep them clean, and maintain a semblance of quiet and order—no small task when dealing with a roomful of toddlers made rambunctious by meals of sugared cocoa and bread or "indian mush sweetened . . . with two table spoonfulls of molasses."[46]

Around 1850 some of the younger women managing the house, perhaps familiar with the ideas of Swiss early-childhood educator Johann Pestalozzi or works on child rearing by American evangelicals—such as Horace Bushnell's *Views of Christian Nurture* (1848)—recognized that the younger children required "amusement rather than instruction" and began to take turns working with the little ones.[47] While still adhering to its goal of trying to reform the adult poor and prevent their children from becoming indolent and intemperate, the House of Industry began to incorporate more flexible notions of child care and early childhood education into its approach.[48]

The Committee of Managers reinforced its influence on the children by sustaining a relationship with them after they had left the nursery. School-age children whose mothers were employed in the workrooms came to the House of Industry for dinner at midday, and before and after school. Indeed, long-term, comprehensive service to children—to entire families, really—became the typical practice in day nurseries until they became more specialized and self-conscious in the early twentieth century.

Though demanding and invasive in its discipline, the House of Industry attracted a large clientele. Even after moving several times into more spacious quarters, it could seldom accommodate the many applicants for the workroom. One reason for its popularity was the material relief women received, for the Female Society took a broad view of their needs. In addition to feeding the women, keeping them warm, and caring for their children while they worked, the committee annually provided all mothers and children with "a stout pair of shoes," "spectacles if needed," and from time to time, clothing, food, and fuel as well. But probably more important was the fact that the society allowed women a greater degree of autonomy than did the Philadelphia Almshouse, which, at least for some, was their only alternative.[49] The almshouse made incarceration and potential separation from their children conditions of receiving relief, while the House of Industry allowed women to live at home with their children.[50]

It should be noted, however, that work at the House of Industry could not in itself support a mother with several dependent children. Open for only four to six months a year, the House did not provide steady employment, and its wage rates were even lower than the market rates for slopwork (the least skilled and most readily available type of waged sewing job). The committee gave their employees no choice as to the type of tasks they were to do or how much they would be paid.[51] Even if mothers labored full time during the entire period when work was available, they could never earn enough to support their families fully. To ensure their survival, poor mothers alternated stints at the House of Industry with periods of voluntary incarceration in the Philadelphia Almshouse. There, however, little work was offered, and the pay was even worse.[52]

The average annual income of an employee at the House of Industry ranged from $5.81 in 1840 to $18.17 in 1888 (table 1.1). To get some sense of the buying power of these wages, we can compare the 1840 figure to a family budget calculated by Mathew Carey in 1836.[53] According to his figures, a woman with two children required a minimum income of $133.60 per year (fig. 1.3).[54] Assuming that the House of Industry covered certain expenses in kind—say, the entire cost of clothing and shoes, and, as a generous estimate,

Table 1.1
Employees, Children, and Average Wages at the House of Industry,
Philadelphia, 1840–1888

Year	No. of Women Employed	No. of Children in House	Average Annual Wage[a] ($)
1840	80	"many"	5.81
1850	122	42	3.65
1860	131	57	7.75
1870	118	36	13.19
1888[b]	93	43[c]	18.17

Source: Annual Reports of the Female Society for the Relief and Employment of the Poor,
Philadelphia, 1840–1888.
[a]The house was open, on average, only four to six months per year.
[b]Year closest to 1890 for which data is available.
[c]Includes 16 older children who came only "to dinner."

one-third to one-half of the annual expense for fuel, food, and drink—a mother employed at the House could reduce her annual need for cash to somewhere between $60 and $75. If she earned only $5.81 in the workroom during the months it was open, that would leave a minimum of just over $54 to be earned during the remaining six to eight months of the year. With the market rate for slopwork running at 18¾ cents per day, she could earn only about $24 during this period (assuming that she took only Sundays off and was able to find employment every other day), leaving a minimum deficit of $30. This was less than the deficit of $84.66 confronting Carey's hypothetical mother, but even so, we must ask what a woman with two or three dependent children would do when faced with a long stretch of unemployment and no savings. Contemplating the fate of such mothers in 1830, *The Ladies' Magazine* demanded, "Must they starve and freeze during the coming winter? or shall they resort to beggary? or be even driven to theft?"[55] Under such conditions it is likely that Carey's mother felt compelled to return to the almshouse during the months when the House of Industry was closed.

Managers of the House of Industry probably kept wages down because they were determined to run their charity as a successful, or at least solvent, business. Financially, it was a curious entity. The managers solicited and received subscriptions and donations in cash and in kind, but the sale of goods produced in the workrooms constituted a substantial proportion of its annual budget (table

Now let us see the hideous result, as regards
a woman with two children.

261 days, at 18¾ cents per day,	.	.	.	$48.93¾
Deficit,	. . .	.	.	84.66¼
				$133 60

Rent, half a dollar per week . .	$26.00
Clothing and shoes for self and children .	20.00
Fire, Candles, Soap, &c. six cents per day	21.90
Food and drink, six cents each per day	65.70
	$133.60

Fig. 1.3. To refute accusations that the poor were responsible for their dependence on charity, Philadelphia reformer Mathew Carey worked out a detailed annual budget to demonstrate that a widow with two children could not possibly live on the wages she might earn from the sewing work generally available to women during the 1830s. From A Citizen of Philadelphia [Mathew Carey], "A Plea for the Poor: An Enquiry How Far the Charges Against Them of Improvidence, Idleness, and Dissipation, Are Founded in Truth" (Philadelphia, December 18, 1836), 6; courtesy of the Library Company of Philadelphia.

1.2). From 1840 to 1888, this proportion ranged from 17 to 43 percent of total income, while donations made up from as little as 5 to 22 percent (the remainder came from income generated by an endowment). Thus, although the House of Industry and its nursery were presented to the Philadelphia community as a charitable organization, its services were at least partly supported by the *recipients* of its charity, who were its own employees.

Clearly, for the managers of the House of Industry, the word *industry* had a double meaning, one that was simultaneously material and moral. In linking benevolence to financial enterprise, the Female Society for the Relief and Employment of the Poor was typical of eighteenth- and nineteenth-century Quaker charities, both male-run and female-run. In combining forms of relief—indoor and outdoor, material and cash—the society was somewhat innovative, although not so radical as to attract criticism. The feature that was most unusual, and likely accounted for much of its attraction to working mothers, was the nursery.

By distinguishing women's needs from men's and tailoring an institution specially for women, the Female Society drew attention to the gendered nature of poverty and its causes. For mothers, poverty was the result partly of the low wages paid for "women's work" and partly of the double burden of having to care for *and* support children. The middle-class managers of the Female Society acknowledged that poor women, like themselves, had maternal respon-

Table 1.2

Wages, Sales, and Donations as a Proportion of Annual Budgets, House of Industry, Philadelphia, 1840–1888

Year	Total Expenses ($)	Wages ($)	Wages (%)	Total Income ($)	Sales ($)	Sales (%)	Donations ($)	Donations (%)
1840	1,818	465	26	2,187	514	24	431	20
1850	2,597	445	17	3,075	1,333	43	678	22
1860	3,021	1,015^a	34	4,116	1,524	37	825	20
1870	4,791	1,556^a	32	5,383	1,816	34	743	14
1880	3,937	1,260^b	32	6,238	1,439	23	762	12
1888	11,929	2,180^a	18	12,820	2,205	17	686	5

Source: Annual Reports of the Female Society for the Relief and Employment of the Poor, Philadelphia, 1840–1888.

^{a}Includes matron's salary of approximately $100 [?] per annum.

^{b}Does not include matron's salary of approximately $208 per annum.

sibilities. The House of Industry was designed to make the two roles, wage earner and child caregiver, compatible.

In essence, members of the society were defining and accepting a class difference in how maternal duties were to be fulfilled. By making this distinction between themselves and their laboring-class sisters, the female philanthropists were able to avoid a potential conflict between their own maternalist ideology and the "message" of their charity. In the course of enabling poor women to keep their families intact, the philanthropists were actually affirming their own commitment to motherhood.

INFANT SCHOOLS

The Boston Infant School, founded in 1828, took a somewhat different approach to wage-earning mothers and their children. Although the school's primary function was educational, its constitution stated explicitly that it would, in addition, "be of eminent service, both to parents and children. By relieving mothers of a part of their domestic cares, it would enable them to seek employment."[56] Moreover, according to William Russell, an educational theorist, journalist, and one of the school's promoters, infant schools, by caring for children as young as eighteen months, not only relieved the mother of caring for "that member of her family which is the most difficult for her to superintend and manage—the one between the youngest infant . . . and the child who is old enough to go to primary school, . . . [but also] by this means, often released [a sister] from premature domestic care, and left [her] free to attend school for her own improvement."[57]

It is important to note the specific terms in which Russell conceived of the child care functions of the infant school. He explicitly condoned maternal employment; indeed, he seems to have taken it for granted among poor and laboring-class women. Nevertheless, he was concerned about how it affected children's welfare and their opportunities for education. Rather than discourage mothers from working, however, he sought to enable them to do so without harming their children. Thus, although he would not have advocated child care as a public service to ensure mothers' right to compete equally in the labor market, he did promote infant schools' care as a means of protecting children's right to education—while acknowledging that mothers would also benefit from placing their children in the school.

The idea of the infant school came from Great Britain, where it had been developed by the utopian Scottish industrialist Robert Owen. The school he established in New Lanark, Scotland, in 1816 was intended to "train children from their earliest infancy in good habits of every description (which will of course prevent them from acquiring those of falsehood and deception)."[58] The "Institute for the Formation of Character," as he called it, would lay the foundation for a new kind of cooperative and egalitarian society. But it also had a pragmatic side. He told the inhabitants of New Lanark that the school was "devised to afford the means of receiving your children at an early age, almost as soon as they can walk. By this means many of you, mothers of families, will be enabled to earn a better maintenance or support for your children; you will have less care and anxiety about them; while the children will be prevented from acquiring any bad habits, and gradually prepared to learn the best."[59]

The twin goals of protecting the children of working mothers and setting them on the right social path appealed to other British reformers, who set up two more infant schools in England and then formed an Infant School Society (ISS). By 1825 the society had established at least fifty-five infant schools around the British Isles. These schools gave priority to children's education, while regarding their child care functions as secondary: "[The] immediate use [of the infant school] is to put the infant heart under the influence of an awakening process. . . . Its subordinate uses are to relieve and assist industrious mothers."[60]

Though generally structured on Owen's model, ISS schools differed in one significant respect: the philosophical context in which they were developed.

Both Owen and the ISS regarded the schools as an instrument of poor reform, but for Owen, this reform was to lead to utopian change—to a new society, which ostensibly had gender equality as one of its major tenets.[61] The goals of the ISS, while lofty, were far more circumscribed; they hoped to alleviate, but not necessarily eradicate, the industrial conditions that had given rise to the need for infant schools in the first place. Because ISS schools far outnumbered those of the Owenites, the British infant school became closely identified with conservative philanthropy, not radical reform.[62]

When the idea of infant schools was transplanted to American soil in the mid- to late 1820s, it was the ISS version, not Robert Owen's, that took hold.[63] Owen's plan was replicated in the experimental community he set up in New Harmony, Indiana, in 1825,[64] but it was through the publicity the ISS-inspired infant schools received in the American press that the idea attracted national attention. Their chief exponent was William Russell, who gave the idea prominent play in the pages of his new publication, the *American Journal of Education*. Russell never mentioned Owen's pioneering efforts but rather gave the impression that the infant schools were wholly the product of the ISS. In an effort to gain support for establishing similar institutions in the United States, Russell reported on British examples and reprinted long excerpts from the writings of William Wilson and Samuel Wilderspin, two early teachers in the British system who had been enlisted by the society to train others in the proper method of running an infant school.

According to Wilson and Wilderspin, the infant schools promised vast improvement over the "Dames'-Schools" to which British working parents had been compelled to resort in the past. The ISS saw these as unsavory enterprises typically run by an "old woman" who kept from ten to thirty children "shut up, perhaps in a close apartment," charging parents at the exorbitant rate of two pence to four pence per child per day.[65] The infant school, by contrast, was to be housed in "an airy and spacious apartment, with a dry, and, if possible, a large play-ground attached to it." Masters and mistresses were to be selected for their "mildness, patience, forbearance, and kindness of disposition"; it was expected that their "tone and manner shall be uniformly those of parental affection." The school itself was to be "not a place of irksome restraint and confinement, but . . . a scene . . . at once of activity and amusement, of intellectual improvement and moral discipline."[66] In general, the design of the infant school was to be tailored to the needs and capabilities of small children. The superintendent was "to convey much useful knowledge to his pupils . . . *without oppressing* their faculties . . . or resorting to any harsh expedients."[67]

If in practice infant schools had lived up to these prescriptions, then they would have avoided the regimentation and dourness that typified so many early nineteenth-century institutions on both sides of the Atlantic. British advocates invited the public to visit any of a number of infant schools where they could view children who were "clean, healthy, joyous; giving free scope to their buoyant spirits; their very plays made subservient to the correction of bad and the growth of good dispositions."[68] "It is possible," said Wilderspin, "to have two hundred, or even three hundred, children assembled together, the eldest not more than six years of age, and yet not to hear one of them crying for a whole day."[69] Visitors could, moreover, "contemplate the striking re-action of the improved manners and habits of the infants on the older branches of the family." British historian Anna Davin challenges Wilderspin's claims, however, arguing that London's infant schools, at any rate, remained rather rigid throughout the century. More liberal Froebelian ideas were introduced in the 1870s, but their implementation was hampered by the large size of classes in these schools. Moreover, in keeping with Victorian ideology, activities also became more differentiated by gender as the century wore on.[70]

Russell, however, took the ISS at its word. After devoting many pages of the first volume of his journal to laudatory descriptions of British infant schools, he reported enthusiastically as American reformers took his cue and began to set up infant schools in cities up and down the Northeastern seaboard. In a retrospective on "The Progress of Education during the Year 1826," Russell exulted, "A new world has here been opened to the survey and the efforts of benevolent minds. Two years ago a proposal to establish schools designed for infants of two years or eighteen months, would only have excited ridicule or astonishment. But such schools are now in successful operation in our own country as well as abroad; they have more than realised the highest expectations of their founders."[71] By the early 1830s, there were infant schools in Hartford, Philadelphia, New York, Boston, and Richmond, as well as in some smaller outlying towns and villages. For the most part these were charitable institutions, which restricted admissions to the children of the poor and stressed their beneficial influence on that segment of the population. All told, they served perhaps several thousand children, including a number of African Americans, who were taught in separate institutions in Boston and Philadelphia.[72]

As charities the schools emphasized the rehabilitative aspects of their work. One supporter invited "citizens as are desirous to rescue an interesting portion of the rising generation from early habits of vice and immorality" to visit the infant school on Chester Street in Philadelphia, where they might "behold from one hundred to one hundred and fifty interesting children, from two to six years old, assembled together in an orderly, regular manner, clean and comfortably clad in general, cheerful and happy, acquiring useful instruction and virtuous impressions—and to contrast the results of this system with those of an education in the streets, where they would be every hour under the influence of the worst examples, and contaminating each other."[73] The *Ladies' Magazine* appealed to the women of Boston to "remember . . . the poor little ones who have no nursery and no mother deserving of the name . . . [and to] come forward and afford your aid to their cause, and not rest till every section of the city has its Infant School."[74]

Advocates also insisted that the children of the rich as well as those of the poor could benefit from an infant school education.[75] A reviewer in the *American Journal of Education* (probably Russell) commented, "We hope . . . that the circumstance of infant schools having been first opened to children from the poorer classes, will not prevent an enlightened and efficient endeavor to offer the same advantages to all classes of the community, without distinction. All mothers need aid and relief in their arduous and exhausting duties; and to the children of the wealthiest residents in any city, moral, intellectual and physical cultivation is not less important than to those of the poor."[76] But only in Boston were private, tuition-charging schools established for the children of the middling and wealthy classes.[77]

Ironically, it was the effort to universalize infant schools that ultimately led to their demise. In its attempts to popularize the notion that young people were educable, the movement aroused fears that the schools had become hothouses that fostered precocity. This perception conflicted with the growing stress on childhood as a discrete stage that had to be prolonged in order for children to develop properly under the watchful eyes of their mothers. As a result, middle-class support for infant schools, both financial and moral, declined, and they gradually died out in the 1840s.[78]

MODELS FOR THE FUTURE

The child care institutions that began to emerge around mid-century came closer to our modern notion of day care centers. They took neither the House of Industry nor the infant school as their model, for they lacked workrooms and left formal education to others.[79] The first institution designed along these new lines was probably the Nursery for the Children of Poor Women, founded in New York City in 1854 (this is the "Infant and Child's Hospital" Elinor

Guggenheimer referred to in her speech of 1960, although it was not until 1856 that the founders of the nursery organized the Child's Hospital to accommodate the many sick children among their charges).[80] The New York nursery was followed by a rapid succession of similar institutions in cities across the country: the Chicago Nursery and Half-Orphan Society in 1860,[81] the Day Nursery of Philadelphia in 1863, and the Infant Shelter in San Francisco in 1871. Boston, curiously, seems to have been without a day nursery until the late 1870s, by which time most other major cities boasted more than one.

The goal of the day nurseries was to enable poor women with children to work and thus prevent them from becoming dependent on charity or public welfare or turning to prostitution. The Philadelphia Home for Little Wanderers expressed its mission melodramatically:

> What can a mother do with a young babe or child unable to care for itself? She cannot go to work and take it with her, as few persons would employ one with such an encumbrance, and she has no one to leave it with and be assured of its safety. What a relief to her mind and benefit to her and the child, to be permitted to bring it to our nursery and have it cared for during the day while she goes out to work. In this way a larger proportion of these classes are saved from crime by relieving them in a time of deep distress, than any other. Hunger, like "necessity," knows no law. It will find ways of relief honestly or otherwise. And but for the help of this kind which we have rendered, many mothers with families must have gone to the almshouse, or done worse. We have saved them from this, and from the mortification or disgrace of being cared for by the commonwealth.[82]

Some institutions, like the Margaret Etter Crèche in Chicago, helped women find employment.[83] Others, such as Philadelphia's Day Nursery for Children, restricted admissions to the children of women who already had work.[84] But the day nurseries' endorsement of employment for mothers was conditional: it was acceptable only when they were in crisis, on the brink of poverty, or already poor. In 1874, for example, the Day Nursery for Children intoned, "In these times of unusual scarcity of employment for men, it necessarily devolves upon the women to do what they can in support of their families."[85] Typically, day nursery philanthropists represented employment as something that mothers sought only in times of emergency—not as part of "normal" family life, even for poor and laboring-class families.

Studies of family economic strategies in Philadelphia and elsewhere suggest that married women did tend to avoid working for wages *outside the home* when they could afford to—that is, when wage-earning husbands were present in the household or when the women could depend on the earning power of other family members, such as older children.[86] But even then, working-class women felt the need to bring cash into the household coffers, which they tried to do through occupations that were compatible with family obligations, such as industrial homework or the keeping of boarders.

Although child care would have enabled domestic entrepreneurs and home-workers to pursue their cash-earning work more efficiently, day nursery managers focused their efforts on the women for whom such occupations were not an option: widows and deserted wives, who were unlikely to have the where-withal to engage in some form of independent domestic industry and thus were compelled to seek employment outside the house or to labor more intensively at industrial homework if they were to earn a sufficient income.[87] Given limited resources, the priorities established by the day nurseries were no doubt as equitable as any. But their rhetoric obscured the fact that for many married women, as well as single female heads of household, wage earning was not a stopgap but a permanent necessity if they were to keep their families intact—that it was, in fact, a way of fulfilling maternal responsibility.

For wage-earning mothers, even the minimal fees charged by most day nurseries were probably a financial burden, but at the same time the payments allowed them to regard themselves as clients, not beneficiaries, of child care services. The freestanding nurseries, like their nursery/workroom predecessors, were not then wholly charitable, although donations and subscriptions subsidized the fees they charged parents. In the budgets of most institutions, fees constituted only a small proportion of total income, and managers tended to trivialize even those amounts in presenting their charities to the public through annual reports, which were, of course, intended to attract contributions. Because the parents who used the nurseries had no such avenues of expression, the overwhelming public image of the nurseries was more likely to be that of a charity that "rescued" the children of desperate mothers than that of a voluntary social service meeting everyday needs.

Managers further underscored the charitable aspect of their work through a continuing emphasis on reform and prevention. From the early days of the House of Industry, nursery philanthropists sought to use their institutions to save both mothers and children. As the century wore on, this dual focus yielded to a more single-minded concentration on the children. This usually dictated a change in nursery structure.

In the beginning, staffs typically included a matron, who was to take full charge of the nursery, including meals, cleaning, laundry, and supervision of the children; and, depending on the number of children admitted and the financial resources available, one or several "nursemaids" or "housemaids," who would assist her in these tasks. Matrons tended to be middle-aged women, sometimes single, sometimes widows, with no formal training for their work, who were expected to run the nursery efficiently and treat the children with kindness, but not necessarily act as teachers. Education was provided, if at all, by volunteers.

When education became more important to day nursery philanthropists, nurseries that could afford to do so hired the occasional trained "kinder-gartner," or matron with some type of teaching experience or training. As the value of this type of personnel rose in the eyes of managers, so did the salaries of matrons and teachers. At the Philadelphia House of Industry, for example, the matron's annual salary rose from about $50 in the early decades of the century to $208 in 1880.

At the same time, the goals of rehabilitation and reform were expressed in increasingly secular terms. The content of nursery programs shifted from Bible reading as a means of instilling Christian virtue to kindergarten methods aimed at educating the children "in a desire to become honest, industrious, law-abiding citizens."[88] One day nursery described its techniques thus: "For the noisy, quarrelsome play of the sidewalk and gutter, which is the training of so many of our children, [the kindergarten] substitutes games and occupations just as congenial and varied, so as to avoid weariness or constraint, by which the children are unconsciously but steadily educated in habits of system, order, and submission to authority, of quick and accurate observation, and of manual dexterity."[89] This same nursery also stressed that the children trained in its kindergarten would later perform successfully in school, but as the quotation makes evident, the chief goal of the program was to instill the qualities needed for good industrial workers. Much of this self-consciously modern methodology was, then, simply old wine in new bottles.

The major exception to this pattern was the network of day nurseries and charitable kindergartens founded in Boston by the noted philanthropist Pauline Agassiz Shaw, starting in 1878. Shaw believed that day nurseries should not only keep children safe and clean but should also educate them. According to one of the matrons, "The aim, from the first, was to give the child not only the best physical care, but to consider his whole nature."[90]

Anticipating the definitive distinction that later would be made between nursery and kindergarten children, Shaw and her colleagues recognized that very young children should not be lumped together but had different needs at different ages. At the five day nurseries Shaw set up, programs were tailored for children of various ages. Those of "kindergarten age" (at that time probably considered to be three to six) attended kindergarten full time, while younger children, "under the care of a kindergartner, divided their time between elementary kindergarten, free play, and sleep."[91]

The programs differed in content as well as schedule. As the matron of the North Bennett Street Day Nursery described it, "A morning in our Day Nursery is much like a morning in a kindergarten, with simpler plays and more freedom. We also have a larger supply of dolls, blocks, carts, etc. Chief among our valued playthings is a big box full of beach stones too large to be swallowed."[92]

Shaw's emphasis on education—and her apparent willingness to back up her philosophy with an adequate financial commitment—also affected the way her institutions determined criteria for admission. Day nurseries commonly restricted their services to families whose dire circumstances compelled mothers to work and leave their children without adequate care. This policy followed the principle that mothers were the preferred caretakers, and if day nurseries accepted children when it was not strictly necessary, they would undermine poor women's sense of maternal responsibility. By contrast, in at least one of Shaw's institutions, the North Bennett Street Day Nursery, children were "allowed to attend the Nursery during the morning with special reference to the educational value of the training received . . . even if the mother [was] not working."[93] By making the interests of the children a priority over accepted principles of philanthropic practice, Shaw was blurring the line between school and charity, overwriting the welfare goals of the day nursery with those of early childhood education.

Frances Willard, the dynamic president of the Woman's Christian Temperance Union (WCTU), also sought to combine the benefits of education with those of a social service to working mothers. Willard called the kindergarten movement the "greatest theme, next to salvation by faith, that can engage a woman's heart and brain."[94] Under her leadership in the 1880s and 1890s, local chapters of the WCTU established a chain of free urban kindergartens that also offered day nursery or crèche services to the children who needed full-day care and served as sites for teacher training. There were facilities in San Diego, Denver, Baltimore, and Poughkeepsie, New York, and in Hamilton, Ontario.[95] By 1890 one of the largest, in San Francisco, had enrolled more than 1,500 children. The national organization set up a separate Department of Day Nurseries to "systematize this work." According to Helen L. Hood, the day nursery superintendent, "It is indeed a grand work to rescue from sin those whose lives have been spent in wickedness; but to take the *sinless* little ones of these parents and train them for God, is labor which will yield a much more abundant harvest."[96] Ruth Bordin, Willard's biographer, argues, however, that "temperance recruitment was only a small part of the motivation" for Willard's interest in kindergartens; by the early decades of the twentieth century, the organization was focusing almost exclusively on the educational aspects of the program.[97]

Combined day nursery–kindergartens like those established by Shaw and Willard were all too rare. In most institutions, condescension and charity hung heavy in the air, and routines seem to have been designed with little thought given to their emotional effects, which touched parents as well as children. Typical were the protocols followed at the Fitch Crèche in Buffalo, New York: "The mother brings her baby about seven o'clock in the morning. She enters the reception-room, not coming into the institution proper at all. A nurse, tidily dressed, with no curl papers in her hair, though it be pretty early, meets the mother, and relieves her of the child, which is taken at once to the bathroom, where its clothing is removed. It is bathed, put into the crèche clothing, and taken into the play-room."[98] The children's own clothing would be hung in "specially ventilated closets," intended to "fumigate" them and presumably rid them of vermin, or at least prevent them from contaminating the rest of the nursery. At the end of the day, before dressing her children for the trip home, a tired mother might find "a cup of good tea" waiting for her behind a pass-through between the reception room and the nursery kitchen. And "once in a while, if she be clean enough, she is taken into the building to see the beauty of orderly and cleanly rooms."[99] Not surprisingly, many mothers felt that the nurseries alienated them from their children.

WITHIN THE AFRICAN AMERICAN COMMUNITY

Significantly, the class tensions that characterized the nurseries run by and for white women were largely absent in those run by and for African Americans. This atmosphere was not due to an absence of class divisions between the black reformers who ran the nurseries and the laboring-class families that formed their clientele; the reformers—most of them members of black women's clubs and civic organizations—readily affirmed their superior class position.[100] But African American philanthropists tended to view the objects of their benevolence more sympathetically than whites did theirs, understanding their charities as part of the overall project of racial uplift.[101] In particular, black clubwo-men accepted maternal employment as natural or at least inevitable. They knew that for the low-income mothers of their race, wage-earning labor was not a stopgap but a permanent fact of life. At the same time they were appalled by the conditions in which most poor blacks lived, and by the high infant and child mortality rates they suffered. Many infant and child injuries and deaths, they understood, were the result of children being left unsupervised while mothers were at work. And although they deplored the necessity of such arrangements, they did not blame black mothers or accuse them of neglecting their children.

Maternal employment was nothing new for African Americans. Under slav-ery, women as well as men were compelled to work, and Southern planters begrudged them only minimal respite for pregnancy, parturition, and postnatal care of themselves and their infants. To ensure that slave mothers would labor with the least possible interruption, owners, especially on larger plantations, devised regular systems of child care.[102] They assigned slaves who were deemed incapable of field work—older men and women, or children not yet strong enough—to look after infants and toddlers; "baby keepers" and nurses were frequently listed among the occupations of plantation workers.[103]

Historian Dorothy Sterling has gathered excerpts from slave narratives, interviews, letters, and other sources that provide a vivid picture of child care practices on plantations: "Dey had a nuss house whar dey put all de young chillun 'till dey wuz old enough to work. Dey had one old 'oman to look atter us and our some'p'm t'eat wuz brought to dis house. Our milk wuz put on de floor in a big wooden tray and dey give us oyster shells to eat wid. All de chillun would gather 'round dis tray and eat." According to Sterling, "on large planta-tions, these primitive day-care centers might house as many as 100 chil-dren."[104] Institutional regimes were developed for hygiene as well as nutrition: "They took all the children to the spring and set them in a row. They had a tubful of water and they washed them and dried them and put on their clean clothes. They used homemade lye soap and greased them with tallow and mutton suet. That made them shine."[105]

Recently parturient mothers were allowed to spend brief intervals with their nurslings, either in the fields or back at the quarters,[106] but older children seldom saw their parents between dawn and dusk. They either played in supervised groups or were set to work at various tasks such as gathering feed for livestock as members of a "hogmeat" or "grass gang," or caring for younger children.[107]

This arrangement served masters' interests in several ways: it maximized the productivity of adult female slaves while protecting and training the future labor power of their young chattels. As one former slave put it, "The white folks was crazy 'bout their nigger babies 'cause that's where they got their profit."[108] This system also allowed planters to carry out the functions of social reproduction without depending excessively on, or encouraging, family ties among African Americans themselves.

Under this system, African American mothers had little control over methods of child care, although they may been able to convince some planters that it was in their interest to see that slave children were looked after properly. Yet it was not unheard of for girls as young as four or five to be pressed into service holding babies or rocking them to sleep, and as a result, neglect and minor injuries were commonplace.[109] As one former slave recalled, "I nuss so many chillen, it done went and stunted my growth."[110] Another admitted, "I'd get tired and make like I was asleep, and would ease the cradle over and throw the baby out. I never would throw mammy's out, though."[111] A slave lullaby reveals the concerns of mothers who left infants in the charge of older siblings:

Mammy went away—she tol' me to stay.
An take good keer of de baby,
She tol' me to stay an sing dis away,
O, go ter sleepy, little baby.[112]

In some cases, especially on smaller plantations, the planter's wife might supervise slaves' offspring, particularly if she saw a value in training them for work at an early age. Not surprisingly, white caretakers used disciplinary methods that slave parents perceived as abusive.[113] When African American children became orphaned because their parents had either died or been sold away, planters simply took custody of them and either provided minimal care themselves or allowed the children to become absorbed by the caretaking system in the quarters. According to one former slave whose mother had died in childbirth, "Any woman what had a baby 'bout my age would wet nurse me, so I growed up in de quarters an' was a well an' happy as any other chil'."[114]

It is one of the famous and cruel ironies of the slavery system that while African Americans were denied the right to rear their own children as they saw fit, they were repeatedly pressed into service to nurture the offspring of their masters.[115] According to the prevailing stereotype, the black "mammy" loved her white charges and cared for them cheerfully, even taking them to her breast.

Conveniently obscured were the mammy's own children, who were routinely deprived of their mother's comfort and suckling.

Such arrangements did not end with Emancipation. Black women continued to work outside the home at a far greater rate than white women, with a high proportion in domestic service, and although few were hired exclusively as mammies, they were expected to look after white children as part of their duties (fig. 1.4).[116] Now, however, they could no longer rely on the primitive child care system of the plantation, paternalistic though it was. In 1897 a male minister explained the dilemma faced by urban working mothers:

> Unwillingly these mothers leave their children all day and part of the night in the place they call home, all alone to care for themselves. . . . With great anxiety and confusion [the mother] tears herself away from them and hastens to her work while they cry for her to come back, and often they are quarreling and fighting among themselves before she is out of sight. No one but a mother knows how painful it is to leave children alone under these unfortunate circumstances, but there is nothing for her to do but go. . . . It is not long after the mother is gone before the children, being left to themselves, leave the house, go into the streets, . . . get into mischief and commit sin . . . without realizing that they have done wrong. . . . The anxious mother comes home to find that her children are not there. She does not know where they are and starts out in the dark to look for them in the streets. Often she finds them in the city jail or station house.[117]

White employers who depended on black domestic servants tended to ignore their dilemma as mothers, preferring to perpetuate the mammy stereotype. In 1912, a group of white Southerners proposed to erect a statue in Washington, D.C., to honor "the black nurse of slavery days." The nascent National Association for the Advancement of Colored People (NAACP) denounced the gesture as hypocritical and ran an irate editorial in its monthly magazine, *The Crisis:* "This appreciation of the black mammy is always of the foster mammy, not of the mother in her own home, attending to her own babies. . . . She existed under a false social system that deprived her of husband and child. . . . It was a perversion of motherhood. Let the present-day mammies suckle their own children."[118]

Whereas the NAACP reinforced the (white) middle-class ideal of the stay-at-home mother, black clubwomen took a different tack. Acknowledging maternal employment as a permanent feature of black life, they set about creating a practical solution: establishing day nurseries for black children.[119] The need for such nurseries was pressing not only because of the high rate of employment

Fig. 1.4. At an early age, African American females were trained to care for white children (sometimes barely younger than themselves). The names of the two "child-nurses" in this photograph taken in Macon, Georgia, in 1903 were not recorded; their charges were two cousins named John and Allie Lamon. Courtesy of the Georgia Department of Archives and History.

among African American women but also because most white-run nurseries, in both North and South, were segregated. From the 1890s onward, under the aegis of the National Association of Colored Women (NACW) and with impetus from its national council, local affiliates set up a number of urban day nurseries for African American children.[120] Their work was especially important in the South, where, by the late nineteenth century, the concentration of black female-headed households was high in urban areas.[121]

MATERNAL INVENTION

Through the efforts of both African American and white female philanthropists, by the late nineteenth century dozens of day nurseries were operating across the country. Still, because of their limited capacities and scattered, often inconvenient locations, they could not meet the needs of all working mothers with small children. Nurseries also excluded certain children on the basis of religion and ethnicity as well as race, or rejected mothers on moral grounds. Few, for example, would accept children known to be illegitimate. Thus many working women were compelled—or perhaps chose—to find other sources of care for their children. In resorting to what we might generally call "maternal invention," they helped construct networks of informal care. Indeed, the provisions they developed probably served more children than did the nurseries. But their functioning was (except in certain notorious cases) less visible, and thus they had less impact on public child care discourses.

Maternal invention took at least two forms: mothers using institutions intended for another purpose to meet child care needs, or mothers relying on non-institutional care offered by independent providers or kin, usually in their own homes. Maternal invention cropped up when mothers found existing child care options to be unavailable, inadequate, or unsuitable. Child care in nurseries and schools suited women who had homes and jobs with fixed hours, but many poor women were homeless or had occupations that prevented them from looking after their children on a daily basis, such as domestic service, wet nursing, or prostitution. In such cases they often preferred to place their children in boarding programs or institutions such as orphan asylums, foster care agencies, children's shelters, and homes for infants.

Boarding institutions constituted a particularly important resource for urban African American women, who, with employment opportunities even more restricted than those of white women, most often found themselves in domestic service and were frequently required to live in their employers' homes.[122] Unless they had nearby kin (less common in the North than the South) or were willing to give up their children for indenture, they had no option but to board them.[123]

The earliest boarding institution for African American children was established in Philadelphia by the Association for the Care of Colored Orphans, another organization of white female Quakers, in 1822.[124] Around mid-century, white philanthropists set up other orphanages for African American children in New York City, Providence, and Avondale, Ohio, as well as a second one in Philadelphia.[125] Evidence suggests that the black community of New York soon joined white philanthropists in supporting the city's black child care institutions, and it is possible that the same pattern was true elsewhere.[126] By the late nineteenth and early twentieth centuries, African American women were independently establishing orphanages and other types of specialized shelters for the children of their community; one of the earliest was the Carrie Steele Orphan Home, begun in Atlanta in 1888 and named after its founder and benefactor, a former slave.[127]

It is evident from their records that orphanages for both black and white children served child care functions.[128] According to a history of the Colored Orphans' Asylum of New York, "The problem of the half-orphan came up early in the existence of the Asylum. Poverty-stricken widows, or despairing fathers of a motherless brood, would often bring their children to the Asylum for care because they were unable to work and take care of their young families at the same time. The half-orphans were admitted to the Asylum as space permitted, and partial support from the surviving parent was gladly accepted."[129] Whereas the history of the New York asylum pointed out its benefits to both fathers and mothers, another Quaker institution, the Home for Destitute Colored Children in Philadelphia, founded in 1855, expressed its mission in self-consciously maternalist and interracial terms:

> Essentially a woman's society, we have been effective in relieving and assisting women. Mothers, grandmothers, aunts and friendly guardians have availed themselves of the advantages offered for better physical and moral training of their children, while at the same time the release thus obtained has enabled them to continue in families, or apply for places suited to their ability, and thus earn their regular wages, where before they were only able to obtain a precarious livelihood which had often to be eked out by the contributions of charity. "I cannot," said one of these, a widow with two children of three and five years, "board them [privately] out of a dollar and a half a week, and keep myself decent, so as to keep my place."[130]

By the second half of the nineteenth century, the boarding of half-orphans, both white and black, had become commonplace across the country. The 1877 report of the Massachusetts Board of State Charities indicated that three-quarters of the state's thirty-two children's homes and asylums took children with one or both parents living, on either a temporary or long-term basis, for fees that ranged between two dollars and eight dollars a month (a few charged nothing).[131] An 1890 report on charities for children in San Francisco found similar practices on the West Coast.[132]

Some institutions refused to take older children because they were hard to discipline, but even fewer accepted infants and toddlers.[133] The first to do so was the New York Nursery and Child's Hospital—the philanthropy described by Elinor Guggenheimer—which had opened its doors in 1854. According to both Mary Delafield Du Bois, Guggenheimer's heroine, and historian Virginia Quiroga, the nursery was originally intended to rescue the children of wet nurses from the perils of being "farmed out" (that is, sent to "baby farms," informal child care arrangements often denounced by reformers).[134] In an account of the nursery's beginnings that is at once more modest and more complex than Guggenheimer's, Du Bois describes how a series of newspaper stories roused her to take action; one in particular described "a wet-nurse's child found in a damp basement room, in a basket under the bed, on which a woman lay ill with small-pox, whose own infant had died of that frightful disease. This poor woman was paid a high price for the care of the infant, whose mother was not allowed to visit it for fear of carrying contagious disease from a tenement house to the child of a wealthy mother."[135] According to a leading physician of the day, the infants of women who became wet nurses usually died of neglect. Du Bois was not insensitive to the class-related dimensions of this situation. She declared indignantly, "The children of the poor were sacrificed to the children of the wealthy."[136]

The New York Nursery, as Quiroga puts it, "functioned as a day care center, a home and employment agency for wet-nurses, and a refuge for infants whose mothers were ill or deceased."[137] It accepted children between the ages of six weeks and six years. Women who had recently given birth could choose to hire themselves out as wet nurses or remain in the institution, where they received room and board in exchange for nourishing one infant in addition to their own. In 1873 a group of Philadelphia women set up the Home for Infants (fig. 1.5), modeled along the same lines as the New York Nursery.[138]

Mothers' immediate and positive response to both institutions indicated the dire need for such services. Initially, however, the infant mortality rate was alarmingly high, owing to the uncertainties of artificial feeding and ignorance of the need for precautions against infectious contagion. In Philadelphia, infant deaths hovered at around 50 percent.[139] It took several years of tragic and bitter experience before the managers and their staff and medical advisers developed techniques for keeping a population of frail newborns properly nourished and free from fatal disease.

At the Home for Infants and elsewhere, many mothers left their children behind and paid board for a number of months or even years, until they were in a position to retrieve them. In nearly every philanthropic institution, subsidies

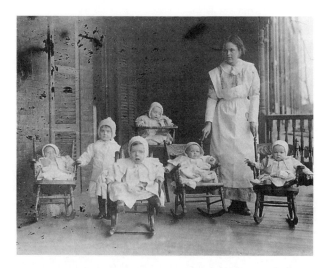

Fig. 1.5. The Philadelphia Home for Infants, founded in 1873, was one of the first American boarding institutions for infants. As this photograph suggests, one adult often had many charges, and even very young children were regimented. From the Children's Aid Society Collection, courtesy of the Historical Society of Pennsylvania.

from donations, endowments, or sometimes municipal or state funding kept fees low, often less than it would cost a parent to keep a child with her.[140] But for some parents even this amount was too high. In a study of three New Orleans orphanages, historian Priscilla Clement found that two of the institutions kept children on even when parents could no longer pay, whereas the third automatically discharged children in such cases. Clement comments, "Herein may be a difference between an orphanage managed by men and one directed by women. Faced with comparable financial exigencies, the male managers survived by shifting the burden to poor parents, while the female directors . . . collected room and board fees only when they could [and] donated more of their own money to keep the asylum functioning."[141] Whatever amount the parents paid, their contributions toward their children's support meant that these institutions, like the day nurseries, were not wholly charitable but involved parents in a form of self-help.

Parents' use of orphanages for child-caring purposes became so widespread that by the second half of the nineteenth century, "half-orphans" (children with one living parent) outnumbered full orphans in most asylums.[142] Moreover, in most cases, that one surviving parent was the mother; in Clement's study, for example, more than three-quarters of the half-orphans had no father.[143] Most parents applying to such institutions were poor or working-class; they often explicitly listed "poverty" as the reason for placing their child in the institution.[144] Not surprisingly, it was single mothers, with their limited earnings, more often than single fathers who felt compelled to take this step.

Many parents found boarding expedient, but like all types of institutional care for children, it bucked the trends in late nineteenth-century welfare as anti-institutional sentiment began building afresh. Child welfare wisdom had been vacillating between institutions and out-placement for more than a century. Eighteenth- and early nineteenth-century poverty officials considered indenture to be far preferable to almshouses in the treatment of "friendless" children, not only because it was more economical (although this was an important consideration) but also because, ideally, placement in families assured them a chance to learn a trade and be exposed to persons of "good moral character."[145] To spare children too young for indenture the unhealthy influences of the almshouse, poverty officials favored separate children's asylums; the first public orphanage was founded in Philadelphia in 1820, and New York and Boston soon followed suit. According to one observer, "'The good effects of this change upon the health and morals of the children are very perceptible.'"[146] Nevertheless, many children remained in almshouses, prompting condemnation by such critics as Dorothea Dix and a scathing 1856 report by a New York State Senate select committee, which called the poorhouses of the state "the worst possible nurseries."[147]

Around the same time Charles Loring Brace, the founder of the Children's Aid Society in New York City, launched his scheme to rescue footloose urban children—"street arabs," as they were often called—by transplanting them to "wholesome" families in rural settings that were often far from their families of origin. By the mid-1890s, Brace had "saved" some ninety thousand children, often sending them to distant placements in the West.[148] Anti-institutional sentiment eventually triggered a nationwide campaign to remove children from almshouses. In dozens of states, laws barring children from almshouses were passed and alternative types of care for dependent children established. Still, as late as 1890 nearly five thousand children remained in almshouses around the country.[149]

The privately sponsored orphan asylums and children's homes that boarded the children of the poor and laboring classes were intended to provide a positive alternative to the almshouses. Nevertheless, they attracted some of the same criticism. In his 1877 report on children's institutions in Massachusetts, charity official Sidney Andrews declared, "Institution life in its best estate is but a poor substitute for family life," and it frequently fell far short. Continuous turnover of children disrupted whatever programs of education and vocational training institutions attempted to carry out, and there was concern that a child "may come to regard an institution of some kind as his proper home, and support by the public as his rightful heritage."[150] Frank Sanborn, another member of the Massachusetts State Board of Charities, told the audience at the 1880 meeting of the American Social Science Association that "nature herself pointed to the home as the only place" for children.[151]

If children could not remain in their own homes, child welfare experts recommended that they be "placed out" in families. Experts distinguished placing-out from indenture, which, by the last quarter of the nineteenth century, had also come into disfavor. According to Homer Folks, a leading turn-of-the-century welfare official and historian of social welfare, it was "clearly not in harmony with the spirit of [the] times to 'bind' any one to serve another person for a definite term of years. The bound child has often been alluded to as typifying loneliness, neglect, overwork, and a consciousness of being held in low esteem."[152] Ideally, children placed out in foster homes were to be treated not like servants or apprentices but like a member of the family.

Nevertheless, many parents preferred to board their offspring in orphanages or children's homes rather than seek placement for them. To be sure, such institutions had disadvantages. Distance or strict regulations limited parents' visits with their children. A parent also risked losing custody of a child if she could not keep up with boarding fees. But institutions, by their impersonal nature, did not threaten to displace the natural parents in the child's affections, as foster parents might. Moreover, the quality of foster homes appeared to be as uncertain as that of institutions. Societies engaged in child-placing work complained about the expense and practical difficulties involved in selecting and adequately supervising numerous far-flung homes, and perhaps they could not assure parents that their children would be well taken care of.[153]

For these reasons, parents continued to use charitable boarding institutions for child care well into the early twentieth century. The population of the Home for Destitute Colored Children in Philadelphia peaked in 1868 owing to an influx of soldiers' orphans and then leveled off to an average of 35–45 from the 1870s through the 1890s.[154] The Franziska Children's Home in Nicetown, Philadelphia, which admitted only half-orphans, was filled to its capacity of 25 as soon as it opened in October 1893, and it quickly expanded; by the next year it was serving 31 children.[155] Despite criticism from experts in the field of child welfare, the Jewish Orphanage of Rhode Island continued to admit children until just before World War II.[156] The population of the Chicago Nursery and Half-Orphan Society, which began as a day nursery in 1860 and instituted "around-the-clock care" two years later, grew from 75 children in 1868 to almost 140 in 1874. But for the next decade it deviated from the pattern just described, declining to an average of 85–90 children annually.[157] The records do not indicate why the numbers dropped, although it is possible that some parents were discouraged by growing anti-institutional sentiment. It is unlikely that day nurseries took up the slack, because Chicago had very few until the 1890s.

Although placing children in orphanages was hardly an ideal solution, critics felt that parents abused the asylums. In an address to the American Association for the Advancement of Science in 1888, one welfare official claimed, "Every delinquent mother and every drunken father now knows that he or she can indulge their vices, and get rid of their children. Thousands of widowed mothers, learning that they can marry again if not encumbered with children, are putting their little ones in asylums."[158] Thus parents who placed their children in long-term child care were presented to the public as acting irresponsibly, not choosing the best of undesirable alternatives dictated by practical and economic necessity.[159]

INFORMAL CARE

This image was perhaps one reason why many parents turned to the less public form of child care given by home-based providers—what today we would call family day care. Throughout the nineteenth century, this type of care appears to have increased as rapidly as institutional forms. Formal facilities simply could not keep pace with the increasing need for care, particularly for infants, that arose with the tremendous growth of urban populations due to migration, immigration, and the spread of industrialization and commerce, which in turn created more employment opportunities for women.

Moreover, certain groups of working mothers were more likely to choose informal care. Although independent providers did not necessarily charge less than day nurseries, neither did they require the invasive and intimidating application process and investigations that had become routine at charitable institutions. And unmarried mothers, barred from most day nurseries on moral grounds, had no alternative. Non-English-speaking mothers sought speakers of their own language with whom to leave their children, and in general, laboring-class mothers probably felt more comfortable with their socioeconomic peers. Neighborhood providers were often more convenient and their hours more flexible. Most important, they were unlikely to vaunt their expertise, attempt to exert authority over their clients, or "quarantine" them within the child care setting.

Such providers seldom kept formal records; their services come to light only through the accounts of investigators from reform organizations such as the Society for the Prevention of Cruelty to Children (SPCC) or scurrilous newspaper reports of "notorious baby farms," which became increasingly frequent during the 1880s and 1890s.[160] These accounts portrayed shady operations through which infants were bought and sold, or where they perished as a result of poor nutrition or abuse. Newspapers occasionally reported on the "responsible" baby farmer who, after hearing nothing from a parent for several weeks, turned abandoned children over to the authorities, but reporters failed to acknowledge the legions of individual women working in their own homes who were the chief source of child care for many poor urban neighborhoods and did not warrant disparagement as "baby farmers."[161]

In addition to investigating allegations of baby farming, SPCC chapters also specialized in following up reports of abusive parents, often mothers, who regularly left children on their own for long hours. As one might expect, such parents were usually working women who had no access to child care and could see no alternative—mothers like those described by the African American minister quoted earlier. But unlike the minister, the SPCC lacked sympathy for these women and their situations; instead, in their annual reports the organization portrayed such mothers as neglectful and irresponsible.[162]

Taken together, the stories of neglected children and baby farms in newspapers and philanthropic reports gave both wage-earning mothers and child care a bad name. Formal institutions such as day nurseries and homes for infants fared somewhat better, but even their own pamphlets and publicity could not efface their philanthropic identities and persistent ambivalence toward maternal employment. In the public mind, these charities remained very much on the margins, indelibly associated with the lower classes, familial crisis, and the need for uplift. Women of the middle and upper classes might manage day nurseries, but they would never consider sending their own children to one.[163]

This is not to minimize the importance of philanthropic child care during the nineteenth century. For countless mothers it was an essential element of their strategies to work *and* keep their children. The existence of institutions like the Philadelphia House of Industry enabled them to avoid incarceration in almshouses; day nurseries meant that they would not have to board their children; and even orphanages and foster care placements allowed them to retain custody of their children during difficult times instead of surrendering them for indenture or adoption.

Yet, with the exception of the women of the National Association of Colored Women, most day nursery philanthropists insisted on presenting their services as a welfare measure—a temporary expedient for poor mothers and families in crisis. They failed to see that paid employment and the concomitant need for child care were endemic in the lives of low-income women, much less that child care would enable these women to participate more effectively in the labor market.[164] Nevertheless, to expect nineteenth-century female reformers to embrace a universalistic ideology of social citizenship for women would be ahistorical. Dedicated exponents of women's rights overlooked the question of child care, although they did take up other aspects of women's labor, such as hours and wages. Most trade unions ignored or excluded female workers, but even those with women's auxiliaries, such as the Knights of Labor, concentrated on young single women who worked in factories, not mothers who *might* have become industrial workers had they found child care.

Wage-earning mothers seemed unable to organize on their own behalf to express a demand for child care in their own terms, probably because they lacked the resources (both time and money) as well as the inclination to form associations as readily as did middle- and upper-class women. Instead, these mothers used institutional care where they could find it, created alternatives where they could not, or attempted to survive by engaging in domestic entrepreneurship or industrial homework and caring for their children simultaneously. Around the turn of the century, however, as industry and commerce became increasingly centralized and homework came under regulation, these occupations and strategies became more precarious and the need for public child care provisions more insistent than ever.[165]

But prospects for addressing this need were dim, for the legacy of nineteenth-century child care was an ambiguous one. Hardly a golden age, this period was nonetheless rich in innovation and invention on the part of parents, philanthropists, and reformers. Child care enabled mothers to escape the worst aspects of poverty and social upheaval. But much of this care grew out of a middle-class concept of women's maternal responsibilities—one that regarded wage-earning women as mothers, not workers, and upheld the ideal of the male breadwinner. Moreover, child care remained firmly lodged within the context of social welfare, not, like public education, a provision that was fast becoming a universal right of citizenship.[166] Thus this nineteenth-century institution—or, rather, set of disparate practices—could not lay the foundation for claiming child care as a woman's right in the twentieth century.

Chapter 2 The Road Not Taken: A Turning Point in Policies Toward Wage-Earning Mothers

One of the most popular exhibits at the 1893 World's Columbian Exposition in Chicago was the Model Day Nursery, where, for twenty-five cents, parents could bring their children to spend all or part of a day. Located in the Children's Building, the nursery was, according to a promotional pamphlet, "equipped with everything necessary to carry on the work properly—dainty wire swinging cradles, cribs, swinging chairs, a pound in which the little ones who can walk are placed with toys to amuse them."[1] There were also a mothers' room and rooms for older children. The equipment was immaculate, and the "nurse girls" in attendance, dressed in striped uniforms and starched white caps, had been carefully trained. Glass partitions allowed passersby and visitors to observe children enjoying all the benefits of modern child care (figs. 2.1 and 2.2).

To the late nineteenth-century public, the typical charitable day nursery was a dreary, highly regimented institution reeking of carbolic disinfectants and overcooked vegetables and crowded with pale, bored, and listless children who had nothing to play with but a few broken, discarded toys. It was a place to which no middle-class mother

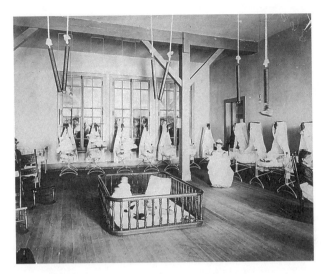

Fig. 2.1. The Model Day Nursery in the Children's Building at
the World's Columbian Exhibition held in Chicago in 1893
featured the latest equipment and child-rearing techniques. The
philanthropists who set it up sought to emphasize both the
hygienic and the educational aspects of the exhibit. The
windows behind the swinging bassinets at the rear allowed
spectators to view modern child care methods in use. Courtesy
of the Chicago Historical Society.

would consider sending her children. The Model Day Nursery, with its spacious, well-equipped rooms, cheerful caretakers, and carefully planned educational activities, was deliberately designed to counter such an impression. Set
up by a group of New York City's leading day nursery philanthropists, the
exhibit was intended to demonstrate the most up-to-date, "approved methods
of rearing children from infancy on."[2] Children from all classes would benefit
from spending a day in this ideal setting.

The moving force behind the nursery was Josephine Jewell (Mrs. Arthur)
Dodge, the founder of two day nurseries in New York City. In 1892 she
convened a conference on day nurseries in New York City and then, as chair of
the Committee on Philanthropies of her state's Woman's Exposition Board, she
lobbied the all-male National Columbian Commission to gain approval for the
special exhibit. Her task was not easy. Not only did American day nurseries
have an unsavory reputation, but the Paris Exposition of 1889 had set an
unfortunate precedent when its nursery became notorious as a depot for aban-

Fig. 2.2. When filled to capacity, the Baby Crèche in the
Children's Building appeared far less serene, although the adult-
to-child ratio was quite high. Here both African American and
white women cared for the children. An advertisement for the
special cribs and bassinets used in the nursery is posted on the
wall to the right. Lantern Slide #74, gift of Mrs. Mae Olson;
courtesy of the Chicago Historical Society.

doned children. The managers of the Chicago Exposition wanted neither
scandal nor the odor of charity to taint their modern "White City," and they
had to be convinced that the nursery would provide an important service to
fairgoers before they agreed to include it as a "department of public comfort."[3]

Public response to the nursery more than vindicated the enthusiasm of the
Woman's Board; during the six-month duration of the fair, parents brought
more than ten thousand children to the nursery, which could accommodate
only fifty at a time.[4] According to one observer,

> The nursery was the tired mother's paradise. Here she could leave her little ones,
> feeling that they were as safe and well cared for as they would be at home, while she
> viewed the sights of the fair.
>
> It was crowded every day . . . and at times children were turned away for lack of
> room. Before the windows in front of this department a constant stream of visitors
> passed or stood during the day, watching the gambols of the little ones inside.[5]

But Dodge was not satisfied with merely providing a service to mothers "enjoying the wonders of the Exposition" or serving up amusing *tableaux vivants* of

childhood innocence. Rather, she hoped to "inspire thousands of philanthropic women with time and money at their disposal to establish in their own cities and towns similar nurseries where poor women obliged to labor for the support of their families may leave their little ones in safety."[6] The Model Day Nursery, an embodiment of progressivism, would serve as an exemplar of what day nursery philanthropists could accomplish.

A MOVEMENT IS BORN

After their triumph in Chicago, Dodge and her associates decided to launch a national child care movement, setting up the Association of Day Nurseries of New York City (ADNNYC) in 1895 and the National Federation of Day Nurseries (NFDN) in 1898; Dodge served as president of both.[7] Following her lead, day nursery philanthropists in Chicago, Philadelphia, and Cleveland formed affiliated chapters.

The Model Day Nursery, along with the formation of a national and city-wide associations, marked a new phase in the self-consciousness of child care philanthropists. By creating public awareness of nurseries and the specific benefits they could offer, these women hoped to expand the scope of their charity and raise its stature. They offered advice and encouragement to would-be nursery founders and worked to improve conditions in existing institutions. While remaining wedded to the nineteenth-century goal of providing tempo-rary relief to families in crisis, the NFDN also defined a new purpose for the day nursery: to Americanize the growing population of immigrant children.

From the 1890s on, maternal employment rose gradually. Many mothers entered the labor force for the same reasons they had in the preceding de-cades—because male breadwinners were absent or unable to earn a "family wage." Increasingly, however, mothers were motivated by what historian Lynn Weiner calls "relative economic need—the desire to better the standard of living for their families."[8]

Until about 1920, mothers often chose to work at home, either practicing "domestic entrepreneurship"—keeping boarders or taking in laundry—or doing industrial homework. These sources of income declined, however, with the tapering off of immigration (a major supplier of boarders) and regulation of industrial homework.[9] Another source, the wages of children, was also cut off as compulsory school laws and child labor prohibitions spread. At the same time, falling birth rates reduced the childbearing phase of women's lives, making it somewhat easier for mothers to respond to changing economic conditions by taking jobs outside the home.[10] From 1890 to 1910, the proportion of married and once-married women in the labor force rose from 31.8 percent (1.2 million) to 39.8 percent (3.1 million). Although precise figures are not available, most historians assume that a substantial proportion of these female workers—perhaps more than half in some areas—were mothers, many with small children.[11] Typically, employment rates for African American mothers were higher than for whites.

Meanwhile, the number of day nurseries was also increasing. In 1892, there were fewer than 100 across the country, but by 1901, there were 175; by 1906, 280; by 1912, 500; by 1914, 618; and by 1916, 700.[12] The growth in institutional child care should not be attributed entirely to the efforts of the NFDN. As a segregated organization, it excluded African American women, who started many facilities with the support of the National Association of Colored Women, which was founded at around the same time as the NFDN. The NFDN also had little influence over the numerous Catholic charities that set up day nurseries. Despite the increase of day nurseries under every type of aegis, there were not enough facilities to accommodate all the children who needed child care, even when the narrowest criteria for admission were applied.

In defining and responding to the demand for more nurseries, both the New York and national organizations took their direction from Josephine Dodge. During nearly thirty years in office, she stamped the child care movement with her particular conservative brand of maternalism, a politics that had class- as well as gender-based components. She insisted that women's primary role should be that of motherhood, defined as the care of children in the home, and she opposed governmental intervention to correct social problems, preferring to leave such matters in the hands of private charities run by the social elite.

Dodge was an expert at operating in the world of philanthropy. She began her work in day nurseries soon after her marriage to Arthur Dodge, a founder of the New York Charity Organization Society (COS) and scion of a wealthy family renowned for its charitable works.[13] Although Josephine Dodge considered philanthropic activity entirely appropriate to her sex and class, she strongly believed that women should remain aloof from politics, lest their credibility and moral authority as reformers become tainted or their energies diverted. Putting organizational power behind her convictions, in 1911 she founded the National Association Opposed to Woman Suffrage, over which she presided for six years.

From this platform Dodge asserted that "reform work, welfare work . . . are not the sole end of government. . . . Government is not reform legislation. In the last analysis government is concerned with the protection of persons and property."[14] The implication was that social reform and welfare should remain in the civic sector. Dodge's desire to keep these functions out of governmental hands was nurtured by her ongoing association with the COS, which generally regarded official government efforts at providing charity as irresponsible when not actually corrupt.[15]

On many points, Dodge's views on motherhood and politics place her in the category of female activists whom historian Molly Ladd-Taylor has labeled "sentimental maternalists."[16] Ladd-Taylor takes as the paradigm for this group the National Congress of Mothers (NCM), whose members, like Dodge, embraced a traditional view of the family and never endorsed women's suffrage (although the organization did not unanimously oppose it). The NCM differed, however, in one important respect: it believed that the state should be involved in social provision for women. Thus the organization played a leading role in the campaign for mothers' pensions. By contrast, the NFDN, under Dodge's firm hand, remained adamantly opposed to yielding responsibility for social welfare to the state.

This position helps to explain why the NFDN never made a concerted effort to win government funding for child care programs. At first Dodge seemed to favor such a course; at the NFDN Conference of 1905, she referred favorably to the municipally sponsored crèches of France and Russia: "Is the American public less keen to recognize the value of this work than the municipalities of Paris and St. Petersburg—both giving sanction and large concessions of money? Up to the present time, there has been no public financial recognition of the importance of day nurseries [in the United States]."[17] Other reformers also advised the NFDN to seek public funding for nurseries. At its 1912 conference, infant mortality expert Edward Bunnell Phelps exhorted the nursery movement to expand its services and suggested that it could win governmental support by taking its cue from successful campaigns for workmen's compensation and municipal milk stations.[18]

At the same time, voices outside conventional child welfare channels were also calling for publicly supported child care. Right-wing socialist John Spargo, in his influential 1906 study of the impact of poverty on children, *The Bitter Cry of the Children,* argued that whereas private philanthropy was making a concerted effort, it was "exceedingly little when compared with the magnitude of the need." He did not think that philanthropists should stop trying, but rather that "the municipality or state should accept final responsibility in the

matter, and provide [day nurseries or crèches] wherever the failure of philanthropy makes such a course necessary."[19]

In spite of these urgings, the NFDN never attempted to secure governmental
support for child care. In part, its leaders may have been unwilling to acknowledge that they could not meet growing needs through their own efforts. They
may also have feared that government funding would deprive them of flexibility in running their nurseries and dealing with applicants on a case-by-case
basis.[20] In any event, the records of both the NFDN and its local chapters
throughout the Progressive Era and into the 1920s give no indication of
significant efforts to lobby for public funding for day nurseries at the municipal, state, or federal level.[21]

ENLISTING THE STATE TO REGULATE

There was one area in which the NFDN did turn to government for assistance:
regulation. The organization needed the authority of the state to put teeth into
its campaign to upgrade day nursery conditions. As a first step, the group drew
up specifications for member nurseries concerning such matters as sanitation,
hygiene, diet, equipment, and staff qualifications.[22] Although the NFDN
threatened to withhold membership from any nursery that failed to comply, its
words were not particularly compelling, partly because expulsion of its members would have weakened the fledgling organization and partly because many
of the nurseries the NFDN sought to regulate did not, for one reason or
another (usually lack of funds), belong to the organization in the first place.[23]
Acknowledging their own lack of power over member nurseries, local chapters
lobbied municipal and state governments to transform the NFDN's voluntary
standards into law, with early successes in New York City, Chicago, and Richmond, and statewide in California.[24] These laws, in turn, served as models for
other communities.[25]

Regulating bodies varied. In some cities or states, a board of charities in-
spected nurseries; in others, health- or education-related agencies enforced the
law; in still others, administration depended largely on voluntary organizations. Wide variations in modes of administration and enforcement, as well as
in regulations themselves, created problems for officials attempting to establish
nationwide standards. In 1919, S. Josephine Baker, the pioneering New York
City public health physician, complained, "In the United States there are no
universal standards [for nurseries] at the present time. In fact, very few of our
States or cities have established any standards at all." Baker saw this as less of a

problem for philanthropic nurseries, which were benevolently motivated, than for commercial nurseries, which were "maintained for gain, and sometimes to the actual detriment of the children who are cared for."[26] Without the force of law behind them, it was difficult for reformers to put baby farms out of business or to police operations that were run solely for profit.

But laws alone did not guarantee that facilities for children could be effectively regulated. In its 1917 investigation of so-called baby farms, for example, the Juvenile Protective Agency of Chicago (JPA) used social service agencies to target 137 uncertified boarding homes for children. Investigators found many with substandard conditions. Through the baby farms, infants were bought and sold "in a regular commercialized traffic," and children were kept in

> filthy, unsupervised homes, where the foster mothers neglected them and some died of sheer starvation; . . . the women who conducted these homes were ignorant and utterly unfit to be entrusted with the care of children; . . . some of them were prostitutes and . . . others drank and chewed tobacco; . . . the babies in these homes were in every stage of neglect and disease, some with rickets, some with venereal and other infectious diseases sleeping in the same beds with other children; some feeble-minded, some tubercular; . . . many of the parents were not interested in what became of their children, and . . . some of the parents were diseased and criminal.[27]

What was perhaps most upsetting was the discovery that existing statutes were inadequate to deal with the conditions that had been exposed. Chicago city ordinances covered only those homes where more than three children under age three were boarded for periods longer than twenty-four hours (these were required to be licensed by the Health Department). Thus homes that boarded three or fewer children, or mostly older children, were not technically subject to regulation.[28]

Although authorities moved quickly to try to plug these loopholes, the JPA investigation may have done more harm than good. On the one hand, it uncovered shocking practices and conditions, but on the other, it made local authorities appear impotent to eradicate them. Ultimately, the lasting impression may have been that much public child care was unsavory but that neither the government nor voluntary child welfare agencies could do much to stop abuses.

NEW AIMS, OLD METHODS

Except for exploiting the government's regulatory powers, the NFDN preferred to rely on more traditional organizational structures and methods to improve child care services.[29] Movement leaders believed they could raise standards by educating the philanthropists and practitioners involved in day nursery work through frequent local, regional, and national conferences. At the same time, they felt that there was something to be gained by aligning nurseries more closely with the "most progressive" forms of child welfare, health, and education. In particular, they looked to the kindergarten movement, which also had its roots in charity but which had gained widespread recognition by the late nineteenth century, attracting parents of all classes who sought the benefits of education for their young children.[30] Although NFDN leaders remained focused on the lower classes, they hoped that some of the kindergartens' favorable reputation might rub off on day nurseries. Josephine Dodge asserted in 1897, "As kindergarten training has appealed to the public's intelligence, it has been included in the nursery regime."[31]

Dodge was exaggerating. Although the NFDN devoted many conference sessions to the methods of the nineteenth-century kindergarten pioneer Friedrich Froebel and later to the ideas of the Italian nursery innovator Maria Montessori and various American progressive nursery educators, few nurseries offered full-fledged educational programs, and most were slow to absorb the principles of the emerging pedagogy of early childhood.[32]

There were several reasons for this situation. For one, progressive education, with its emphasis on free play and creativity, conflicted sharply with the NFDN's vision of what was appropriate for poor and working-class children, especially those from immigrant families. What these youngsters required was not activities that fostered the imagination but didactic lessons in patriotism and middle-class customs and manners. This conflict led the organization to send out mixed messages. While Dodge exhorted member nurseries to modernize, Marjory Hall, who ran both the New York and the national offices of the NFDN, advised, "The lower the home, the greater the need of the child. It is someday to be an American citizen, and to this end it ought to be given the trend toward personal cleanliness and order."[33]

Local affiliates were more inclined to follow Hall's advice than to try to fulfill Dodge's self-serving claims. For example, the Young Women's Union of Philadelphia, a group formed by German Jewish women, decided that the best way to help their Russian Jewish brethren would be "to make of the children good American citizens, to imbue them with the best American ideals."[34] Accordingly, they trained children in their day nursery to associate "patriotic songs with cleanliness, order, thrift, and adherence to rules."[35]

But even nurseries with more progressive-minded boards and managers found it difficult to put educational techniques into practice, for they lacked the requisite staff and funding. Trained kindergarten and nursery school teachers were hard to come by and commanded salaries far higher than those of the low-skilled nursery maids who made up the bulk of their staffs.[36] Nurseries that could not set up educational programs on their own premises often sent older preschool charges to nearby kindergartens (sometimes located in the same settlement house) for part of the day, but younger children were then left with little relief from what was likely to be a rigid and monotonous routine.[37]

On the whole, the NFDN's efforts to foster educational improvement bore little fruit. In 1906 Dodge felt compelled to admit, "The kindergartens of our nurseries . . . are not what they should be." But real improvement would have entailed a fundamental shift in the philosophy of the nurseries, which stressed that their purpose was to offer *temporary* relief. As Dodge herself admitted, "One can hardly expect the best of trained kindergartners to devote their time where conditions are impossible to control, and all our best workers are obliged to adapt their methods to the irregular attendance of the pupils."[38] What she failed to note, of course, was that "irregular attendance" was the inevitable by-product of the NFDN's policy on eligibility. Had the organization conceded that maternal employment was an ongoing necessity for low-income families and encouraged nurseries to admit children on a long-term basis, conditions for teaching would surely have improved.

Although nursery managers found it difficult to undertake a wholesale re-structuring of their programs for educational purposes, they did manage to incorporate the protocols of the advancing child health movement.[39] NFDN standards required a physician's examination before admission and regular monthly exams thereafter (local physicians usually volunteered their services); in addition, each child was subjected to a daily health inspection by the nursery matron. Physicians' warnings about the transmission of germs only reinforced the nurseries' long-held concern with cleanliness. Well into the twentieth century, nurseries continued to follow the custom of stripping children of their "home clothes" and replacing them with nursery garb. The NFDN stipulated that each child be given her own towel, toothbrush, and eating utensils, and prescribed a specific "dietary," with copious amounts of "fresh, pure milk," for the children's meals. Nurseries also enlisted mothers' cooperation in keeping children robust and free from disease by offering classes or clubs where mothers could learn to practice proper hygiene and nutrition at home.[40]

Nurseries in Chicago and Boston went even further in their efforts to ensure the health of their charges. They pioneered in setting up cooperative programs with district nurses who went into the homes of nursery families to reinforce health advice, identify medical problems, and trace paths of contagion. Visiting nurses also referred needy families to nurseries when they felt it was appropriate.[41] The Philadelphia Association of Day Nurseries formed an Infant Mortality Committee, which investigated milk shops in the neighborhoods of its member nurseries and brought about city regulation of milk sales.[42]

In addition to an emphasis on health, NFDN leaders felt that it was important to gain legitimacy in the field of child welfare. Welfare leaders, for their part, viewed nurseries favorably because they permitted mothers to earn wages. This, in turn, kept families intact—a goal that was very much in accordance with progressives' growing distaste for institutionalizing children.[43] In deterring mothers from seeking relief and becoming pauperized, nurseries upheld the principles of groups like the Charity Organization Society. In his influential volume *The Principles of Relief,* Edward Devine, general secretary of New York COS, commented that the day nursery was "a comparatively new form of assistance, but it had speedily become popular, and its usefulness is unquestionable."[44] In 1902, eight New York City districts requested the establishment of day nurseries, and at the 1905 NFDN Conference, Dodge proudly noted that according to Josephine Shaw Lowell, founder of the New York COS, day nurseries served the state "in keeping children out of the institutions by providing a day home."[45] At the same conference, Devine paid tribute "to the breadth of view and the thoroughness of the leaders in the Day Nursery movement, to the absence of amateurishness, and to the genuine need for the service which you [Dodge and the NFDN] perform."[46]

In spite of Devine's flattery, Dodge was well aware that she and her colleagues in the NFDN lacked the professional training and status that were becoming de rigueur in welfare work. When her organization was invited to hold a session at the 1906 National Conference of Charities and Corrections, the most important convention in the field, Dodge modestly stated that the NFDN was appearing "for the first time among a body of experts, and as comprising perhaps the largest body of amateurs who have ever attempted an extensive work." She appealed for "advice, interest and co-operation from all educational and philanthropic bodies."[47]

One of the day nurseries' main weaknesses, in the eyes of some welfare experts, was its propensity to dispense charity without first doing proper casework. Even the generally favorable Devine expressed reservations on this score: "It has already become reasonably clear that indiscriminate aid in the form of care for children in day nurseries is nearly as objectionable as any other form of indiscriminate relief."[48] What Devine seemed to be implying was that nurseries sometimes accepted the children of mothers who left the home to work for "frivolous reasons."

As a defense against such accusations, the NFDN moved to bolster investigations into applicants. At first, leaders thought that this task could be accomplished by hiring "a better grade" of matrons,[49] but it soon became apparent that matrons, no matter how well qualified, could not perform such research along with their other duties, which generally included supervising nursery personnel and overseeing the daily routine. So the organization advised member nurseries to assign this responsibility to someone else—possibly a trained nurse or a board member who had some experience in "friendly visiting." But such personnel were not up to the task; the changing scope of social work demanded a greater degree of professional specialization and training.[50] Most nurseries, however, could barely afford to hire one professional, much less two or more, so they asked specialists to combine functions. According to Linda Goldmintz, a scholar of social work, "a nurse would often be hired to do the work of a nurse and a social worker, in addition to acting as a consulting physician." Similarly, the duties of teachers and social workers were thought to be interchangeable.[51] At the 1916 NFDN conference, one member lamented that the "nurseries . . . lagged behind [the] movement to advance the national wealth through scientific study and through conservation of its child life. We still follow . . . old methods and hold up old aims."[52]

PROFESSIONAL AMATEURS

Yet the NFDN seemed to cherish its amateur status, and it remained committed to traditional notions of the virtues of private charity. A 1902 article in the *Century Illustrated Monthly Magazine* reveals some of the complex motivations at work in the field of child care philanthropy. The author, Lillie Hamilton French, remarked after touring dozens of day nurseries in New York City:

> I never realized so fully as after one of these journeys the difference that prosperity makes in institutions of an eleemosynary character. It is to be detected at once in the air of the matron who receives you. When she has a board of rich managers behind her, or the exchequer of a well-to-do church to draw upon, there is that in her manner which is not to be mistaken. It is like the bearing of the happy wife who has never been harassed by anxiety. "All that I have to do is ask for what I want, and I get it. The children have only the best of everything," one of these matrons said to me; and I

realized she spoke truly when I looked into the happy faces of the children, and at their pretty beds, and into the closets filled with their clothes—linens of every kind, dresses and underwear, and even little coats of quaint and charming fashion, meant for use in the roof garden when the day is cold.[53]

This description evokes the "dainty swinging cradles" prominently featured at the Model Day Nursery in Chicago; indeed, many New York women had been involved in setting up the exhibit in Chicago. Back at home, they seem to have married the Victorian nursery with that late nineteenth-century "palace of consumption," the department store (fig. 2.3).[54]

French's deft use of detail suggests that some philanthropists were not interested in simply providing necessities for their charges but sought to use their charities for vicarious display of their own wealth—as a theater for their good works. (Ironically, in the view of contemporary sociologist Thorstein Veblen, upper-middle-class and upper-class women were themselves also being used as "vehicles for display" of their husbands' wealth, their philanthropic activities serving as a form of "vicarious leisure" for their husbands.)[55] Well-heeled NFDN women were no doubt sincere in their desire to improve day nurseries, but it was also true, as historian Anne Firor Scott notes, that "women's clubs were sometimes a road to social status."[56] Although Josephine Dodge was secure in her position in the highest echelon of New York society, many members of the NFDN came from the middle class and had chosen day nurseries as "their" charity.[57] This may help to explain why they were reluctant to seek government funding for nurseries; it would have been a point of class as well as gender pride that they were able to support their projects without public assistance.

Certainly, not all day nurseries could serve as vehicles for conspicuous benevolence. As French herself reported, with a Dickensian sense of pathos,

> The case is sadly altered . . . when a day nursery's board of managers has to economize. The matron may be as conscientious and as kind, and the children as tenderly loved; but everything, even to the matron's manner, betrays the pinched and the troubled. To realize this you have only to look at the way in which the children's food is prepared; at the way the bread is broken and put into the galvanized iron cups waiting for the soup.[58]

It was not good intentions that the matrons and managers of such nurseries lacked, but financial resources. Public funding might not have brought all nurseries in New York City to the same level, but it would no doubt have narrowed the gap between the poorest and the lavishly endowed.

Fig. 2.3. A series of highly romantic drawings of New York City day nurseries by children's book illustrator Jessie Willcox Smith matched Lillie Hamilton French's lyrical descriptions of these institutions. This scene portrays nursemaids and children in the garden of Grace Church, whose well-heeled congregants generously funded its nursery. From Lillie Hamilton French, "While the Mother Works: A Look at the Day Nurseries of New York," *New Century Magazine* (December 1902): 181.

Class differences played out not only between nurseries but within the child care movement as a whole. National meetings of the NFDN were dominated by upper-class volunteer board members, nursery managers, members of visiting committees, and paid members of the NFDN staff, while the matrons and other nursery employees who actually provided services had little voice in setting policy, and nursery mothers remained invisible altogether.[59] Although board membership was presumably based on a woman's interest and expertise in the field of child care, it was clearly a perquisite of the middle and upper classes.

Restricting decision making in this way affected mothers, staff members, and the child care movement as a whole. To mothers, it was both alienating and insulting. In her 1914 study of working mothers on New York City's West Side, feminist reformer Katharine Anthony observed, "The women regard the day nursery as a type of institution, and, as such, distrust it. It must be said that the attitude of the management too often shows the strain of autocracy with which we are prone to dilute our charity. . . . Some [mothers] made very intelligent and just criticisms, and there were several who might very well have served on the visiting committee of the nursery. These were women who had long been in domestic service before their marriage and were well trained in the care of children."[60] The West Side at this time had two day nurseries with a combined capacity of 120 children. Yet Anthony found that only 40 of the 221 preschool children of working mothers in the district were sent to the nurseries. Mothers' distrust of these institutions led them to prefer the "haphazard" care of neighbors and relatives.[61]

The exclusion of staff members from decision making had broad implications. As with the mothers, perceptions of social status prevented volunteers from accepting matrons and superintendents, who generally came from lower-middle-class or working-class backgrounds, as equals in the cause of child care.[62] Indeed, board members seem to have regarded their employees more like servants. In her analysis of the New York Nursery and Child's Hospital, historian Virginia Quiroga astutely compared its internal procedures to "those of a large middle class household."[63] Within this model, the volunteer managers played the same role they did within their own households, directing the paid staff (many of whom lived on the premises, like domestic servants) to carry out their orders.

Although Quiroga was describing a mid-nineteenth-century institution, French's reportage, along with dozens of annual day nursery reports, suggests that the working conditions of nursery staffs had changed little by the early twentieth century. Matrons were still expected to live in the nurseries (indeed, food and lodging were calculated as part of their compensation). Some had the assistance of a cook and one or two nursery maids, but many performed all the daily work of the nursery—caring for and feeding dozens of children, even doing laundry—by themselves. And in addition, they were expected to be extremely dedicated and self-sacrificing (not unlike mothers). Nursery managers, cognizant of how much the success of their institutions depended on these exemplary individuals, were lavish in their praise. But in the eyes of one observer, matrons were still nothing more than "glorified housekeepers."[64]

This image created a quandary for Dodge and other movement leaders, for it indicated that nursery personnel were out of synch with those in other fields of child welfare. Dodge tried to paint a different picture of nursery work, claiming that college girls and educated women were coming to regard the position of day nursery matron or superintendent as "just as much a calling and goal to work for as the Settlement or other social work."[65] But movement records suggest that this was wishful thinking on her part; young middle-class "new women" seeking careers were not flocking into the field of child care. Because it remained unprofessionalized and continued to bear many of the characteristics of domestic service, day nursery work continued to lack social cachet.

Yet while they bemoaned the status of their staff members, neither the NFDN nor its affiliates made a concerted effort to improve staff quality through specialized training. Instead, most of their educational efforts took the form of conferences to which only managers and board members were invited.[66] Nor did nursery workers themselves attempt to break away from the NFDN to form their own organization, set professional standards, or establish training programs, as did social workers, early childhood educators, and other groups of women involved in delivering social services within philanthropic settings during this period.[67] Such moves would have displaced upper-class volunteers from their predominant role as the primary spokespersons for the field of child care. But at the same time they would have lent nursery staff members a professional identity and a degree of authority that they—and child care as a field—otherwise lacked.

Had matrons and staff been allowed (or claimed) a greater part in making nursery policy, it might well have taken a different direction. As historian Anne Durst has argued, staff members did not always see eye to eye with the leadership, particularly around such issues as maternal employment. Because many staff members came from class backgrounds similar to those of their clients and had direct daily contact with them, they were conversant with their problems and tended to be more sympathetic and less judgmental than the managers. They understood, for example, that the reason most mothers worked was not family crisis but chronic financial hardship, and thus among low-income families the need for nurseries was ongoing.[68] Because of such attitudes (and also probably because of a lack of time), matrons were not always as scrupulous in carrying out home visits and screening applicants as nursery managers expected them to be, and they admitted families that did not strictly fit eligibility criteria. Still, while resisting official policy in practice, nursery employees stopped short of challenging it openly.

Inaction on the part of both volunteers and staff members meant that the NFDN continued to operate as a philanthropic and advocacy group, rather than as a professional organization. The NFDN's leaders, ambivalent toward the role that professionals should play within nurseries and uncomfortable in using the kinds of scientific discourse that were becoming common elsewhere in the field of child welfare,[69] preferred to look outside their own movement for both legitimation and guidance. But even here, their response to external critiques was selective. If a proposed change appeared to enhance the prestige of the day nursery, they might accept it, but if it conflicted with deeply entrenched principles, they might not. Dodge, for example, rejected physicians' advice to exclude infants from nursery care, even though they offered compelling statistical evidence that the mortality rates for bottle-fed babies were far higher than for breastfed infants.[70] She pleaded with member nurseries, "Do not drop the first work for which we came into existence, the care of the baby."[71]

As the second decade of the twentieth century neared its end, it was apparent that the persistent dilettantism of the NFDN's leadership was causing strains in the day nursery movement as a whole. At a 1919 forum on child welfare standards, Myrn Brockett of the Mary Crane Nursery of Chicago criticized amateur philanthropists for running nurseries that had a "makeshift character," growing complacent with "gratifying returns in child welfare and happiness," and failing to make the effort needed to upgrade plant, equipment, and staff. "There has been a proneness to isolation and a too great reliance upon sentiment for guidance in methods," she chided.[72] To members of the NFDN, Brockett's remarks must have been especially stinging because the nursery she represented was part of Hull House, then the center of progressive reform and the model of enlightened social service for the entire country.

OTHER VOICES

In spite of such critiques, the NFDN, as the sole national organization devoted wholly to the cause of child care, continued to dominate discourse in the field of child care for many decades, blocking out more progressive perspectives. As a result, its central principles—that child care should be offered only on a temporary basis, that day nurseries should remain private charities, and that upper-class volunteers should set policies for low-income families—persisted. Dissident voices could be heard, usually at the margins of political discourse, but their support for child care was also often conditional. Socialist John Spargo believed that day nurseries should receive public support, although he called for ultimately eliminating the need for them through the institution of some type of mothers' allowance. Feminist Katharine Anthony took a similar position. She criticized nursery managers for their high-handedness toward mothers and defended women's absolute right to work. Later, however, she became one of the leading American advocates of an endowment of motherhood—state payments to all mothers, which would eliminate the need for maternal employment.[73] Thus over time neither Spargo nor Anthony served as an effective advocate for mothers' right to employment or more adequate child care provisions.

Leading female African American philanthropists, in contrast, advanced an unequivocally positive view of child care. Accepting maternal employment as a fact of life, they believed that the most important task was not to discourage mothers from working but to free them from anxiety by keeping their children safe. Their principal organization, the National Association of Colored Women (NACW), took the position that day nurseries had a permanent place within the black community, and from the 1890s on, local affiliates were active in establishing numerous urban day nurseries for African American children (fig. 2.4). According to Mary Church Terrell, first president of the NACW, the day nursery was "a charity of which there is an imperative need."[74]

The differing positions on child care taken by the NACW and the NFDN are all the more striking because of the similarities between the two organizations. Founded at around the same time, both sought to attract a middle- and upper-class membership, and both employed a maternalist politics.[75] Unlike the NFDN, however, the NACW counted among its members many women who were or had been employed during a major portion of their adult lives.[76]

Their own working experience was only one source of the African American

Fig. 2.4. African American reformers took an active interest in child care. The Day Nursery for Colored Children—or "N" Street Day Nursery, as it was known—was started in 1904 by a group of white female philanthropists of Washington, D.C., but was taken over by two African American organizations, the Alpha Charity Club and the Social Purity Club, the following year. Black clubwomen made a special effort to recruit neighborhood families and added a vacation school for older children. Photograph from *The Crisis* (February 2, 1912): 166.

women's motivation. Many decided to undertake child care projects after attending the Atlanta University Conferences, which were held annually from 1896 to 1905. There they heard papers—including a number devoted specifically to the welfare of children—on the deplorable mortality rates and social and physical conditions of urban African Americans, and they came to believe that at least some of these problems could be alleviated by day nurseries and kindergartens.[77] Aware that few white-run nurseries accepted black children, these women responded eagerly to Terrell's call to action.

African American day nurseries differed from those run by whites not only in philosophy but also in their mode of operation and relation to the community. Instead of relying on a few major benefactors, as many white philanthropies did, African American nurseries were deeply embedded in their communities, which worked constantly to keep them afloat. In Atlanta, for example, women from a middle-class philanthropic organization, the Neighborhood Union, started five free kindergartens between 1905 and 1908. Although full-day nurseries were really what was needed, the organization could not afford them and decided that "care during part of the day was better than no care."[78] In 1918, one of these kindergartens, the Gate City Free Kindergarten Association, finally began to offer full-day care.

For nearly twenty years, until they were picked up by the newly organized Community Chest in 1924, the kindergartens were supported by dozens of "working circles" located throughout the city. These groups ran countless bazaars, turkey dinners and other socials, athletic events, baby contests, and sales of homemade foods, handicrafts, and recycled goods such as soap wrappers.[79] The largest single donation came from Herman Perry, the founder of one of the first black insurance companies, who gave forty dollars each month to cover rent for one of the kindergartens. Despite constant fundraising, "for ten years [the black women who ran the nurseries] never had any sum of money in view on which they could count."[80]

Through donations in kind, the Neighborhood Union kept expenditures to a minimum; only rent, fuel, and teachers' salaries were paid in cash. In 1909, the total annual budget for *all five* of their kindergartens was $1,200. By comparison, the same year the budget for *one* of Atlanta's white nurseries, Sheltering Arms, amounted to more than $11,000.[81] When the black kindergartens were finally taken into the Community Chest, a cash value was placed on the in-kind donations that had come in over the years, and the black institutions' budgets were recalculated at more then $10,000 per year.[82]

Fundraising was much easier for white people than for black people. Not only did Sheltering Arms receive funds from the city of Atlanta ($1,800 in 1909), but it could draw on the resources of a much wealthier community. Sheltering Arms raised more than $4,700 from its "tag day," while the black working circles raised only $100 from theirs. Because of the greater wealth of the white community, Sheltering Arms and similar institutions could manage with only a few annual events; the black fundraisers had to keep going year round.

Nevertheless, the black community did not allow a lack of funds to compromise the quality of programs they offered to children. The largest single item in the Sheltering Arms budget, salaries, was $2,350—nearly twice the *total* budget for the five black institutions. Salaries for black teachers, by contrast, were described as meager.[83] To compensate, the community attempted to improve the teachers' working conditions through volunteer work; numerous students and teachers from local colleges and public schools regularly assisted in the kindergartens and nurseries.

The African American civic leaders of Atlanta used what historian Edyth Ross calls a "community development approach to social work and social welfare."[84] This approach tended to make them more sensitive to communal needs than their white counterparts in Atlanta and other Southern cities—even those who were directly involved in organizing charities for black communities. For example, beginning around the turn of the century, the white women who belonged to the Women's Home Mission Society of the Methodist Episcopal Church, South, organized a number of settlement houses in black urban neighborhoods throughout the South. Committed specifically to helping women and children, these settlements (which were called Bethlehem Houses, Centers, or Community Centers, to distinguish them from similar facilities restricted to whites) often offered kindergartens and supervised playgrounds, but apparently none had day nurseries.[85]

The philanthropic style of African Americans also contrasted sharply with that of the middle- and upper-class whites who belonged to chapters of the NFDN.[86] White benefactors and even managers often related to their "pet charities" in a distanced and ritualized way, speaking in lofty terms about the benefits they could bestow, attending teas and other fundraising events, but seldom actually visiting the nurseries or spending time in direct contact with either the children or their parents. Black nursery philanthropists, like their white counterparts, used the rhetoric of uplift and child saving: the nurseries "aided in building the health and character of . . . underprivileged children, and sheltered them from the influence of 'curbstone education.'"[87] But through their ongoing activities and regular involvement, these middle-class women developed a much more intimate relationship with the institutions they supported, and as a result they tended to be far more accepting of the parents who used them. Also, they understood from their own experience the discrimination and intimidation that African Americans encountered on a daily basis as they went about the business of making a living.

Although the NACW and local groups like the Neighborhood Union demonstrated a deep and longstanding interest in child care throughout the Progressive Era, there is no evidence that the NFDN ever exchanged views on the subject of day nurseries with any of the leading African American philanthropists, much less that the NFDN altered its staunch elitist and conservative convictions in response to black women's position. Like nearly all white women's organizations of the period, the NFDN barred African Americans from membership. Still, it is not inconceivable that the two organizations might at least have acknowledged one another's presence. Race, however, proved to be an impermeable barrier. The lack of communication did not appear to impede the NACW's progress, but for the NFDN, it meant a further hardening of its principles.

From neither within nor without, then, did the NFDN feel serious pressure to reconsider its views by accepting maternal employment as a commonplace in "normal" families and reconceptualizing the day nursery as a service that fulfilled an ongoing and increasing need in many communities.

REALIGNMENT IN REFORM

By remaining wedded to a nineteenth-century conception of itself and its mission, the NFDN—and the child care movement as a whole—began to lose ground. Despite efforts to expand and modernize day nurseries, the organization's ambivalence about its own aims, its reluctance to professionalize, and its mixed success in bringing nursery practices up to the levels demanded by experts in other social service fields, combined to undermine the cause of child care. The weakened movement was hard-put to counter objections to day nurseries, particularly when they came from one-time allies.

No less a figure than Jane Addams, the founder of Hull House, was one friend who changed her mind about child care. During the early days of her settlement work in Chicago, Addams had endorsed the establishment of a day nursery in response to the obvious needs of neighborhood women whose children, left alone while their mothers worked, frequently came to harm. But she grew ambivalent about child care and its meaning in the lives of mothers. In a revealing 1905 interview with the influential journal *Charities and the Commons,* she seemed to be seeking some sort of clarification. She condoned the use of child care by young mothers who had worked before marriage and might find it "irksome" to stay at home: "The girl who has always been in a store would no doubt rather go back to the store and earn her living than do the household work. The nursery would give the child much better care than she could give it . . . and she could help along the fortune of the family."[88] But she expressed deep reservations about the solo mothers (widows or divorced, deserted, or never-married women) working in physically demanding jobs:

> The day nursery is a "double-edged implement" for doing good, which may also do a little harm. . . . The conduct of day nurseries is full of little temptations to blunder with human life. How far the wife can be both wife and mother and supporter of the family raises the question of whether the day nursery should tempt her to attempt the impossible. . . . The earnings of working women are very small at the best. . . . [And what of] the careers of children after leaving day nurseries[?] One . . . investigation made in Chicago has disclosed results which are neither encouraging nor reassuring.[89]

The marital situation and type of employment available to each mother seemed to determine whether Addams felt that the day nursery was appropriate. If it led to an intolerable double burden for the mother and increased suffering for her children, clearly it was not.

Addams was led to take this position by her experiences with the some of working mothers she had encountered through her work at Hull House. She frequently recounted the tragic tale of "Goosie," a small boy who would come to the nursery covered with down from the feather brush factory where his mother worked. One windy day, as he was helping his mother hang out laundry on the roof of their tenement, Goosie was blown off and fell to the alley below, breaking his neck. As Addams tells it,

> His mother cheerily called to him to "climb up again," so confident do overworked mothers become that their children cannot get hurt. After the funeral, as the poor mother sat in the nursery postponing the moment when she must go back to her empty rooms, I asked her . . . if there was anything more we could do for her. The overworked, sorrow-stricken woman looked up and replied, "If you could give me my wages for tomorrow, I would not go to work in the factory at all. I would like to stay at home all day and hold the baby. Goosie was always asking me to take him and I never had any time." This statement revealed the condition of many nursery mothers who are obliged to forego the joys and solaces which belong to even the most poverty-stricken. The long hours of factory labor necessary for earning the support of a child leave no time for the tender care and caressing which may enrich the life of the most piteous baby.[90]

Addams and certain other leaders in the fields of maternal and child welfare were coming to believe that child care no longer presented a viable general solution for the problems of poor women. Indeed, several of Addams' Hull House colleagues were convinced that it simply created more problems. Florence Kelley, an advocate of protective labor legislation for women and children, denounced day nurseries for taking mothers away from their youngsters and sending them into shops and factories. "No money earned in the United States costs so dear, dollar for dollar, as the money earned by the mother of young children."[91] Elaborating on this theme, she asserted, "Family life is sapped in its foundations when the mothers of young children work for wages."[92] In a similar vein, Sophonisba Breckinridge and Edith Abbott, leading social work educators, linked maternal employment with children's delinquency.[93] It was not only the day nurseries themselves, but the plight of working mothers— their low wages, their weakened health and exhaustion due to overwork— coupled with the poor quality of their family's lives—the physical dangers and social risks—that led to dissatisfaction with child care and the search for an alternative.

THE MOVEMENT FOR MOTHERS' PENSIONS

With regard to policies toward wage-earning mothers, the Progressive Era proved to be an important "switch point." As the day nursery movement stagnated, the idea of mothers' pensions—government payments to mothers who lacked other means of support—rapidly moved into position as the predominant paradigm in the field of child welfare.[94] The fortunes of the two policies were not unrelated, for criticism of maternal employment and child care often turned into approval for mothers' pensions.

One of the earliest critics to make this connection was Lee R. Frankel of United Hebrew Charities. At the 1905 NFDN conference he explicitly denounced the day nursery as "only a make-shift. The great issue is the family, and the proper place for development is the home. Any system that permits the breaking up of home surroundings must be make-shift."[95] Frankel went on: "Why is it necessary for the mothers to work? It is a very unfortunate thing that under modern industrial and economic conditions it may be impossible for a man to earn enough to properly support his family, and it is most deplorable that as a result it becomes necessary for the mother to go out into the world and work for those lives entrusted to her care." His alternative was "a system of pensions that shall give a widow the chance to rear her own children."[96]

At the same conference Julia Lathrop, a child welfare reformer and resident of Hull House, anticipated Jane Addams' sentiments regarding child care and working mothers: "The fact is that the working mother is the most melancholy figure in the working world, not alone because she is unskilled, ill-paid and harassed by . . . unspeakable anxieties . . . but because the records of the world show that her children recruit the ranks of youthful delinquents and later of adult criminals."[97] Citing Australia, Germany, and Switzerland as examples, Lathrop recommended the adoption of a policy of mothers' or widows' pensions.

Lathrop's position on mothers' pensions was particularly significant, for she would soon have an opportunity to implement it at the national level. When the U.S. Children's Bureau (CB) was established in 1912, she became its first chief. Although the bureau's power remained limited for decades by a lack of funds and continuous political opposition, its imprimatur carried symbolic value. As a central clearinghouse and coordinator for voluntary and statewide initiatives in various areas of maternal and child welfare, the bureau also served as a fulcrum of political power.[98] During the campaign for passage of the Sheppard-Towner Maternity and Infancy Protection Act of 1922, the CB demonstrated that it could in fact mobilize federal support (at least temporarily) for the type of child welfare policies it favored.[99] Thus the bureau's lukewarm opinion of day nurseries meant that prospects for any kind of national child care policy were dim.

The idea of establishing state payments to mothers also gained favor among reformers outside the social welfare establishment. John Spargo was motivated by what he perceived as the deleterious effects that mothers' work had on their children. Both factory employment and industrial homework caused what he called "the blighting of the babies." He graphically depicted risks to working mothers and their infants during the perinatal period and quoted public health officials who attributed high rates of infant mortality to the "unavoidable neglect" by working mothers forced to leave infants in the care of older children (fig. 2.5). Dramatizing the danger in such practices, Spargo described one little girl who fed a four- or five-month-old sibling "soda water, banana, ice cream, and chewed cracker—all inside of twenty minutes."[100] To prove that this was not an isolated case, he presented a schedule of "five typical cases from one town" (fig. 2.6). For Spargo, an adequate set of social provisions for mothers would include paid maternity leave, municipal crèches, and mothers' pensions. He drew many of his ideas for reform from foreign models, including industrial crèches in France, factory-sponsored maternity leaves in Germany, and laws prohibiting maternal employment immediately following childbirth in Switzerland and England.

Feminist Katharine Anthony had initially endorsed maternal employment as part of her overall support for women's right to work, which she saw as key to

Fig. 2.5. Socialist John Spargo deplored the use of "little mothers" such as this one to care for small children. He claimed that this practice led to high rates of infant mortality and child neglect among the poor. From John Spargo, *The Bitter Cry of the Children* (New York: Macmillan, 1906), 73.

their independence from men. But her research for *Mothers Who Must Earn* convinced her that wage-earning mothers were paying too high a price for their freedom.[101] In her view the best solution was the endowment of motherhood, an idea she borrowed from the British feminist Eleanor Rathbone and promoted actively in the United States.[102] Because endowment of motherhood

Name	Age	Average Weekly Earnings	Husband's Work, Wages, etc.	Total Number of Children Born	No. of Children having Died	No. of Children now Alive	Nationality of the Parents	Age of Youngest Child	How Children are cared for while Mother Works	General Remarks
Mrs. M.	43	$7.00	Mill laborer. Wages $9.00 week, but is often sick. Drinks heavily.	5	5	—	Mother, Irish; Father, Scotch.	—	—	All five died under 18 months of age; three of them under 6 months. All the children were cared for by other children while mother worked. Three died of convulsions, two of diarrhœa.
Mrs. K.	38	$6.50	Laborer. Often unemployed. Average wage the year round not more than $7.00 week.	7	5	2	Mother, Irish-American; Father, Swede.	10 months.	By girl, aged 9 years.	All five that died were under 12 months of age. Two of them died of convulsions, one of acute gastritis, two of measles. The baby is a puny little thing.
Mrs. C.	34	$7.00	Deserted wife.	6	4	2	Mother, German; Father, Austrian.	18 months.	By oldest girl, aged 9 years.	One child was scalded to death while mother was at work; one died of convulsions and two of bronchitis.
Mrs. S.	29	$6.00	Sick two years and unable to work. Was a laborer formerly.	6	3	3	Mother, English; Father, American.	2 years.	By father and girl of 7 years.	The first two children and the last born are alive; the third, fourth, and fifth are dead, each of them dying within the first year. Mother says they were poor, puny babies. Causes of death: Debility, 2; convulsions, 1.
Mrs. H.	41	$6.00	Dead 6 months. Was a laborer, often sick and unemployed. Widow does not think he earned $6.00 a week the year round.	8	5	3	Mother, American; Father (deceased), French-Canadian.	20 months.	By oldest girl, 11 years old.	The first two and the eighth born are alive; the five intervening are dead. Four of these died within the first year. Causes of death: Debility, 2; intestinal dyspepsia, 2; bronchitis, 1.

Fig. 2.6. Spargo used this table, "Five Typical Cases from One Town," to dramatize the condition of children in a factory town in upper New York State. From John Spargo, *The Bitter Cry of the Children* (New York: Macmillan, 1906), 40–41.

was universal in application, it avoided the stigmatizing effects that other types of payments to mothers (that is, those targeted at a specific group) entailed.

Nearly all the critics of maternal employment and child care looked abroad for alternative policies, in effect rejecting the precedents for mothers' or widows' pensions that already existed in the United States. In fact, payments to destitute mothers, whether in cash or in kind, had been common practice in nineteenth-century social provision, both public and private. In some cities, maternalist associations formed expressly for the purpose had offered widows outdoor relief as early as the antebellum period. In other cities and in rural areas, public outdoor relief was sometimes available.[103] The widows of Civil War veterans received federal pensions, usually more generous than allotments from other sources.[104]

All these payments were intended to substitute for the earnings of the absent male breadwinner, the assumption being that a woman alone could not support a household. However, both public and private relief tended to be sporadic and inadequate (federal pensions were more reliable, although these, too, could be cut off under certain circumstances).[105] As a result, poor female-headed families, particularly those of widows, were regularly broken up, with children being sent off to orphanages or foster homes (indenture had become more or less obsolete) so that mothers could work and support themselves.

This was the cycle that advocates of mothers' pensions hoped to break. Over and over, reformers lamented the folly of removing children from "worthy" mothers simply on account of poverty. As early as 1894, the suffragist minister Anna Garlin Spencer cautioned an audience of welfare officials that in breaking up families,

> you waste all that long, careful training of the ages which the parent has had in parental affection; you waste by cutting the close tie, which grows stronger and stronger as the years go on, between parent and child; you have struck a blow at that which, in our Anglo-Saxon civilization, has given us our strength, the unity of the family. . . . If the mother . . . is only poor in purse, if she is competent in other ways to deal with her child, let us make it possible in some way to hold the family together. Do not let us think that we can parcel out human beings as we do bales of merchandise.[106]

The popular press dwelled on the pathos of separating mothers and children. Typical was a 1913 article from *The Outlook* describing a court scene in which the judge had just ordered a family to be broken up: "One of the children was a boy seven years old and the other a girl four years old. The mother begged to be allowed to keep them. The little boy threw himself into her arms, sobbing, 'Oh, mamma, I can't leave you.' But it was of no use. The mother was too poor to care for the children properly. So the law tore them apart."[107] Judges were hardly inured to the emotional pain they were compelled to inflict. Referring to "the tragic separation between mothers and children," Judge Merritt W. Pinckney of the Chicago Juvenile Court admitted, "Words cannot begin to draw the child's fear and the mother's agony, the collapse of all things strong and holy at such a time."[108]

Family breakup also came under fire because it usually led to some form of institutionalization for children. According to reformer Mary Conyngton, "Even a very poor home offers a better chance for [a child's] development than an excellent institution."[109] Dissatisfaction with the regimentation, inefficiency, and corruption of institutions had begun to crystallize by the last quarter of the nineteenth century, leading many child welfare experts to support foster homes for dependent children. But it was also clear that neither foster homes nor large-scale institutions made economic sense. It was far cheaper—half as much, by some estimates—to pay women for keeping their own children at home, through a policy of mothers' pensions.

CAMPAIGN BY COALITION

Most historians mark the 1909 White House Conference on the Care of Dependent Children as the moment when a full-fledged campaign for mothers' pensions was launched. As the first such meeting to be sponsored by the federal government, the conference drew national attention to the plight of poor mothers and children. President Theodore Roosevelt, reiterating reformers' concerns with existing policy, told representatives, "Surely . . . the goal toward which we should strive is to help the mother, so that she can keep her own home and keep the child in it; that is the best thing possible to be done for the child." But Roosevelt left open the question of how pensions should be funded and administered: "How the relief shall come, public, private, or by a mixture of both, in what way, you are competent to say and I am not."[110] It was generally agreed, however, that the resources of private charity were inadequate, so supporters quickly moved in the direction of public funding. As for administration, it would evolve on an ad hoc basis, drawing on both public and private structures.

Unlike the day nursery movement, which was virtually paralyzed under the leadership of the NFDN, the mothers' pension campaign was run by multiple organizations working in coalition.[111] Although the National Congress of

Mothers (NCM) and the General Federation of Women's Clubs (GFWC) took the lead, a number of other groups were involved, including the National Consumers' League and the Woman's Christian Temperance Union. Labor organizations also lent limited support. Endorsements from juvenile court judges Pinckney, Ben Lindsey of Denver, and E. E. Porterfield of Kansas City, and from Progressive politicians including Roosevelt, Robert LaFollette, and Louis Brandeis, added momentum.[112] The linkage between the media campaign, waged especially effectively by progressive reformer William Hard in the pages of a popular women's magazine, *The Delineator,* and the sophisticated and highly efficient political methods of the women's organizations, was what ultimately produced numerous legislative successes.[113]

From the outset, reformers aimed to establish pensions at the state, rather than the federal, level. There were several reasons for this. They probably wanted to avoid any association with the Civil War pension bureaucracy, which, by the late nineteenth century, had become notoriously corrupt.[114] Moreover, two states had already tested the waters for mothers' pensions: New York, where in 1898 the legislature passed a bill (vetoed by the governor) that would have paid widowed mothers the equivalent of what it cost to keep their children in institutions, and California, where by 1906 several counties were already providing aid to children who were cared for in their own homes.[115]

But the most important reason for the state-by-state strategy was that the maternalist politicians who spearheaded the campaign were most comfortable working at that level. The NCM and the GFWC, though national in scope, were both structured along state lines and relied, in this pre-suffrage period, on spheres of influence in municipal and state politics to exert their greatest pressure.[116] By mobilizing affiliates in nearly every state, these organizations were able to coordinate their efforts to create a domino effect—the rapid passage of legislation in state after state.[117]

The mothers' pension movement enjoyed strong support from many quarters of the social welfare establishment. One notable exception was the COS, which, since its founding, had argued that paying relief to poor women, whether from public or charitable sources, would "pauperize" recipients. According to the theory of "scientific charity" by which the COS operated, "outdoor relief" (that is, relief provided outside of institutions) undermined its recipients' will to work and become independent.[118] To them, pensions were simply another form of outdoor relief.

Advocates of mothers' pensions had to find a way to counter such charges. At the 1905 NFDN conference, Lee Frankel pointed the way: "No woman who has three or four or five children should be asked to earn her living. She has done her duty to the State and the State should recognize it, and help her bring up those children in a way that will make good citizens of them."[119] Clubwomen took up this theme, asserting that pensions should be regarded as a form of salary or wages for the *work* of motherhood—work that must also be regarded as a form of service to the nation.[120] Mary Wood told the 1912 biennial GFWC convention that pensions "would relieve the stigma of pauperism—felt under existing Charity relief. . . . The woman who produced citizens and soldiers should be placed in a class with the disabled soldier, during the period she is unable to earn for herself and children."[121]

Underscoring this point, William Hard argued that motherhood had a civic value, although he did not specifically compare it to military service. Hard pointed approvingly to the British conceptualization of social provision, quoting the formulations of New Liberal sociologist L. T. Hobhouse: "We no longer consider it desireable to drive the mother out to her charring work if we possibly can, *nor do we consider her degraded by receiving public money. We cease, in fact, to regard the public money as a dole; we treat it as a payment for a civic service.*"[122] Hard also believed that a pensioned mother should be seen not as a dependent of the state (as critics of the policy would have it) but as "an independent citizen kept from self-support only by the presence of future citizens at her knees and requiring, in order that as she fulfills her instinctive duty to them she may also fulfill her indirect civic duty to the state, the means of support really for them and only incidentally for herself."[123]

As presented by Hard and the women of the GFWC and the NCM, mothers' pensions had the potential for transforming social provision for mothers from a form of charity into one of entitlement—compensation for service to the state.[124] Had this line of argument been carried through, mothers' pensions might have become the female equivalent of men's Civil War pensions, with the citizen-mother becoming the female counterpart of the citizen-soldier. In practice, however, mothers' pensions fell far short of the ennobling vision of their architects. They not only failed to endow motherhood with a new aura of dignity but ended up creating the foundation for a welfare state that discriminated against women in two ways: by inscribing them within the state exclusively as mothers (as opposed to, say, workers or worker-mothers) and by apportioning them payments inferior to those received by men.[125]

On the whole, popular support for mothers' pensions was not based on a conceptualization of motherhood as service to the state that entitled women to compensation. Rather, it drew on sentimental encomiums to motherhood and widowhood that perpetuated a view of pensions as a form of charity (though one supported by the state). As Katharine Anthony wryly observed, "The widow enjoys great honour in American public life, although it usually turns out to be rather a spurious and sentimental homage. . . . [Thus] the [state] legislatures were in no position to resist an appeal on behalf of the poor widow." Anthony also believed that the lawmakers were "so nicely narcotized . . . by their traditional tender-heartedness that they failed to perceive the socialistic basis of this new kind of widow's pensions."[126] But here she was being overly optimistic; their sentimentality was laced with hard-headed pragmatism that ended up reinforcing a conventional view of gender roles while also granting legislators blanket permission to keep the costs of mothers' pension programs as low as possible in the name of greater economy.

The radical potential of mothers' pensions was further eroded in the course of implementation. Initially, pension legislation in most states was enabling but not mandatory. Funding levels, usually left up to municipalities or counties, were seldom adequate to cover all potential recipients, so choices had to be made. The rhetoric of the mothers' pension campaign implicitly offered an image of the ideal recipient: a "worthy" woman who had been widowed or otherwise deprived of the support of a male breadwinner through no fault of her own; virtuous, hard-working, self-sacrificing, devoted to her children; without resources and therefore dependent upon the state. For many, this image no doubt brought to mind white, native-born, middle-class women—much like those who were advocating for pensions. In practice, however, applicants for pensions came from different class, ethnic, and racial backgrounds and did not readily adhere to the norms and styles of motherhood inherent in the ideal. If they did not appear to be amenable to change or willing to learn, they would be denied pensions. Historian Joanne Goodwin found that in the early days of mothers' pension administration in Chicago, numerous women were rejected on moral grounds or for lack of cooperation with the authorities, but even more were denied because they appeared to be *too* self-sufficient; that is, they were deemed to be "adequate earners" and thus not in need of pensions.[127] Either way, they fell short of the ideal.

Problems also arose in the constitution of pension bureaucracies. After passing legislation, each state had to scramble to set up its own administrative apparatus. In some, authority was granted to juvenile courts; in others, entirely new agencies had to be formed, often at the county or municipal level. Most states required a thorough investigation of each applicant before a final decision could be made. This task was usually assigned to a charity worker who had experience in making home visits;[128] the findings were then reported to the pension-granting authority.[129]

Eligibility boards appointed by courts or state welfare agencies generally comprised male welfare officials and business leaders, and prominent women who had been active around welfare issues.[130] But reformers who had supported mothers' pensions as a means for equalizing women's status seldom ended up in positions of power. In Illinois, for example, such leading progressive reformers as Sophonisba Breckinridge and Edith Abbott, who had been central to the formulation and passage of pension legislation, suddenly found themselves boxed out, helpless to influence the administration of pensions.[131] Abbott was highly critical of the fact that, owing to a lack of properly trained social workers, applicants were put through haphazard, arbitrary, and unnecessarily harsh investigations and then had to endure ongoing surveillance.[132] "There was an idealism back of the demand for widows' pensions that saw in such legislation a step toward a finer social justice than was to be found in our old pauper laws," she reminded the National Conference of Social Work in 1917. "A pension granted only on proof of destitution after searching investigation and under continued supervision is not what most wage-earners wish for their wives and children."[133]

Political scientist Libba Gaje Moore argues that such practices came to constitute a kind of "sub-policy" that allowed local prejudices and values to dictate who would receive pensions.[134] African American mothers were systematically denied benefits, although more of them headed families than white women. In 1917, fewer than 3 percent of the nearly one thousand families on pension rolls in Chicago were black. By 1931, the proportion of black families had reached 3 percent nationwide, but percentages were lower in Southern states.[135] Many foreign-born women failed to meet residency requirements; others were taken onto the rolls but then closely supervised.[136] For all women, gaining initial approval was no guarantee of security; a mother could be dropped from the pension rolls if at any time authorities deemed that she was no longer "fit." Moreover, the laws themselves were highly mutable; categories of eligibility could change, or levels of funding could drop, leaving large groups of mothers without resources. As Moore notes, "The poor . . . had no contractual rights to relief, only limited statutory claims."[137]

Aware that such practices undermined the spirit of mothers' pensions, at least as they had been initially envisioned, welfare advocate Sophie Loeb offered impassioned testimony before a U.S. Senate committee considering a mothers' pension bill for the District of Columbia in 1926. Loeb, then president of the

Child Welfare Committee of America, had helped formulate pension legislation for New York State and had studied pension and social insurance policies from across the United States and Europe. She claimed that in the early days, when pensions were administered by the public welfare agency in New York City, "the best mothers. . . . refused to come to us. The very mothers that we were anxious to reach, good mothers, that would rather put their children in institutions if they had to than accept from the Board of Charity."[138] Eventually, New York State had to amend its law and set up an independent agency to administer pensions. Loeb urged the Senate not to repeat New York's mistake, noting that when a pension is delivered discreetly and without stigma, "it is a civic function, and it creates that spirit in that family that the local community is getting behind that mother and giving her the help of her own home to bring up her own children. . . . We are trying to make it possible for these people to wear the same badge of honor as the mother in Denmark [who receives respect as well as a generous pension]; that she is not coming as a beggar, but . . . like a great soldier who is trying to bring up her children in the best way she can."[139]

According to Loeb, entrenched welfare practices tended to drag mothers' pensions back into the quagmire of charity. Rather than constitute a break with the stigmatization and moralism that had characterized the nineteenth-century treatment of indigent mothers, the new policy only perpetuated them. The application process, with its invasive questioning and embarrassing investigations, was hardly calculated to enhance the dignity of applicants.[140] Ongoing supervision and changeable laws produced feelings of uncertainty rather than entitlement and pride in recipient mothers. Loeb, along with other visionary reformers, had looked to mothers' pensions as a means of elevating the status of poor women and gaining for all mothers the recognition and gratitude of the state. But their hopes were harshly and utterly dashed by the actual administration of the policy. Without political or judicial power, women reformers could not control the direction of the very programs they had helped create.

CHILD CARE OR MOTHERS' PENSIONS?

For a time it appeared that the advent of mothers' and widows' pensions in state after state might eliminate the need for day nurseries altogether.[141] After all, the stated purpose of the legislation was to allow mothers who lacked a male breadwinner to forego paid employment so that they could remain at home with their children. In this sense, the government would be subsidizing women to provide child care in their own homes. In practice, however, the policy did not have that effect. A sizable proportion of poor and low-income mothers derived no benefits from pensions because they preferred to work, did not fit the criteria, or the pool of funds in their states was exhausted.[142] As Josephine Dodge commented wryly in 1912, "The pension system . . . is well enough theoretically, if the plain ordinary mother possesses even a fair proportion of the qualities desirable in every mother."[143]

Many pension recipients continued working for wages because the amounts granted were too low to support their families.[144] In Pennsylvania, for example, a 1927 study found that the wages of mothers on pensions constituted 21 percent of their families' total income and Mothers' Assistance grants (mothers' pensions) 40 percent, with income from boarders, children's wages, and lodge or union death benefits making up the balance.[145] The same year, Sophie Loeb testified that in New York City 3,479 out of 8,640 pensioned widows held jobs outside the home because pension levels were inadequate. Many states nonetheless explicitly prohibited recipients from working.[146] Others advised them to seek only part-time work or, if their children were very small, to take in industrial homework. Such restrictions and recommendations channeled women into the lowest-paid, least stable, and least desirable of jobs, when they were not barred from the labor market altogether.[147]

There was little consensus as to how pension rates should be calculated. Some states regarded payments as an allowance for children, on the more or less implicit assumption that the mother would somehow support herself.[148] Joanne Goodwin found that in Illinois, legislators actually shifted their concept of the level of support from being the "amount necessary for proper care" to one that would provide only "partial support," with the remainder of a family's income to come from wages, including those of the mother.[149] It was taken for granted that supplements were necessary because women could not be expected to earn a "family wage." Few reformers questioned the concentration of women in low-paying occupations or challenged deeply entrenched gender-based wage differentials. Indeed, although pensions clearly eased the burdens of recipients, their very existence undercut possible claims for increasing women's wages on the grounds that they, too, had dependents to support. The right to a "family wage" remained a male prerogative.[150]

Instead of discouraging the use of day nurseries, pensions sometimes had the opposite effect. In states that allowed maternal employment, administrators tried to prohibit mothers from taking jobs outside the home if their children were not properly supervised.[151] This policy placed an added burden (unaccompanied by added funding) on day nurseries. Elsewhere, strict rules for eligibility either barred many low-income women from receiving pensions or discouraged them from applying in the first place, leaving them no choice but to continue working.[152] In 1916, the Association of Day Nurseries of New York City reported, "The granting of pensions . . . has as yet made no perceptible difference in the nursery situation. Three hundred and eight-four widows are now receiving a pension, but as far as we are able to learn, only three or four were nursery mothers. The larger appropriation that is expected in the near future will have no appreciable effect on the nurseries."[153]

But the ADNNYC was wrong; the establishment of mothers' pensions did affect day nurseries, in terms of their public support, visibility, and status as a "policy of choice" among child welfare experts. Moreover, the shift away from day nurseries occurred at a critical moment in the development of the American welfare state. The need to oversee mothers' pensions led to a major expansion of administrative capacity at the level of state and local government. Once this apparatus was in place, bureaucratic momentum kept it going, and official eyes focused on mothers' pensions rather than child care as the government's principal policy toward low-income mothers and their children.

Nowhere was this more evident than at the U.S. Children's Bureau. Julia Lathrop had announced her preference for mothers' pensions before assuming the position of bureau chief; once in Washington, her views did not change. While maintaining contact with dozens of national women's organizations concerned with maternal and child health and welfare,[154] she paid little attention to the NFDN, and the issue of child care seldom appears in the early records of the agency. Thus although the CB advocated forcefully for many issues of social reform, there was no possibility that it would take up the cause of public child care.

At the time, only a few social observers recognized the political danger to women that was inherent in the shift from child care to mothers' pensions. One critic was Charlotte Perkins Gilman, who argued that pensions commodified motherhood. "Motherhood is not an economic function," she wrote in *The Forerunner* in 1914; "it is physiologic and psychologic. It is not, nor should it be, for sale or for hire."[155] Instead, the state should establish "baby-gardens," which would be far more economical and would provide positive benefits for children. In keeping with her fundamental insistence on women's need for economic independence, Gilman argued that, in general, child care should be provided for mothers who want to work.[156] She still believed, however, that "the care of children belongs to women," although not all, she conceded, were equally suited for the task.[157]

Another feminist and radical, Benita Locke, pinpointed the gender implications of mothers' pensions. In the first issue of Margaret Sanger's *Woman Rebel,* also published in 1914, Locke argued:

> There is little doubt but that, if the pension scheme be adopted, it will restrict the freedom of the mother. It will also prohibit her from working outside the home, with the result that, as the benefits will not provide complete support, the sweated industries will be subsidized. . . . Prohibition of work for wages and enforced home-keeping are tyrannous extractions to place on the worker, and are some of the signs of that new slavery which an institutional state is endeavoring to impose. . . . Mothers' pensions will create a capitalized interest in one kind of legislation. Let that interest find and join hands with public sentiment—and then will rally all the seekers of special privilege. The tide of pensions will grow.[158]

Locke's prophesies proved to be remarkably accurate. Mothers' pensions ended up limiting mothers' options and slotting them into the least desirable sectors of the labor market. Moreover, pensions, buoyed by widespread public support for a traditional notion of motherhood, gained a monopoly on state policy toward women. Yet critics like Locke and even Gilman were too marginal to shift the course of public opinion or stop bureaucratic momentum.

Curiously, little or no opposition to mothers' pensions was voiced by the National Woman's Party (NWP), despite its firm position in favor of the inalienable right of women—both married and single—to employment and its opposition to all forms of protective labor legislation on the grounds that it interfered with the right to work. When it came to mothers, the party veered away from its usual stance. Party leaders refused to explore fully the social implications that arose when *mothers* exercised their right to work, or to take the logical next step of calling for universal child care to support maternal employment. Instead, at least some subscribed to a maternalist view. Mrs. Harvey Wiley, chair of the NWP Homemaker's Council, wrote in *Equal Rights* in 1923, "In my opinion women with young children should stay at home, unless they are compelled to go out and earn money. . . . Personally I do not believe in the combination of a career with the rearing of young children unless stern necessity compels the mother not only to make her contribution of service to the home but also to supply the money with which to create it."[159]

Wiley seemed to be reverting to the NFDN's position that only extreme circumstances justified maternal employment. Nor did she and other members of NWP regard mothers' pensions as a form of protective legislation, even though it effectively discouraged or even prevented many women from working. The NWP not only supported pensions but went one step further. Acknowledging that most mothers, even those driven by "stern necessity," would probably be found ineligible for pensions as they were currently being administered in the United States, the party endorsed a European-style endowment of motherhood on the grounds that it would be universal.

WAR AND CHILD CARE

Opposition to maternal employment among child welfare officials and child care advocates was so strong that it even withstood calls for more women workers and day nurseries in order to free mothers for defense work during World War I. Many child welfare leaders, including Dr. S. Josephine Baker and Josephine Dodge, grew alarmed as dozens of "emergency" and industrial nurseries sprouted up in cities and towns where defense work created a demand for female workers. Either commercially run or started by factory managers for purposes of recruiting mothers, these nurseries were often exempt from any type of regulation and, even worse, refused to submit to the unofficial jurisdiction exerted by the NFDN.

Child care leaders deplored the low material and personnel standards of the new nurseries, but what exasperated them most was that industrial and commercial recruiters implicitly condoned maternal employment. They made no effort to go through the usual social work protocols of ascertaining family need or suggesting to would-be working mothers that perhaps there was another solution to their families' financial problems. Instead, they took at face value mothers' stated desire to work and attempted to supply the necessary services to facilitate their employment.

Entrenched day nursery leaders moved decisively to try to curtail the growth of "upstart" facilities. In a rare moment of contact with the federal government, Dodge met with CB chief Julia Lathrop and forged a pact concerning child care policy in wartime. Both women were particularly concerned about reports that French factories were setting up not only on-site crèches but also special rooms where mothers could nurse their infants, and they vowed to prohibit American factories from following such a practice.[160] Dodge promised Lathrop that "as long as [she] had any power [she] would see that women were not exploited in industry for war purposes."[161]

For Dodge, this meant campaigning against the creation of emergency industrial nurseries that were intended to bring mothers into the factories. She centered her efforts on Connecticut, where a sizable armaments and military equipment industry had stepped up the demand for female workers. According to Dodge, "there was much consideration of starting emergency nurseries, [but] we worked hard to prevent them from being started. Not a single day nursery was started in a munition town to fill Government contracts."[162]

Dodge's self-congratulatory statement reveals how the NFDN's class-based, maternalist support for child care could easily work to the detriment of wage-earning mothers. She obviously did not stop to consider that low-income women might not regard skilled jobs for higher wages as a form of exploitation. Nor did she seem to realize that women would seize the opportunities open to them regardless of the availability of child care.

In any event, Dodge's claim about blocking day nurseries appears to be overstated. A number of factory nurseries were apparently opened during the war years, and according to a 1920 report by the state's Department of Labor, they maintained high standards. "Infants of as tender an age as four and six months were left in factory nurseries where they undoubtedly obtained better and more scientific care and greater attention to their cleanliness than if their mothers remained at home and cared for them." Everywhere, the report claimed, children's health and habits improved. "In fact, there was no day nursery in any plant which was not excellent."[163] Given the difficulty of maintaining high standards in pre-existing nurseries, one suspects that the virtues of these ad hoc facilities may have been overstated. Nevertheless, if the report was at all accurate, Dodge's efficacy was far less than what she asserted.

After the war, the NFDN attempted to use its newfound power, which, according to Dodge, "our prominence in the war emergency has given us as a child saving agency," to lobby for day care licensing bills in Connecticut and Massachusetts.[164] It should not be surprising that its initial attempt in Connecticut failed; state officials, factory owners, and the public at large may well have perceived the organization as meddlesome and obstructionist.

But the NFDN did get the last word in Connecticut. The same report that praised the state's industrial nurseries for providing high-quality care denounced mothers for seeking to continue employment and shirk their maternal responsibilities during the postwar period. Whatever advantages the nurseries might offer, "the practice of young mothers going out to work and leaving their children in the care of any sort of institution is a bad one and will result in lessening of the proper regard for the home. Many of these women work for the finest of motives, but the cold truth is that many of them are perfectly willing to shun all the responsibility they can."[165] According to the State of Connecticut, maternal employment was justified only in cases of national emergency or when a mother lacked a male breadwinner owing to death, desertion, or disability. Now that the war was over, mothers who sought to keep their jobs were suspect. Although the state obviously wanted to have it both ways, the NFDN could at least claim consistency: it had refused to be deterred from its principled opposition to maternal employment, even in time of war.

Had day nursery philanthropists embraced a broader view of women's roles, they might, with their organizational strength, have been able to push at the limits of public opinion and gain support for a panoply of policies that allowed mothers the option of remaining at home with their children, adequately supported, or competing freely on the job market while their children received good care. Given the gender segmentation of the American labor market during the Progressive Era, women would have had limited job opportunities at the outset. But the ready availability of child care (assuming it was well run and affordable) would have granted them a degree of security and enabled them to pursue more or less continuous employment, which, in turn, would have situated them more favorably in the struggle for better wages and working conditions.

As it was, motherhood, whether actual or potential, was repeatedly used as a rationale for relegating women to the least stable positions in the least-skilled, lowest-paying occupations.[166] Given the grinding nature and paltry rewards of most of the jobs that were open to women, some mothers chose pensions over employment, and more might have done so had the payments been adequate and readily accessible. For those who received them, pensions provided a degree of latitude—escape routes from abusive relationships and unbearable situations, or a much-needed supplement to low wages.[167] But it was not mothers' wishes and responses that were paramount in the minds of most policy makers. Mothers' pensions succeeded because they affirmed women's maternal role within the home, whereas child care (had it been allowed to appear on the public agenda) would have challenged that gender-based assignment. The policy that received the government's imprimatur and all-important bureaucratic support was the one that upheld a traditional division of labor between women and men.

In spite of the stigma that came to be attached to mothers' pensions, the stinginess of funding, and the condescending and discriminatory manner with which they were administered, governmental payments to poor mothers soon became a social right for American women—for good or for ill.[168] Publicly supported child care, however, never achieved that status.[169] By the end of the Progressive Era, mothers' pensions had gained the backing of federal, state, and local welfare officials, as well as that of leading child welfare experts. Child care, by contrast, was left behind in the private sector, supported by an outmoded and self-contradictory organization. The NFDN's reluctance to encourage maternal employment, along with its deep-seated aversion to governmental intervention into day nursery work, accorded perfectly with the position of key agencies like the CB. This convergence between public and private social policy left a growing population of wage-earning mothers with few viable resources for the care of their children.

Chapter 3 Studied Neglect:

Federal Inaction in the 1920s

The paradigm of mothers' pensions, which emerged from the Progressive Era as the policy of choice toward poor and low-income mothers, took on new significance in the "semi-welfare state" that developed in the United States over the following decades.[1] As the proportion of public to private welfare spending increased, social welfare debates shifted decisively from the voluntary sector to the government.[2] Moving into expanding state and federal welfare bureaucracies was a second generation of maternalist reformers, more professionally minded than their predecessors yet equally committed to the principle of keeping mothers out of the labor force and at home with their children—even when they were financially needy.[3] To address problems such as poverty, child labor, and child neglect, these reformers repeatedly fell back on mothers' pensions rather than call for governmental support to expand and improve child care and thus assist mothers who wanted to work for wages. Even the demand for women's labor during World War II did little to soften their principled opposition to maternal employment.

This chapter (covering the 1920s) and the next (covering the Depression and World War II) examine the different forces that shaped public policy toward mothers and children during a critical period of American welfare-state development. Throughout this period, the U.S. Children's Bureau (CB) served as the federal voice of neo-maternalist reformers. Although the bureau was often marginalized in deliberations over national policy, its views were nonetheless influential, finding support among politicians and officials who had their own reasons for upholding the status quo of gender relations and helping to shape federal responses to social problems and to the crises brought on by economic depression and war.

While the prevalence of neo-maternalist views kept child care off state and federal policy agendas, a steady increase in maternal employment made the need for child care more acute than ever. It was during the 1920s that the transformation of the female labor force "from working girls to working mothers" began.[4] The ranks of working mothers, once dominated by poor women, widows, and divorcees, now included many women whose husbands were present and employed but who sought to raise their families' standard of living.[5] As opportunities for industrial homework and domestic entrepreneurship declined, these mothers increasingly looked for jobs outside the home.[6] Between 1920 and 1940, the number of married women workers (at least half of them probably mothers)[7] grew from 1.9 million to 4.6 million.

The trend in voluntary day nurseries did not keep pace. In 1923, there were 613 facilities with a capacity of almost 23,000 children.[8] This meant that even in a city like Philadelphia, which had a relatively large number of nurseries, it was possible for only about one-third of children ages five and under with wage-earning mothers to receive nursery care.[9] The Depression weakened philanthropic support for nurseries, causing many to close their doors; the total number of voluntary facilities plummeted from a peak of 800 in 1931 to 600 by 1940.[10]

At the same time, the federal government launched its first program for young children, the Emergency Nursery Schools of the Works Progress Administration (WPA), which served both educational and child care functions for more than 60,000 children nationwide. During World War II, these schools formed the basis for a federal child care system of more than 3,000 centers with a capacity of 130,000 children. Despite this boost, however, the combination of public and voluntary child care could not accommodate the millions of children whose mothers were now employed outside the home.[11]

Even more dramatically than World War I, World War II revealed that the voluntary sector lacked the resources to meet wartime child care needs. But

World War II also showed that the federal government could, under pressure, overcome political opposition and muster sufficient funding and administrative capacity to run a national child care system. However, the persistence of neo-maternalism, reinvigorated by what I call the discourse of the democratic family, prevented the program from gaining enough momentum to continue into the postwar period.[12]

Some of the patterns and players who were prominent during these decades will be familiar: volunteer organizations and child welfare experts, the CB, and after World War I, the U.S. Women's Bureau (WB). Others came on the scene only during the crisis years: ad hoc agencies like the WPA and its wartime successor, the Federal Works Administration (FWA). Child welfare discourses shifted in response to the influence of early childhood educators, psychologists, and social workers, but neo-maternalist views remained a constant theme.

THE PARADOX OF MATERNAL EMPLOYMENT

The mandate of the CB was to "safeguard" the health and welfare of American children. It examined the condition of children in a variety of situations it deemed stressful, identified problems, and formulated solutions. During its early years (1912 through about 1930), the bureau divided health and welfare into three major policy areas: maternal and child health, child labor, and child welfare. Parallel with these concerns, the CB sought to promote three major types of legislation: provisions for maternal and child health, child labor regulation, and mothers' pensions.[13]

In attempting to fulfill its mandate, the CB developed a kind of tunnel vision when it came to women: they were important only in their role as mothers. The establishment of the WB, which dealt with women's labor issues, served to reinforce this conceptual as well as bureaucratic division of labor. In its studies and policy recommendations, the CB sometimes focused on both parents (as in studies of child labor and child welfare, where the income and circumstances of the entire family came into consideration), sometimes solely on mothers (as in *maternal* and child health). In either case, this narrow view of women had the effect of "overfeminizing" them, that is, presenting them as mothers to the exclusion of any other role, such as that of worker, which might detract from what the bureau saw as their central and defining responsibility.[14] Thus, when the CB concluded that children suffered as a result of their mothers' gainful employment, its response was to lobby for greater funding and improved administration of mothers' pensions rather than for child care, which would have allowed mothers to continue working *and* have the assurance that their children were receiving adequate attention.

As the first federal agency dedicated to social welfare and the first headed and largely staffed by women, the CB had to find its own way in Washington. Not only were its powers circumscribed by a small budget and weak administrative capacity, but its political influence (especially in the pre-suffrage years) was uncertain or at least untried. Under the circumstances, CB chief Julia Lathrop turned to a political method that she and her Hull House colleagues had found effective in bringing about reform in Illinois: the social investigation.[15] In its first twenty years, the CB published more than two hundred bulletins based on its research and conducted dozens of other studies whose results never appeared in print but were used in lobbying. Much of the research was devoted to maternal and child labor and its impact on children's welfare, health, and educational opportunities.

The bureau's findings created a paradox within its own ideology. On the one hand, many of the studies pointed to a trade-off between maternal and child labor; that is, the greater a mother's earnings, the less likely it was that her children would work—and vice-versa. On the other hand, the same studies documented the deleterious effects of maternal employment—inadequate child care, unavoidable neglect, high rates of accidents and infant and child mortality, sporadic school attendance, and juvenile delinquency. These findings challenged the basic principles the bureau was pledged to support; it seemed impossible to eliminate both child labor and maternal employment simultaneously.

In theory, this is what mothers' pensions were intended to do, but the policy was no panacea, for few recipients could afford to live on pensions alone. Moreover, a number of low-income women were ineligible because they had husbands present, even though their wages were insufficient to support the entire household. Thus many women with fully employed husbands still sought jobs outside the home to meet expenses. Faced with this reality, the CB could have decided to continue campaigning against child labor while making maternal employment more acceptable by eliminating its deleterious effects through the establishment of comprehensive child care. But the bureau's opposition to maternal employment, which could be traced back to the Progressive Era switch from day nurseries to mothers' pensions, proved intransigent. Although the CB continued to work for the elimination of child labor, it did little to expand or improve child care.

The bureau's politics limited the ways its research was used, particularly the recommendations derived from each collection of data. Yet the studies themselves contain much "surplus" information that allows us to see how working families fared, given the available social services. Inevitably, this information also prompts speculation about how different types of policies might have affected the mothers and children being studied.

Studies by the CB of conditions in industrial and agricultural employment were of two types. One looked at child labor as an isolated phenomenon, while the other examined the work of children in conjunction with that of mothers. Studies of child labor alone investigated agricultural enterprises that included truck farming, vegetable and fruit growing, and such specific crops as cotton, tobacco, and hops. They also examined child labor in coal mining, canning, industrial homework, and the street trades. Studies of mothers and children looked into shrimp and oyster canneries, beet fields, and truck farming. Researchers crisscrossed the nation, from New England and the Southeast through the Midwest and all the way to the Pacific Northwest. Although both types of studies yielded data on the relation between child labor and parents' earnings and on the impact of child labor on health and school attendance, it was the combined studies that provided the sharper insights into how working mothers dealt with the issue of child care.

According to the CB's findings, child labor occurred more commonly in occupational sectors that also had a preponderance of female labor, such as certain types of agricultural production, canning, and industrial homework.[16] There were both economic and practical reasons for this. With regard to economics, the lower the mothers' wages, the more their children needed to earn. Although women could easily find jobs in agriculture and food processing, these occupations paid very poorly (which also explains why they attracted fewer male workers), so families needed both children's and mothers' wages to survive.[17] In practical terms, it made sense for children to work where their mothers did, often alongside them. The more open the workplace to children, the younger the ages at which they could be found earning wages.

The unevenness of child labor laws during this period generally favored such practices. In 1916 Congress passed the Keating-Owen Act, which regulated labor for children under sixteen, but two years later the law was found unconstitutional. The Child Labor Tax Act (Pomerene Amendment), passed in 1919, met a similar fate in 1922. Many states also passed child labor statutes during the 1920s, but these varied tremendously and enforcement was notoriously erratic. It was well known among reformers that inspection was lax, and that parents conspired with employers to evade the law.[18]

The studies of the CB revealed that in the industrial and agricultural sectors dominated by women, the line between child labor and child care often became blurred. Mothers seem to have put very young children to work primarily as a way of keeping them occupied, with actual earnings a secondary consideration. Mothers were drawn to occupations and to specific workplaces that made it possible for them to combine work and child care, either because those workplaces made some sort of provision for children (ranging from simply tolerating them on the premises to designating a specific area where children could stay) or allowed them to work.

This is not to ignore the many other factors that determined women's occupational choices (if we may call them that): geography, opportunity, wage levels, skills and education, the gender conventions of a workplace, and various types of discrimination.[19] Nevertheless, all things being equal, a mother who had no other form of child care available to her might well choose a job that allowed her to combine wage earning and child care.

A DANGEROUS PLACE FOR SMALL CHILDREN

The CB's 1919 study of six shrimp and oyster canning communities on the Gulf Coast (in Florida, Mississippi, and Louisiana) illustrates this pattern of occupational selection and its implications for both mothers and children.[20] Men, women, and children could all find employment in the shellfish industry; wages and job assignments conformed to predictable gender, age, and racial hierarchies. Men, who worked on oyster or shrimp boats or did certain jobs around the canneries or wharves, earned between $12 and $25, or more, per week. Women, who shucked oysters or picked or peeled shrimp for canning, averaged between $5 and $7.50 per week. Children also worked in canning, making between $2 and $5 per week. The older the child, the higher his or her wages. In nearly every category, African American workers (who made up between one-third and one-half of the total labor force) were paid less than white workers.

The study, which covered 423 families with 1,350 children, found that 40 percent of the children were employed, nearly two-thirds of them on a regular basis. Only two of the working children were under the age of six (one was four, one five). School attendance was sporadic, and as a result, 25 percent of the children between the ages of ten and fifteen were illiterate. When asked why so many children were kept out of school and sent to work, parents cited their own low wages and erratic opportunities to earn—weather affected the catch and created frequent intervals of unemployment. In addition, nearly one-quarter of the mothers were the primary breadwinners in their families. Many had been widowed or deserted, but mothers' pensions were not an option for them, as none of the three states had a mothers' pension law at the time the survey was conducted.[21]

The work patterns of some children appeared to be somewhat casual: "A 4-year-old girl, who 'sometimes plays around at home and sometimes goes to work with her mother and shucks a little and makes 5 cents for candy,' probably does not work as much as a 10-year-old girl whose mother says she does not allow her to work but that the girl sometimes goes in with friends and works for one or two hours 'on the sly.'"[22] Other children, however, arrived at the plant half an hour before starting time to be assured a place at the processing tables. Regular child workers sometimes had to spend brief periods playing around the cannery while they waited for boats to come in, but then it was down to business. As Viola Paradise, the author of the study, noted, "Even the part-time work . . . was real labor and not play, involving as it did the standing and bending postures, the monotony, wetness, and dirtiness of the task, the stench of the shrimp, and the frequent early hours."[23]

When Paradise asked parents about the extent of their children's labor, they tended to minimize it. They were underreporting, she suspected, because they feared legal reprisals. As it happened, the study was conducted during the interval after the first federal child labor law was declared unconstitutional and before the Pomerene Amendment went into effect.[24] Nevertheless, many parents mistook CB agents for factory inspectors. Those who were willing to speak to Paradise indicated that they took child labor for granted. Some even claimed that they allowed their children to work in the interests of the industry; according to one mother, "The children save the oysters from spoiling."[25]

The child care functions of child labor were explicitly acknowledged; one grandmother told Paradise that "if she had any young children she would take every one of them to the canneries and make them work all day long." "'This is the worst place for kids,' she said, 'they git awful mean around here. See, there ain't hardly a winder left around this place; the kids smash 'em. . . . They should be sent to the canneries to keep them from getting mean, and then if the Government kicked about it, I would make the Government take care of them.'"[26] To this woman, it seemed obvious that the children of working mothers should be the government's responsibility.

For smaller children, mothers made several different arrangements (fig. 3.1). Some availed themselves of the few day nurseries in the area. Although fees were

Fig. 3.1. This Louisiana mother and her three children were on
their way to work. The mother would drop the toddler at a day
nursery and take the infant and older child, aged seven, to the
cannery with her. From Viola I. Paradise, *Child Labor and the
Work of Mothers in Oyster and Shrimp Canning Communities on
the Gulf Coast,* Children's Bureau Publication No. 98
(Washington, D.C.: GPO, 1922), facing p. 64.

reasonable (five cents per day per child) and mothers felt they were "a good
help," they were crowded, and the hours were inconvenient. Factory owners
made allowances for mothers who could not come to work until after the
nurseries opened at 7 (the regular starting time was 4:30 or 5 A.M.), but these
women had to accept less advantageous places at the processing tables.

As a result, many women "made a practice of taking their small children and babies with them to the wet and drafty picking and shucking sheds." Paradise commented,

> Sometimes the mothers, being obliged to work and having no one at home with whom to leave the children, had no alternative but to take them to the canneries. Some did not realize that this practice endangered the health of their children. One mother with three children—aged 5 years, 2 years, and 7 months respectively—said, "I take the children to the factory and they play around. It's a good place to keep the baby, but last week I put it in a drafty place and it caught a bad cold." Another mother took her 6-month-old baby with her; she said there was a "clean cement place" for babies. This mother, who had lost a 3-year-old child several years ago, said, "My husband claims that taking the child to the factory caused its illness, but I think not."[27]

This mother might have been right; children left behind were also at risk. One woman explained that she took her seven-month-old to work with her because "the mosquitoes would eat her up" at home. "I have a cradle for her at the factory, and she seldom cries and doesn't bother me in my work," the mother assured Paradise. "I stop once in a while to nurse her. Sometimes I leave her with her 8-year-old brother."[28] Other mothers kept infants in boxes, rocking chairs, carriages, or other conveyances. Those who left babies at home nursed them before and after work, and at lunchtime if they lived close by (many had places in company camps).[29]

These practices earned the disapproval of fellow workers. One woman complained, "People don't care for their children. They bring them in gocarts to the factory and they cry all day long." Another said, "I tell you, the factory is terrible on children. One Italian mother has seven little children. She keeps the baby in a box, and it cries all day. She goes out and nurses it and gives a piece of bread to the others and then starts work again. The poor kids are in awful shape."[30] Although this observer implied that the Italian mother deliberately neglected her children, it was more likely the pressure of working for piecework wages that induced her to treat her infant as she did.

Some factory owners seem to have tolerated the presence of children in their workplaces because they depended on having an abundance of workers on hand to prevent spoilage of highly perishable shellfish. Because the women were not being paid by the hour, employers allowed them to interrupt their work to attend to their children and sometimes even allocated space and offered primitive equipment for purposes of child care (fig. 3.2). The accommodations, however, were less than gracious. One employer complained that children refused to stay in the room he had provided for them, but according to

Fig. 3.2. The owner of this cannery designated one corner as an "on-site day nursery," where mothers could leave infants in makeshift perambulators and where older children were supposed to play. From Viola I. Paradise, *Child Labor and the Work of Mothers in Oyster and Shrimp Canning Communities on the Gulf Coast,* Children's Bureau Publication No. 98 (Washington, D.C.: GPO, 1922), facing p. 65.

Paradise, it was "absolutely bare, having no chairs or other furniture."[31] In another factory, "a little free space in a stall-like division, cluttered with barrels, boxes, and a miscellany of factory properties, was assigned to the children. No cannery visited had a well-equipped nursery, and usually no provision was made for the babies, who lay in boxes, baby carriages, gocarts, or on trucks in some corner of the shed. In cold weather some of the factories allowed the mothers to put their babies near the steam box [used as part of the canning process]."[32] Conditions in even the most modest day nursery would have been superior to those Paradise described.

Some owners regarded the children as a nuisance and would not allow mothers to bring them into the workplace at all. They seemed little concerned about how such restrictions would affect the children. "Sometimes [the mothers] leave them outside the factory with a couple of [older] kids, or else they leave them with a neighbor," one employer told Paradise nonchalantly. "That's very common around here."[33] Another owner was more candid; he refused to allow children to "skylark around the cannery" because he feared a lawsuit if they were injured.[34]

Mothers themselves tried to avoid bringing toddlers into the plants because "there is no one to look after them, and they run loose."[35] Hazards were ubiquitous. Children were in danger of being run over by heavy cars pushed roughly by workmen. According to one mother, "The steam is often so thick they can't see what is in front of them."[36] Oyster shells, shrimp thorns, and other waste strewn over the floors caused countless cuts and bruises (fig. 3.3). Those youngsters who took part in the processing suffered lacerations and bruises; abscesses were common. To add to the danger, canneries were located next to piers and wharves, where there was always the possibility of "falling

Fig. 3.3. To keep their children in sight, mothers working in the canneries allowed them to play near the packing tables, but wet floors strewn with discarded shells made this a hazardous place for children to play. From Viola I. Paradise, *Child Labor and the Work of Mothers in Oyster and Shrimp Canning Communities on the Gulf Coast,* Children's Bureau Publication No. 98 (Washington, D.C.: GPO, 1922), facing p. 13.

overboard." Mothers lost precious work time as they strained to keep an eye on children while they worked.

But, according to Paradise, "the children who were not brought to the factories . . . were often left more neglected at home."[37] More than half the 269 children under six in the sample had caretakers who were under the age of sixteen, and some "as young as 2 years, were left entirely alone."[38] The mother of one such toddler was hardly sanguine about her decision. "I risked it because I needed the money so," she told Paradise.[39]

As the 1920s wore on, employers' attitudes toward children in the workplace began to change. In addition to a fear of lawsuits and child labor inspectors, many became aware of the principles of scientific management and sought to rationalize labor processes by minimizing interruptions and eliminating employees who could not "work up to speed." While shortening the length of the working day, they intensified the pace of work and attempted to keep it steady. This shift in working conditions created new problems for working mothers, who had, within the relatively loose structure of the paternalistic, pre-Taylorization workplace, been able to construct makeshift forms of child care. Now very small children were no longer welcome in the workplace, either to play or to work.[40]

Several CB studies of fruit and vegetable canning in the mid- and late 1920s illustrated the impact of these changes in one industry.[41] Technology in canning factories had remained static since about 1919. Machines ("requiring" male operators) had taken over many operations, but sorting, trimming, and other parts of the process still had to be done by hand. This work drew in women and older children. In many states, children under twelve were prohibited from working, but some did anyway. Besides being illegal, this situation meant that the very youngest children were left alone in labor camps for the entire work day. Among other dangers, the camps were usually located close to active railroad tracks. Cannery owners and managers made spasmodic attempts to supervise the younger children (it would be an exaggeration to call these efforts child care), not because they were concerned with their welfare but because they wanted to keep them out of the plants. There were reports of scaldings, burns, and other serious accidents to those who wandered in. Some owners built fences to keep children in the camps; others hired caretakers or watchmen to act as guards. But most of these means were ineffective, and the behavior of children left to themselves in the camps all day verged on anarchy.

In 1930, the CB concluded that conditions like these had been ignored for too long. However, the agency made no recommendations for federal action to institute or improve child care for these children. Instead it suggested that all states follow the model of California, whose Department of Industrial Relations had drawn up guidelines for day nurseries and playgrounds that some of the state's canners had followed.[42] But few states bothered to comply.

CHILDREN IN THE FIELDS

Officials of the CB considered agricultural camps safer for children than cannery camps, because they did not carry the risks of railroads or unguarded machinery.[43] But the children of agricultural workers still faced the hazards of being left by themselves or in the care of siblings while parents worked. "Occasionally," according to a CB report, "[an agricultural] family would report that 'the dog takes care of the children.'" It was unclear whether they meant this seriously.[44] Children left behind frequently fell ill owing to cold, improper nutrition, or accidents.

Those who accompanied their parents to the fields were generally safer, although they had to keep the same long hours their parents did (mothers might return to the camp before other family members to prepare the evening meal, bringing smaller children with them). Depending on the crop and the specific types of labor involved, parents were able to make different kinds of arrangements for their children. In the beet fields of Colorado, for example, they put up small canvas tents for infants, as no other shade was available (fig. 3.4). Mothers tried to keep their children within sight, but toddlers had a tendency to wander off. The CB's study of beet field workers found at least two cases in which toddlers had drowned in irrigation ditches.[45]

Child labor was also common among agricultural families, partly for eco-

Fig. 3.4. Beet workers set up canvas tents to shelter their children from the elements while they toiled in the fields. According to the CB investigator, this was "a rare instance of careful provision for the baby's protection." From Ellen Nathalie Matthews, *Child Labor and the Work of Mothers in the Beet Fields of Colorado and Michigan,* Children's Bureau Publication No. 115 (Washington, D.C.: GPO, 1923), facing p. 67.

nomic reasons, partly because, again, it served as a form of child care for younger children (fig. 3.5). Parents had the alternative of leaving children with minimal or no supervision, or bringing them to the fields. Reporting on Michigan beet workers, a CB researcher commented, "In some families no child was considered too young to count as a . . . worker." Of 763 children studied, three-fourths of the boys and more than three-fifths of the girls between six and sixteen worked on crops; older girls were kept at home to do child care and housework.[46] On the truck farms of Norfolk, Virginia, parents acknowledged that they put their children to work because "that was the easiest way to watch them."[47]

At the same time, the value of children's labor was not always negligible. Among resident farm families in the cotton-growing areas of Texas, some children became prodigious pickers: "The average day's work for 153 children ranging in age from 3 to 15 years was slightly under 100 pounds of cotton each. . . . Even the 8- and 9-year-old children could pick from 50 to 75 pounds a day, and most of those who were younger could average 50 pounds. Working 12 hours, a 6-year-old girl, who had begun field work at the age of 4, picked 80 pounds a day, and 4-year-old twins . . . working beside their mother . . . put into her bag an average of 12 or 15 pounds a day."[48] Cotton farmers used their own children in lieu of hired labor; at the rate of two dollars per hundred pounds, their work represented significant savings to parents. It also did double duty as cost-free child care.

It was difficult for the CB to develop generalizations about children's work in agriculture because the sample sizes varied widely, as did the length of the working day, the number of days worked, and other working conditions. Nevertheless, Nettie McGill, who conducted several of the studies, concluded

Fig. 3.5. In the cranberry bogs of southern New Jersey, the oldest children commonly worked while the next oldest took care of younger children. From Children's Bureau, *Work of Children on Truck and Small-Fruit Farms in Southern New Jersey,* Children's Bureau Publication No. 132 (Washington, D.C.: GPO, 1924), facing p. 34.

that child labor was common in agriculture everywhere except in the corn and wheat belts, where heavy machinery was in use. Age ranges differed little from one region to the next; everywhere there was a sizable proportion of children under ten. "Little fingers," McGill noted, "can pick strawberries as well as cotton, can worm tobacco as well as thin beets."[49]

The CB also found parents using work as child care among industrial homeworkers in Rhode Island. Mothers had long regarded home production as a relatively simple way to combine wage earning with supervision of children; for many, it was preferable to sending their children to day nurseries.[50] Yet, even though they were at home, these women did not want to let their children roam the streets while they worked. So, like agricultural workers, they involved their children in wage earning "to eke out insufficient family incomes" and to keep them safe—" 'busy,' 'off the streets,' or 'out of mischief.' "[51]

FEDERAL INACTION

The CB studies left no doubt that child labor and a lack of adequate child care were both extremely hazardous to children caught up in the general exploitation of labor in agriculture, food processing, and industrial homework. Moreover, it was obvious that the two phenomena were inextricably linked. Desperate parents who put small children to work were probably less interested in pocketing their meager earnings than in keeping them safe. Yet when it came to recommendations and action to alleviate this dual problem, the CB focused single-mindedly on the issue of child labor.

In the absence of governmental initiative on child care, voluntary organizations like the Council of Women for Home Missions moved into the breach, founding centers that offered child care and youth recreation programs to the families of migrant workers. "The chief objective at first was to furnish care for babies and small children who were neglected while older members of the family worked in fields and canneries. It soon became evident that directed activities were needed for young people during hours when they were not working, so recreation programs for them became part of the Center schedules."[52] Starting in about 1920, the first eight centers, located in four eastern states, were open only during the summers. In 1924 another seasonal program was set up in Oregon. These programs sparked other services for migrants, including a mobile nursing service in California that followed workers from camp to camp throughout the year-round growing season. Local committees were usually able to house the summer programs in rural school buildings that were not being used, and they arranged for donations of food, milk, and other supplies from nearby churches. Much of the staff was voluntary.[53] The need for services for migrant workers did not diminish; by 1940, Women's Home Missions Boards were supporting sixty centers in fifteen states, and evidence suggests that at least some of these continued through the immediate post–World War II era.[54]

Awareness of the importance of child care also remained high within African American communities. In the late 1920s, white philanthropists John D. Rockefeller and Julius Rosenwald initiated model housing projects for African Americans: the Paul Laurence Dunbar Apartments in New York City and the Michigan Boulevard Garden Apartments in Chicago, respectively. Plans for both projects included on-site day nurseries (fig. 3.6), as well as playgrounds and club rooms for older children. Rockefeller and Rosenwald provided the overall financing for the two projects, but it is not clear who sponsored or ran the nurseries. It is likely that they were self-supporting, because the two philanthropists expected a return on the money they had put into the buildings, and tenants were expected to pay more or less market rates for their housing.[55]

Part of the CB's inaction around child care can be explained by the agency's sense of its own mandate. When the Keating-Owen bill was passed in 1916, its administration was assigned to the Department of Labor, which turned it over to the CB. To carry out the task, the bureau appointed Grace Abbott, a Hull

Fig. 3.6. The day nursery at the Paul Dunbar Apartments in
New York City, built in 1928, was modern and well equipped.
This photograph suggests, however, that the adult-to-child ratio
was low (one adult for ten children here) and that children of
mixed ages were cared for in a single group. Photograph by
George H. Van Anda, in *Negro Housing: Report of the Commission in Negro Housing,* ed. John M. Gries and James Ford
(Washington, D.C.: President's Conference on Home Buildings
and Home Ownership, 1932), facing p. 158.

House alumna, to head a special Child Labor Division.[56] Child labor stayed on
the bureau's agenda even after Keating-Owen was struck down in 1918, eliminating the CB's oversight assignment, and it remained there even after administration of the 1919 Pomerene Amendment went to the Treasury Department.[57] The bureau continued to initiate maternal and child labor studies,
using the data in its ongoing legislative campaign. Driving the bureau, in
addition to its own momentum, were outside forces like the National Child
Labor Committee and the Consumers' League, of which Florence Kelley,
another Hull House colleague, was general secretary.[58] When Abbott succeeded Julia Lathrop as chief of the CB in late 1921, the bureau's ongoing
commitment to the child labor issue was assured.[59]

The bureau's connection to child care was very different: the CB received no
mandate from the administration concerning child care, nor was it under
outside pressure to focus on the issue. Quite the contrary. The nation's sole
child care advocacy organization, the National Federation of Day Nurseries,
was averse to seeking government support and, with the exception of the pact
between Lathrop and NFDN president Josephine Dodge concerning mothers'
employment during World War I, had largely eschewed contact with the CB.
The NFDN's position accorded perfectly with the CB's principled opposition

to maternal employment. Thus, in contrast to child labor, the issue of child care held no brief in the bureau, with the result that it was unlikely to consider federally sponsored day nurseries as a solution to any of the problems its own research documented.

Neo-maternalism drove the rest of the CB's agenda, which included maternal and child health and mothers' pensions. Like child labor, these two issues also had champions both inside and outside the agency, ensuring them a claim on its limited resources and political capital. This hierarchy of issues not only set the CB's legislative and research agendas but also determined how its data would be interpreted. The preoccupation with maternal and child health was evident, for example, in a 1923 study of infant mortality in Baltimore, which showed that the children of homeworking mothers fared better than those whose mothers were employed outside the home. The reason, the report strongly implied, was that group child care conditions were unhealthy.

Anna Rochester, the author of the Baltimore report, directly attributed higher rates of miscarriage, premature birth, stillbirth, and infant mortality to mothers' out-of-home employment. "The baby whose mother works away from home or during the baby's first year," she concluded, "pays dearly for the physical strain to the mother and for the lack of a mother's care."[60] Yet she was hard put to explain precisely the correlation between maternal employment and infant mortality, despite abundant data gathered in numerous tables and statistical breakdowns.

The data revealed, for example, that there was an obvious link between methods of feeding and mortality rates: "So far as employment either at home or away increases early weaning it will inevitably raise the infant death rate. And the earlier the baby is deprived of breast milk the greater will be the hazard he must face throughout the year."[61] Yet, according to Rochester, "the greater prevalence of artificial feeding accounts only in part for the special hazard" to infants of employed mothers.[62] It was not clear what accounted for the *rest* of the "special hazard." Rochester discussed "the babies' surroundings" in general terms, describing the physical conditions and ethnic breakdowns of neighborhoods, but she failed to examine specific aspects of child care practices that might directly affect infants—the age and skill of caretakers; the physical conditions of places where infants were kept (such as heating, risk of infection from other children, unguarded windows); methods of artificial feeding; and so on. Indeed, child care, whether in day nurseries or in informal settings, hovered as a kind of phantom presence throughout the report, unarticulated but implicitly blamed for infant mortality.

Had child care been explicitly invoked and analyzed, Rochester might have been able to recommend practical changes in day nurseries or in informal care by friends and neighbors that would produce better outcomes. But she was headed toward a different set of conclusions. She wanted to use her research to demonstrate that what these working mothers needed was better health care and education, which, among other things, would presumably induce them to stay at home with their infants instead of going out to work. Rather than proposing higher standards for sanitation, hygiene, and preventive health measures in day nurseries and supervision of family-based care, this and other studies used data to call for better prenatal and confinement care and more education of mothers concerning infant welfare. The explanation, of course, was that child care was not on the CB's agenda, while health care was. The bureau was caught up in defending the Sheppard-Towner Maternity and Infancy Protection Act, which, since its passage in 1921, had been under constant barrage from Congress.[63]

In other instances, it was the CB's longstanding preference for mothers' pensions that blinded the agency to the need for more and better child care. In the study of maternal and child labor on the truck farms near Norfolk, for example, the bureau deplored the fact that poverty drove so many mothers into general farm work, with its long hours and low wages. Their young children were inadequately cared for, while older children, unregulated by any state or federal laws, worked "longer hours than is generally deemed advisable for the immature." In addition to calling for an extension of protective legislation to cover children in agricultural work, the study urged, "Fatherless families actually in need of the children's earnings should receive assistance under the State mothers' pension act, so that the temptation to employ the children would be reduced."[64]

Because more than a third of the families in this survey were fatherless, they could presumably have met the criteria for pensions, were they not also predominantly African American. In recommending pensions for this group, bureau agents ignored what was by then fairly well known, especially among federal welfare experts—that discrimination among blacks was routine in pension administration, particularly in the South.[65] Nor did the agents stop to consider what should be done for the remaining two-thirds of the families, where fathers were present but the household's income was still inadequate.

In all these studies, the CB's neo-maternalist agenda determined the uses to which data would be put. Their intent, however, did not seem to circumscribe the nature of the research itself—how data would be collected or what questions would be asked. Indeed, the findings sometimes exceeded or even contradicted the bureau's rather narrow political goals. But each study's policy recommendations had to fit neatly within the agenda, even when its contents cried out for considering something else—something like organized child care.

THE THERAPEUTIC TURN

Much of the systematic exclusion of child care from the federal child welfare agenda can be attributed to the policy switch of the Progressive Era and to the leadership of the CB, with its deep roots in maternalism and pattern of alliances with advocates of mothers' pensions and child labor reform. In addition, two other factors should be considered in analyzing changes in attitudes toward child care both in the CB and within the voluntary sector. One was the "therapeutic turn," which recast the meanings of motherhood in psychological terms, strengthening opposition to maternal employment. The other was the growing popularity of nursery schools, which, with their innovative approach and largely middle-class clientele, put day nurseries in a bad light.

The therapeutic turn occurred around the time of World War I, as leaders and practitioners in the fields of child welfare and social work began to move away from the broad environmental and sociological approaches to social problems that had characterized progressive thinking, especially within the settlement house movement, and toward more narrowly focused, family-centered methods.[66] This move paralleled the shift within social work from "friendly visiting" to professional, "scientific" methods that crystallized in "casework." Children's practitioners, concerned with preventing social and psychological pathology before it could form, saw great potential in the new disciplines of child development and child psychology. Joining forces with colleagues in psychiatry and the mental hygiene movement, they established a new field, child guidance.[67]

Day nursery leaders, ever alert to changing trends in child welfare, recognized in this new emphasis an opening for their own services. Still ambivalent about encouraging maternal employment through provision of child care, they sought to create a special niche for the day nursery as an aid to "family adjustment." At the 1919 NFDN conference, one speaker pointed toward the day nursery's new function: "Like all progressive social agencies we have as an ideal our eventual elimination and a chance for every mother to stay in her home, but until the social evils which brought us into existence have been wiped out by more vigorous community pressure, we must still exist to protect children who might otherwise be neglected or families who might still be disorganized."[68] When the "social evils" were eliminated, mothers would, presumably, choose to remain at home. Although this speaker still saw external conditions as the major cause of problems such as maternal employment, she used the term "disorganized," a keyword within the discourse of the emerging fields of counseling and child psychology, to describe their ill effects.

As the therapeutic paradigm took hold, a mother's decision to work came to be seen not as a rational—if regrettable—response to poverty but as evidence of psychopathology; the cause of her behavior did not lie outside her or her family but was internal. Change, therefore, required not social reform but psychotherapy. By positioning itself as an essential element of therapeutic programs for troubled families, the nursery could now play an active and direct role in eliminating maternal employment by participating in the process of individual and familial transformation. In addition to lending the nursery a much-needed professional identity, this new function promised to resolve the old conflict between simultaneously facilitating maternal employment and seeking to eliminate it. Not surprisingly, the NFDN eagerly directed member nurseries to give preference to families that demonstrated psychological— rather than financial—need.[69]

Officials of the CB, while certainly aware of the sea change within the field of child welfare, did not immediately rush to embrace a therapeutic approach. Julia Lathrop and her successor, Grace Abbott, were closely linked to the Chicago School of Social Administration, which, unlike most schools of social work during this period (and since), remained wedded to a more broadly environmental approach rooted in quasi-socialist principles.[70] Nevertheless, in preparing the 1921 revision of its famous child-rearing manual *Infant Care,* the CB drew on the ideas of psychologist John Watson, the father of behaviorism, and also published a study by Dr. Douglas Thom, head of a Boston "habit clinic," recommending that child guidance services be made generally available to families.[71]

One of the central tenets of child guidance was that both the child and his or her parents (especially the mother) should become involved in the child's treatment. As Thom put it, "The home must be considered the workshop in which the personality of the child is being developed; and the personalities of the parents will make up, to a very large extent, the mental atmosphere in which the child has to live."[72] Thom offered a typology of "parents who contribute largely to the inadequate development of the personality of their children." Notably, the first "type" he described was the mother, "worn and wearied by her routine household cares, who tries to supplement the family budget by putting in a few hours scrubbing floors when she should be in bed and who has little energy, either physical or mental, left for her children's welfare."[73] Though now phrased in therapeutic terms, this image was highly reminiscent of the working mother whom Lathrop in 1905 had called "the most melancholy figure in the working world."

Therapeutic discourse did not permeate the CB as thoroughly as it did the voluntary sector of the child welfare field, but it nonetheless influenced CB officials and certainly reinforced their inclination, already present, to seek alternatives to maternal employment. The bureau held to this course not only throughout the period of grave financial insecurity among poor and working-class families documented by its own studies of the 1920s and early 1930s, but also during the storms of national upheaval that were to come during the Depression and World War II.

Ironically, maternal employment came to be seen as psychologically abnormal just as it was approaching a sociological norm. In 1922 economist Edgar Sydenstricker reported that "less than half of the wage-earners' families in the United States, whose heads are at work, have been found to be [solely] supported by the earnings of the husband or father."[74] From the end of the Great War on, the percentage of mothers who were employed outside the home grew steadily.[75] As in earlier decades, most were taking jobs because of economic need, but perceptions of what constituted need were being transformed by the values of mass consumerism.[76] Local and nationwide studies of breadwinning mothers conducted between 1915 and 1925 showed that the new attitudes were already widespread. A 1918 community survey of the stockyards area of Chicago found that 80.5 percent of the 590 mothers working outside the home had sought employment because of financial hardship, even though more than half had husbands present. Their reasons broke down as follows: insufficient income, 42.2 percent; widowhood, desertion, divorce, 19.7 percent; debts occasioned by death or illness, 8.5 percent; husband's illness, 10.1 percent. Another 17.8 percent said that they worked to buy property, pay for children's education, or build up savings.[77] Fewer than 40 percent of these women gave as their reasons "conventional" forms of family crisis such as widowhood or illness, while nearly 20 percent were explicitly seeking upward mobility and a higher standard of living for themselves and their families. Those who said they had "insufficient income" might well have fallen into either category.[78]

Philadelphia mothers employed in industry in the early 1920s had similar motivations. In a study of 728 such women, Gwendolyn Hughes, a Bryn

Mawr–trained expert in social economy and social research, found, "These mothers are true exponents of the economic independence of women in that they are doing their best to meet their domestic financial difficulties. They find the economic status of their respective families unsatisfactory and, recalling their industrial experience before marriage, they go back to the work by which they formerly supported themselves."[79] According to Hughes, mothers shared far more of the economic responsibility for families than was commonly supposed. "The struggle to live on the husband's wage, in most industrial families, is a failure," she asserted. In a preliminary canvass of more than eleven thousand working-class families, her research team found that "only six per cent . . . was of the conventional statistical type, husband, wife, and three children under sixteen years of age, supported by the husband alone."[80]

Other studies showed that patterns of maternal employment did not change as dramatically over the life course of a family as might be expected. Mothers of preschoolers were almost as likely to work as those with older children—at least until children were old enough to become wage earners themselves.[81] In two national WB studies published in 1923 and 1925, between 40 and 60 percent of the working mothers had children under five. Most also had wage-earning husbands present.[82]

Although information of this sort came from highly reputable sources and was widely disseminated in reform circles, it had only limited impact on the neo-maternalist thinking of child care leaders; few were induced to accept maternal employment and child care as part of "normal" family life. By 1930, the NFDN had begun to acknowledge an increase in the number of families in which both parents worked; because women "in all grades of society [were] entering business and professional life," the day nursery and nursery school had "come to stay."[83] Yet the organization's leadership, intent on maintaining the image of nurseries as an emergency service, still discouraged nurseries from accommodating two-earner families in addition to their usual clientele of single mothers and families in crisis.

Local nurseries, for their part, tended to ignore this directive, preferring to take in "normal" children from two-earner families rather than seek out those who were diagnosed with psychological problems and then hire the staff to deal with them. In response to growing demand, the number of voluntary day nurseries climbed to an all-time high by the early 1930s, yet day nursery leaders clung to their message of pathology and the need for therapy, resisting the grassroots trend toward acceptance of both maternal employment and child care.

POOR COUSINS

A second factor that discouraged child welfare experts from promoting day nurseries was a growing preference among parents for nursery schools run according to the principles of progressive early childhood education. Day nursery leaders and managers had not found it easy to incorporate any sort of pedagogical principles into their programs, much less keep up with developments in this dynamic field. One child care leader later recalled that well into the 1920s, nursery care still consisted chiefly of "herding children, feeding one end and wiping the other."[84] The orientation toward therapeutic services further distracted child care leaders from the goal of upgrading the nurseries' educational dimension.

The relation between early childhood education and child care had a mixed history. The kindergarten movement, whose roots were deeply intertwined with those of charitable day nurseries, had begun to move off and establish itself separately during the last quarter of the nineteenth century. By 1900 or so, kindergartens had become incorporated into hundreds of public school systems. Still, because kindergartens shared with day nurseries a common birthright in philanthropy and became affirmatively democratic when they gained public support, kindergartens' advocates never repudiated day nurseries but rather presented them as supplementary or complementary institutions.[85]

The trajectory of the nursery school movement was different. As the schools became more established, nursery school leaders took pains to differentiate their institutions from day nurseries. They feared that association with these "custodial" institutions would not only discourage the middle-class clientele they were hoping to attract but would also cast suspicion on the lofty educational benefits nursery schools purported to offer. In narrowing their appeal to the middle class, these early childhood educators effaced the decidedly heterogeneous class origins of their movement, for some of the earliest nursery schools did in fact serve "mixed" or nonpoor populations. In late nineteenth-century Boston, for example, parents of all classes clamored to send their children to Pauline Agassiz Shaw's nursery schools or day nurseries. In the same city, Abigail Eliot's Ruggles Street School, founded in 1922 and modeled along the lines of Margaret McMillan's London nursery schools, served a largely poor population.[86] But most of the American schools established between 1910 and 1930 sought children from families that could afford to pay some amount of tuition, and whose mothers were free to participate in parent education classes while their children were in school. These institutions had no intention of tailoring their programs to fit the needs—especially the hours and calendars—of working mothers.[87]

Early childhood educators did sometimes turn to day nurseries when they needed laboratories for new methods and materials or sites for teacher training; at the same time, a handful of nurseries took the initiative to incorporate progressive pedagogy into their programs.[88] But such instances of cooperation and overlap were rare and had little effect on the educational offerings of the average day nursery.

Even in New York City, where much of the educational experimentation was centered, day nurseries remained educationally underdeveloped, as became evident in a 1929 report on programs for young children in the city. The authors of the report, Dr. Mary M. Reed and E. Mae Raymond, two early childhood experts from Teachers College, Columbia University, used the principles of progressive nursery education as their criteria in judging the quality of the programs. Commissioned by the city's Welfare Council, they examined day nurseries, nursery schools, and kindergartens located in six settlement houses. The survey, frustrating for the historian of child care, made no distinction among the three different types of facilities, referring to all of them as "schools."[89] It is reasonable to assume, however, that the programs with the weakest educational components were probably the day nurseries, as education was not their primary goal. The detailed report, though deeply flawed in other respects (not least the smallness of the sample and the fact that all the facilities were sponsored by settlements), does give some idea of what services were being offered to poor and low-income New York City children during this period. It also reveals how progressive early childhood educators viewed contemporary child care practices.

Settlement houses, which were among the most progressive of civic organizations, might have been expected to emphasize education, but Reed and Raymond found much to criticize in their programs for young children. Staff members, for example, lacked appropriate professional qualifications. Four of the programs had teachers with either kindergarten or nursery school training, but one was directed by a registered nurse, whereas the staff at the sixth had "received a little professional training in the use of Montessori material supplemented by a few lessons by an 'expert' employed by the store which sells the material. . . . In some of the schools," the report noted with disapproval, "untrained maids and volunteer workers without special training were assisting the teachers," a practice that had been common in nurseries since the nineteenth century but which the NFDN, among other groups, had been working to eliminate.[90]

Everywhere, adult to child ratios were low and the staff overworked. At one school, "a nurse and two maids were responsible for 35 children ranging in age from three and a half months to four years"; in addition to caring for the children, they were supposed to clean the rooms and prepare and serve their food. At another school, "one teacher cared for a group of 25 children, including toddlers of 15 months and boys and girls of six." Along with the inadequate supervision, the schools were criticized for mixing children of widely different ages.[91] Curriculum, such as it was, also fell far short of the authors' standards. Most schools offered little opportunity for outdoor activity or for "the development of large muscles" and failed to offer time for rest as well as activity, or provide adequate napping facilities. Accepted hygiene practices were ignored, and the diet varied from excellent to poor.

Given sufficient desire and money, such practical matters as equipment and scheduling might have been remedied fairly easily. But inadequacies in the educational, psychological, and social aspects of the programs would prove far more recalcitrant, for they revealed deeper problems in the educational philosophy (or lack of it) in each school. Citing Douglas Thom's stress on the importance of early childhood for normal mental development, the report noted, "In only two of the schools . . . was the atmosphere characterized by observers as being happy and unrepressed."[92] Similarly, "in some of the schools there was little or no opportunity for the children to learn to do things for themselves or to make decisions," fundamental activities for developing independence. At one school, "the only activity for the youngest children (three to four years) . . . seemed to be getting on and off chairs. The assistant spent much of her time trying to keep the children seated."[93] In the worst case, "there were absolutely no toys or play materials and no play activity was provided for. . . . The children in this school were required to remain seated on chairs, with no occupation, during the entire morning.[94] Overall, Reed and Raymond found that to varying degrees the programs they observed fell short on nearly every criterion they applied. Because these criteria clearly represented the "progressive point of view," the study indicates that the principles and methods of progressive preschool education had made few inroads in these six "schools," four of which were actually day nurseries.

Although Reed and Raymond's sample was small and skewed, there is reason to believe that the nurseries they studied were not that unusual. In 1931 the

Association of Day Nurseries of New York City reported that seventeen out of forty-two member nurseries it surveyed apparently had no paid nursery school teacher. Of the seventeen, eleven used outside private or public kindergartens, but this meant that there still was no educational program for children of preschool age.[95] The situation was similar in Philadelphia, where information gathered by the Association of Day Nurseries from 1925 to 1930 indicated that nurseries were much more likely to hire social workers than nursery or kindergarten teachers. In 1925 and 1927, only three of twenty-one institutions reported a nursery school teacher on their staffs, while at least thirteen had social workers. By 1930, several had added nursery school programs, but several others had dropped theirs, so the net figures remained identical. At the same time the number of nurseries with social workers had risen to fifteen.[96] The Philadelphia data show that one effect of the therapeutic turn in nursery work was a marked preference for social workers over professional teachers.

The educational deficiencies of day nurseries became even more glaring as nursery schools grew in both number and reputation. The relative status of the two types of programs was spelled out at the 1930 White House Conference on Child Health and Protection (WHC), a gathering of the nation's leading experts on child welfare and education. John Anderson, who headed the Institute of Child Welfare at the University of Minnesota, discussed the day nursery in sympathetic but ultimately condescending terms.[97] Using language that suggested familiarity with Reed and Raymond's report, he noted that in most nurseries teachers and matrons were overworked, the adult-to-child ratio was low, and provisions for play were inadequate. The NFDN's new emphasis on mental health and its longstanding attempts to improve educational standards were not lost on him, but he felt that day nurseries had a long way to go and needed outside guidance in the process.[98]

When Anderson turned to the subject of nursery schools, his tone perked up noticeably. He commended the schools for making "an effort to meet the new social conditions characteristic of modern life"—conditions that, notably, included maternal employment. "Ventures in nursery school education should be encouraged," Anderson concluded, omitting any suggestion that the field needed outside help.[99]

In retrospect, the WHC appears to have been stacked against the day nursery. Many members of the main conference committee were early childhood educators, whereas the sole representative of child care—Mrs. Herman Biggs, successor to the NFDN's long-time president, Josephine Dodge—died before the conference was actually held. (The CB was notable in its absence, although this probably made little difference with regard to the child care issue.) With no one to make their case, day nurseries appeared in the worst possible light—backward, problem-ridden, and bearing little resemblance to nursery schools. Not surprisingly, the CB later reported, "the White House Conference classified day-nursery service definitely as one of relief to dependent families."[100]

Child care's poor showing would have long-term implications, for this WHC marked a significant moment in the history of American policy making for children. Not only did it serve as a gauge of mainstream child welfare discourse for the early 1930s, it also laid guidelines for New Deal thinking about programs for children. Unfortunately for the cause of child care, nursery schools had become the darling of child welfare experts, while day nurseries remained "poor cousins." Despite their growing numbers and capacity, the nurseries had actually lost status. The CB, while deploring the condition of children with working mothers in both industry and agriculture, eschewed child care in favor of efforts to strengthen mothers' pension provisions. Day nursery leaders attempted to salvage the reputation of their work by converting day nurseries into vehicles for the new therapeutic practices, but such goals fit neither the clientele nor the treasuries of most nurseries. Thus, as had occurred during the debate between day nurseries and mothers' pensions, when the Depression brought policies toward mothers and children to another "switch point," child care once again emerged on the lower track, this time with nursery schools in the ascendant.

Chapter 4 Uncle Sam's Cradles: New Deal and Wartime Policies

The Depression and then the onset of World War II strained the infrastructure of America's "semi-welfare state" almost to the breaking point. For the first time since the Civil War, public officials began to consider policies that would involve the federal government in massive social and economic interventions and, implicitly, refigure the welfare state. Among their chief concerns was the welfare of children and families; accordingly, blueprints for both New Deal and wartime social policy included programs for young children. The Works Progress Administration Emergency Nursery Schools and the Lanham Act Child Care Centers were the result.

The Emergency Nursery Schools (ENS) were one of several educational programs for children, youth, and adults set up under the New Deal. Though intended primarily as a form of work relief, all the educational programs had the secondary goal of promulgating what reformers regarded as modern values, whether vocational, social, or cultural.[1] The nursery schools were closely related to the WPA's programs of family-life education for parents.

As the architects of the New Deal began planning for children, they turned to the nursery school, not the day nursery, as an institutional model. In one sense, the choice was surprising, for the day nursery, despite its drawbacks, had a long history of serving families in crisis and had earned the White House Conference imprimatur as a form of relief. Nursery schools, by contrast, were relatively new, far fewer in number, and more clearly associated with the middle and upper classes than with the poor. Whereas the stock of nursery schools was nowhere near adequate, existing day nurseries could, with sufficient public funding, have been expanded and modified to meet the enormous need for children's services identified by government officials. Indeed, a Children's Bureau survey found that because of widespread unemployment, day nursery use in twenty-seven areas had declined markedly between 1929 and 1930, so there were many openings.[2]

Nevertheless, it was characteristic of the New Dealers that they preferred innovation over the tried (and what they considered failed) forms of charity of the past. So in designing the project for young children, they passed over the day nursery and opted instead for the nursery school, whose star was newly risen in federal policy circles. The decision pushed the day nursery even farther to the margins of the realm of social policy, spelling disaster for voluntary day nurseries, whose numbers fell by one-quarter between 1931 and 1940.[3]

The ENS operated from 1933 to 1943, when many were discontinued and others converted into wartime child care centers. Some parents used the WPA schools as child care, even though they were not intended as such and their design made this somewhat difficult. Most schools were open for only half a day or until three in the afternoon at the latest, and admission was restricted to children whose families were financially distressed. If one or both parents obtained jobs, the children might lose their eligibility. Women employed on WPA projects, however, were encouraged to enroll their children in the ENS, which gradually came to be regarded as a concomitant of the work program.

Prior to the establishment of the WPA program, fewer than 300 nursery schools (in contrast to approximately 800 day nurseries) were operating in the entire country, most of them privately supported, enrolling fewer than 6,000 students.[4] From 1933 to 1934, nearly 3,000 nursery schools were set up under federal auspices, serving more than 64,000 children.[5] These schools were then consolidated, and from 1934 to 1935, an average of 1,900 schools were in operation, with a capacity for some 75,000 students.[6] Eventually the program spread to forty-three states, the District of Columbia, the Virgin Islands, and Puerto Rico.[7]

Whereas private nursery schools had primarily served a well-to-do clientele, those sponsored by the government were explicitly geared toward children of low-income parents, especially those on relief. Announcing the program in October 1933, Harry Hopkins, head of the Federal Emergency Relief Administration (FERA, predecessor to the WPA), explained, "Young children of pre-school age in the homes of needy and unemployed parents are suffering from the conditions . . . incident to current economic and social difficulties. The education and health programs of nursery schools can aid as nothing else in combatting the physical and mental handicaps being imposed upon these young children."[8]

In addition to serving children, each ENS was to offer parent education, which, according to Hopkins, would relieve parents "from their anxieties resulting from the worry of inadequate home provisions for their young children" and include them "in an educational program on an adult level which will raise their morale and that of the entire family and the community."[9] It is worth noting that in spelling out the mission of the nursery schools, Hopkins appeared to be drawing on the therapeutic rhetoric of the day nursery movement as much as the cognitive and developmental theories of early childhood education.

Although such public pronouncements emphasized benefits to children and parents, the nursery schools, like all FERA and WPA projects, were intended first and foremost to function as an employment program. Accordingly, the federal government provided funds only to pay the salaries of teachers, who were to be drawn exclusively from the ranks of the unemployed (the general economic downturn had forced many public schools to close, putting their faculty members out of work). Local communities were to initiate plans for establishing the schools and to provide plant, equipment, and, after the first year, food as well.[10] Supervision would come from local and state boards of education.[11]

"NOT SIMPLY CHILD-MINDING"

Aside from the financial stipulations, the federal government kept the parameters of the program rather vague. Its content and structure were left to the early childhood and parent education movements to define. Thus what started as a general concept in the minds of relief officials took concrete form in the hands of educational professionals.

There are conflicting accounts of how and where the idea for the WPA nursery schools originated, but it is abundantly clear that, once it became policy, leaders in the field of early childhood education moved rapidly to help determine the shape of the program.[12] As it happened, many of these experts were attending a conference in Toronto when the ENS program was announced. They immediately saw that a national program could offer early childhood education an unprecedented opportunity for expansion, but at the same time they understood that if the quality of the schools could not be controlled, such a program ran the risk of doing their cause a disservice. As educator Christine Heinig recalled, the Emergency Nursery Schools were to be "recognized as educational institutions. No one wanted [them] to be simply child-minding or baby-sitting centers."[13]

Heinig's remark underscored the rift between early childhood education and child care, revealing the widespread assumption—among early childhood educators, at any rate—that it would be disastrous for the reputation of nursery schools if they were mistaken for day nurseries. Fearful that governmental programs could all too easily lapse into the kind of custodial anarchy associated with the nurseries, early childhood and parent educators sought to position themselves so that their influence would be felt. They quickly volunteered the services of a National Advisory Committee on Emergency Nursery Schools (NAC), comprising representatives from three sponsoring organizations: the Association for Childhood Education, the National Association for Nursery Education (NANE), and the National Council of Parent Education. This distinguished group included many of the most prominent members of the early childhood education movement.[14]

Because the FERA had been set up to promote general welfare, not education, its administrative structure was quite permeable and allowed this extragovernmental body a good deal of input. Because the Emergency Relief Act of 1933 provided no funds for supervision, during the first year of the program NAC took the initiative in raising private funds to pay the salary of Mary Dabney Davis, a member of NANE on loan from the U.S. Office of Education, who served as an ENS Specialist in the FERA. Private funds also paid the salaries of twenty-one state supervisors, nine regional supervisors, and two federal supervisors (see appendix A). In 1934 the FERA took over Davis' salary, and Hopkins gave a dispensation allowing each state commissioner of education to hire one or more trained nursery specialists who were not necessarily eligible for relief.[15]

Bureaucratic consolidation did not cut off the NAC's influence but merely shifted the financial burden for administration from private to public funds, leaving in place most of the same personnel, all carefully selected from the tightly knit group of early childhood educators. At the same time, the NAC set up a kind of shadow bureaucracy made up of regional advisers "loaned" from the various institutions and agencies with which its member organizations were affiliated.

Once in place, the educators lost no time in putting their stamp on the program and clarifying its identity. As one early WPA bulletin stated flatly, "The Nursery School is not a day nursery, neither is it a play school. It has definite educational aims and objectives. . . . It does not attempt to substitute for the home but it supplements the home."[16]

The NAC's insistence on establishing and maintaining high educational standards sometimes put it at odds with the WPA's mandate to give priority to relief. One of the principal stumbling blocks was staffing.[17] Although there were many unemployed teachers to be found, few had specific experience in early childhood education. During the first year of the program, the NAC persuaded the FERA to hire a large number of trained nursery school teachers who were not eligible for relief, arguing that because "the nursery schools set up under the relief program would serve as a demonstration of what nursery school service could accomplish, it was . . . extremely important that this demonstration be on a high professional basis and that whatever was done in the . . . schools . . . should be so sound educationally as to be a contribution to education, at the same time serving a relief need."[18]

The number of non-eligible teachers declined as state supervisors established training institutes, which prospective relief-eligible teachers were required to attend for four to six weeks before entering a classroom. The institutes, mostly affiliated with colleges, universities, normal schools, or teachers' colleges, gave early childhood leaders an opportunity to promulgate their own approach to preschool education.[19]

To a great extent, the professionalism of NAC members reflected their sincere desire to create a governmental program that would actually provide educational benefits to the thousands of children it reached; however, it also revealed a good deal of self-interest. By insisting on special training for teachers and ensuring that supervisors would be drawn from their own ranks, early childhood educators were attempting to protect their professional status and reputation and to continue to police the boundary between nursery schools and day nurseries.

In spite of the networks and training programs that were established, it was difficult to maintain homogeneous methods and high standards in a program as geographically diverse and heterogeneously staffed as the Emergency Nursery Schools (see appendix B). Some schools lacked suitable quarters or adequate equipment; others could not find appropriate personnel. The ideal teacher followed progressive principles, allowing children to play freely and use materials imaginatively in an environment scaled down to their size and designed with their interests in mind. Although there was a definite daily schedule, the timing of such events as meals and naps was approximate, and teachers were urged to be flexible. The schools were expected to stress nutrition, health, and hygiene, but these concerns were to be integrated into the normal routine in the form of playful learning experiences.[20] However, not all teachers—particularly the poorly trained or less experienced—felt comfortable dealing with groups of children in classrooms with only minimal structure, and many quietly resisted directives from Washington. ENS Specialist Grace Langdon found evidence of "more regimentation than is desirable for 2 and 3-year-old children" at some of the schools she visited.[21]

Although teacher training eventually became more or less regularized, the program continued to be plagued with staffing problems. Many of the nursery schools in the North as well as the South were segregated, and local authorities had difficulty finding qualified teachers who were willing to work at schools serving black children.[22] Turnover was a constant issue as funding priorities shifted or teachers were forced to quit because they had lost their eligibility for relief or were offered positions in private schools.[23] (WPA regulations compelled them to accept such positions, even when wages and working conditions were inferior to those in the Emergency Nursery Schools.)[24]

Turnover became an even greater problem in the final years of the program, as defense industries began luring teachers away to more lucrative jobs.[25] The coming of war also made inroads on the nurseries' clientele, reducing the population of families who still qualified for relief. Between 1936 and 1942, the number of nursery schools declined from 1,900 to 944.[26] Like other government officials, Grace Langdon began turning her attention to the children of defense workers, but she remained mindful of the needs of low-income children and stressed the importance of retaining services for them.[27] Schools that served this group exclusively were, however, phased out when the WPA was disbanded in April 1943.

RELIEF OR EDUCATION?

The staffing problems and withdrawal of support were symptomatic of the internal contradiction that had plagued the WPA program from the start—the contradiction between alleviating social crisis and providing education. As its very name never allowed the public to forget, the Emergency Nursery Schools program had gained legitimacy from the crisis out of which it was born. Nevertheless, many leaders in early childhood education cherished fond hopes that the program would become permanent. They took encouragement from Harry Hopkins, who, in announcing the funding for state supervisory positions in 1934, asserted, "It is my desire that the emergency educational program covering various phases of adult education and nursery schools shall be so administered in the states as to build toward a permanent and integral part of the regularly established public school programs."[28]

Experts on child welfare and early childhood agreed that public nationwide preschools were desirable. NAC member George D. Stoddard, director of the Iowa Child Welfare Research Station, wrote in 1935, "At the present time few homes and few mothers appear to be equipped for doing what needs to be done." Only professionally staffed nursery schools, complemented by parental education, could effectively guide children and their parents through the preschool years. Thus, Stoddard concluded, "We have before us the hard task of welding, once and for all, the needs of five million preschool children to the great body of public education."[29]

That union, however, never materialized. According to Mary Dabney Davis, the fact that the WPA program was funded and to a great extent administered outside the public education bureaucracy precluded its integration into local systems. Its unique structure, Dabney and her colleagues wrote, "left the double impression that nursery schools were good things for the economically underprivileged but that they were a service which local schools could not undertake without federal aid."[30] Officials of the NAC, well aware that communities would have to take over support of the schools if they were to continue, repeatedly urged local sponsoring committees to take more responsibility for the nonpersonnel expenses of the schools.[31] Many communities managed to mobilize considerable resources, but they were seldom sufficient to maintain schools once federal funding was withdrawn. At the same time, the ENS program became marginalized within the WPA, because it was administered under a separate educational division and mediated by the NAC. The schools' independence did not, however, protect them from the threat of extinction as all relief programs began to be phased out.

Potentially the opening wedge for a permanent public nursery school program, the Emergency Nursery Schools failed to find an appropriate bureaucratic home or a source of ongoing financial support. Moreover, they could not avoid the stigma that sponsorship by a federal relief agency carried with it in the 1930s. Nevertheless, the schools succeeded in promulgating the idea of nursery education more broadly than ever before, making the public more comfortable with the notion of sending small children out of the home for at least part of the day. In addition, the ENS showed that, with careful administration, high standards could be achieved in a public program. Left in place was a band of federal bureaucrats who were firmly committed to upholding the principles of high-quality early childhood education in any future governmental services for young children.

Unintentionally, the ENS were more successful in laying the groundwork for federal child care policy. Although the early childhood specialists had initially taken pains to dissociate their project from day nurseries, the schools ended up providing child care for thousands of mothers who were working in WPA jobs. In a series of films made in 1936 and 1937 to document its achievements in individual states, the WPA proudly included scenes of children's activities in the ENS, which were interchangeably referred to as nursery schools and day nurseries.[32] The inclusion of child care in the nursery schools broke down two key barriers to government policy. First, it finally put the federal government into the business of providing child care, if only for women employed on relief projects. And second, it bridged the gap between child care and early childhood education, demonstrating that the functions and benefits of both could be combined in a single program. The coming war would offer the government a chance to test this new policy direction further.

DEBATING THE NEED FOR CHILD CARE

Although child care was clearly an important aspect of the ENS, the early childhood specialists tended to downplay it, preferring to promote the educational dimensions of their work. As the defense economy geared up, however, child care came to occupy more of their attention.[33] Aware that the need for services would soon become critical, they attempted to move into an obvious administrative gap in the federal government.

The timing of their move, beginning in mid-1940, suggests that the specialists may well have been motivated by a desire for bureaucratic self-preservation. Because the nursery schools, like other relief programs, were rapidly losing support, they needed a new raison d'être, and child care presented itself as a logical choice. Moreover, theirs appeared to be the appropriate agency to take the lead. But this was not an instance of sheer opportunism; in taking up the issue of child care, the specialists employed rhetoric and strategies consistent with the belief in the value of early childhood education that they had demonstrated throughout the New Deal. With public schools unwilling to take over the Emergency Nursery Schools, the best alternative for maintaining and expanding education for very young children appeared to be government-supported child care. Significantly, the model they envisioned was based not on the voluntary day nursery but on a modification of the Emergency Nursery Schools. By initiating and administering their own program, the specialists could ensure its quality and adherence to high educational standards.

The administrators of the ENS, though based in Washington, became aware of the dimensions of the child care problem at an early date through reports from the field as well as their own travels. In June 1940, Specialist Grace Langdon told L. R. Alderman, director of the Education Division, "There is no doubt that a new need for day nurseries is imminent, which the WPA can take leadership in meeting."[34] Several months later, she drew up a plan for expanding the WPA Family Life Education Program to meet defense needs by offering child care. Anticipating possible objections to having the Education Division undertake this new type of provision, Langdon assured her director that "existing trends in the day nursery field . . . are toward educational emphasis" and that the NAC considered day nurseries to be an "educational project."[35]

In attempting to pave the way for a child care program run under the auspices of the Education Division of the WPA, Langdon was venturing into territory that she and her fellow early childhood educators had once disdained and that was still jealously guarded by the day nursery movement. That movement, however, was in no position to protest, for the Depression had taken its toll on voluntary child care. Since 1930, the number of day nurseries had fallen from an all-time high of 800 to 600, and in 1938 the National Federation of Day Nurseries was compelled to merge with its New York chapter, forming the National Association of Day Nurseries (NADN).

In spite of, or perhaps because of, its weakness, the day nursery movement interpreted proposed government support not as an opportunity to extend their own efforts but as encroachment onto their professional turf. Less than a month after Langdon's memo to Alderman, she and CB chief Katharine Lenroot both received indignant letters from Elizabeth Clark, executive secretary of the NADN. Clark expressed her alarm over a radio address in which Florence Kerr, assistant commissioner of the WPA, mentioned the possibility of using the WPA's Housekeeping Aide projects as day nurseries. "This would seem to mean day care is to be given by the WPA in some other division than the nursery education department, and by wholly inadequate personnel," Clark told Lenroot. "We feel this is extremely serious for child care standards, concern for the stability of family life, for the very existence of privately supported day nurseries."[36] Lenroot and Langdon both confronted Kerr on this issue, and in early August Lenroot wrote back assuring Clark that, according to Kerr, "the WPA has never promoted and is not now promoting day nurseries."[37]

This was not strictly accurate; many of the WPA's nursery schools were already operating as child care centers and Langdon was busily planning for many more. But WPA officials were, apparently, not interested in taking Clark into their confidence at that moment, even though her letters to Langdon and Lenroot implied that the NADN *would* approve of government-sponsored child care if it were administered by the Education Division. Langdon did not want to alienate the NADN completely, however, so in her recommendations for expanding the WPA's existing child care centers, she stipulated that policies regarding admission and fees should be set up "in accord with the accepted standards of the National Association of Day Nurseries."[38] At the same time, she made sure that the philosophy of early childhood education would predominate in the government's wartime nurseries by taking steps to convert the remaining Emergency Nursery Schools (which by then outnumbered the surviving voluntary day nurseries). To meet the needs of working mothers, she called for extended hours of service.

FOOT-DRAGGING AT THE CHILDREN'S BUREAU

The WPA was well in advance of other federal agencies in drawing attention to child care as a critical defense issue for both women and the nation. By 1940 the Women's Bureau had also become concerned with the impact of defense industry on women, but it focused on working conditions and safety standards.[39] Although it struggled to gain a voice for women in the nation's "manpower" policies, the WB never raised the issue of child care. Longtime WB chief Mary Anderson supported care for the children of working mothers but did not make it a priority, apparently out of deference to the government agencies explicitly concerned with children.[40] This division of labor meant that although it was wartime maternal employment that created the need for day care and after-school programs in the first place, the programs themselves would, chameleon-like, derive their rationale and identity from the agencies that actually administered them. Thus, at least within federal circles, child care would be seen not as a labor issue or an entitlement for working women but as a matter of child welfare.

The other likely source of support for wartime child care was the Children's Bureau, but unlike the WB, the CB sought to ignore maternal employment as long as possible, despite its impact on children. In this, the CB was remaining true to type; it had, of course, never approved of mothers working. For two decades, the bureau had avoided the implications of its own research, which pointed to the need for expanded child care provisions as a remedy for wide-spread child labor and child neglect. Instead, CB officials took the neo-mater-nalist position that mothers' pensions would solve these problems. During the 1930s, the CB played a major role in the successful campaign to transform state-based pensions into federally supported Aid to Dependent Children,[41] and on the eve of war, it appeared that the agency was determined to maintain its neo-maternalist trajectory. At the 1940 White House Conference on Children in a Democracy, CB officials joined the chorus calling for preservation of the security of "the democratic family," a concept that implicitly entailed keeping mothers in the home.[42]

It was not until mid-summer 1941—a full year after the WPA's Grace Langdon had drawn up her plan for defense-related child care—that the CB finally acknowledged that the situation was becoming critical and decided to convene a conference on Day Care of Children of Working Mothers. The conference might never have come about but for the urging of Charles Schott-land, a former assistant CB chief who had been appointed bureau liaison to the newly established Office of Defense Health and Welfare Services. Although the CB set the agenda, it was clear that its support for maternal employment and child care remained lukewarm.

The CB found support for its views among other conference participants, who included federal- and state-level government officials as well as representatives from a number of private-sector organizations concerned with children (see appendix C).[43] It was perhaps no surprise that its staunchest ally was the NADN; indeed, the neo-maternalist solidarity between the two organizations was reminiscent of the World War I pact between Josephine Dodge and Julia Lathrop. The two organizations were especially opposed to work for mothers of children under two. "It is a very serious situation to take these mothers out of the home," warned the NADN's Elizabeth Clark.[44] The allies jointly proposed counseling prospective working mothers in order to help them determine whether employment was a good idea for their families as well as themselves.

Mary Anderson, chief of the WB, took strong exception to this suggestion.

For most mothers, she said, the thought of leaving their children was a "terrific worry," and they welcomed help. But, she argued, if it came in the form of interrogation about their families, some women might become suspicious and resistant, fearing, "They won't take me if I tell them those things. . . . That is particularly true because of the fact that the women work for the same reason that men work. They work to live. They work to get bread and butter not only for themselves but for dependents. . . . For that reason I am not at all sure we ought to be so very strict and try to do all of these counseling things, because I don't believe we could do them anyway, and I wouldn't set up more barriers than there already are against women's working."[45] Sensitive to the implication that she was being insufficiently patriotic, Clark retorted, "None of us in the Day Nurseries Association stands for putting any obstacles in the way of defense, but we do want to make sure that we are not creating a lot of emotionally ill and neglected children in the process."[46]

For many conference participants, attitudes toward maternal employment were reciprocally linked to their views on mother-child separation, the impact of child care, and what type of services was most appropriate. On the one hand, those who approved of maternal employment believed that mother-child separation was not in itself harmful if children received adequate care in the interim. This group was convinced that child care could be educationally beneficial and argued that services should be designed to enhance those benefits. On the other hand, those who disapproved of maternal employment claimed that mother-child separation was inherently harmful. They were dubious about the educational value of child care and contended instead that, to offset potential psychological damage, services should replicate as closely as possible the "natural" setting of the child's home.

Grace Langdon of the WPA quickly took the lead in explaining child care's educational potential. She claimed that child care centers could provide the same educational benefits as the Emergency Nursery Schools. The nursery schools had, in fact, been so successful that even higher-income families sought admission for their children. However, Langdon conceded, an educational program demanded more planning, supervision, and equipment than the typical custodial nursery; ideally at least a portion of its staff would have professional training. All these requirements made programs difficult to establish and costly to run and supervise, and it was likely that the tension between quality and expediency would increase in proportion to the number of mothers demanding child care as they entered defense industries.

Langdon's opponents dismissed the potential educational benefits of child care centers because they entailed keeping children in large groups and depended heavily on trained professionals. Representatives of the CB, NADN, and other organizations preferred placing children a few at a time in foster day homes or sending housekeeping aides into their own homes. Such services, they argued, were not only more homelike but offered greater flexibility than group care. Margaret Batjer, chief of the WPA's Home Economics Division, sketched several likely scenarios: What would happen if a child became ill, or if the mother's working hours did not coincide with those of the day care center? Housekeeping aides, Batjer contended, could provide emergency help to working mothers whose children became sick or who could not find child care. Katharine Lenroot, chief of the CB, concurred: this type of service was crucial for the care of school-age and preschool children in nonroutine situations.

The NADN's Elizabeth Clark particularly favored foster day care for children under two.[47] She was joined by Howard Hopkirk of the Child Welfare League of America (CWLA), an organization that had long considered foster care preferable to institutional care and generally opposed maternal employment. Hopkirk added that foster day care allowed sibling groups to remain intact. "Often an older child has a warm relationship that could be conserved if you have flexibility in your day program."[48]

But foster care also came in for its share of criticism. The CB's own medical adviser, Dr. Martha Eliot, reported that Britain's wartime experience had led to a preference for "nursery centers"—"a compromise between a nursery school and a day nursery"—over foster homes. Foster homes evoked the image of "child minders," who had fallen into disfavor among "all the people with any interest in children" (that is, professionals). To address the problem of children's illness, the British set up "sick bays" to care for those with minor ailments. Despite professional opinion, foster homes had sprung up in wartime England, but the government required "minders" to register and submit to a health inspection. Even so, Eliot concluded, "the difficulties of such a minder system are obvious."[49] One of these, according to Paul Benjamin of the Buffalo, New York, Council of Social Agencies, was psychological. Foster homes could be convenient in certain situations, but they might "in many instances be quite confusing to children and should be used with discrimination." Nursery school pioneer Abigail Eliot (Martha's sister) also sounded dubious about the idea, noting that in Boston foster homes were found to be more expensive than group care.[50]

Even the advocates of foster care admitted that there were problems in finding suitable homes. They had to be conveniently located so that parents could drop children off on their way to work (this was also a consideration for child care centers, but policy planners had some latitude in choosing sites for centers, whereas they had to take foster homes wherever they could find them). Moreover, in high-demand areas, the same·employment opportunities that attracted mothers also drew in potential foster day care providers; fewer women would be willing to remain in this low-paying, traditional form of women's work. Finally, private-sector social workers, who had customarily been the ones to find homes and place children, could not deal with the volume of demand created by defense industries. There was little government help available at any level, and only one state, Connecticut, had regulations regarding "private day homes."[51]

In spite of these reservations, Lenroot urged communities to consider foster care an important element of their social service repertoire. "Certainly you wouldn't be meeting the needs of the working mother, and certainly not in a stepped-up defense program, if she had to take a child back home because he was excluded at the door of the nursery [because of illness]," Lenroot pointed out.[52] Because foster day care and homemaker services were provided in dispersed locations, they could not be readily supervised, yet the CB seemed willing to sacrifice oversight for what it saw as more homelike provisions.

AN UNEASY COMPROMISE

Failing to reach consensus, the forty-three conference participants finally issued an equivocal ten-point program. On the one hand, they asserted, "Mothers who remain at home to provide care for children are performing an essential patriotic service in the defense program." But, recognizing that mothers might well be needed for defense work, they also conceded that "it is more than ever a public responsibility to provide appropriate care of children while mothers are at work."[53]

Although the ten points appeared to represent a compromise on the issue of maternal employment, they barely papered over the deep divisions on the goals and uses of group child care. Participants called upon communities to plan "as many forms of day care as are required to meet the needs of children of all ages for whom such provision should be made" but then assigned "nurseries, child centers, and other forms of community day care" a lower priority than care "by relatives and friends" and stated that if the community was called upon, it should integrate child care programs with other social services.[54] This hierarchy represented a victory for the CB, which, along with the CWLA and

NADN, persisted in viewing group care, or day nurseries, as a form of social welfare to be used only as a last resort. Moreover, the insistence on linking child care with other social services meant that such care was to be embedded in the context of social work, which continued to pathologize child care and the families who needed it.

The conference resolutions implicitly gave short shrift to the position of the WPA Early Childhood Specialists, who, along with the National Association for Nursery Education and a few other educational groups, conceived of group care as a force for good, an opportunity to foster cognitive and emotional growth in preschool children while, coincidentally, freeing their parents for vital national work. Fulfillment of the educators' vision necessarily involved a certain level of professionalism, which explains why individuals like Grace Langdon were so strongly opposed to using foster day care and housekeeping aides on a regular basis.

The divisions among policy makers did not go away but continued to play themselves out over the next few years. The conference had called for the establishment of a Joint Planning Board to consult on child care and welfare issues related to defense, with the CB, Office of Education (OE), and WPA each sending representatives. Two weeks after the conference, Katharine Lenroot invited the WPA to join the other two agencies in setting up a national child care program. Joint administration with the WPA would have been advantageous for the CB and OE, because the Emergency Nursery Schools represented the federal government's only previous venture into children's programs on a national scale. From the WPA's perspective, however, the project did not make sense, for Grace Langdon and Florence Kerr realized that their philosophical differences, especially with the CB, could not be easily resolved. Moreover, after successfully running the nursery schools for seven years, they had already begun to make the transition to child care with no help from anyone else. So they declined Lenroot's offer.

Kerr and Langdon were gambling that, on its own, the WPA would be able to obtain enough funding to expand the nursery school system to meet wartime needs. The Lanham Act, passed in 1941, funded community facilities in "war-impact areas," but it was not until early 1943 that these provisions were interpreted as being applicable to child care centers. In the interim, the WPA was operating on limited funds, with schools closing down because of a lack of personnel and reduction in the number of families eligible for relief. To oversee the expansion and transformation of the nursery schools from relief work to defense, the WPA set up the Child Protection Program, with Langdon as consultant. From mid-1941 through 1942, she toured the country, inspecting local projects and consulting with regional and state supervisors. Over and over again, she found officials besieged with requests to provide child care by keeping existing nursery schools open or establishing new ones in areas where there were none. With no federal funds forthcoming, some states had begun to undertake the expense.[55]

Federal support finally arrived in mid-1942, when, at the urging of Representative Mary Norton (Democrat–New Jersey), Congress came up with $6 million for expansion of the nursery school program through the Emergency Appropriation Act.[56] In April 1943, the entire WPA was liquidated, but the child care program was transferred to the War Public Services Bureau of the Federal Works Administration, where it was jointly administered by Langdon as chief of the new Child Care and Protection Program (CCPP) and Kerr as head of the War Public Services Bureau.

As soon as Kerr learned about the new funding, she called a national conference to assess needs and plan for expansion. Unlike the 1941 conference, this one was intended not to debate the general direction that policy should take but to develop practical procedures for the CCPP. Most of the participants were former WPA and FWA personnel from Washington or state or regional offices, with a few handpicked outsiders, including representatives of several state departments of education, three prominent early childhood educators, and members of the National Advisory Committee that had overseen the Emergency Nursery Schools. One of the first items of business was to reconstitute the advisory committee. The new body, now called the National Commission for Young Children, included a few members of the NAC and was chaired by Rose Alschuler, a pioneer in early childhood education who had started the nation's first public nursery school in Chicago in 1924.[57] Notably absent from the committee were representatives of the CB, the CWLA, and the NADN.

One of the main themes of the conference was maintaining educational standards. Participants understood that with increased demand for female labor in defense industries, staffing problems would undoubtedly worsen, so they agreed to rely on volunteers and high school and college students. College students, it was thought, could earn credits in home economics or education by working in child care centers. In order to retain qualified head teachers, Kerr would see to it that WPA regulations were modified so that they could be classified as "key personnel" for "constructive training for reemployment."[58] To train new personnel, conferees were urged to cooperate with colleges, universities, and training schools, many of which had previously offered training for WPA teachers.

Not only did the conference place a positive emphasis on education, it discouraged anything that smacked of social work or social welfare. The procedural guidelines stated that while a sliding scale for fees should be worked out by program sponsors, the WPA, and an appropriate social service agency, fees should be determined without taking a case history, "unless for some reason such a case history seems to be indicated."[59] Although the CCPP clearly had a huge task before it, participants seemed to be united in a spirit of cooperation. Unlike the 1941 conference, which had ended in uneasy compromise, this one concluded on a note of energy and optimism.

But while FWA officials forged ahead, their opponents also began to gather their forces in an effort to wrest away control of the child care program. By spring 1943, Lanham funding had become available for child care centers. According to the terms of the law, localities had to seek certification as "war-impact areas," and then local sponsors had to apply for funding for specific projects. As the result of an awkward arrangement, the CB and OE were given jurisdiction over certifying applications for programs, which the FWA would then administer. The FWA, however, was not authorized to establish a network of regional supervisors such as the one that had overseen the WPA nursery schools. Instead, the two certifying agencies tried to extend their control over local projects by working indirectly through state education and welfare agencies. Because the WPA had already established contacts with state governments and in many cases had even put nursery education specialists in place at that level, this situation created much overlap and confusion.[60]

Frustrated by their lack of direct control, the OE and the CB tried to get Congress to revamp the bureaucracy of the child care program so that the FWA would be bypassed altogether. Under the terms of the War Area Child Care Act (the so-called Thomas Bill), which was introduced into the Senate in May 1943, child care centers would no longer be funded through the Lanham Act but rather would be entirely approved, funded, and administered by the Federal Security Agency, the umbrella structure that now housed the OE and the CB. On the surface, the proposed bill appeared to be a boon to child care, for unlike the Lanham Act, it explicitly called for federal funding for child care services. But its administrative details proved controversial, as the ensuing debate revealed.[61]

Speaking in favor of the Thomas Bill, Bess Goodykoonz, assistant commissioner of education, argued that states, working through public schools, could make plans for nursery and after-school programs that would be better coordinated than those that resulted from reliance on local initiatives. Another supporter, Dr. Martha Eliot of the CB, claimed that her agency had already developed standards for day care and could readily institute them at the local level by tapping the working relationships it had been developing with state welfare and health departments since passage of the Social Security Act in 1935. Moreover, the Thomas Bill called for measures that the CB had been advocating since the joint conference in 1941, namely, foster day care for infants, information and advisory services, and a network of regional consultants.

Florence Kerr testified in opposition to the bill. She pointed out that the FWA was already running a successful child care program and objected to adding another—unnecessary—layer of bureaucracy to the program on the grounds that it would slow down allocation of funds and construction of new facilities. A quarter of a million children were already being cared for, she averred, and that number could be quadrupled within six months if the FWA were allowed to function unimpeded.[62]

The Thomas Bill passed in the Senate but died in the House in the summer of 1943. At the urging of President Franklin Delano Roosevelt, the warring parties eventually reached a compromise outside the legislative process: the OE and CB would continue to review proposals for children's programs, but the FWA would have the final authority to approve them.[63] Once again, those who viewed child care within the context of early childhood education appeared to have triumphed.

PERSISTENCE IN THE PRIVATE SECTOR

Nevertheless, those who persisted in pathologizing maternal employment and casting child care as a form of social welfare would not rest. Though outmaneuvered at both the legislative and bureaucratic levels, they had not exhausted their armory. Not only did representatives of the CB and OE continue to serve as mouthpieces for their position throughout the rest of the war, they enjoyed strong support from private-sector organizations, mainly in the fields of family and child welfare, which, through social workers across the country, could still influence policy at the local level.

Here the weakness of the FWA structure, working through the procedures dictated by the Lanham Act and modified by President Roosevelt, became apparent. The FWA could not act until a local committee had taken the initiative to seek funds (and even then, bureaucratic procedures could delay funding, not to mention construction, for many months). Moreover, because the federal government covered only 50 percent of operating costs, communities had to find sponsors who were willing to underwrite the other half.[64] (This arrangement was not dissimilar to the one used for the Emergency Nursery Schools, but in that case the federal government covered a greater proportion of the costs.) Many municipalities established community defense councils or similar bodies to formulate policy and handle such matters as applications for federal funds, but members of these groups were often inexperienced and felt themselves at a loss in dealing with the federal government. In many cases they were simply opposed to the idea of encouraging maternal employment by providing child care. Together, these factors led to long delays in getting child care centers under way, when they did not block progress altogether.

From the earliest discussions of wartime social problems, the CB and the OE had called on the private sector for advice and assistance. Now it was the turn of private-sector professionals to attempt to uphold the position against child care that was shared by those government agencies.[65] Local social workers, though geographically dispersed, kept abreast of the views of their respective professional organizations (the American Association of Social Workers, the American Public Welfare Association, the Family Welfare Association of America, or one of a dozen more specialized groups) through publications and conferences. Because many welfare professionals at the state and community level belonged to pre-existing networks or had worked together on fundraising drives or other cooperative projects, they tended to form natural caucuses on ad hoc defense committees and thus reinforced one another.

One of the most dominant voices in the field of child welfare—and one of the most conservative on the question of child care—was that of the Child Welfare League of America. In the fall of 1942, the CWLA absorbed the National Association of Day Nurseries.[66] It was a fitting swan song for child care's most venerable advocate, symbolizing its longtime ambivalence toward the very cause it was pledged to support. In a study commissioned by the CWLA the same year, social worker Henrietta Gordon affirmed the partnership by reiterating the tenets of the therapeutic stance that both organizations had endorsed since the 1920s. "Placement of children [by private agencies] so that their mothers may go out to work," she wrote, "is a departure from accepted practice."[67] Agencies usually offered care only to families in which parents were physically or emotionally incapacitated and therefore unable to care for their children, or when children suffered from certain psychological problems that agencies thought a day nursery could alleviate. "We cannot too easily overlook the principles that a child's own home is the best medium for his development," Gordon wrote, "and that children should not be deprived of home life except for urgent and compelling reasons."[68] The crisis of war did not qualify.

Affiliates of the CWLA and other organizations that shared its views influenced the delivery of child care at the community level in several ways.[69] Their representatives sat on local defense councils, where they could block proposals to apply to the federal government for child care centers. In many communities, social workers were in the best position to assess day care needs and, if facilities were required, initiate applications for Lanham funds. However, their own professional ideology frequently prevented them from taking this step.

If they could not prevent centers from being established, social workers could intervene in their usage by doing "intake"—screening applications and offering counseling to potential clients. Typically, social workers regarded mothers applying for day care with suspicion or presumed that they were pathological. Even "financial stress" was seen as a dubious reason for leaving one's children to go out to work. The alert social worker could detect "inappropriate" or "insincere" motives in an interview with an applicant and perhaps persuade her (for it was usually the mother who applied) to seek counseling or apply for public aid instead of working. One social worker expressed concern that maternal employment might upset the balance of power within families. If the husband were unemployed, earned less than his wife, or simply derived "great ego satisfaction in being the sole provider," his wife's employment might cause friction, and thus the counselor should advise against it.[70]

Social work leaders did not rest content with their part in day care intake; if, in spite of their efforts, a child was actually admitted to a center, many professionals felt that they had a continuing responsibility to aid the mother in "adjusting" to having her child in day care and counsel her regarding any behavioral problems the child might experience—as reported by the nursery teacher. All these interventions served to discourage mothers from using child care centers or made them feel somewhat uneasy when they did.

Thus, although the funding and administration of the wartime child care program came to rest in the hands of federal officials who, for the most part, believed that child care could not only serve an important defense need by freeing women to work but also offer substantial educational benefits to children, their efforts were stymied by rivals at both the federal and local levels. Community initiative and delivery of services were subject to the influence of the pro-therapeutic social work perspective, which looked upon child care clients as abnormal and day nurseries or child care centers as, at best, temporary solutions to unfortunate or pathogenic situations.

DEMOCRACY'S THRESHOLD

Proponents of the therapeutic perspective were hard put to sustain their opposition to maternal employment in the face of the persistent demand for female workers in defense industries. Given the critical need, how could they rationalize counseling mothers to remain at home? To shore up their position, social workers and other family professionals turned to the "discourse of the democratic family," a system of meaning that linked the family to the defense of freedom and mothers in the home to the family's survival and stability.[71] Picking up on the language of the 1941 CB conference, one CWLA author suggested, "Women advised to remain at home were to be consoled with the thought that mothers, too, performed 'an essential patriotic service.' "[72] Stressing the psychological dimension of their task, she maintained, "The conservation of stable family life is the basis of our democracy." Thus, taking women away from the family to work, even in vital defense industries, automatically assumed a lower priority and "should, in most cases, be looked upon as a temporary plan."[73]

By casting essentially private, individualistic activities in public, altruistic terms, this discourse justified attempts to keep mothers out of the paid labor force. As in the past, therapeutically oriented social workers maintained their opposition to maternal employment without taking economic circumstances into account. The war exacerbated the usual financial straits of low-income families by removing male breadwinners for military service. Although soldiers' families received dependents' allotments from the government, most needed additional income to sustain themselves. Discussions of psychological well-being—now linked to the health of the entire nation—masked these more practical concerns. In asking families to make financial sacrifices (in the form of mothers' wages), the discourse was placing the democratic valence of the family above its financial security.

The discourse of the democratic family was particularly powerful because it traversed a number of terrains, from social work and policy making to politics to popular culture. Multiply resonant, it was capable of uniting disparate groups for the common purpose of keeping mothers out of the labor force. The themes of the discourse were first articulated even before the United States formally entered the war. At the 1940 White House Conference on Children in a Democracy, President Franklin D. Roosevelt stated, "A succession of world events has shown us that our democracy must be strengthened at every point of strain or weakness. All Americans want this country to be a place where children can live in safety and grow in understanding of the part they are going to play in the future of our American nation." Because children were an essential element of a democratic society, Roosevelt continued, their physical, intellectual, emotional, and moral development was a concern for the entire nation.[74] Elaborating on FDR's remarks, other speakers pointed out that "home and family are the first condition of life for the child." The family could, therefore, be "the threshold of democracy . . . a school for democratic life."[75] Thus private was inextricably joined to public within a conceptual framework which revealed that the therapeutic stance had become influential in the highest reaches of American government.

At the popular level, the discourse of the democratic family took the form of advice to parents. The American public, ever alert to experts' advice on child rearing, had for some time been hearing warnings about the dangers of maternal deprivation from prominent child psychologists like Arnold Gesell and Leo Kanner.[76] With the anticipation of wartime social upheaval, such warnings now took on added urgency. Experts described the chaotic experience of British children who had been separated from their parents during the mass evacuations from urban bombing targets and taken to foster homes in presumably safe areas in the countryside. Both the popular press and professional journals were filled with reports claiming that the psychological effects of dislocation may have been more harmful than the blitz itself.[77] American donors to the Foster Parents' Plan for War Children received a newsletter in which psychologist Anna Freud and her associate Dorothy Burlingham described the traumatized children they were caring for at London's Hampstead Residential Nursery. Their studies concluded that parental—and especially maternal—deprivation produced a range of psychopathologies in children.[78]

Bringing it all back home, Anna Wolf, head of the Child Study Association of America, told American parents that the war could well have similar effects on their children. In her popular manual *Our Children Face War*, Wolf minimized the fact that, from the beginning of the war, the Hampstead nursery had taken only "problem" children—those who could not adapt to their foster homes—and, as the war continued, orphans. She also overlooked the experiential differences for children between being placed, solo, in a strange family or institution, and attending a child care center for part of the day while continuing to live within the bosom of their families—even one in which the mother was employed. Conflating the two situations, Wolf drew broad conclusions from the Freud-Burlingham studies and translated them into prescriptions for the American public at large: "A child's mental and emotional well-being depends upon his parents' ability to remain emotionally integrated. When the parents, and especially in the case of young children, the mother, can face danger, the child almost without exception feels secure and contented. . . . For a young child's world is bounded on all sides by his mother. So long as she offers him herself unchanged, he will feel safe. When she leaves him, no matter how well cared for he may be, he is likely to become anxious and upset."[79] Although the danger of leaving children in group care was not mentioned explicitly, it was clearly implied.

Reports from Germany also fueled concern about maternal deprivation. As early as the mid-1930s, observers began pointing out the inconsistency between the Nazis' emphasis on increasing Aryan marriage and birth rates and preserving family life (the infamous *Kinder, Küche, Kirche*)—all to the greater glory of the state—and the harsh conditions of women's employment. Clifford Kirkpatrick, a University of Minnesota sociologist who had spent a year's sabbatical in Germany, reported that "thousands of German mothers stand at the machine for long hours at miserable wages and bear children to be neglected or to be cared for by relatives and day nurseries. Under such conditions, the scant contact of the exhausted mother with her children is not the joyous relation idealized in National Socialist propaganda." Nazi leaders, he concluded, were not "willing to pay the price of a complete restoration of the wife-mother role in the patriarchal family."[80]

American leaders, however, *were* prepared to pay the price of maintaining traditional family structure—at least as long as the war effort could afford it. Paul McNutt, chair of the War Manpower Commission (which excluded women, even those who belonged to its own advisory board, from its deliberations), stated in a 1942 directive: "No women responsible for the care of young children should be encouraged or compelled to seek employment which deprives children of essential care until all other sources of supply are exhausted."[81] Other official pronouncements drew on and simultaneously reinforced conventional views of the family, with fathers firmly at the head. Brigadier-General Lewis B. Hershey, director of Selective Services, solemnly assured the American public that he had admonished local draft boards "almost prayerfully to consider the necessity for maintenance of the family in the national interest—to remember the harm that may result from separating a father from his child, a husband from his wife."[82] In a similar vein, McNutt intoned, "The first responsibility of women with young children in war and in peace is to give suitable care in their own homes to their children."[83] Although much of the "manpower" mobilization campaign was directed at women, McNutt sought to exempt mothers, who, according to the discourse of the democratic family, had a more important national task to fulfill in the home. But hundreds of thousands of mothers were already voting with their feet, forcing the federal government to concede that if they did take defense jobs, their children were entitled to receive public care.[84]

POLICY OUTCOMES

The discourse of the democratic family proved to be a powerful shaper of popular opinion. It served as a counterbalance to economic demands for more—and more efficient—workers, forming the context within which federal agencies and voluntary organizations waged their political battles over wartime family policy. In terms of child care, the discourse performed important ideological work by undermining public demands for services, thus slowing the conversion of nursery schools and establishment of new centers and fostering uneasiness among the parents who placed their children in group care.

At the same time, the discourse upheld policies that were clearly aimed at supporting the traditional family. In 1941, for example, the CB, at the urging of Dr. Martha Eliot, initiated a program of Emergency Maternity and Infant Care (EMIC) for the wives and children of lower-ranking servicemen. Eventually put into operation in 1943, the program was intended to raise servicemen's morale by relieving their anxiety over the health of their pregnant wives and young families. By 1946 it had paid for the hospital births of more than one million babies.[85] Although the combined images of "babies and soldiers" caused legislative and bureaucratic hurdles to crumble in its path (Congress ultimately appropriated $140 million for the program), EMIC's success was due mainly to the CB's wholehearted support. The program's goals were consonant with the bureau's longtime concern for maternal-child health and welfare and entirely in keeping with the spirit of neo-maternalism.

Federal child care, by comparison, made slow progress, hampered by its unwieldy administrative apparatus and lengthy application process as well as ambivalence and lack of sustained initiative at the local level. Federal guidelines recommended one child care slot for every ten female defense workers, but provisions never reached that level. According to historian Karen Anderson, in 1942 Seattle had only ten child care centers with a capacity of 350 children for

75,000 women workers, Tacoma had one center for 20,000 employed women, and Baltimore had about twenty centers for 140,000 women workers. By 1943, Detroit had only seventeen public child care centers, all of them converted from WPA nursery schools, to accommodate the needs of 350,000 female employees.[86] Nationwide, the female labor force peaked at 19 million in 1944. Theoretically, this number should have been matched by nearly 2 million child care slots. But at their height, federally supported child care centers numbered only 3,000, with a capacity for 130,000 children.

Considerably more successful, though not as well known, was the Extended School Services program (ESS) initiated by the OE and the CB for school-age children. This program, which was less controversial than group care for younger children, immediately attracted enthusiastic cooperation from state and local agencies. Granted less than half a million dollars by the federal government in 1942, the ESS was serving 320,000 children, 60,000 of them preschoolers, a year later. When federal funds ran out, states and municipalities took over, maintaining the program's momentum.[87]

Opponents of public child care were fond of pointing out that facilities were more than adequate but too often underutilized. This, according to the critics, proved that American mothers rejected the idea of group care, preferring to make private arrangements for their children or remain at home. In fact, the explanation had little to do with parental preferences or child-rearing philosophies. Minority parents, including African Americans and Chicanas, routinely encountered racial barriers in admissions policies and had no choice but to seek nongovernmental facilities. Some mothers eschewed public centers because of their persistent association with the WPA and the specter of relief. Others found that hours or locations were simply inconvenient. Moreover, the quality of centers was undeniably uneven. The National Commission for Young Children, using a guide prepared by its head, Rose Alschuler,[88] sought to advise center directors on how to arrange facilities, design and build equipment, hire staff, and organize daily routines. Despite these detailed instructions, many facilities fell short. The staffing problems that had plagued the WPA in the late 1930s only worsened during the war, and hastily furnished spaces in school basements and other public buildings were often unsuitable and unappealing.[89]

Few centers ever approached the level of the Child Service Centers at the Kaiser Shipyards in Portland, Oregon—indisputably the jewels of wartime child care. Even though they were federally sponsored, their status was unique. Built at the behest of Edgar Kaiser, son of Henry J. Kaiser, an industrial innovator who also founded one of the nation's first health maintenance organizations (Kaiser Permanente),[90] the centers avoided all the delays and red tape involved in federal Lanham Act applications, and their administrators had a free hand and a deep pocket in designing and running the facilities. Edgar Kaiser sought approval for the facilities directly from the U.S. Maritime Commission, which had urgent orders under production in the shipyards he managed, and he simply added the expense to the government's bill on a cost-plus basis.

The two Kaiser Centers were both architecturally and philosophically distinctive in their positive, creative approach. With a combined daily capacity of 1,125, they cared for children from eighteen months to six years old while their parents worked nearby. Located close to the workplace to save time and precious fuel, the facilities were "purpose-built" according to a wheel-and-spoke design that ranged a series of playrooms around a protected central outdoor play space (fig. 4.1). All the furniture, plumbing, fixtures, and even the windows were scaled down for small children. To accommodate round-the-clock shifts at the shipyards, the centers offered twenty-four-hour care, charging a fee of only seventy-five cents per shift for the first child, fifty cents for each additional one. They even catered to parents' needs, offering them cooked meals for purchase at a modest price when they picked up their children at the end of an arduous shift (fig. 4.2).[91]

In addition to these practical adaptations, the centers prided themselves on their educational benefits. According to James L. Hymes, Jr., a center administrator, "In the past, good nursery schools have been a luxury for the wealthy. The Kaiser Child Centers are among the first places where working people of average means have been able to afford nursery education for their children."[92] The curriculum was designed by director Lois Meek Stolz, a leading early childhood educator who had taught at Columbia Teachers College and the University of California at Berkeley. She in turn appointed Hymes, a former student, manager of the Child Service Department and Dr. Miriam Lowenberg, who had worked for years at the Iowa State College Nursery School in Ames, chief nutritionist.

The centers were able to recruit and retain a qualified professional staff of teachers and registered nurses, in part because of their excellent facilities and progressive outlook and in part because Kaiser paid center employees the same wages that factory workers earned. "Much was done, too, to keep alive the significance of their teaching jobs for the war effort," Stolz later recalled. Staff members were taken on tours of the shipyards and invited to launching lun-

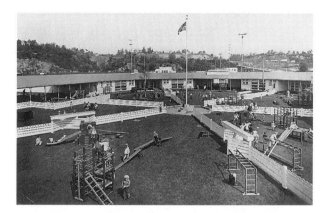

Fig. 4.1. The Child Service Center at the Kaiser Shipyards in
Portland, Oregon, featured a wheel-and-spoke design with
classrooms ranged around a protected inner court where each
group of children had its own play space and access to a wading
pond at the hub. The design concealed the center's industrial
setting from the children's view. Courtesy of the Oregon
Historical Society, neg. no. 80379.

cheons; several actually got to christen ships. "At these launchings teachers were
the maids of honor."[93]

Advocates of child care frequently cited the Kaiser Centers as a model to
which all might aspire; in 1944 the prestigious magazine *Architectural Record*
featured the project prominently. Unfortunately, none of the Lanham facilities
could boast the same architectural panache or lavish professional resources. A
museum exhibition mounted in 1995, "World War II and the American
Dream," has suggested that wartime architectural innovations had a profound
impact on the postwar built environment.[94] Although this may well have been
true for designs in other sectors of American society, the Kaiser Centers, despite
their acclaim, were not duplicated in the following years, for the motivation to
push ahead in child care was weak in the postwar era. Indeed, it would be
almost three decades before *Architectural Record* (or any of the other major
magazines in the field) again found reason to examine designs for U.S. child
care centers.[95]

With the notable exception of the Kaiser Centers, wartime public child care
provisions generally lacked uniformity, their facilities were unattractive and
inconvenient, and their policies were often racially discriminatory. Given the

Fig. 4.2. An unusual feature of the Child Service Center was its food service, which offered ready-to-eat meals to tired parents picking up their children at the end of a shift. Courtesy of the Oregon Historical Society, neg. no. 80373.

shortage of the centers and low utilization figures, it was clear that hundreds of thousands of working mothers had no access to any kind of formal child care for preschool children. There were, inevitably, scandals about children locked in cars parked in factory lots and ubiquitous images of forlorn "latchkey children" coming home from school to an empty house.[96] Overwhelmingly, however, mothers were not neglecting their children but were once again turning to maternal invention, making arrangements that might not be apparent to the casual or even expert observer.[97] Many women were able to ensure coverage by alternating shifts with spouses or other working mothers, sometimes doubling up for housing as well. Others relied on their own mothers or other relatives, who often crossed the country to join them in areas where lucrative defense jobs were available. Some had little choice but to pay exorbitant fees to babysitters with dubious qualifications or, worse, to unlicensed, unregulated commercial (proprietary) day nurseries. Absenteeism and quitting were common among mothers with defense jobs as child care arrangements—or the transportation needed to reach them—broke down.

Certain groups of mothers chose not to use either public or proprietary child care even when it was available. This was particularly true for African American mothers. As historian Gretchen Lemke-Santangelo explains, "black . . . women had long relied on friends and relatives to provide care. Children were viewed as part of a communal trust and thus were only reluctantly placed in the care of outsiders."[98] This may explain why even the Kaiser Centers failed to attract black children. Lois Meek Stolz came to understand too late that an absence of black staff members was off-putting to black families. "We learned, near the end, that our buildings looked so grandiose to black mothers. At that time they couldn't quite believe the Centers were for their children too. And some, we learned, were afraid that our white teachers would hit their young-sters."[99] African American mothers were adept at creating their own child care resources. For example, the Southern women who migrated to the West Coast for defense jobs soon established networks that included both reciprocal and paid arrangements.

In the San Francisco Bay Area, this network even took in white children. As long as black caregivers confined their activities to their own community, they did not attract notice, but when they began to serve white families as well, the authorities moved in. In 1943 welfare officials from San Mateo County began to harass a group of black providers who were caring for black and white children together. The officials claimed that this practice was illegal, citing bogus municipal, county, and state regulations. The local chapter of the Na-tional Association for the Advancement of Colored People took up the issue and obtained affidavits from some of the white mothers who were involved. These women not only attested to the excellence of the providers but com-plained about being forced to place their children in other situations that were less convenient, lower in quality, and more expensive. Eventually the providers were able to obtain licenses from the county, but the NAACP went on to complain to state authorities about the racial discrimination that had occurred. State regulations, they pointed out, required that children be placed with caretakers of the same religion "where practicable" but said nothing about race.[100]

The impediments to locating and retaining good care in wartime were many. Those who found high-quality care, whether in public centers or through private arrangements, were fortunate; children flourished and mothers could face the demands of defense work without added worry about the welfare of their offspring. For most wage-earning mothers, however, in-adequate child care provisions compounded the ordinary difficulties of war-time. Although defense work offered them access to skilled, high-paying jobs, daily life was filled with stress and hardship for both themselves and their children. Holding a job under these conditions was not something most women wished to prolong or repeat.

THE POLITICS OF WARTIME CHILD CARE

American mothers' mixed experience with public child care centers, together with the strain of combining paid employment with family responsibilities, no doubt goes a long way to explain why working women did not organize to demand more public child care during the war, or, with a few exceptions, to seek its continuation afterward. Also, the discourse of the democratic family created widespread ambivalence in mothers who placed their children in group care. Many may have preferred to avoid the subject of child care once their own need for it had passed. In addition, two other factors should be taken into account: the obstacles to feminist mobilization in the 1940s and the bureaucratic context within which child care was eventually provided.

Although the discourse of the democratic family in both its popular and professional versions remained hegemonic throughout the war, women's dissenting voices could occasionally be heard exploiting patriotic rhetoric for their own purposes. Working mothers in particular had several allies in Congress, including Representatives Mary T. Norton (Democrat–New Jersey) and Edith Nourse Rogers (Republican–Massachusetts).[101] In June 1942, Norton appealed to Congress for funds to convert two thousand WPA nursery schools scheduled for closing into nurseries for the children of defense workers, arguing, "Unless the mothers are assured of the welfare of their children, it will be impossible for them to extend their best efforts to the production of those essentials necessary to win the war."[102]

By contrast, employed mothers received only minimal support from organized labor. Trade unions were potentially the most significant locus for gathering feminist forces, given the large numbers of female industrial workers and the paucity of feminist organizations and activities that survived the 1930s.[103] But coalitions like the Congress of Women's Auxiliaries of the CIO (CWA) faced opposition within the ranks of labor.[104] Male unionists were more likely to sabotage than support women's causes because they believed that men's jobs would be threatened if women became a permanent presence within the industrial workforce.[105] Nevertheless, women unionists were occasionally able to break into policy debates on their own. At the Thomas Bill hearings in 1943, CWA head Eleanor Fowler contended, "The establishment of child-care centers [would] enable women to make their maximum contribution to the defense of our country." More pragmatically, Catherine Gelles of the United Auto Workers–CIO pointed out, "The fact that the Government allowances to wives of men in the armed forces are utterly inadequate means that thousands of wives of draftees will have to get jobs." Further, as she and other witnesses noted, without public subsidies, fees for child care would take about half of women's wages, even including overtime. "We believe it is incumbent upon the Federal Government to take the main burden of seeing to it that child-care needs are met," Fowler concluded.[106]

Norton, Fowler, and Gelles were all posing a direct challenge to the discourse of the democratic family, Norton and Fowler by asserting that factory work, not child rearing, was mothers' most valuable contribution to the war effort, and Gelles by exposing the financial hardship imposed on servicemen's wives if they were prevented from taking waged work because they lacked child care. But efforts to transform the political discourse surrounding child care and to frame it as a feminist demand were only partially successful. Norton's appeal won a temporary reprieve for the WPA nursery schools, but in less than a year more than one-fourth of the converted centers had lost their funding because they were not located within designated "war-impact areas."[107] Around the same time, the Thomas Bill died in the Senate.[108]

Far more effective in breaking down the multiple legislative and bureaucratic barriers to federal child care policy was the approach taken by WPA Education Division officials Grace Langdon and Florence Kerr, which foregrounded child care's advantages for education, health, and safety. By maintaining near-silence on the fact that child care allowed mothers to work, the educational approach avoided raising conservative hackles. This meant, however, that government-sponsored child care won support primarily because it was good for children, not because it enabled mothers to earn wages.

Even so, rival views on what was good for children slowed the progress of child care policy. Although WPA and FWA officials had support from the nation's leading early childhood educators, philosophical differences in the field of child welfare along with interagency rivalry within the federal government prevented the educational approach from gaining consensus. At the war's end, the CB and a number of outside groups remained skeptical about child care.

The continuing conflict among policy makers and children's experts recapitulated more than three decades of unresolved debate over public responsibility toward children, mothers, and families. The CB, upholding a neo-maternalist position, consistently advocated policies that would encourage mothers to remain at home with their children. Influenced by trends within the field of social work, CB officials increasingly adopted therapeutic language in arguing against group care for children. This discourse, in turn, led them to downplay the realities of poverty, child labor, and child neglect and oppose maternal employment under nearly all conditions, including war.

The WPA, through the Emergency Nursery Schools, attempted to lay the groundwork for a positive view of public programs for young children by distinguishing nursery schools from day nurseries. Emphasizing the educational advantages of the nursery schools, the agency offered a fresh and plausible rationale for separating preschool children from their mothers for a portion of the day and also for using federal funds for the program. Operating under the umbrella of early childhood education, the ENS were able to expand their functions to include child care without attracting opposition.

In spite of their modern look, the ENS could not eradicate the stigma of charity that day nurseries had carried for so long. When they began to accept children whose mothers were employed on relief projects, they were implicitly reverting to the old day-nursery principle of providing care for the children of poor mothers so that they could work and therefore help themselves—offering "a hand up instead of a handout." Regardless of whether the schools were providing only preschool training or simultaneously serving as child care, it was well known that the basis for eligibility was poverty. This reinforced the association between the ENS and relief—something that private nursery schools on their own had avoided but which would come back to haunt the government's wartime child care program.

By focusing attention on their educational and relief-related dimensions, the Depression-era nursery schools were able to function without objection, even when they quietly branched out into child care. But the war raised the twin issues of maternal employment and child care more publicly and explicitly than ever before, making it difficult for WPA and then FWA officials to continue to rationalize their programs as they once had. Some of the most vocal opposition came from the Children's Bureau and its private-sector allies like the National Association of Day Nurseries and the Child Welfare League of America, organizations whose neo-maternalist views resonated with conservatives seeking to contain women's drive toward economic autonomy. These views were reinforced by the discourse of the democratic family. Mixed messages from government officials as well as civic leaders produced uneven and half-hearted policies, which, in turn, failed to inspire public confidence in government-sponsored child care. Two national crises—the Depression and World War II—had expanded America's semi-welfare state, focusing a good deal of attention on policies to promote children's interests but doing little to advance the cause of mothers' rights.

Chapter 5 Should Mothers
Work? Prescriptions and
Practices in the Postwar Era

World War II placed the issue of child care prominently on the nation's agenda for the first time, but it failed to establish a precedent for permanent government provision. Once the war was over, the most obvious rationale for federally supported services quickly evaporated, even though mothers, after the initial wave of layoffs, were still entering the labor force in substantial numbers. Attempts to extend public funding for child care through both local protests and congressional lobbying met with only limited success. They did, however, provoke a broad-ranging debate about motherhood, paid employment, and child care that eventually led to the formation of a national child care movement.

The debate focused on a series of interlocking questions. Was the upswing in maternal employment a predictable sequel to wartime social change or was it an anomaly, something that had to be explained afresh? Why did mothers work? What was happening to their children? And, perhaps most important, was the federal government still obliged to provide child care?

Testimony and letters from parents, organized labor, and professional and civic activists presented at Senate hearings on the 1946 Maternal and Child Welfare Bill prefigured the lines of debate. Among other things, the bill called for federal support for child care. Mrs. Eleanor Vaughan, vice-chair of the Congress of American Women, a newly formed left-wing feminist organization, argued that the government should provide services because a high proportion of women working in defense industries planned to remain employed. Their intentions were shaped primarily by severe financial need, not merely because "they liked to work and feel independent." Because of a lack of child care, Vaughan pointed out, "war widows and other mothers, self-respecting and able to work, are being forced to stay at home, to accept the ignominy of public assistance or private charity."[1]

This "need-to-work" line of argument harkened back to the antipauperism discourse of the early day nurseries. In contrast, representatives of a day care center in Cleveland stressed both mothers' rights and children's interests: "A democracy which professes no discrimination because of race, sex, or creed and in which coeducation is prevalent has a responsibility to provide the service women need to enable them to express themselves in the way for which their talents, education, and skills enable them, especially when this service contributes positively to the development of their children."[2] And in still another mode, one CIO union made the case for child care in light of social good, claiming that day care and other services for children would "cut down on juvenile delinquency."[3]

Even before the Korean War began in 1950, the need for child care had again reached near-crisis proportions. As of March 1947, defense-related centers continued operating in nine cities: New York, Chicago, Philadelphia, Detroit, Los Angeles, San Francisco, Denver, the District of Columbia, and Baltimore.[4] Within a few years, however, all but those in New York, Philadelphia and California had shut down, stranding the children of more than a million working mothers—some former defense workers who had shifted to lower-paying and less-skilled jobs, others first-time employees. Commercial and voluntary or philanthropic services attempted to take up the slack, but demand perpetually outstripped supply. In 1951, the Child Welfare League of America reported that "for every child now in a day-care center, there is one or more on a waiting list." In the eight cities it surveyed, "applications for day-care services . . . increased over a period of 5 months at rates ranging from 10 to 166 percent." The need for child care was, according to the CWLA, desperate.[5]

Although the seriousness of the situation was obvious to both family experts and policy makers, there was no immediate call for the government to assist in expanding the supply of child care. Throughout most of the 1950s, the two federal agencies charged with overseeing policy toward women and children, the U.S. Women's Bureau and the U.S. Children's Bureau, closely monitored women's participation in the labor force and acknowledged the social problems created by the growing trend in maternal employment. But except for a brief, unsuccessful flurry of activity during the Korean War, neither agency proposed legislative remedies to address the child care crisis. Indeed, child care per se had virtually disappeared from the political agenda.

Outside organizations, preoccupied with other matters, were also slow to take up the issue. For social work agencies like the CWLA, child care was but one of many kinds of services demanding their attention. Trade unions with large female memberships were concentrating on increasing pay equity and breaking down occupational segregation by sex. A few West Coast locals fought successfully to retain state-supported child care services in California, but their national organizations made no effort to extend the child care campaign.[6] The attention of other feminist activists was divided between civil rights and race issues at home and peace abroad.[7]

During the same period, however, a freestanding child care movement was gathering momentum, and by the late 1950s it began to have an impact in Washington. A group of child care advocates, mostly from the East Coast, formed the Inter-City Council for the Day Care of Children (ICC), the first national organization dedicated to this issue since the National Association of Day Nurseries (which had been absorbed by the CWLA in 1942). By forging a strategic alliance with the CB and the WB, this political newcomer soon gained access to top-level policy-making circles and reclaimed a place for child care on the public agenda.

But legislative gains were still slow in coming, partly because of the political weakness of the child care coalition and partly because child care was "nested" within other contentious issues. These included government's responsibility for social services in general and, at the most fundamental level, definitions of female roles and the appropriateness of maternal employment.[8] Without unequivocal acknowledgment that mothers belonged in the labor force—not merely for personal reasons but because they served a distinct national purpose—there could be no mandate for public child care provisions. The Korean War momentarily offered such a rationale, but when it ended in 1953 a new policy had yet to be defined. For the rest of the decade, the twin issues of maternal employment and child care continued to be debated.

The discussion drew on four distinct discourses, each with its own problematic. One, rooted in the newly ascendant fields of child psychology and psychiatry, assessed the effects of mothers' work and group care on children and analyzed mothers' desire for employment outside the home in terms of their unconscious motivation.[9] A second discourse, liberal and feminist in its implications, also explored mothers' motives for employment but accepted the desire for work as a natural outcome of women's increasing educational attainments. Numerous magazine articles and newspaper columns explored the meaning of paid work in women's lives and wondered if it was legitimate to aspire to be "more than a mother" and whether women could successfully combine motherhood with careers or jobs. In this context child care was seen as a problem that women should solve individually.

In contrast, the third discourse, which stemmed from discussions about the nation's need for "manpower," saw both maternal employment and child care as matters of national policy. Labor analysts and government officials generally endorsed the idea of recruiting more female workers, but when it came to mothers, their plans hit a snag and they were forced to weigh the nation's requirements against experts' concerns about the welfare of children, political precedent, and popular opinion.

The fourth discourse, that of federal social agencies, looked at the labor market from the reverse angle, starting with the condition of working mothers and their children. The WB and the CB did not ask whether or not mothers should work but documented the extent of their employment and the consequences that flowed from it. Following the curiously hybrid style that had come to characterize their publications over the decades, they used statistics and social categories to impose order on the situation but allowed images of distressing situations to irrupt into the texts through striking anecdotes interspersed with the tables and charts. Yet, despite many dramatic and disheartening revelations about shortages and inadequacies of existing child care provisions, the two agencies refrained from calling for wide-scale federal intervention.

All four discourses played across numerous terrains: professional journals, popular magazines (especially those with female readerships), and governmental, advisory, and academic studies and policy reports. As the debate heated up, familiar domestic icons were challenged. Surveys showing that large numbers of women were either self-supporting or heads of households or both contradicted the notion that the financially beleaguered paterfamilias still deserved credit for singlehandedly supporting the American household. Descriptions of disenchanted college women and guilt-ridden housewives undermined the "myth of the happy housewife heroine."[10] Each discourse strained to absorb and contain these contradictions.

Yet the center mostly held. Despite changing realities, the presumption that mothers belonged at home with their children remained strong. This view, temporarily muted during the war, gained new momentum from the piece of Cold War ideology that linked strong families to national security.[11] Some commentators denied that maternal employment was becoming a normal, permanent feature of American society, insisting instead that it was a social problem which, properly understood and addressed, could and should be eliminated. Others grudgingly conceded that working mothers were here to stay but attempted to rationalize their jobs in terms that simultaneously preserved more traditional aspects of their familial role.

Among those who condoned maternal employment, rationales divided along class and racial lines. For middle-class mothers, most of whom were white, employment was seen as a choice, a means to self-fulfillment that could actually enhance their responses to their children. By contrast, low-income and working-class mothers, many of whom belonged to ethnic and racial minorities, "had to work" out of financial need, but in so doing they brought economic security to their families. This distinction was reminiscent of the class-differentiated concepts of motherhood propounded by nineteenth-century maternalists, although this time the middle-class version also included paid employment. For poor women, however, little had changed; once again, they were to be "allowed" to work in order to preserve their families and avoid becoming "dependent."

Class distinctions carried over to attitudes toward child care. Middle-class working mothers expected (and were expected) to make private arrangements—babysitters, nursery schools, and the like—while policy makers acknowledged that the financial needs of working-class and low-income mothers gave them a claim to some sort of subsidized provision, whether governmental, civic, or charitable. With the constituency for child care thus divided by class, the chances for developing a universal policy with full public support were reduced. It was possible, however, to link federally supported services with efforts to reduce the welfare rolls.

The next two chapters concern the politics of child care in the postwar period. In this chapter I analyze the discourses that emerged around the entwined issues of motherhood, employment, and child care, showing how ambivalence and uncertainty left an opening for a class- and race-based approach to policy that could compel poor mothers to seek paid employment while denying that women in general had a right to work. In the following chapter I trace the development of the national child care movement and the public-private partnership between voluntary advocacy organizations and certain federal agencies, explore how they deployed the discourses of maternal employment and child care within the political arena, and assess their overall effect on child care policy.

THE PSYCHOPATHOLOGY OF THE WORKING MOTHER

The most vehement and explicit opposition to both maternal employment and child care could be found within the psychological discourse. The literature of the 1940s and 1950s reveals, however, that expert opinion was far from unanimous. Professionals in psychology and social work were divided between advocates of children's interests, who focused almost exclusively on what they saw as the deleterious effects of maternal employment on children, and dissidents (often feminists), who took a more benign view and called for broader consideration of the needs of mothers within the dynamics of marriage and families.

Advocates of children's interests tended to be strongly influenced by the famous wartime studies of "maternal deprivation" conducted by John Bowlby, René Spitz, William Goldfarb, and Anna Freud and Dorothy Burlingham.[12] This research suggested, among other things, that group care accelerated children's motor coordination but slowed their language acquisition and toilet training. At an extreme, separation from parents for a week or more caused children to become depressed and withdrawn. While the circumstances of the children and infants in these studies were generally conceded to be more dire than those of the children of working mothers (most of the subjects lived in institutions, and those in Freud and Burlingham's sample were actually war orphans), the graphic depictions of children suffering from syndromes like "hospitalism" and "anaclitic depression" still tended to dampen enthusiasm for group care.[13]

Professionals in this group also blamed maternal employment for the growth in rates of juvenile delinquency and adolescent maladjustment. Sheldon and Eleanor Glueck, in their well-known 1951 study *Unravelling Juvenile Delinquency,* maintained that mothers' work outside the home implicitly challenged their husbands' authority within it, disturbing the men's relationships with their sons and producing antisocial behavior.[14] Whereas the Gluecks focused on boys, a study of three hundred adolescent girls also found that those with employed mothers had more difficulty adjusting to family life. Psychologists Mary Essig and D. H. Morgan observed a "greater feeling of lack of love, understanding, and interest between many parents and their daughters if the mother works." When mothers were not on hand to greet their adolescent daughters after school, the girls were "encouraged to loiter on the way home," perhaps with "undesirable companions," doing "things which might not be approved by the parents." This situation led to suspicion on the part of the parents and deception on the part of the girls—behaviors that were exacerbated by a lack of time for "family discussion."[15] At its worst, the study implied, maternal employment could produce sexual promiscuity in daughters.

Some advocates of children's interests even went so far as to argue that a history of employment prior to marriage and motherhood unfitted a woman for her maternal duties. According to Johns Hopkins psychiatrist Irving Berger, a mother with office experience tended to apply "impersonal modes of work" to domestic situations and, to compensate for her "dissatisfactions and resentments" with marriage, strove "to make the child a success, as exemplary as her own efficiency."[16] Faced with "perfectionistic" and "exacting" mothers, children developed a raft of symptoms including eating and digestive disorders, phobias, tics, and stuttering. Although fathers' foibles could aggravate these problems, Berger regarded the mothers' attitudes and behavior as primarily determining.

IN DEFENSE OF THE WORKING MOTHER

The second group of psychologists and social workers—the dissidents—objected to the tone of such studies, asserting that they had hidden ideological agendas. Psychiatrist Hilde Bruch, for example, argued that alarmist predictions about the harm done to children when the mother-child bond was broken, even briefly, "is a new and subtle form of antifeminism in which men—under the guise of exalting the importance of maternity—are tying women more tightly to their children than has been thought necessary since the invention of bottle feeding and baby carriages."[17]

Developmental psychologist Eleanor Maccoby defended working mothers on several fronts. Turning the Gluecks' conclusions on their heads, she noted that their own data showed that the percentage of working mothers was actually the same for both delinquent and nondelinquent boys. Mothers of delinquent boys, however, tended to work only sporadically. According to Maccoby, the decisive factor was not whether or how long mothers worked "but something about the family's characteristics which led both to the mother's sporadic employment and her child's delinquency."[18] Looking more closely at these cases, she found that mothers' erratic employment patterns were merely a symptom of deeper emotional disturbance and "antisocial characteristics." It was these factors in family life, rather than the mothers' work per se, that she saw as the root of juvenile delinquency. Moreover, Maccoby argued, whatever the mother's employment status (from housewife to full-time worker), delinquency was related to the quality of supervision she provided for her children, whether she cared for them herself or arranged for others to do so. If supervision was good, delinquency rates were low; if poor, rates were higher.[19]

Maccoby also took on the maternal deprivation studies, pointing out that the circumstances of children caught up in the crisis of war and those of youngsters with working mothers were not identical. Children living at home usually enjoyed their mothers' affection and attention (if not that of *both* parents) during nonworking hours. "Unless [a child] is cared for in a large group during the day and neglected grossly by his mother in the evening, he would not be likely to undergo the kind of deterioration observed among institutional children."[20] Maccoby conceded that separation from mothers was bound to produce anxiety in young children, but if it were properly handled (with adequate group care, for example), she felt that it would not create serious disturbances.[21] She was one of the first psychologists to transpose concern with maternal absence into an analysis of the structure, content, and emotional quality of substitute care, and to apply her insights to a discussion of actual services for children. In this way she was able to avoid rejecting maternal employment outright simply because it led to mothers' absence and instead ask what provisions would be made for the children of working mothers.

Maccoby's enthusiasm led her to claim that high-quality group care could in some cases be preferable to mothers' care; it might, for instance, counteract excessive dependency on the part of either parents or children. "Often the persons in charge of children's groups are better trained, more patient, and more objective in dealing with the children than the mothers. A child can be allowed greater freedom to run, climb, and throw in a nursery school than in a home full of breakable objects."[22] Although Maccoby was obviously eager to demonstrate the virtues of group child care, she was treading on dangerous ground when she suggested that it might be superior to what certain types of mothers had to offer. Such arguments were not uncommon in the history of child care reform; nineteenth-century nursery managers claimed that they were better suited than poor parents to give children moral training, while their

Progressive counterparts argued that nurseries exposed immigrants' children to the American values and customs of which their families were ignorant. Maccoby's reasoning was less explicitly biased in terms of class and culture; rather, she seemed primarily interested in seeing that children had access to an educational environment designed along progressive lines. Nonetheless, her position was risky, for at its logical extreme, it could be used to justify programs of social control whereby mothers would be compelled to take paid employment while the task of socializing their children was given over to some extrafamilial authority.[23]

Whereas Maccoby focused on group care's benefits to children, other psychological dissidents sought to remove the blame from mothers by considering the emotional dynamics of family situations from the mothers' perspective. In a much-cited 1949 article, two Chicago-based family professionals, psychiatrist Irene Josselyn and social worker Ruth Schley Goldman, challenged the notion that all women were naturally suited to motherhood. Seeking to depathologize mothers who did not appear to take to their role instinctively, they argued that there was a wide range in women's motivations for having children, their capacity for mothering, and their feelings toward their children. "Most mothers who are classified as rejecting mothers are actually *ambivalent* mothers. They are confused in their relationship with their children. . . . Why is guilt aroused if one's child is not accepted? A rejecting mother cannot overtly manifest the rejection, in part because of fear of society's condemnation. . . . There is, in most cases of so-called rejection, some positive nucleus in the relationship to the child."[24] Many women, they added, had a reasonable amount of aptitude and inclination for mothering but needed support and outside interests in order to maintain satisfactory relationships with their children.

Although Josselyn and Goldman were less judgmental than many of their colleagues, their analysis of maternal employment was built on a rather conventional concept of motherhood. They resisted accepting at face value the fact that many postwar women were, through their life choices, implicitly redefining the duties of motherhood to include financial support as well as physical and emotional nurture.[25] Even in low-income families, they contended, the motivation to work ran deeper. For some women, financial independence was a sign of adulthood; for others, it was a way to avoid "the stigma of 'charity' with its implication of inadequacy and condemnation." There were also mothers who sought employment because "they feel the need to achieve in fields other than their homes. Maternity alone does not completely satisfy them." They could give to their children emotionally, but only for brief, intensive periods of time. Such women were still considered normal: they were "actually better mothers because they do work."[26]

Also acceptable, if only marginally, were mothers who took jobs to avoid caring for their children: "If [a woman] cannot bear the role of motherhood and is unable to give to her child except in terms of material benefits, she may be giving as much as she can by working. On the other hand, through help in understanding herself she may be able to re-evaluate her relationship to her child, so that she can give more than financial support to him."[27] While apparently seeking to avoid judgment, Josselyn and Goldman clearly implied that for women (though not necessarily for men), merely providing financial support did not fulfill the parental role. Although mothers might choose to perform their family duties in many different ways, responsibility for children was still primarily theirs.

Within this insistently psychopathological framework, employment was not to be regarded as an end in itself either because it met financial needs or because it fulfilled a mother's vocational or professional aspirations. Rather, it should be seen as a form of therapy, one that might "offer a wise solution to mounting strains in the child-parent relationship. . . . [It] should be considered as a tool to be used if it fosters a healthy child-mother relationship and should be discarded if it is a detriment to such an adjustment."[28] The two experts called for high-quality child care, again, not as an end in itself, but to "relieve the mother of anxiety" while she is out of the home.[29] According to this logic, child care became primarily an adjunct, an aid to therapy—certainly not a social right for mothers.

Josselyn and Goldman cautioned that availability of "suitable care" should not per se be allowed to determine a mother's decision to work. Social workers, for example, should not use child care to compel mothers to work simply to keep within public or philanthropic budgets.[30] By the same token, a mother should not choose to work simply out of financial need; her decision "must be based on a full evaluation of the emotional and social needs of herself and her child."[31] However, it was "dangerous to assume . . . that a mother of small children should *not* work. There are too many factors involved to make a dogmatic statement or a generalization. Some mothers," they concluded, "should work and some should not."[32] Even if they chose to work, however, these women were still regarded primarily as *mothers*.

Finally, dissidents within the psychological professions refuted the contention that holding a prior job "de-skilled" women as mothers. Faye Higier von Mering, a social psychologist who taught at Smith College, studied patterns of maternal behavior among women who were currently professionally active, those who had previous professional experience, and those who had none. Using a functionalist approach, she argued that all three sets of women defined the purpose of mothering similarly—to serve the interests of the child—but that, based on the full range of their life experiences, they "selectively adapted" in different ways to achieve that purpose, all within the range of "normal": "The professionally-active mothers emphasize the discipline and independence training functions of the parent, and . . . the mothers currently identified with the maternal role exclusively emphasize the protective, empathetic, and under-standing functions."[33] Based on her findings, von Mering challenged psychiatrists like Irving Berger who persisted in typing professional women as non-maternal. She argued, "The sentiment is often expressed in psychoanalytic and even anthropological quarters that women who are 'sober' and 'intellectual' with their children will never know what 'true motherliness' is, implying that 'true' maternity is basically 'emotional,' basically a unitary quality which some women possess and others don't." Simply because women were associated with certain social roles did not mean that they were "biologically or psychologically non-maternal types."[34] According to von Mering, professional women could still be adequate mothers.

THE NECESSITY FOR CHILD CARE

"Depathologizing" the working mother was one thing; "normalizing" child care was another. It was anthropologist Margaret Mead, drawing on her vast store of cross-cultural data, who pointed to an alternative way of thinking about group care that avoided portraying it as a poor second to a middle-class mother's care in the home. According to Mead, the kind of exclusive mother-care associated with Western culture was not the only way to guarantee that children would grow up well adjusted. Writing in 1954, she noted that "cross-cultural studies suggest that adjustment is most enhanced if the child is cared for by many warm friendly people."[35] Optimally, this is what would occur in a day care center.

Closer to home, Ethel Verry, executive secretary of the Chicago Child Care Society, made the case for child care as a normal part of modern society. Although she was writing during the Korean War, she claimed that providing services for children was no longer an "emergency need": "Mobilization is an accepted part of our national economy, full employment a fact, and increasing incentives, both positive and negative, are pressing upon women, including the mothers of young children, to go to work. We can therefore safely assume that for the indefinite future substantial numbers of little children will be without the care of their own mothers during part of the day and large numbers of school children will be without the supervision of their mothers for hours preceding and following the conventional school day."[36]

To this pragmatic rationale for child care, Verry added a nod to the 1950s zeitgeist along with a plug for feminism: "We believe that it is important for mothers to stay at home and that their most important job is to care for their children, but we do not disapprove of a mother's going to work if good care for her children can be provided and she prefers it that way. Day care programs should be planned to implement this freedom of choice."[37] Here, for perhaps the first time, was a clear articulation of the principle that women needed child care provisions in order to define themselves without constraint, to combine work and motherhood if and as they saw fit. Unlike Josselyn and Goldman or Maccoby, Verry appeared to consider child care a woman's right, not a service tethered either to her family's financial needs or to her own psychological condition. Verry also avoided the pitfall of claiming that group care was superior to what certain groups of mothers were providing for their children at home.

Although Verry's article appeared in a mainstream professional journal, *Child Welfare,* her position was not widely shared by her colleagues. Few of the "demi-experts" (the phrase is Hilde Bruch's) and professionals in psychology and social work could bring themselves to take such an unequivocal position in favor of maternal employment and child care. Some of the most damaging myths about maternal employment were dispelled, at least temporarily, but only a handful of the experts projected a vision of women's lives in which paid work assumed a place parallel to that of motherhood, a truly "normal" place. Similarly, although child care was beginning to emerge as a neutral or even positive (if compensatory) service for children, it was still far from being regarded as an ordinary part of everyday life in the United States—or as a mother's right.

THE MASS MEDIA DEBATE

Discussions of the psychological implications of maternal employment and child care, though specialized and often technical, affected millions of American families who increasingly turned to professionals for counseling and guidance during the postwar period.[38] The professionals' influence was further amplified by exposure in the popular media, where their opinions shared space with proto-liberal-feminist views about the place of employment in the lives of modern women. It was here that the second of the postwar discourses on motherhood emerged. Typical was an article in the July 1955 issue of *McCall's* that mapped the contours of the entire debate for the lay reader. Turning to children's experts, judges, and working women—feminists and conservatives alike—journalist Elizabeth Pope put the central question quite bluntly: "Is the working mother a threat to the home?" She found disagreement on every side.

Psychiatrists took their by-now-familiar positions at opposite poles. Dr. Leo H. Bartemeier maintained that a small child whose mother left her to go to work, even if she were properly cared for, would "carry the scars of this experience for life." Bartemeier, who was medical director of the Seton Institute, a Catholic institution in Baltimore, argued that "a mother who runs out on her children to work . . . betrays a deep dissatisfaction with motherhood or with her marriage. Chances are, she is driven by sick, competitive feelings toward men, or some other personality problem."[39] By contrast, Dr. Lauretta Bender, senior psychiatrist in charge of children's services at Bellevue Hospital in New York, refused to diagnose the working mother as pathological. "It's lack of love that leaves scars, not Mother's workday absences," she told Pope. "Having a job actually increases some women's capacity to love and also their children's awareness of being loved."[40] For Bender, it was the quality, not the quantity, of a mother's interaction with her child that counted.

Millicent McIntosh, president of Barnard College, also weighed in on the issued of quantity versus quality. Herself the mother of five and wife of a prominent pediatrician, she admitted that in the past colleges had allowed young women to become "hopelessly confused" because their psychology courses taught them that mothering was a "twenty-four hour job." Now, however, psychology professors had changed their message "because it has been so thoroughly proved that quality is more important than quantity in a mother's relationship with her children."[41]

Interviews with wage-earning mothers who had young children indicated that the psychological discourse had percolated down to the lay public; those who spoke to Pope sounded like disciples of Bender, Maccoby, and McIntosh. Several stated that they enjoyed being with their children more at the end of a working day than when they stayed at home, and they believed that their children seemed to appreciate them more as well. Further, they asserted, attending nursery school fostered independence in their children.

The *McCall's* article also explored the relationship between working mothers and older children, challenging the assertion that maternal employment was a major cause of juvenile delinquency. Pope cited a Detroit study of twenty thousand juvenile delinquents which found that approximately 25 percent had working mothers—a proportion no greater than that found among average adolescents. To her, these results made perfect sense: "If the woman in such a situation has enough gumption and self-respect to go out to work—on top of her regular housework—it means she's still struggling. Her children have something to cling to. There is some hope in their lives." Justine Wise Polier, a judge in the New York Family Relations Court, concurred: "There are plenty of things that are worse for children than finding Mother at work when you come home from school. Perhaps the worst is finding her resigned to hopelessness."[42]

Whereas Polier and most of the other family professionals, even those who were neutral or favorable on the issue of maternal employment, regarded wage-earning mothers as mothers first, Millicent McIntosh viewed them from a different perspective. As head of an elite women's college, she believed that "each woman should chart her course individually, according to what's right for her, not only as a mother, but as a human being." No woman, in her view, should "tether herself unhappily to her own hearthstone out of a sense of duty."[43] This was, in effect, an early articulation of the liberal feminist discourse that would draw millions of middle-class adherents in the 1960s.

But Judge Polier, along with Dr. Marie Jahoda, associate director of the Research Center for Human Relations at New York University, pointed out that it was not personal inclination but financial necessity that drove most women into the workforce. "The overwhelming majority of mothers can't afford to choose. They work because they need the money." Chief among this group were women who were divorced, separated, or widowed and had to support their children—about one-fifth of all wage-earning mothers. Others had husbands whose income fell below the "health and decency level" set by the Labor Department.[44]

Assumptions about class clearly affected the experts' views of child care. McIntosh's focus on women's self-fulfillment tended to limit her understanding of the real-world constraints faced by working mothers. No doubt with Barnard graduates in mind, she counseled them to take steps to prevent their children from feeling unwanted. These proposed steps included dovetailing working schedules with a child's school hours, being available by telephone, remaining at home with a sick child or one who seemed especially needy "even if it interferes with your work," and taking leave from work during a child's infancy (but not too long; "three years seems about right") and maintaining contact with one's profession in the meantime.[45]

Although McIntosh was sensitive to many of the practical concerns that faced working mothers, she seemed to assume that child care would simply take care of itself. This was probably true for middle- and upper-class women, but not for the low-income women whom Jahoda and Polier had in mind. To ease the practical problems these mothers faced, Jahoda proposed making available more part-time jobs, creating a "vast network of first-rate day care centers for preschool children . . . and day foster homes for . . . babies," and trying to mobilize more grandmothers to provide care.[46]

"Is the Working Mother a Threat to the Home?" was a breakthrough, not only in terms of mainstream 1950s ideology but particularly for *McCall's*, a magazine that had historically hovered close to the ideal of the female home-maker and male breadwinner. Pope turned to experts who convincingly countered the most damning arguments against maternal employment and child care—those concerning emotional damage to children and the linkage between working mothers and juvenile delinquency. While she allotted space to "eminent psychiatrists" on both sides of the debate, she tended to give the last word to those who found nothing inherently wrong with maternal employment.

The article did add one proviso: mothers should, if possible, wait until their children reached the age of three before going out to work. A final quotation from Barnard sociologist Mirra Komarovsky counseled patience: "It is a continuous process. . . . In the beginning, when there are babies, it takes a very exceptional woman and very exceptional circumstances, to be able to do a good job as a mother and a worker at the same time. As children grow older, the task becomes easier. Finally, when they are away from home much of the day, the entire situation has been reversed. By then it is the exceptional woman who can maintain her own and her family's equilibrium *without* a job."[47] Motherhood, clearly the priority in this scenario, is the driving element of the narrative, while the chief endorsement for maternal employment is psychological. Of the people Pope interviewed for *McCall's*, Millicent McIntosh came closest to declaring employment as a woman's right and a matter of free choice. The other supporters preferred to cast it in financial, psychological, or social terms. Notably, it was only Marie Jahoda who raised the issue of child care.

For the most part, it was the plight of middle-class, not working-class, mothers confronting the competing demands of family and employment that fascinated the popular writers of the 1950s. This was not surprising, given the middle-class orientation of most mass-market magazines; nevertheless, it left an overall impression that women's problems were primarily individual, not social. Much attention was paid to college-educated women who were attempting to reconcile their broader aspirations with the demands of motherhood, very little to low-income mothers faced with daily insecurities and economic constraints.

A 1957 *Ladies' Home Journal* article, for example, pointed to widespread anxiety among female college students who were exposed to an incessant harping on motherhood in both popular culture and expert discourses. Unlike Millicent McIntosh, psychologist Nevitt Sanford, the author of the article, contended that psychologists and psychiatrists were still issuing "grim warnings about mothers' responsibilities to their young children."[48] The emphasis on women's futures as wives and mothers, even in campus culture, prevented young women from becoming deeply committed to their studies or imagining professional careers for themselves. This observation led Sanford to wonder, "Is College Education Wasted on Women?"

Nor did these conflicts end when women left college; if anything, according to child study expert Sidonie Matsner Gruenberg and her daughter Hilda Krech, women felt even more torn after they entered family life. In a 1957 Public Affairs pamphlet, they identified "the modern mother's dilemma." Having been "stimulated by the sights and sounds of our civilization, by our political, social and economic issues as well as by our sports and our entertainments, [young women] have begun to wonder whether marriage and motherhood are all-consuming. Though their families come first with them, they long to use some of their other abilities and to play a significant part in the world outside the home."[49] But social conventions conspired to prevent them from combining domestic responsibilities and work outside the home, leaving them feeling "vaguely dissatisfied and disappointed at not having a chance to go on with interests they developed before marriage."[50]

Gruenberg and Krech, like Sanford, blamed family experts for exacerbating the dilemma.[51] "Some women were disturbed by the very *wish* to do more and to have more than they already do and have," because such a wish implied that they were "unconsciously rejecting their children." The professional woman might enjoy some exemption from this expectation, as society recognizes her contribution to the general good as well as the "values and benefits" she confers upon her children, but "ordinary" women had more difficulty in justifying time spent away from their children.[52]

The two authors called for a broader conceptualization of motherhood, a recognition that "there are more ways than one to be a good mother." However, echoing Mirra Komarovsky, they counseled mothers to be patient: "Develop a sense of perspective; recognize that [a] woman's life typically falls into several distinct phases."[53] Motherhood would come first, but when the children were grown, women would still have the opportunity and the energy to pursue other interests—provided that work or other interests were properly kept "outside" the family, pursued on women's "own time." The husband of "the bogged-down young housewife" could play a key role by helping her to grasp the long-term picture. He should help her with the demanding tasks of raising young children, but she should not forget that "Father is still the breadwinner."[54]

These examples confirm historian Joanne Meyerowitz's finding that mass-culture authors of the 1950s did not totally dismiss the idea of combining work and motherhood but, rather, tended to present it within a context that left no doubt about where women's primary responsibility lay—with their families.[55] They also bear out Meyerowitz's contention that much popular writing about working women drew attention to their individual achievements rather than to their collective predicament.[56] For McIntosh, Sanford, and Gruenberg and Krech, work meant "career," and its primary purpose was not financial gain but "self-fulfillment." Thus, although it was surely important to their individual happiness and probably to the satisfactory "adjustment" of their children, employment for these mothers was not regarded as critical to their families' survival or even to the maintenance of a certain standard of living. They were, presumably, middle-class women who could depend on full-time, adequately paid male breadwinners.

Such an image of working mothers was not conducive to building arguments for publicly supported child care. For one thing, the issue itself was seldom raised; finding adequate services did not seem to be a problem for middle-class women. Moreover, the emphasis on individual satisfaction deflected attention from whatever social benefits might be derived from mothers' entry into the labor force. These individuals were not self-sacrificing defense workers but bored housewives seeking an alternative to card parties and bargain hunting. Gruenberg and Krech did stress the contributions of professional women, but the child care problems of this small minority (if indeed they encountered any) would not have been sufficient to warrant a general solution. Finally, the mass media implied that most women were working for "non-essential" reasons, so any problems relating to their situation, including low wages, discrimination, and unsatisfactory working conditions, as well as difficulties in finding child care, could safely be ignored by policy makers.

WORKERS NEEDED—
SHOULD MOTHERS APPLY?

While the mass media tended to trivialize mothers' participation in the labor force by reducing it to the personal level, the third postwar discourse, that of national security and public policy, presented mothers' wage earning in a different light. Government officials and civic and business leaders, facing a labor shortage due to the rapid expansion of the postwar economy, saw the female labor pool as a valuable resource. Although heavy industry, the engine of economic growth, was generally inhospitable to female workers, there was a demand for women in light industries and in the clerical, service, and sales sectors, whose growth was linked to that of heavy manufacturing.[57] Moreover, the opening of new occupations to women was creating chronic shortages in such traditional "women's fields" as nursing.[58] Both the Korean War and the Cold War accentuated all these tendencies, for in the eyes of many, the nation's security depended greatly on its economic strength.

Once again, the defense of the nation seemed to open up employment opportunities for women, although they were more limited than they had been during World War II. Because the Korean War did not drain off large numbers of male workers for an extended period, the labor force remained highly segregated by gender. Moreover, as before, efforts to tap the pool of female workers had to contend with prevailing gender ideologies, and government officials were not convinced that the labor shortage was critical enough to warrant the mobilization of women. This was particularly true when it came to recruiting mothers; as in World War II, stable homes and families were regarded as an essential element of America's bastion against the enemy (in this case, Communism), so it seemed self-defeating for the nation to urge mothers to abandon their domestic responsibilities in order to become paid workers.[59]

Although both the economy and the gender system were driven by Cold War politics, there was a tension between them, and this soon became evident to the National Manpower Council (NMC), a blue-ribbon panel set up in 1951 at Columbia University by the Ford Foundation to study the problem of labor shortages. As the council quickly became aware, recruiting female workers to fill labor shortages was complicated by public attitudes toward maternal employment.

The council drew its membership from the academic and publishing worlds as well as the ranks of medicine and government. Dr. Leo Bartemeier was a member, and Millicent McIntosh, as president of Barnard College (part of Columbia University), played an active role in setting up the study itself. Elinor

Guggenheimer, president of the Day Care Council of New York and later of the Inter-City Child Care Council, was the only conference participant specifically identified with child care. In addition to nationally known figures, dozens of local notables participated in some sixteen regional conferences on women in the labor force convened across the country by the NMC in 1955 and 1956.

Faced with conflicting views on the impact of maternal employment on families, the NMC found it difficult to reach consensus on the issue .[60] They believed that while most Americans had come to accept that a major social shift had occurred and that "married women were in the labor market to stay," public opinion still adhered to a "male breadwinner" ideal and the notion that every infant and young child required "a warm, intimate, and continuous relationship with his mother (or *permanent* mother-substitute)."[61] Did this mean that mothers of small children should definitely be discouraged from working? Or did the nation's security and mothers' own financial needs offset psychological considerations?

The question of the propriety of female employment was clouded by the issue of motivation. At a 1957 NMC conference titled "Work in the Lives of Married Women," Frances Feldman, a professor of social work at the University of California at Los Angeles, suggested that while paid employment was optional for most mothers, either because their income was *supplementary* to that of a primary (male) breadwinner or because working satisfied some psychological need, they nevertheless worked to improve their families' standard of living. Their income might enable a family to establish credit for major purchases, shop for goods (particularly clothing) that they might otherwise have to make at home, and provide children with "cultural and educational advantages." Such expenditures were not considered essential, but they did permit ascendance from the working to the middle class.[62]

While Feldman was careful to stress that maternal employment benefited the entire family (rather than merely satisfying individual aspirations), other conferees were uneasy with the picture she presented. Some could see the practical value of accelerated consumption of manufactured goods, but others were troubled by "the idea of insatiable [material] aspirations as a force leading wives and mothers to work outside the home. . . . They wondered what the future held for a society in which married women wanted more, worked more, worried more, and had to work more in order to get more."[63] Instead of being swept up in materialism, women ought to be doing something more worthwhile—like staying at home to care for their children.[64]

All discussions seemed to lead back to one central issue: the impact of maternal employment on children. Psychiatrist Leo Bartemeier, who had earlier voiced his opinions in *McCall's*, reiterated his assertion that mothers' employment and group care were harmful, while psychologist Eleanor Maccoby again argued the reverse.[65] She stressed that differences between the children of nonworking and working mothers might be due not to maternal employment per se but to the type of care each group received. The quality of care varied according to class. "When middle-class mothers work," Maccoby pointed out, "they usually are in a position to arrange reliable care for their children. Thus their children do not suffer from the neglect which often follows upon the employment of working-class mothers, who cannot so easily afford sitters, housekeepers, or nursery-school care." While centers with overcrowded conditions and poorly trained staffs were obviously harmful, well-run group care, according to Maccoby, was actually good for children.[66]

Maccoby's ally in this round of the debate was Katherine Brownell Oettinger, the newly appointed chief of the U.S. Children's Bureau. Oettinger indicated that her agency, which had long been adamantly opposed to child care, was beginning to soften its position. In her opinion, mother-child separation was not inherently damaging if "adequate care" was provided, although for children under three, that was almost impossible to find.[67] For older preschool children, group care was improving and the "horror stories" of the past were diminishing; fewer children were being neglected or subjected to excessive regimentation in overcrowded situations.[68] As a result of greater vigilance by the CB and other agencies, both public and private, more state and local governments were imposing standards for licensing and supervision, although these standards varied from one place to another and usually failed to address the problem of after-school care for older children. Nevertheless, Oettinger ruled out the scarcity of child care as a sufficient reason to oppose maternal employment, although she did concede that a lack of provision in specific instances might prevent mothers from entering the labor force when they would otherwise choose to do so.[69]

CLASS, RACE, AND POLITICAL STRATEGY

Oettinger, who had been dean of the School of Social Work at Boston University before coming to the CB, was well aware of the psychological aspects of maternal employment and child care. Nevertheless, she was determined to shift the issue onto the political plane. Responding to insinuations that women worked simply for materialistic reasons or to escape child-rearing responsibilities, she insisted that when mothers of very small children sought employment, it was more likely to be out of necessity than choice. This fact had clear implications for policy. Society must decide whether it was preferable to have such mothers in the workforce, very likely earning a low wage, or to pay them some sort of "maternal allowance or support." If these women were expected to work, public policy must accommodate them. When mothers themselves could not arrange some form of child care, Oettinger argued, "then either the community must foot the bill for daytime care or foot the bill for the consequences of inadequate care."[70]

Like psychologist Marie Jahoda, Oettinger sought to justify maternal employment and the use of child care on the basis of a family's financial need. But Oettinger took this argument one step further by pointing out that maternal employment was an alternative to welfare, and if this alternative was preferable, then the government must support child care to allow mothers to work outside the home. Oettinger's reasoning exploited what she conceded was a double standard in public attitudes toward maternal employment: in general, Americans denounced work for mothers, but they made an exception for "mothers who are widowed, divorced, or separated" (and therefore have to support themselves).[71] Oettinger was not prepared to declare that all women should have the right to work, but she did assert that the "responsible" working mother (the one who was working out of financial necessity) should have the right to decide what child care arrangements were best for her children. "She is not able to exercise this right if no provisions exist or if she cannot afford satisfactory ones."[72] In other words, for such mothers there should be some sort of public guarantee that child care would be both available and affordable.

Most of the NMC concurred with Oettinger on this point, but there was disagreement about whether making claims on behalf of low-income women was the best strategy for improving child care provisions. Although existing day care centers were "generally inadequate in number and in the quality of care they offer," local communities felt little inclination to upgrade services when the greatest demand came from poor mothers, who wielded little political influence. Aid to Dependent Children (ADC) might alleviate this problem, but as one member pointed out, monthly grants were insufficient to keep mothers out of the labor force.[73]

The subtext of this discussion was race as much as class. Traditionally, those in the category "widows, divorcees, and separated women" were presumed to be white—the "worthy widows" whose image had helped advance the campaigns for mothers' pensions during the Progressive Era and for benefits under the New Deal.[74] But in reality the ranks of poor mothers were increasingly filled with African American women, many of whom had never married.[75] Whereas most white widows were eligible for survivors' benefits under Social Security, most African American women, even widows, were barred from the program because they did not have husbands who had worked in jobs covered by Social Security.[76] African American women also had difficulty qualifying for ADC benefits, particularly in the South.[77] Thus NMC members' remarks about the political weakness of poor mothers—those most in need of finding paid employment—may well have been a coded reference to the presence of many African American women in that category.

The discussion of employment among low-income women left the NMC on the horns of a dilemma: should the council call for an expansion of child care facilities or for increases in ADC grants? Was it better if the mother left the home to earn and thereby raised her family's standard of living, or if she stayed at home with her children, struggling to get by on a pittance from ADC? Though troubled by these questions, the council backed away from answering them on the grounds that its main concern was not alleviating the plight of poor mothers but finding ways to use women to alleviate the labor shortage. Even on this issue, however, the group equivocated. When the need to recruit women ran up against gender bias, whether explicit or couched in "expert opinion," the NMC tended to retreat. Its final recommendations revealed just how far its members were willing to challenge convention. They advised employers to "experiment with part-time and flexible work arrangements, so that they can draw upon the potential supply of women who want to work, but are not available for regular, full-time employment."[78] This vision rested on the image of the middle-class woman who simply wanted to work during the hours when her children were in school and did not require day care. It did not take into account the many mothers who were eager to work full time (whether out of vocational aspirations or financial need) but could do so only if the supply of child care were increased.

During World War II, it was the nation's need for defense workers that eventually overcame most of the resistance to maternal employment and public child care.[79] Either the acute labor shortage by itself or in combination with the Korean War or the Cold War might have served the NMC in the same way, but the council chose not to call for radical changes in public policy. Members may have felt that such a step was not warranted by the scope of the labor shortage, however severe, or they may have been unwilling to face a barrage of criticism for breaching the ideology of domesticity.[80] Thus, after nearly seven years of generously funded research and consultation on the part of a prestigious council and leading academics, businesswomen and businessmen, civic activists, and professionals, the NMC failed to reach consensus around a new national policy toward working mothers or, more important, to recast the issue as one of employment policy, not welfare.

POLICY MAKERS WEIGH IN

Oettinger was unwilling to concede defeat. Her remarks before the NMC served as a trial balloon, allowing the CB to test reactions to a new approach to maternal employment and child care. Long opposed to both in principle, the CB could no longer deny the new reality: more mothers were working than ever before, and the pattern was not about to reverse itself. The agency's attitude toward child care was shifting from grudging provision to qualified approval. In a series of studies, which constitute the fourth discourse of the postwar era, the CB, along with the WB, acknowledged an ongoing and even increased need for services. As in the 1920s, however, neither agency showed much inclination to move from investigating and analyzing the situation to mobilizing the political resources necessary to push new programs through Congress.

Their inertia had both external and internal sources. The CB and the WB, underfunded and politically marginal from the outset, had been frequently bypassed in the bureaucratic maneuvering of the New Deal and World War II; thus they entered the postwar period with little political capital to risk on questionable causes like governmental support for child care.[81] Moreover, lingering maternalist attitudes, especially within the CB, prevented newer staff members from expressing unqualified enthusiasm for programs to encourage maternal employment.

Ironically, this atmosphere changed somewhat under the Republican women appointed by Eisenhower to direct the two agencies. In 1953 Alice K. Leopold, a longtime advocate of equal pay, succeeded labor economist Frieda Miller at the WB, and in 1957 Katherine Oettinger replaced Dr. Martha Eliot at the CB.[82] Unlike any of their predecessors, both Leopold and Oettinger had the experience of combining careers with raising families, so they were especially sensitive to the issues surrounding maternal employment and expressed as much, if not more, interest in the needs of working mothers as the Democratic women who had preceded them.

By the time Leopold and Oettinger took over, the two bureaus were already using the financial rationale to explain the presence of so many mothers in the labor force. In 1947 the CB found that most mothers whose children attended public day care centers in California were working "because they have to do so to make ends meet." According to the report, "Some were the wives of veterans struggling to get re-established in business or jobs. Some were the wives of GI's attending school under the Bill of Rights. Many were the sole support of families."[83] Similarly, in 1951 a nationwide WB study of nine thousand female workers, all of them union members, showed that more than half helped to support one or more dependents in addition to themselves, and from 14 to 21 percent were the only earners in their families.[84] Many women interrupted their working lives to bear and rear children, returning to work once their children entered school, but a sizable minority took up employment before their children were safely ensconced in first grade.[85]

Increasingly, both the CB and WB focused on financial need as the single factor that drove mothers to seek paid employment. The public statements of Frieda Miller, who succeeded Mary Anderson, the founding chief of the WB, in 1944, reveal this subtle but important evolution in the bureau's position.[86] Addressing the American Academy of Political and Social Sciences in 1947, Miller asserted that most women worked for the same reasons men did: out of financial need, to support themselves and often dependents as well. However, she noted, striking a liberal feminist note, a minority sought employment out of a "desire for self-expression, the need to make a contribution to society in a field adapted to one's individual personality."[87] While minimizing the significance of this group, she granted that their motives were understandable, given women's increasing access to higher education. Moreover, she claimed, this desire reflected the popular opinion "that a woman should work, certainly when she has no other means of support, *and even when the factor of support is removed*."[88] But when writing for the National Parent-Teacher Association five years later, Miller dismissed personal motives. Sketching the work history of six female workers, she noted: "self-expression, career fever, and the feminist ego are conspicuously absent in these women's tales. One reason alone is given: they work because they need money—by no means, in most cases, for themselves alone."[89]

Miller's shift here cannot be explained in terms of audience, which in both cases was educated and middle class. Nor should it be attributed entirely to the rise in inflation, which undoubtedly worsened the financial situations of many women. Rather, it suggests that both WB and CB officials were becoming more strategic in their presentation of employed mothers as they sought to develop a rationale for their right to work. This meant steering away from the liberal feminist discourse of life enhancement and self-fulfillment, which ran the risk of trivializing maternal employment, and instead emphasizing that most women, especially mothers, took jobs out of necessity.

ASSESSING NEEDS

Both the WB and the CB pointed out that mothers would have difficulty in exercising the right to work if they lacked child care. During the five years between Miller's pronouncements, the two agencies, along with representatives from the Office of Education and the Bureaus of Employment Security and Public Assistance, formed an interdepartmental subcommittee on the children of employed mothers to conduct research on the extent of child care needs.[90] In a report issued in 1953, they found that 4 million of the 18 million working women had children under the age of eighteen; of these, 1.5 million had children under age six.[91] The need for child care far exceeded the capacity of existing facilities. Indeed, according to WB director Miller, a child care crisis was fomenting.

World War II and the Korean conflict had given rise to the mistaken notion that this crisis was a social problem that emerged only in times of national emergency, but many communities were now coming to the realization that they had "a permanent need to provide services for children of employed mothers."[92] Several factors contributed to the "substantial increase in the number of young children whose mothers [or caretakers were] at work" and who needed care.[93] For one thing, there were simply more children in the United States than ever before. Although the record-breaking birth rate of the immediate postwar years had subsided somewhat by the early 1950s, it was still high, with the result that the number of children under five in 1950 was 53 percent greater than it had been in 1940 (16,163,571 compared to 10,541,524).[94] Most children under age ten in 1950 lived in urban areas, where their mothers were more likely to find employment.

Another factor was the trend toward smaller, two-generational (rather than multigenerational) households. This meant that it was increasingly unlikely that an adult other than the parents would be available to look after children. Such was the case for single parents, two-thirds of whom lived with their children and no other adults. Existing social welfare programs did not entirely address this problem; 16 percent of mothers receiving ADC were employed either full time or part time.[95] There was also a sizable number of single working women who were taking responsibility for youngsters not their own.

Among married couples, the committee found, there was also a trend toward maternal employment. Young people were marrying and completing their families earlier, leaving more years during which mothers were likely to seek employment. In addition, couples had different expectations than in the past. Many fully anticipated "partial dependence on the wife's earnings to aid in the establishment of the home in its initial stages, with her employment sometimes continuing after children had arrived."[96] There were more than twice as many working couples as in the previous decade (22 percent or 8 million in 1950, compared with 11 percent or 3 million in 1940).

Married mothers were less likely than their single counterparts to be the sole support of their household; nonetheless, they, too, worked for financial reasons, including the pressure of inflation on household finances, or such particular family needs as funding a child's education or making major purchases. Like Frances Feldman, federal officials did not regard such motives as frivolous; instead, they pointed out, "These economic conditions give every evidence that the necessity for married women's employment will continue."[97] Moreover, because most of these mothers were working out of necessity, they were entitled to community support, including "adequate facilities for care of their children during the mother's working hours."

LOCAL RESPONSIBILITY FOR NATIONAL PROBLEMS

Although federal officials presented maternal employment and the need for child care as national issues, they held out little hope that the federal government would underwrite community child care in peacetime. Indeed, the report, tracing the history of federal involvement in child care from the WPA nurseries onward, implicitly criticized the government for being erratic and ultimately leaving many children without organized services. In addition to the well-known story about the abrupt termination of Lanham Act programs, it described other instances where highly successful programs had foundered for lack of funds and bureaucratic continuity. For example, child care provided to migratory families in Farm Security Administration camps beginning in 1936 dried up when the War Food Administration took over the camps in 1943.[98] Similarly, many day care centers located in housing projects funded by the Public Housing Administration had stood idle since Lanham Act funds were withdrawn in 1946.[99] The point of this sorry recitation was to warn federal agencies that they would have to pursue another course if they hoped to develop a successful child care policy for the postwar period.

It was readily apparent that the number of "adequate" facilities across the country was woefully small. "Many children," according to the study, "are left without the care or supervision they need, or are placed in homes or centers that are not safe for them."[100] Few facilities were supervised or regulated. But there was little indication that federal policy makers were prepared to take up the challenge alone. It would fall to community agencies, then, to undertake "local studies of the situation of working mothers, followed by planning for adequate child-care facilities [and funding] to suit the needs found."[101] To improve conditions and quality, the subcommittee recommended that programs should be carefully planned through the cooperative efforts of private, local, state, and federal authorities.

Once again, federal officials attempted to foist the better part of responsibility for child care on other levels of government or on the private sector. Though concerned with the quality of care, they did not even set specific standards. It would be up to local authorities to define needs, initiate day care projects, and arrange for—if not actually provide—funding. Although some federal funds were available to states through grants-in-aid for child welfare services, the amounts were insufficient to "provide for the development of day-care programs commensurate with the known need for such services." Moreover, before federal funds could be used, communities had to find matching funds, either locally or from state treasuries. The only way to bring in additional federal money was to make the case that the growing need for child care was related to a national emergency. The committee vaguely suggested that this might be possible, because many working mothers were employed "in areas affected by defense activities," but they knew very well that this would only be a temporary solution to what was, by its own account, a long-term problem.[102]

LOOKING FOR CHILD CARE

Although the WB had been represented on the Interdepartmental Committee, it was not content to let the question of child care policy rest with the joint publication of a pamphlet on planning services. The WB's stake in the child care issue was perhaps greater than that of any of the other agencies involved because its officials understood that paid employment was not merely an option but a daily reality for many mothers, and their ability to negotiate successfully in the labor market depended on the availability of decent provisions. Along with access to basic housing and transportation, proper training, job opportunities, legal protections, and suitable working conditions, the bureau considered local child care services essential for allowing women to take and retain employment.[103] Thus it was important for the WB both to establish a strong, noncontingent rationale for child care and to demonstrate that communities were unable to meet the growing demand.

Accordingly, in 1953 the WB conducted its own study to supplement the rather sketchy information gathered by the Interdepartmental Committee, publishing the results in the bulletin *Employed Mothers and Child Care*. This study examined child care facilities in twenty-eight cities scattered across twelve states. In all the cities surveyed, women constituted a substantial and permanent proportion of the non-agricultural work force—from 24 to 41 percent (the national average in 1951–52 was 31 percent). Many of these female workers were mothers of small children.[104] Yet in those same cities, the WB found, child care facilities were on the whole overcrowded, discriminatory, costly, and uneven in quality.

Employment opportunities for women in the postwar economy varied by region and economic sector. Light industry in such customary sites as the small cities of Connecticut continued to demand female workers, while centers of heavy industry like Gary, Indiana, needed few, sending "surplus" women to compete with the resident female labor pools in neighboring towns.[105] The proportion of female workers in the labor force in Bridgeport, Connecticut, hovered around 33 percent, while that in Gary stood at 24 percent. In South Bend, Indiana, a balance between light and heavy industry proved somewhat more favorable to women. Only 13 percent of workers hired at a major aviation plant were women (mostly in clerical rather than factory positions), but a demand for women in rubber, apparel, and automotive industries pushed the city's overall rate for women workers to 27 percent.[106]

Expansion in such fields as health care and financial management, along with the growth of governmental bureaucracies, created rich opportunities for women outside the manufacturing sector.[107] The female labor force of Denver, for example, leaped by 50 percent from 1940 to 1950, owing to the presence of regional offices of several federal agencies, a new and sizable veterans' hospital, and an air force finance center.[108] Hartford, Connecticut, the nation's insurance center, had an above-average proportion of female workers—34 percent in 1951.[109]

Child care provisions varied as widely as jobs for women. In 1950, according to the WB, only 10 percent of child care facilities across the nation were publicly funded, either through states or municipalities, while another 14 percent operated with Community Chest funding (table 5.1). The overwhelm-

Table 5.1

Sponsorship of Nursery Schools and Day Care Centers, 1950

Sponsor	Number	%
Private nursery schools and centers	1,530	43
Community nursery schools and centers	501	14
Public-school nursery schools and centers	360	10
State Department of Education (292)		
Local public schools (68)		
Church-affiliated schools and centers	264	8
Cooperative schools and centers	263	8
Laboratory nursery schools (auspices of university or college)	220	6
Philanthropic nursery schools and centers	46	1
Industrial nursery schools	17	1
Other nursery schools and centers	324	9
Schools for exceptional students (76)		
Summer day camps (19)		
Not elsewhere classified (229)		
Total	3,525	100

Source: A Directory of Nursery Schools and Child-Care Centers in the United States, Merrill-Palmer School, Detroit, 1951.

ing bulk of services were provided by private (commercial) nursery schools and centers (43 percent), or through such voluntary organizations as churches, philanthropies, or institutions of higher education (23 percent in total). Commercial facilities tended to charge more than those that were voluntary or sponsored by the Community Chest, which usually used sliding scales. For example, fees at a Rockford, Illinois, day nursery sponsored by the Community Chest ranged from one to ten dollars per week, while licensed homes in Gary charged ten to fifteen dollars per week.[110] With the median weekly income for women at about thirty dollars, mothers might have to spend up to half their wages on child care, even more if they had more than one child.

The WB estimated that approximately 3,525 child care facilities were in operation nationwide, but more than three-quarters were concentrated in only sixteen states (table 5.2). Not surprisingly, they seemed to cluster in industrial centers where many women were employed; six of the sixteen states had the highest percentages of female workers in the country. But working mothers in areas with a lower density of female employment had few or no resources. Moreover, even where female employment was high, other factors sometimes

Table 3.2
State Distribution of Nursery Schools and Day Care Centers, by Sponsorship, 1950

| | Total | | | | Type of Sponsor | | | | |
State	Number	%	Private	Community	Public education authorities	Church affiliates	Cooperatives	Laboratory	All other[a]
California[b]	626	18	174	—	286	17	75	10	64
New York	503	14	233	76	4	55	50	17	68
Illinois	227	6	151	40	4	17	8	5	2
Pennsylvania	172	5	127	—	5	2	3	16	19
New Jersey	152	4	64	61	—	—	19	2	6
Ohio	138	4	55	37	—	23	5	10	8
Michigan	113	3	38	—	6	9	10	7	43
South Carolina	113	3	51	25	—	19	—	1	17
Tennessee	113	3	40	25	10	21	3	9	5
Washington[b]	95	3	20	7	10	—	54	4	—
Maryland	92	3	46	18	—	4	16	5	3
Connecticut	88	3	76	4	—	2	1	3	2
Minnesota	83	2	25	41	—	10	—	4	3
Massachusetts	78	2	3	8	—	8	2	12	45
Missouri	75	2	24	21	8	12	—	8	2
Florida	75	2	51	13	—	3	5	3	—
Other 32 States and District of Columbia	782	22	352	125	27	62	12	104	100
Total	3,525	100	1,530	501	360	264	263	220	387

Source: A Directory of Nursery Schools and Child-Care Centers in the United States, Merrill-Palmer School, Detroit, 1951.

[a]Includes schools or centers sponsored by philanthropic agencies (46), industrial firms (17), schools for exceptional children (76), summer day camps (19), and nursery schools or centers not elsewhere classified (229).

[b]State public school funds depended on current legislative appropriations and were eliminated in some sessions after this report.

affected the availability of child care resources. In Ohio, for example, there were 138 facilities, 37 of them supported by communities, while in Connecticut, where some cities were reportedly "keenly aware of the needs of working mothers for the care of their children," there were 88. But there were only 49 in Indiana, where demand was strong but community opinion divided, with "an element . . . that opposed spending public money for child-care centers [because it] might encourage more women to enter a labor force already crowded with surplus labor."[111]

Rock Island County, Illinois, provided a graphic illustration of how the unequal distribution of child care resources affected working mothers in one area—and how they coped with the situation. With several thousand women in the workforce, Moline, the county's main city, had *no* large group care facilities and only four licensed day care homes serving a maximum of sixteen children altogether. Most working mothers, as a result, were forced to make private arrangements, but this practice had several disadvantages. For one, it could be costly—as high as fifteen dollars a week—forcing some low-income families to seek foster-home placements for their children. For another, it actually served to block development of community-based services. Local leaders, convinced that there was "a large proportion of long-term residents with relatives and neighbors known as sources of aid to the working mother," felt no need to plan public child care facilities.[112]

It was not only in small cities like Moline that informal arrangements prevailed; a similar pattern appeared in Dallas, where, in the spring of 1952, more than 3,500 children were in some form of care (table 5.3). Texas law required any home that cared for fewer than six children, even part time, to be licensed as a "commercial boarding home" (facilities serving more than six children were designated "commercial day-care centers"). The State Department of Public Welfare reported 80 licensed homes in the Dallas area but estimated that at least 220 more were operating without licenses. Together these homes served 2,500 children. Community Chest and church-sponsored centers, all racially segregated, cared for the remaining thousand or so children; every one of them was operating at or above capacity and turning down requests for places every day.

At the other extreme was California, with a unique state-supported network of preschool and school-age services that limited admission to low-income families and calculated fees on a sliding scale. Its more than 280 centers had been in operation since the war. After Lanham support was withdrawn, the state had picked up the funding, reauthorizing it at two-year intervals. A

Table 5.3
Children in Day Care Facilities in Dallas, Texas, 1952

Type of Facility	Number Enrolled	Fees
Community Chest		
6 for white children	386	$0 to $1.65 per day
2 for Negro children	118	$0 to $1.65 per day
Church centers		
3 for white children	60	$8 to $10 per week
2 for Negro children	500	nominal fees, if any
Commercial homes		
80 licensed	1,500	$8 to $10 per week
Private homes		
220 estimated	1,000	various fees
Total	3,564	

Source: Employed Mothers and Child Care, Bulletin of the Women's Bureau, No. 246 (Washington, D.C.: GPO, 1953).

majority of Californians appeared to favor making the centers permanent, but there was concern that it would be necessary to raise taxes to support them.[113]

Although California's public child care system was by far the largest and most developed in the nation, the WB pointed out ways in which it, too, still fell short of needs. For one thing, even with a sliding scale, high fees put public centers beyond the reach of many families.[114] For another, there simply were not enough places. In San Diego, for example, the female labor force of 55,000 in 1950 was nearly double what it had been a decade earlier.[115] Because many of these workers were new to the area, they tended to look for organized rather than informal services. The city offered a range of facilities, which altogether provided full-time care to about 3,740 children, but in the first ten months of 1952, the public centers *alone* received 5,000 new applications. Many children were automatically excluded because their families did not meet eligibility criteria (admission to the centers was limited to families with annual incomes below $2,700 if one parent was working, or $3,000 if there were two earners), but the remainder could not be accommodated because of space limitations.[116] Although much of the demand for female workers in San Diego stemmed from the surge in manufacturing and naval activities created by the Korean conflict, other industries, such as fish canneries and clothing factories, also employed large numbers of women.[117] Thus officials did not regard the crisis in child care as temporary.

BUSINESS AND CHILD CARE

Across the country, businesses and other institutions tended to rely on the community to initiate services, whether public, voluntary, or commercial. One exception was hospitals, which were so dependent on a female labor force that some had begun to set up their own facilities.[118] But most businesses, less constrained by tight labor markets, were less responsible. In Dallas, for example, employers recognized that a dearth of child care provisions caused absenteeism among mothers and therefore carefully screened the arrangements of prospective employees. They made no attempt, however, to increase the local supply of services. According to the WB, "The plan most frequently preferred is to have a relative in the home or nearby care for young children by specific arrangement. Many employers feel that commercial or public nurseries do not prevent any great amount of absenteeism because the health requirements make it necessary for the mother to keep home a child who shows signs of illness."[119] Such attitudes on the part of employers displayed rational self-interest but did nothing to promote standards of child care and discouraged community-wide solutions to the problem of scarcity. They did, however, help to explain the high proportion of private care received by Dallas children.

The position of Dallas employers gave rise to a vicious cycle. The city's civic leaders were in no position to object to what amounted to discriminatory hiring practices, for public and voluntary centers were operating at capacity, and they did not want to do anything that would increase maternal employment. But employers' implicit opposition to public centers also gave civic leaders a perfect excuse not to open more. "Even should [the city] finance two or three more [centers] in the next few years, . . . these can do no more than alleviate the most pressing needs," the Texas State Department of Welfare lamented.[120]

The situation in Dallas was not unusual. Nationwide, the number of public programs was small and in some cases shrinking. As of 1948, 60 percent of the 1,518 American cities sampled in one survey had public kindergartens (serving five- and six-year-olds), an increase of 30 percent from 1938. But the number of school systems operating nursery schools and child care centers (which served younger children) was much smaller; only 165 cities had nursery schools and 150 had child care centers, many of which were being curtailed by the

1950s.[121] Extended school services for school-age children were somewhat more plentiful, though still inadequate.[122]

The paucity of public programs opened up a huge market for commercial centers and private home providers seeking to offer care at a profit (see table 5.1). Although such services were obviously meeting a need, they caused concern among officials from the WB as well as other governmental and voluntary agencies. In many states, for-profit facilities went unregulated, so standards varied widely. On the whole, providers were free to restrict admission in any fashion they saw fit, often by either setting explicitly discriminatory policies or charging fees that excluded low-income families, which were often minority. In Colorado Springs, for example, the two day care centers supported by the local Community Chest set fees at three to seven dollars a week and had a clientele that consisted mainly of the children of "pink-collar" (service sector) workers. Fees at the four private nurseries in the city, by contrast, were sixty-five dollars a month. In neighboring Pueblo, the Community Chest–sponsored center, which also charged a maximum of seven dollars a week, was badly overcrowded, but a commercial nursery charging ten dollars a week had to close after four months because mothers could not afford its services. Moreover, this nursery excluded Mexican American and African American children, who formed a large part of the local population.

Although commercial child care was often deplorable, other alternatives also had drawbacks. The WB, on the basis of the information it was able to gather about the number of working mothers and the quantity and distribution of day care facilities, made the logical inference that many mothers must be relying on "informal arrangements."[123] This was, they knew, particularly true among foreign-born women, who felt more comfortable leaving their children with family members or neighbors. But such arrangements could also be costly. In Idaho Falls, Iowa, for example, one working mother paid a neighbor fifteen dollars a week to care for her two children before and after school and all day during the summer. "She felt this was high," researchers noted, "but knew the care was good."[124]

Minority women faced unique problems in finding care. African Americans, Mexican Americans, and other women of color who were unable to place their children in segregated private or voluntary centers, turned to those operated by welfare organizations. But if they were fortunate enough to earn decent wages or lived in two-earner households, they might exceed income ceilings. This did not mean, however, that they could readily afford or would be welcomed at the only other alternative—commercial centers.

In areas with large minority populations, the situation reached crisis proportions. In Dallas, each of two black church-based centers took in from two
hundred to three hundred children, and the pastor of one said "if he had the
facilities he could round up another 200–300 still without any care."[125] The
plight of minorities in Pueblo, Colorado, was so dire that WB researchers
included an anecdote in their report to draw attention to it. The story was
drawn from a letter written to President Truman:

> This mother [who was African American] was employed in the ammunition depart-
> ment of the Pueblo ordnance plant, working on the third shift (12:30 A.M. to 8:30
> A.M.) for which she received a pay differential of 6 cents per hour. She had five
> children aged 14 months to 10 years, the two oldest staying with their grandparents.
> Her husband was at home with the three youngest children at night, but left at 7
> A.M., so they were alone until their mother returned at 9 A.M. or later, after a trip of
> over 14 miles from the plant. She had little opportunity to sleep by day because of the
> small children. . . . In the summer she was transferred to a factory clerical job of
> checking materials and to the shift from 4:30 P.M. to 1 A.M., but there still was
> considerable time between her leaving home and her husband's arrival there. She
> reported her problem would be greater in the fall, since the 6-year-old had to go to
> school and the grandparents could no longer keep the two older children. She had no
> room for them in her 2-room house which rented for $10 a month and had no water
> nor plumbing, and they had been unable to locate other accommodations.[126]

Clearly, this woman had to work outside the home in order to support her
many dependents, but because of the lack of child care, she was compelled to
leave her children in a situation that put them at risk. The alternative was to
turn down the work altogether—a devil's choice.[127]

Although there were obvious discrepancies between the number of mothers
with small children who were working and the estimated number of places in
various types of child care facilities, actual need had to be determined at the
local level because the distribution of services across the country was so skewed.
Maldistribution of services also occurred within communities where, in addition to cost and availability, proximity to transportation, workers' residential
areas, and work sites often determined whether facilities would be used. Centers located in more congested areas tended to be overcrowded, while those on
the outskirts of town might close down for lack of enrollment.[128] But unless
they were inconvenient, expensive, or did not suit the hours or budgets of
working mothers, most centers had long waiting lists.

The scarcity of child care resources put pressure on other types of services
that were not intended to fulfill that purpose. Many mothers, frustrated with

interminable waiting lists for day care centers, applied to agencies that arranged foster-home care. Others found more makeshift solutions: "School authorities . . . noted that many children who formerly went home to lunch were now remaining at school through the noon period. The YWCA . . . noted that a large number of smaller children were accompanying older sisters at centers for teenagers. Elsewhere, a city with extensive park recreation services noted that in summer increased numbers of children brought lunch and remained through the day; recreation workers were sure the mothers of many of these children were employed."[129]

The WB deplored such strategies, but they were not new; mothers had long used "maternal invention" to transform all sorts of institutions and programs into child care. Nor was the criticism unprecedented; reformers and social critics had been making similar observations from the nineteenth century through World War II. What was new, however, was the understanding that the problem was an ongoing one, not the result of war or economic crisis, and that it would continue to evoke such responses unless and until it was addressed properly.

ASSIGNING RESPONSIBILITY

Bureau officials' analysis of the relationship between working mothers and their families, in combination with the striking data from the WB study, seemed to point in just one direction: the need for greater public involvement in child care provision. But which part of the public—what level of government—should be responsible?

This was a particularly delicate question for the WB in 1953 because its own political future, as well as that of the entire nation, was unclear. Bureau chief Frieda Miller was about to yield her office to her Republican successor, Alice Leopold (indeed, signing the letter of transmittal for *Employed Mothers and Child Care* was probably one of Miller's last official acts), and she may have reasoned that recommending federal support for child care would not only prove futile but might also draw Republican antagonism toward the WB. Instead, the report urged "communities" to make child care their concern.

The WB attempted to build an argument for local responsibility by showing how child care was related to the community's interest in maintaining economic stability. A lack of services caused high rates of employee absenteeism and turnover. "With business and industry relying on women workers," the

bureau warned, "the problem becomes a salient one for the entire community."[130] This was not, apparently, so obvious to most civic and business
leaders, who, WB researchers discovered, had not reached consensus on how to
meet the growing need for services. They debated whether to use local funds,
seek state or federal support, or urge mothers to come up with individual
solutions with the help of relatives or other adults. When no solution was
apparent, they fell back on the old question, Should mothers work?[131]

To the WB, the answer was unequivocal: not only *should* mothers work, they
would do so, one way or another, because they felt that they had to: "Mothers, as
well as fathers, desire to maintain a good standard of living for their children.
The rising cost of living makes their financial contribution necessary in many
families."[132] Though morally unassailable, this rationale for child care still
lacked political clout; without a stronger incentive backed by federal pressure
and, preferably, funding, communities were not about to take the initiative to
expand child care provisions.

The WB suggested that this incentive could be found by consulting the
welfare rolls. In spite of the relative abundance of employment opportunities
for female workers, the paucity of care for their children was driving many
mothers who were already employed, or those who were potential workers,
toward welfare. Under the regulations of unemployment insurance, mothers
who failed to take proffered work because they could not obtain child care were
automatically disqualified. Yet, according to the WB, "no account was taken of
how their families could subsist without their [unemployment benefits]."[133]
They might well end up on welfare.

At the same time, many ADC recipients were leaving the welfare rolls
because they had found work, but caseworkers were concerned that they took
this step precipitously. "It was not known what was done with the children nor
whether the family subsequently was in a better position financially."[134] The
WB seemed to be suggesting that child care would not only keep some women
off of welfare but would also ensure that those who left the rolls to take jobs
would not be placing their children at risk. The WB, like the National Manpower Council, was considering child care primarily in conjunction with the
problems of low-income women and, increasingly, defining public services as
an antidote or preventive to welfare.

Under Alice Leopold, the WB did not undertake another study of child care
until 1959, when it again collaborated with the CB, now led by Katherine
Oettinger, to conduct research for the bulletin *Child Care Arrangements of Full-
Time Working Mothers.*[135] Their joint survey demonstrated that the trends in

maternal employment predicted by the earlier research were holding steady. From March 1940 to March 1958, the proportion of married women in the labor force nearly doubled, increasing from 16.7 percent to 31.4 percent. From April 1948 to March 1958, the number of employed married women with children under eighteen rose from 4.2 million to 7.5 million, an increase of almost 80 percent. More than half of all women who had at least one child under twelve were working full time—nearly 2.9 million female workers with more than 5 million children. Women with preschool children were less likely to work than those whose children were older, but still, nearly 15 percent of mothers with children under six were employed.[136]

This survey, based on Census Bureau data (for which the CB and WB paid some thirty thousand dollars), provided more detailed information about child care arrangements than earlier studies. Only a small proportion of preschool children were in group care—about 4.4 percent. This figure included 24,000 children under three and 67,000 from three to five. For children over six, the proportion in group care was much smaller—less than 1 percent. Unlike the WB's study, which had dwelled on the prevalence of informal arrangements outside of children's homes, the joint survey drew attention to the overwhelming majority of children who were cared for in their own homes by relatives. Usually these were fathers, but in more than a third of the 1.5 million families in this category, the care-giving relatives were under eighteen—that is, older siblings.[137] This was more likely to be the case in nonwhite families, in which fewer fathers were available to provide care than in white families.[138] Finally, nearly 8 percent of all children under twelve with working mothers were in "self-care"; most of these were over six.[139]

Such statistics could not fully capture the complicated, often inconvenient, and tenuous arrangements mothers made to ensure supervision for their children while they were working. This was particularly true when those arrangements did not fall into any of the standard categories, as was the case for about one-eighth of the children. The joint report described a variety of combinations of care:

• Babysitter takes care of child for one hour until daughter, age 18, returns from school—she then takes over.
• Mother lives in apartment over dry cleaning establishment in which she is the only employee. . . . Mother is able to look after her son while working. [Another mother owned and lived in a motel and was thus able to combine work and child care.]

- Mother is grade teacher. She gets home and leaves the same time as the child does usually—on occasions when she can't be home with the child he stops at his grandmother's house until his mother comes home.
- After school child goes to YMCA and other boys' meetings so is only home 1 or 2 nights a week right after school and then the father or grandmother is there to be with him and his sister—they are never left alone.
- Mother works night shift and is home all day. [When did she sleep?]
- When working in fields brings children along—baby takes nap in car.
- [Child works] chopping cotton with mother.[140]

Clearly, the practice of bringing children along to work had persisted since the early decades of the century, when agricultural workers had commonly taken their children with them to the fields.

What is perhaps most striking about nearly all these arrangements is the extent to which mothers (and often fathers as well) saw to it that their children were seldom or never left alone. For political reasons, however, the sponsors of the study chose to deemphasize such anecdotal evidence, with its positive implications, in favor of the survey data, which revealed the extent of inadequate arrangements and "self-care" among the children of working mothers.

For the CB, more than the WB, these data were cause for alarm.[141] By this time, the two federal agencies were beginning to concur on child care, but divergences in their views came to the surface in early 1959, when the CB began to publicize the results of the survey. A CB press release dated January 25 opened with the statement: "Nearly 400,000 children under 12 have to care for themselves while their mothers work, and 138,000 of these children are less than 10 years old."[142] Alice Leopold of the WB felt that this manner of presentation blamed mothers for leaving their children without care while they worked. In a letter to Oettinger, she complained that the CB's statements did "not appear to express the cooperative interests of our Bureaus with respect to day care." Commenting on the draft for a second CB press release, Leopold charged that it

> implies that many working mothers neglect their children. As you know, we share your concern for safeguards for all children. However, it does not seem that such concern requires overemphasis of the fact that some children are not provided for during the time their mothers may of necessity have to be away from home at paid employment. . . . You will note that our press release contains Census data showing that most mothers, regardless of family income, do not work while their children are very small.[143]

This exchange reveals the inherent conflict between mothers' rights and children's interests, as conceived by the two agencies. The WB was attempting to push for child care services on behalf of working mothers, but without blaming them, while the CB felt that the best way to make the case for child care was by using a time-worn reference to the plight of children, despite its implied critique of their mothers. Leopold's sensitivity on this issue suggests that the difference between the two bureaus ran deep. Yet their awareness of the critical need for day care, regardless of motivation, was also heightened, and it strengthened a mutual desire to overcome their differences in the interest of cooperation. On March 12, 1959, the WB received a revised version of the second CB release, which toned down references to children left to care for themselves. Oettinger apparently still believed that this issue was vital to her appeal for community responsibility, but she was willing to downplay it.

The CB took a similar approach to presenting data about the twenty-four thousand children under three who were in some form of group care. This practice violated the CB's longstanding sanction against group care for children so young, but in this instance CB officials apparently decided to compromise with the WB and keep their concerns to themselves.[144] The bulletin noted that many of the mothers, "and especially those with very young children," worked "out of economic necessity." For this reason communities should provide day care to "protect children."[145]

The purpose of the governmental studies was to document the increase in the proportion of American mothers who were working *and* to show that day care and other services for their children were inadequate. The studies demonstrated this and more. They revealed a side of American society that conventional domestic iconography usually hid from view—a labor force filled with working mothers, hundreds of thousands of children caring for themselves or for others even smaller, and a conglomeration of child care practices that was so chaotic it defied quantification or categorization by federal researchers.

Provisions were uneven in terms of location and the type and quality of facilities, which tended to be poorly regulated, underfunded, and often expensive. For the most part, services lacked coherent direction by either public or private agencies. The motivations of providers ranged from altruism to sheer greed. Minority and low-income families were often blocked from access. In sum, provisions fell far short of meeting the growing national need for child care. Yet, as the CB had done in the 1920s, the two bureaus repeatedly stopped short of calling for federal intervention into the crisis.

The multivoiced postwar discussion of working mothers and child care drew to a close without marking out a clear direction for public policy. In the literature of psychology and the family professions, many of the most serious concerns about the negative effects on children from maternal employment and group care had been addressed. In fact, both maternal employment and group care had been shown to bring psychological benefits to certain groups of mothers, in terms of their self-esteem and self-images, and to children, by way of the higher quality of care offered by professionals and improvements in their families' standard of living. Unfortunately, psychologists persisted in discussing the positive aspects of maternal employment and group care within a therapeutic framework that excluded financial considerations and tended to denigrate particular types of mothers. Equally unfortunate, nothing was heard from early childhood educators, who might have reframed child care as a cognitively enriching experience for "normal" children from "functional" families—that is, in universal, nonpathologizing terms.

Within the liberal feminist discourse, maternal employment was presented positively, but the focus on individual self-fulfillment for a group of young mothers who were primarily middle class and college educated again limited application of the principles that were established. Significantly, this discourse paved the way for a redefinition of middle-class motherhood that included work outside the home as well as child rearing, but it was much weaker when it came to claiming women's universal right to work. Even more problematic was the silence on the issue of child care. By implying that women could work without reconfiguring the family *or* calling for help from society as a whole, liberal feminists effectively removed middle-class mothers from the child care movement, leaving the impression that only working-class and low-income women needed public provisions.

The National Manpower Council had an opportunity to take policy discussions in a different direction by linking maternal employment and, by implication, publicly supported child care, to the nation's general and growing need for "womanpower." Whether it framed its rationale in terms of Cold War defense needs or of the country's overall economic stability, such a move would have endowed working mothers with a higher, even patriotic, purpose that justified governmental support for the care of their children. But the strong influence of a liberal feminist conceptualization of employment as merely one option for mothers, coupled with persistent psychological reservations about maternal absence, played into council members' preoccupation with shoring up the American family as a bastion against Communism. As in other spheres of

American social life, Cold War domestic ideology succeeded in "containing" (to use Elaine Tyler May's apt phrase) threats to the family and compulsory motherhood.

The Children's Bureau and the Women's Bureau also rejected the Cold War as a justification for child care policy, but for different reasons. The experience of World War II made them wary of once again rationalizing public provisions on the basis of temporary, albeit critical, national needs. Both the Korean War and even the much-vaunted labor shortage appeared too evanescent for their purposes. As they cast about for alternative rationales, one in particular kept surfacing: child care as a support for working-class and low-income mothers. Although this approach tapped into Americans' traditional eagerness to prevent pauperism by helping the poor help themselves, it created another kind of problem. By ruling out a definition of child care as a universal provision linked to women's right to work, it reinforced the class-based and racial divisions among wage-earning mothers—between those who could, apparently, resolve their child care needs privately, and those who had to turn to the state for help. This distinction received reinforcement from the strain of psychosocial discourse that advocated child care as the solution not only to financial need and welfare dependency but also to juvenile delinquency, child neglect, and inadequate mothering.

All these discourses were available to the activists, experts, and policy makers who came together to form a child care movement over the course of the "quiet" decade of the 1950s. Which arguments would prevail depended not only on the power of each discourse to persuade but also on the predilections of the political actors who decided, finally, to put child care on the American agenda.

Chapter 6 Making an Issue
of Child Care

Just as discourses of maternal employment and child care were being constructed and deconstructed throughout the late 1940s and the 1950s, so too were the politics of child care (and American women's politics generally) being transformed. The center of political action shifted from local organizations, including groups of citizens and grassroots day care consumers, to a coalition of elite statewide and national advocacy organizations, which eventually came to work hand in glove with federal agencies.[1] This partnership brought new visibility and broader scope to the issue of day care, but it did not necessarily result in increased public support, nor, by itself, could it resolve the growing crisis in day care. As advocates and government officials discussed and debated policy, struggling to determine who might be entitled to child care services and on what basis, they raised the possibility that women's rights might be expanded, but they were also constrained by the discursive and practical limits of America's reluctant welfare state.

The coalition of advocacy organizations that formed around the issue of child care included a number of multipurpose social service organizations such as the National Social Welfare Assembly and the Child Welfare League of America (CWLA), which had been involved in children's issues, including day care, for decades.[2] The most active member of the coalition, and the only one devoted exclusively to child care, was also the youngest: the National Committee on the Day Care of Children (NCDCC). Initially known as the Inter-City Council for the Day Care of Children (ICC), the NCDCC had its origins in several state and municipal organizations, including groups of parents, providers, and civic leaders that formed in the immediate postwar period to oppose closings of wartime child care centers in such cities as New York; Cleveland; Philadelphia; Washington, D.C.; and Detroit; and state-wide in California.[3] Such groups not only staged local protests but in 1946 also lobbied for the Maternal and Child Welfare Act, which would have continued federal funding for day care centers begun under the Lanham Act.[4] The bill failed, but public child care was continued with local support in New York City, Philadelphia, and Washington, D.C., and with state funding in California. Equally important, child care activists realized that, whether or not they had been successful, it was necessary to maintain their mobilization. In California, they continued to focus on the state legislature, while on the East Coast they turned their gaze toward the federal government.

DAY CARE POLITICS, NEW YORK STYLE

Much of the momentum for a national organization came from New York City, where the struggle to maintain public support for child care services during the immediate postwar period gave rise to a lively, determined, and politically sophisticated day care movement. Activists were divided between an elite wing based in the city's traditional upper-class philanthropic and civic circles and a populist wing driven by several left-leaning Popular Front groups. As the movement shifted onto national terrain, it shed the populist wing, which had been most vociferous and most consistent in calling for child care as a universal right for women.

New York City's postwar public child care system was the second-largest in the country (California's was the largest). This system came into being partly through a fluke. Because New York City was never designated a war-impact area, its wartime day care system had followed a unique trajectory. In areas that received the designation, the Federal Works Administration (FWA) took over funding of Works Progress Administration (WPA) facilities, first on an emergency basis and then later according to the terms of the Lanham Act.[5] In areas of upstate New York, for example, WPA nursery schools were converted into FWA child care centers and administered under the state War Council.[6] Because New York City fell outside the category, its 190 nurseries (some public, some voluntary) were ineligible for either FWA or Lanham funds. Instead, the New York State legislature moved into the breach and, through the War Council, appropriated $2.5 million for day care for mothers engaged in defense-related work in the city. A formula was instituted whereby the state would pay one-third, with local contributions (both municipal and private) and parent fees making up the balance.

To administer funds and coordinate the large network of publicly financed but locally sponsored day care centers, a "public-voluntary" system evolved in New York City. At its hub was the Mayor's Committee on the Wartime Care of Children, comprising representatives of city departments and of the dozens of voluntary agencies that actually provided care.[7] The system was notable not only for the large numbers of children it served but also for its ability to establish and maintain standards. Much of this work was done through the pioneering Day Care Unit of the New York City Department of Health, which had been set up in 1943 with Cornelia Goldsmith, formerly a professor of child studies at Vassar, as director.

Goldsmith soon discovered that many of the city's nurseries, having opened their doors during the Progressive Era, had been operating at substandard levels for years, but, mindful of wartime child care needs, she was reluctant to shut them down summarily. Instead she attempted to use regulations "as a leaven to stimulate people to provide programs of ever-increasing quality."[8] Goldsmith's creative and nurturing oversight, accompanied by an infusion of funds for child care from the city's coffers, resulted in better hygiene, more educational programs, and improvements to physical plants.[9] City officials, civic leaders, and especially parents were understandably eager to see that their model system lasted into the postwar period.

Federal funds were withdrawn from all Lanham Act day care centers in February 1946; only a small program for migrant workers was retained and later transferred to the U.S. Department of Agriculture and Markets. In New York City, however, child care centers continued to receive funding from the state War Council through April 1946. At that time, administrative responsibility for the city's centers shifted from the War Council to the State Youth Authority, which sought to recast child care for low-income families as part of its program to prevent juvenile delinquency.[10]

A year later, the Youth Authority released a report recommending that the state withdraw its aid from New York City's day care services because they were too costly, not restricted to "needy" families, and in any case had proven ineffective in delinquency prevention.[11] As far as the Youth Authority was concerned, child care should be considered a local welfare issue. In response to the threatened shutoff, a group of parents and children mobilized under the leadership of the United Parents' Association (UPA), a citywide grassroots organization, staged a motorcade to the private home of Governor Thomas E. Dewey in Pawling, New York, to protest the report and demand that state funding continue.[12]

The demonstration was notable not because of its political success (state funding in fact ended a few months later) but because it was part of a wave of postwar activism in which, for the first time, American parents directly expressed their need for child care in a visible and organized fashion.[13] Through the efforts of the UPA and several affiliated organizations scattered throughout the boroughs, the grassroots coalition persisted into the early 1950s and, in cooperation with several other organizations, became a force in New York City and New York State child care politics. This coalition gave voice to working parents who, during the war, had come to rely on public child care and were unwilling to return to the status quo antebellum, which would have once again left them to their own resources. The movement allowed them to express their needs without the mediation of psychological experts, economic forecasters, or welfare officials.

Although the UPA failed to reach its initial goal of retaining state support for child care, New York City agreed to take over funding, and the program was transferred from the Mayor's Committee to the city's Department of Welfare, where a Division of Day Care was set up to handle it. Many staff members from the Mayor's Committee also went to the new agency.

Under the city's administration the system grew, even though funding was uncertain from year to year. In March 1950, the program was serving more than 4,600 children—3,257 preschoolers and 1,345 of school age. There were some 99 centers run by 60 different agencies; 24 were located in spaces provided and maintained by public housing projects. By the end of the year, the number of centers was expected to increase to 105. Eighty-four percent of the funding (nearly $3 million annually) came from the city and participating agencies, with parent fees making up the remainder. Children were eligible for the program if their families had financial need or their mothers were unable to care for them. The majority had working mothers, most of whom were "the sole or major support of their families."[14]

New York City's "exceptionalism" afforded its child care funding a temporary reprieve from the postwar ax, but supporters still had to find a way to justify its continuing existence. Arguments about financial need had proven effective in the short run, but many "non-needy" families who had relied on city services during the war hoped that a broader-based rationale could be found. The conflict between these two approaches—one based on financial need, the other more universal—was implicit in the discourses of maternal employment and child care. This conflict deepened as it was played out on the stage of practical politics.

The contrasting approaches were embodied in the two wings of the movement that had arisen from the recurrent political struggle to keep the city's day care centers open and funded. The elite wing, which tended to emphasize the financial needs of specific families as a rationale for public funding, was represented by the Day Care Council of New York City (DCC), while the populist wing, led by the UPA, sought to establish day care as a universal entitlement for working mothers. Together these very different organizations kept the system going, but only one, the DCC, would become the core of a new national organization.

The DCC, a coordinating body comprising the voluntary boards of sponsoring agencies, had grown out of a steering committee formed in 1946 to fight for the extension of funding. It was headed by Elinor Coleman Guggenheimer, a "professional volunteer" known for her work in day care. Born in New York City in 1912, Guggenheimer attended Vassar for two years and earned her B.A. from Barnard in 1934. In 1932 she married Randolph Guggenheimer, and the couple had two children. As a young society matron who was well connected in Democratic Party circles, Guggenheimer became active in voluntary work and developed a particular interest in children. This interest crystallized into a focus on day care when, through her excellent political connections, she was asked to join the Mayor's Committee on the Wartime Care of Children.[15]

The DCC acted as a liaison between the public and voluntary components of the city's child care system. As a semi-official body, it was still free to advocate and lobby on behalf of the program. To secure both public funds and private donations, the council chose to present day care as a child welfare measure for low-income families. Its promotional materials depicted "typical" welfare scenarios: "families where the mother or father is dead . . . [or] seriously ill, where the family is broken by divorce or desertion, where the family is living in horribly overcrowded, inadequate tenements with no room for a child to play."[16] In many instances, both parents were present but the father's salary was too low to support the family, and the mother worked to avoid seeking supplementary public assistance. According to DCC rhetoric, day care families belonged to a kind of swing group, a low-income population always hovering just above the welfare line but eager to work and remain self-supporting. Public child care was a critical factor in their struggle to remain independent.[17]

The position of the UPA was subtly but significantly different. Coalition members stressed that making public services available only to the very poor "would presumably aid those mothers who are in particularly desperate straits, . . . [but] would do nothing for the thousands of mothers who could earn enough to provide quite adequately for their children" if they had child care.[18] Insofar as it continued to present child care as a matter of financial need rather than one of pure choice, the UPA's argument for public funding was not quite universalistic. Nevertheless, the range of "legitimate" need it delineated was broader than that of the DCC.

The difference in the positions of the two groups reflected the circumstances of their respective constituencies. Most of the female members of the DCC were child welfare professionals or full-time volunteers and civic leaders like Guggenheimer for whom child care was a "cause," not a daily necessity.[19] The UPA coalition, by contrast, had a membership of working-class and middle-class parents with a fundamental and direct stake in the fate of the centers.

Even more dramatically than its rhetoric, the parent coalition's tactics differed from those of the DCC. While DCC members mined their political and social contacts and worked in official chambers, the UPA and its affiliates mobilized letter-writing campaigns and staged demonstrations. When the state legislature was in session, the UPA drafted model bills and sent lobbying groups to Albany every week.[20]

The coalition's specialty was mobilizing mass support on short notice. When state funding for day care was withdrawn a few months after the much-publicized motorcade from Manhattan to Governor Dewey's home, UPA members set up a picket outside the State Department of Public Welfare office in downtown Manhattan. Local papers carried photographs of this event, which was obviously staged in part for their benefit. One picture, under the caption "Mothers and Children Protest," showed children marching with their mothers, carrying placards with such slogans as "Nursery Children Make Better Citizens."[21] Several months later, parents and children from the Brownsville Child Care Center staged a similar demonstration at City Hall, protesting changes in eligibility rules at city-sponsored centers.[22] Both these demonstrations drew editorial attention from the three major New York papers, the *Times,* the *Post,* and the *Herald Tribune.*[23]

Press coverage was generally favorable, but the coalition's flagrant tactics, particularly the motorcade, may ultimately have backfired. For several years afterward, dozens of bills restoring state funding for child care were introduced into the legislature, but none of them ever made it out of committee. Coalition leaders attributed the blockage to the state's Republicans, who were apparently acting at Dewey's behest. Although Republican opposition was to be expected, it may have taken on added impetus because Dewey was still smarting from the barrage of negative publicity engendered by the Pawling incident.[24]

One New York paper, the conservative *World-Telegram,* was decidedly unfriendly to the grassroots coalition. In January and February 1948, the paper ran a red-baiting campaign against the city's entire day care program. Reporter Walter MacDonald claimed that "well-meaning citizens" had been "duped by Reds" into lobbying for child care. Indeed, he maintained, "supporters of Communist-front organizations have had their fingers in the child care center program" since the Depression, and the *Daily Worker* was active in the current campaign to retain funds, which had "all the trappings of a Red drive, including leaflets, letters, telegrams, petitions, protest demonstrations, mass meetings, and hat-passing."[25]

MacDonald also challenged the assertion that most of the parents, particularly the mothers, who sent their children to the city's centers were financially needy. "Children arriving with their fur-coated mothers afoot, in taxi-cabs, in 1947 automobiles, or being delivered by maids are not uncommon at certain city child care centers," he reported.[26] According to MacDonald, Welfare Commissioner Benjamin Fielding's assurance that 92 percent of center parents met eligibility criteria was based on parents' "flimsy statements" about their income and expenses, which Department of Welfare investigators, under orders from Fielding, were prohibited from checking. Independent investigations by *World-Telegram* reporters revealed that many center children had parents in the professions or in business who paid "ridiculously low fees." Women who claimed to be deserted, according to MacDonald, in fact knew the whereabouts of their husbands; other parents earned far more income and paid far less rent than they reported.[27]

MacDonald's exposé suggested that a group of selfish parents were jeopardizing the rights of the legitimate beneficiaries of public services. While discrediting particular parents, his attack actually served to vindicate the position of the elite wing of the day care coalition, for it implied that if these parents, these mothers, *were* needy, then they would be entitled to child care services.

Sensational though they were, MacDonald's accusations did not succeed in breaking apart the elite-grassroots alliance that had formed around day care, possibly because his barrage not only hit alleged "Reds" but also targeted several city officials whose politics were above suspicion. At the same time, it is apparent that MacDonald's charges about the left-wing ties of some of the leaders of the parents' coalition were, in at least one case, probably on the mark. The papers of Edythe Lutzker, president of the Child Care Parents Association (CCPA), an affiliate of the UPA, and the history of her organization's subsequent activities, suggest that both she and her group did indeed have ties to the American Communist Party.[28] In general, however, MacDonald appeared to be relying more on circumstantial evidence and innuendo than on concrete proof.

In spite of MacDonald's charges, the UPA and the DCC continued to work together for several more years.[29] The energy and determination of the grassroots coalition were obviously an asset to New York City's day care movement. Nevertheless, though the approaches of the two groups could be complementary and mutually reinforcing, they also produced a certain degree of tension. The semi-official DCC wanted to take advantage of the UPA's access to "the masses" to orchestrate displays of popular support into its overall strategies, but at the same time the elite organization strove to temper the flamboyance of its grassroots allies. For example, at a planning meeting to devise tactics for an April 1953 New York City budget hearing, one UPA parent claimed that "city officials have been amazed at the campaign the mothers have conducted. . . . We have made them aware of us."[30] But the DCC's Guggenheimer warned the parent group that their purpose "was not to antagonize, but to look toward the future. We should thank the board for keeping the program intact. The main message of the mothers should be what the program has meant to them and what it means to others who *need* it. We are also to mention that we will fight for state aid."[31] DCC officials, acknowledging differences between the council and the various parent groups, stressed that it was important for coalition members to maintain a united front.

The DCC clearly intended to control that front, in both word and actions. Guggenheimer's warning to parents revealed that she wanted to define the rationale for child care narrowly, restricting it to financial need, rather than allowing them to use the more populist rhetoric of the UPA and its allies, which called for child care as a more general and universal right. Moreover, she seemed to be suggesting that, in keeping with the tenor of the need-based arguments, parents should appear more deferential and grateful.

A FORK IN THE ROAD

The alliance held, somewhat uneasily, through the late 1940s, but around this time each of the two wings began to feel that its struggle could be won only by "going national," and their paths began to diverge. Although both groups saw the need to build a broader movement, they went about it differently. On April 15, 1950, members of the CCPA and the UPA joined left-wing women from across the country at a national "Bread and Butter Conference" held at Chicago's Hull House. In attendance were male and female delegates from eight states and fifteen cities, representing a range of national and local organizations, trade unions, and religious and ethnic groups. Several of these, in addition to the CCPA, had left-wing ties, including the Congress of American Women, the Women's International League for Peace and Freedom, and the Committee of Women of the National Council for American-Soviet Friendship.[32] Others, however, were firmly middle-of-the-road, if not actually conservative: the Salvation Army, the National Save the Children Federation, and the Council of Church Women of Greater Chicago and Illinois. The presence of the National Association for the Advancement of Colored People and the National Council of Negro Women gave the conference an explicitly biracial focus that had, until then, been largely missing from national discussions of child care policy.

The fit between the two New York groups and other left-wing women was not entirely congenial. Participants in the conference were, on the whole, more equivocal about child care and maternal employment than the CCPA and the UPA. Most took the position that communities should not "dictate whether mothers should work or shouldn't work; . . . families have their own right to decide whether they should or should not."[33] While calling on communities to extend "the resources of good child care" to working mothers, they also demanded full employment and sufficient wages (presumably for male breadwinners) to ensure an adequate family income. If wages were inadequate, then governmental supplements in the form of family allowances, Social Security, unemployment compensation, or public assistance should be made available. Casting maternal employment as but a minor element of an overall strategy to establish social supports for families, conferees implicitly signaled an unwillingness to break with class solidarity in order to struggle for child care and employment as women's rights.

This position was far less feminist than the one taken by the Congress of American Women at hearings on the 1946 Maternal and Child Welfare bill. There, Eleanor Vaughan, a vice-chair of the organization, had argued for continuing public support for child care in order to prevent war widows and other mothers, "self-respecting and able to work," from being "forced to stay at home [and] accept the ignominy of public assistance or private charity and . . . maintain their children at inadequate relief levels." Although Vaughan's argument was based on prevention of poverty, not women's universal right to work, it nonetheless foregrounded women's role in supporting their families.[34] By 1950, however, the left in general appears to have returned to an earlier Popular Front ideology that, in the name of class solidarity, subsumed women under the rubric of the family and rendered their wage-earning potential nearly invisible.[35] By leaving decisions about maternal employment up to the *family* rather than to women themselves, the left's position actually came down somewhere to the *right* of liberal feminism, which insisted that maternal employment should be a woman's choice.

The one role that Bread and Butter conferees assigned specifically to women was a traditional neo-maternalist one: accepting "the responsibility of being the leaders in the fight for our children's rights."[36] In her closing remarks, Helen Wortis, a longtime left-wing activist from New York City who had served as secretary of the conference, urged female delegates to become involved in child welfare at both the local and national levels by initiating discussions on such issues as child care in their communities and contacting State White House Conference Committees (a White House Conference on Children was to be held in Washington, D.C., later that year).

If members of the New York City parents' groups had attended the Bread and Butter Conference in hopes of gaining encouragement and support in their struggle for child care, they must have come away sorely disappointed. But the political orthodoxy of their fellow leftists was the least of their troubles. As the virulent effects of McCarthyism began to spread during the early 1950s, self-identified left-wing, and especially Communist, groups were forced to withdraw from public policy discussions of all sorts, including child care.[37] The CCPA and UPA gave up their campaign to win state funding for New York City's child care system, although some of the other coalition groups remained active, and city funding for child care continued.

Whatever the political affiliations of its leaders, the populist coalition succeeded in mobilizing grassroots support and focusing public attention on child care in ways that turned out to be highly effective at the local level. But this same approach backfired in Albany and probably would have been even more out of place in Washington. So it was their rhetoric and tactics, as well as anti-Communist repression, that stymied the political ambitions of New York City's left-wing child care activists. Nevertheless, they made their mark as part of one of the first parent-directed efforts to build public child care.

CHILDREN AND DEFENSE REDUX

Meanwhile, the DCC took the lead in New York City day care politics. Its members began developing broader alliances through contacts in national organizations like United Neighborhood Houses, a league of settlement houses in whose offices the DCC was located, and the CWLA, which was headquartered in New York. In the early 1950s, Elinor Guggenheimer became involved with the CWLA, which was beginning to abandon its longtime opposition to child care, and she was soon appointed chair of its Day Care Committee. As the country once more mobilized for war, the CWLA and other child welfare organizations also geared up, hoping that defense mobilization might again bring federal involvement in social provision and create opportunities for establishing permanent entitlements.

Neither the popular authors nor the professionals whose writings on working mothers and child care were examined in chapter 5 seemed to pay a great deal of attention to the Korean War, no doubt because many of them had come to realize that the "cause" of maternal employment was not World War II but a host of more enduring factors, including families' financial pressures and women's personal ambitions. High-profile advisory bodies like the National Manpower Council were more inclined to take the war into consideration, but their project eventually outlived the war and thus came to focus on other issues affecting the demand for female employment.

Official memory, however, was not so short. Within the federal government were numerous officials who, still haunted by their experiences of World War II, sought to forestall what they regarded as the inevitable disruptions of war. As the nation headed into another armed conflict, conservatives grumbled that defense production would again draw mothers into the workforce, while liberals, including many of the women who worked in the government's social agencies, anticipated a crisis in child care and moved to head it off.

On January 16–17, 1951, the CB and the OE, both then housed in the Federal Security Agency, called a conference on Planning for Day Care and Extended School Services in Areas Affected by Defense Mobilization. The participants, who represented both public and voluntary education and welfare agencies, echoed the position taken by the War Manpower Commission in 1942, namely, that recruitment of mothers of small children "should be deferred until full use has been made of all other sources of labor supply." However, they stated, the government should not "set up barriers" against the employment of such women. "The decision as to gainful employment should in all cases be an individual decision made by the woman herself in light of the particular conditions prevailing in her home."[38] This position represented a slight improvement over that espoused by family professionals during World War II, namely, that mothers should make such decisions only in consultation with social workers or other "experts."

Conference participants also endorsed a set of standards, prepared in advance by the CWLA's Day Care Committee, which embodied the principle that child care programs should be both protective and developmental. Notably, these standards broadened eligibility criteria to include categories that had nothing to do with supporting defense mobilization. They stated that agencies should provide care because of "(1) employment of the mother [pure and simple], (2) illness or absence of either parent, (3) overcrowding in the home or inadequate housing, (4) other factors within the family which have an adverse effect on the child, [and] (5) special needs of the child."[39]

Voluntary organizations like the CWLA saw the war as an opportunity to involve the federal government in child care provision in ways that would not only address the crisis created by the war but also meet the ongoing need for child care. Among themselves, members of the CWLA subcommittee concerned with child care legislation confessed, "While it is the emergency that makes Federal funds necessary at this point, through good administration existing services will be strengthened and at the same time given an opportunity for expanding."[40] To exploit this opportunity to the fullest, it was necessary to be pragmatic: "Everyone felt that anything which we might want to recommend would have to be related to defense in order to pass Congress."[41]

The CWLA was fearful of reproducing the administrative conflicts of interest that had snarled delivery of services during World War II. The Defense Housing and Community Facilities and Services Act (the so-called Maybank Bill) passed in September 1951, which granted funds to the Federal Housing Authority to be used for child care, caused the CWLA's Day Care Committee particular concern. Members felt that the CWLA should take action to see that the day care program was assigned to the Federal Security Agency, where it could be administered by the CB. On October 2, President Harry Truman, following Franklin D. Roosevelt's precedent, issued an executive order granting joint control of both child care and extended day programs to the OE and the CB.[42] As soon as the CB was assigned to administer the Maybank Bill, it asked the CWLA to share any information it had on the growing need for child care. The CWLA legislative subcommittee seized upon this opening to write a letter to the CB stating that the bill represented "a forward step for day care" and offering its cooperation. The letter was not merely congratulatory; it also reminded the CB of a day care meeting held in December 1950, "where it was agreed that joint planning [with nongovernmental organizations] should be a part of any new program."[43]

Eventually, however, both the CB and the CWLA's plans for wartime day care proved to be merely academic. Although they got their way in terms of how the program was to be administered, Congress refused to appropriate funds for establishing or administering day care (in fact, such services were specifically excluded from funding appropriations). So the expected federal boost to day care never materialized, and it was left to local, voluntary, and commercial providers to fill the gap in services created by wartime demands.

In retrospect, it appears that the reason Congress refused appropriations may well have been related to Truman's decision to involve the CB in administering the wartime child care program. During hearings on the Maybank Bill, the Right Reverend John O'Grady, secretary of the National Conference of Catholic Charities and a fierce opponent of both maternal employment and day care, warned that "old-line" government agencies might be tempted "to use the defense program as a means of expanding their own programs." It was evident that the Federal Security Agency, which housed the CB, was one of the agencies he had in mind.[44] Opponents of day care within Congress may have shared O'Grady's line of reasoning and blocked appropriations that would have automatically gone to the CB.

In late 1951, while the CB and the CWLA awaited funding that would never come, the Women's Bureau added its voice to the call for day care. The WB had historically left this issue to the CB, focusing instead on inequities of women's pay and employment opportunities. But now, noting that women's "dual responsibilities [as workers and homemakers or mothers] have been overlooked or underemphasized so frequently in the past," the WB placed a broad interpretation on its mandate to promote the welfare of women working in defense areas. It cautioned that "inadequate provisions for the care of children and other dependents" could cause "turnover, absenteeism and loss of productivity of women workers in industry."[45] Out of deference to the CB, the WB opposed "the active recruitment of women with small children into the labor force. However," it stated, "if women with children do work either through choice or necessity, adequate provision must be made for the care [of their children]."[46] Child care was already "one of the most pressing problems" of domestic mobilization.[47] The WB called on both the federal government and local communities to undertake "exploratory surveys" to see whether these needs were being met and what services should be provided.[48]

WAR AND TAXES

Although children's advocates failed in their efforts to use the Korean War as a lever for federal aid to day care, the conflict did figure into debates over a deduction for child care expenses when Congress undertook a major revision of the income tax code in 1954. Under the new version, working adults (widows, widowers, divorced persons, or married mothers) would be able to deduct up to $600 for child care, "as long as its purpose was to permit the taxpayer to hold gainful employment."[49] The maximum deduction was available to individuals or couples earning less than $4,500 per year.

Some members of Congress objected that the deduction would encourage mothers to delegate their children's care so they could earn money for nonessential purposes, but supporters countered that many of the beneficiaries would be military widows and the wives of veterans who had not yet gotten back on their feet.[50] Others argued that many parents, not just those affected by the war, were in difficult financial straits; according to Representative Carl Elliott (Democrat–Alabama), more and more Americans required child care "in order to earn even a meager living."[51] The deduction would thus assist many families in need.

Even though Elliott based his support for the deduction on the principle that it would prevent low-income families from becoming dependent on public assistance, he and others sought to broaden eligibility or even make it universal. They believed that child care should be considered a legitimate business expense, one of the "ordinary and necessary costs of operation incurred in the earning of a livelihood." Indeed, noted Representative Aimé J. Forand (Democrat–Rhode Island), it was only by historical accident that child care was not already seen this way. "If as many mothers . . . had been working at the time regulations were shaping the meaning of 'ordinary and necessary business expenses' as there are now, the Treasury Department would have permitted deductions for wages paid housekeepers, nursemaids, and expenses of nursery care."[52]

If the deduction were to be considered a business expense, some legislators reasoned, then it should be allowed universally, regardless of a taxpayer's total income or family status; likewise, as with other types of expenses, the amount should not be fixed but determined according to local markets and estimates of "reasonable costs." As Senator Paul Douglas (Democrat–Illinois) argued, "We have long permitted a businessman to deduct the full cost of the salary of a watchman to protect his factory, regardless of the amount of his income."[53] Making an exception for child care by predetermining the amount to be allowed for the expense and indexing the deduction to the taxpayer's income were, he implied, forms of gender discrimination. Testifying in a similar vein at hearings before the House Ways and Means Committee, Julia Thompson of the American Nurses' Association (ANA) deplored the practice of allowing a woman's *employer* to count her salary as a business expense while denying *her* the right to deduct the wages she paid to a housekeeper or nursemaid to care for her child so that she could earn a living.[54]

But efforts to remove the income cap and deductible maximum from the bill failed. Indeed, the cap, at one point set as high as $6,000, was eventually reduced to $4,500. At this level, it still included low-income and some lower-middle-income households, but many mothers felt that this did not go far enough.[55] Nancy Henderson, a working mother from Alexandria, Virginia, reasoned, "Because a woman has been able to acquire an education and has pursued a career along with her family, she should not be penalized because of her capability and ambition and the fact that she earns a salary of $6000 or more."[56] Congress, however, remained implacable on this point.

Efforts to raise the maximum amount for the deduction also proved fruitless. The ANA's Thompson complained that it was inequitable to limit child care expenses while continuing to allow businessmen unlimited deductions for entertainment, gifts, dues, and other business-related costs. Noting that, in major cities, child care could cost as much as $40 per week, she called for raising the maximum from $600 to $2,000 per year.[57] Ranice Davis, a professor at the Johns Hopkins School of Medicine in Baltimore, testified that while cheaper forms of care might be available, they were likely to be unregulated, "and public pressure is being brought against such unlicensed care."[58] But the maximum remained fixed at $600.

Slightly more successful were attempts to expand eligibility. At the behest of Representative (later Senator) Jacob Javits (Republican–New York), divorced women were added to the category of those entitled to take the deduction, which originally included only widows, widowers, and the wives of the disabled. Speaking on behalf of divorcées, Javits prevailed upon Congress to set aside moral reservations and look "just at the question of justice and of the working force of the country."[59] Referring to the nation's labor shortage, he noted that divorced women tended to be younger than widows and therefore more productive. Congress accepted Javits' argument with regard to divorcées but balked at proposals made by others to include wives who had been deserted or were separated.

The idea that child care should be considered a business expense resonated with the popular press, and they were quick to perceive the gender-based inequity of opposing the measure. Columnist Sylvia Porter, writing in the *New York Post,* declared that it was unfair to allow businessmen to take deductions for entertainment, including dues at social and golf clubs and even the expenses of keeping a yacht, while denying the same right to women. "If we didn't hire some person to take care of our children during our working hours, we could not earn the money on which we pay taxes; if we did not earn the money to employ those who help take care of our children, they in turn would not have the incomes on which they pay taxes. (Talk about double taxation.)"[60] But the fine points of caps and ceilings—and their attendant inequities—tended to escape the press. In another column, Porter seemed to accept without question the $600 limit. "I am forced to pay tax on $600 a year that I pay someone else. It is not fair."[61] Similarly, *Redbook* magazine told women that they had an "absolute right . . . to protest bitterly the discriminatory laws that rob them of their earnings" but ignored the further discriminations that were built into the eligibility categories spelled out in the legislation.[62]

Porter and her fellow journalists did object to charges that mothers were simply seeking ways to palm off their child-rearing responsibilities on someone else. "This help is not a luxury," Porter exclaimed.[63] The primary source of this canard was Representative Noah Mason, an Illinois Republican known as his state's "conservative spokesman." As a member of the House Ways and Means Committee, Mason was in a good position to try to block the deduction by impugning women's motives for taking jobs. Typical, he claimed, was the case of "a married lady who insists on working so that she can buy a $750 fur coat because her husband cannot afford it . . . and . . . neglects her children or hires someone who is not capable of handling them and is letting them run the streets and thus bringing about juvenile delinquency."[64] Mason also asserted that "thousands, if not millions" of women married to husbands earning "enough for a pretty fair living" were willing to displace male workers merely so that they could earn money to spend on themselves.[65] Another Republican on the committee, John Byrnes of Wisconsin, argued for limiting the deductible so as to prevent wealthy widows who were earning only token amounts while living off inheritances or annuities from sending their children to "rather fancy nursery schools" and passing the tuition expense on to the government.[66]

In contrast to their suspicious colleagues across the aisle, congressional Democrats emphasized women's selfless dedication to family life. Representative Leonore Sullivan (Missouri), who wanted to extend the child care deduction to all women regardless of marital status, pointed out that married women's tendency to work was inversely related to their husbands' earning power; the lower the men's income, the more likely that the women would work. "Nearly a third of the married women are working today in order to assist in giving their children a decent standard of living," Sullivan testified.[67] Representative Edna Kelly (New York) insisted that the deduction would be used not for babysitting but for child care. "This means . . . while the taxpayer is at work," not, presumably, out shopping or enjoying leisure-time activities.[68] Finally, Representative Kenneth Roberts (Alabama) accused the government of insensitivity for allowing "a lawyer to deduct entertainment fees lavished upon a prospective client, [or] a professional golfer to deduct his equipment in tournaments . . . [while denying] this privilege to the weary mother who toils all day in the factory and works for her family in the evening in the hope that her children may have a better life."[69]

Supporters of the deduction, unwilling to rest their case simply on the needs of wage-earning mothers and their families, also invoked the nation's interests. With nearly full employment, there were labor shortages in many fields, including traditionally female-dominated occupations such as nursing, teaching, and stenography. "We are on the one hand appealing to mothers to take these jobs and at the same time penalizing them for doing so by refusing to deduct the cost of child care," Senator Douglas pointed out.[70] According to Thompson of the ANA, one-fifth of the 335,000 registered nurses currently working had children under eighteen. The deduction would not only ease their financial burden but would also encourage another 100,000 inactive nurses with small children to return to duty.[71]

The ANA was unequivocal in its support for the deduction and its denunciations of the inequities in the existing code, but other labor organizations were divided on the issue. The American Federation of Labor supported an increase in the tax code's dependency exemption, which applied to all children, on the grounds that a deduction specifically for child care expenses would be difficult to administer and would invite "wholesale evasion." The Congress of Industrial

Organizations, in contrast, endorsed the child care tax deduction but did so halfheartedly, because its leaders believed that the measure would encourage more women to enter the labor force, thus undermining the union's perpetual struggle for a (male) family wage.[72]

The debate over how to treat child care expenses within the tax code dovetailed with other 1950s discourses on maternal employment and child care. Within Congress, positions ranged from liberals who wanted to make the deduction universal and unlimited, to conservatives who regarded it as an affront to men's privileged position as breadwinners. Even among supporters, however, attitudes toward maternal employment were still ambivalent. Paul Douglas conceded that "mothers' place is in the home caring for their children . . . assuming that economic conditions make this possible."[73]

The prevalence of such views made it difficult to modify or eliminate the various qualifications and limitations. Removing the income cap and making the deduction universal would have decoupled maternal employment from financial need, implying blanket federal support for wage-earning mothers, a step that most in Congress were not prepared to take.[74] Raising or eliminating the maximum allowable for the expense would have opened up knotty questions about the quality of care. Among at least some members of Congress, there seemed to be a sense that the children of wage-earning mothers were not entitled to anything more than "custodial" care, as if offering them something better would somehow condone their mothers' behavior.

By allowing only minimal expenditures and keeping the income cap low, Congress was able to craft a child care deduction that functioned as a surrogate anti-poverty measure, one that signaled an important shift in policy toward poor and low-income women: instead of supporting them to remain at home with their children (as did Aid to Dependent Children, the successor to mothers' pensions, which became federal law in 1935), Congress now encouraged them to become wage earners by underwriting the expense of child care. At the same time, most legislators made it clear that they did not condone maternal employment in general. Instead, the deduction created a precedent for linking public support for child care to mothers' financial status and the prevention or reduction of the need for public assistance.[75]

BUILDING A NATIONAL ORGANIZATION

The tax reform measure turned out to be the most significant breakthrough in child care policy of the 1950s, and it was to have far-reaching consequences. For many years the tax deduction (after 1976, the dependent care tax credit) constituted the single greatest federal expenditure for child care.[76] Yet tax legislation, by its very nature, could do nothing to address such issues as the supply, distribution, affordability, or quality of child care. Tellingly, throughout the tax-reform debates, whenever child care was mentioned, it was usually understood to refer to "nursemaids" or "housekeepers," rarely day care centers or day nurseries. As in the liberal feminist discourse described in chapter 5, members of Congress seemed to assume that child care problems would be resolved privately and individually. But it was unlikely that the low-income and single-parent families being targeted by the bill would be hiring domestic servants for child care. One reason that group care received scant attention in the debates was that no child care advocates were invited to testify at the Republican-controlled hearings. Voluntary organizations like the CWLA began to understand that if they wanted to see improvements in child care provision, they—not the federal government—would have to take the initiative. This was, of course, what such federal agencies as the CB and the WB had been saying all along.

Leading the voluntary drive was Elinor Guggenheimer, who was by this time moving from municipal and state politics onto the national stage. Her stint as chair of the Day Care Committee at the CWLA had exposed her to congressional politics and the federal bureaucracy.[77] Working within a large, multi-issue organization convinced her that the only way to incite action on child care was to establish a national organization devoted solely to that issue. In the fall of 1956, Guggenheimer began circulating a CWLA planning proposal which stated that child care had become "a permanent need and deserves careful consideration and long-range planning." Accordingly, she called for the formation of a national citizens' committee, which, in conjunction with either the CB or the CWLA, would conduct research and stimulate the expansion and upgrading of child care.[78] At the National Council of Social Work conference in Philadelphia in May 1957, Guggenheimer met informally with several other child welfare leaders who were specifically interested in child care, and early in 1958 a new organization was announced, taking the name Inter-City Committee for Day Care of Children.

One of the purposes in seeking a national platform at this point was to block what the CWLA saw as a dangerous trend toward linking child care with efforts to reduce the welfare rolls. "There is evidence," said the planning proposal, "of public misuse of [child care] facilities to encourage eligible women to leave ADC."[79] The CWLA and its allies in social work had long argued that low-income mothers should not be categorically compelled to take jobs outside the home but instead should be counseled to make a careful decision based on their own needs and those of their families—just as mothers who were financially secure could do.[80] Such cautions, while scrupulously democratic, still partook of the fundamental disapproval of maternal employment that had its roots in the maternalist politics of the Progressive Era, and they may have had the unintended consequence of undercutting the struggle for day care by arming its conservative opponents. Notably, Guggenheimer's implicit endorsement indicated that moving to the CWLA had induced her to shift her position from the one she had taken only a few years earlier when, as head of the New York City Day Care Council, she had urged members of the United Parents Association to stress financial need as a justification for public child care.

FORGING A PUBLIC-PRIVATE PARTNERSHIP

During its first year, the ICC's membership was based primarily in Eastern cities—New York City; Hartford; Springfield, Massachusetts; Philadelphia; Baltimore; Trenton; and Newark. In addition to Guggenheimer, the group included many activists who had long been associated with the day care issue: co-president Sadie Ginsberg, a leader of the Child Study Association who chaired a Maryland child care committee; Cornelia Goldsmith, who, as a New York City Health Department official, had been instrumental in establishing a system of licensing for child care institutions; and Winifred Moore, a child care specialist who had worked for both the CWLA and the CB.[81]

In November 1957, as plans for the ICC were beginning to take shape, members of several voluntary organizations met with federal officials to discuss ways they might cooperate on programs for children of working mothers. The CWLA was represented by its executive director, Joseph Reid, and by Guggenheimer, still in her capacity as chair of the CWLA Day Care Committee. Katharine Oettinger, director of the CB, and Alice Leopold, assistant secretary of labor and director of the WB, along with members of their respective staffs, represented the federal government.[82]

It was agreed that the upcoming 1960 White House Conference on Children and Youth (WHC) could serve as a "focal point for stimulating interest" in child care. Advocates could begin by raising the issue at regional pre-conference meetings. To make their case, they would require updated information about existing facilities and projected needs.[83] Guggenheimer suggested that such information should include the number of working mothers and their children, broken down by age; availability of facilities and how they were operated; licensing; sources of support; and community opinions with regard to responsibility. Officials of the CB agreed to try to obtain some of this information through the Census Bureau, and the WB planned a publication on the subject in 1959.[84] This turned out to be *Child Care Arrangements of Full-Time Working Mothers* (discussed in chapter 5).[85]

The influence of the CWLA, and particularly of Elinor Guggenheimer, on the federal agencies was clear. Guggenheimer's questions helped shape the CB's research agenda and also spurred cooperation between the CB and the WB. A month after the initial meeting, Oettinger told Guggenheimer that the two agencies had formed an ad hoc committee "to look into the present position of each Bureau with respect to working mothers" and determine whether the Social Security Administration should develop policy. Oettinger promised to keep Guggenheimer informed of the agencies' progress so that the ICC (still in its formative stage) could tailor its efforts accordingly.[86]

This initial meeting between Guggenheimer and federal officials laid the groundwork for continuing public-private exchanges on the subject of child care. The desire for cooperation was mutual, and Guggenheimer was almost always at the center of it. In early 1958, when the ICC began holding regular meetings in New York City, the fledgling organization invited members of the federal ad hoc committee to participate. Laura Dale of the WB and Clare Golden of the CB attended often, reporting back to their respective agencies. In spite (or perhaps because) of their presence, other members of the ICC freely discussed their aims with regard to federal involvement. They decided to push for inclusion of day care on the agenda of the upcoming White House Conference, for establishment of a position for a day care consultant somewhere within the federal government, and, eventually, for federal funding for day care.[87]

Dale and Golden were careful to point out that they could not "commit their Bureaus to any course of action [or] give personal approval to any course of legislative action other than proposed by their agencies," but their attendance at ICC meetings implicitly signaled CB and WB endorsement of the ICC's agenda while simultaneously serving to keep those agencies apprised of the ICC's plans and actions. At the same time, the federal staffers funneled useful information to the new organization. At one meeting, for example, Golden told the group that plans for the WHC were "still quite nebulous, awaiting the appointment of an executive so that more definitive plans can be made." She emphasized that it was essential for groups like the ICC to bring children's issues to the fore.[88] Just as the DCC had once used the UPA coalition, now the federal agencies relied on the ICC, also an outside group, to act as a spur and take definitive positions that the agencies themselves might feel uncomfortable assuming. The agencies could also point to the ICC as a barometer of grassroots support for action on day care.[89]

Golden's intervention pushed the ICC to clarify its aims with regard to the White House Conference. The organization agreed that child care needed financing and improved standards and quality. These, in turn, were related to public perceptions of services. But what was the best way to situate and present child care? In preliminary private discussions, the ICC formulated a two-pronged approach that conceptualized day care as both a service for working mothers and a form of therapy for troubled families.[90] But in public statements of its scope and purposes, the group presented day care "as a service which both substitutes for and supplements or complements the family. Day care is an all-inclusive consideration and must be concerned with the well-being of all children and families."[91] By omitting mention of troubled families and allowing "well-being" to be interpreted as psychological, economic, or simply neutral, this definition of day care sounded more universal. But the final version of the statement was somewhat bland; day care became "a service which provides daytime care for children of families who need the service as an essential aid in maintaining and strengthening the family. . . . Day Care is a means to the end of preserving individual and family values."[92] Significantly, nowhere in the document was day care explicitly linked to maternal employment.

The ICC was sensitive to accusations (either actual or anticipated) that day care encroached on family autonomy. Such accusations, which were not unfamiliar to day care advocates, were no doubt spurred by Cold War domestic ideology.[93] The ICC's statement paid lip service to this concern: "Any form of day care must be developed in relation to the principle of the family as the base of our society. . . . The more responsibility a person or family gives up the more it relinquishes his rights to the community and state. As day care is encouraged, the degree of responsibility which is assumed by the service should be carefully evaluated in terms of the amount of responsibility it may usurp from the family."[94] This rhetoric not only affirmed the importance of the American family but also served to distinguish child care from traditional forms of social service, with their condescending tones and threats of social control.

With an anodyne and neutral platform on which to operate, the ICC was prepared to detach child care from its traditional moorings in the field of child welfare and broaden its base. To open up new avenues of influence, the organi-

zation began to reach out to other agencies, both governmental and nongovernmental. In May 1958 Elinor Guggenheimer and Sadie Ginsberg met with
Charles Schottland, commissioner of Social Security (and a veteran of World
War II–era social agencies), who proposed convening an ad hoc advisory group
on day care that would include, in addition to the CB, the WB, the CWLA, and
the ICC, representatives from the Department of Agriculture, the Social Secu-
rity Administration (SSA), and the Family Services Association of America.
Schottland also supported the idea of appointing a child care specialist to the
CB staff and appeared willing to help the ICC get day care on the agenda of the
White House Conference.[95] Around the same time Guggenheimer wrote to
Arthur Flemming, secretary of the Department of Health, Education, and
Welfare, requesting his support.[96]

Guggenheimer was clearly a force to be reckoned with in federal circles. At
Flemming's request, Katharine Oettinger wrote back to her in June outlining
various developments within the CB and the SSA with regard to day care.
Many of these were, of course, already known to Guggenheimer because the
ICC had requested them in the first place. These included the appointment of a
part-time CB research specialist who would analyze data on the effects of
maternal employment on children and on the relation between working
mothers and juvenile delinquency; a national survey to be undertaken by the
Census Bureau; and formation of an SSA Committee on Working Mothers,
which would prepare a report.[97] In October 1958 Helen Witmer, director of
the CB's research division, sent Guggenheimer copies of the first publication on
the planning of the White House Conference, and Guggenheimer assured her
that the ICC would continue to feed suggestions to the conference planners.[98]

Reaching into another important field, Guggenheimer and Ginsberg also
met with Hazel Gabbard of the U.S. Office of Education (OE). Gabbard raised
several different issues. She expressed concern about the lack of after-school
services for children up to age eleven, and about inconsistent qualifications for
day care personnel, proposing the use of teacher certification to raise standards
in the field. Herbert Espey, who headed research for the OE, told ICC leaders
that it might be possible to channel some funds into the study of the educational aspects of day care. Officials of the CB and the WB appeared to view with
equanimity the ICC's efforts to reach out to other government agencies, even
when it meant going over or around them.[99]

With Elinor Guggenheimer and the ICC at the forefront, the public-private
partnership on child care policy was solidifying, and legislative efforts to improve and expand day care were going forward. At an ICC meeting on May 28,

1958, Guggenheimer announced that Jacob Javits, now a senator from New York, would introduce a bill "to provide facilities for the children of working mothers."[100] Guggenheimer was concerned that reference to working mothers in the bill's title would "make support for it very difficult." In keeping with the CWLA's approach, she sought to deemphasize maternal employment and instead stress children's needs, in effect shifting the rationale for child care from upholding women's rights to serving children's interests. Accordingly, she proposed that Javits change the wording to "children who need day care outside of their own homes."[101]

The Javits bill called for an appropriation of $25 million, which would take the form of grants-in-aid to states, and designated the CB to administer the program and develop standards. Although prospects for passage in the Eighty-fifth Congress were dim, the ICC was told that a bill could be reintroduced in the Eighty-sixth "if sufficient interest were generated." In any case, ICC leaders believed, the mere fact that Javits was willing to introduce the bill and speak in support of it "would focus attention on the need for child care."[102]

The following year, as Javits prepared to reintroduce the bill, the ICC reconsidered its terms and decided that designating the CB to administer a federal child care program might prove problematic. Because many existing state- and community-sponsored programs were currently being operated under the auspices of educational authorities, they would fear being excluded from a system operated under a federal *welfare* agency. Thus, despite its initial alliance with the CB, the ICC asked that the bill be modified to channel funds through the OE instead.[103]

The ICC also stressed the need for support from other legislators, particularly in the House. "The more identical bills that are introduced in the House from different states, the better."[104] In April 1959, ICC leaders met with Roy Millenson, Javits' administrative assistant, who urged them to help mobilize grassroots support for the bill. According to Millenson, Javits did not want the bill to go into hearings until "it has sufficient support to assure its being considered favorably. To have it considered unfavorably would be a serious matter."[105] Guggenheimer mobilized the ICC network to launch a nationwide letter-writing campaign to key members of Congress (whose names had been supplied to her by WB director Alice Leopold).[106] "This is our first all out effort to demonstrate that there is national interest in day care," Guggenheimer told her colleagues.[107] The ICC was poised for action, and the public-private partnership allowed the group to serve its own interests and those of the OE and a key legislator simultaneously.[108]

CONSOLIDATING THE INTER-CITY COUNCIL

Working with Javits on the first child care bill gave the ICC a sense of its own potential and helped to focus its energies; by the time the second bill was introduced, the organization had already moved to solidify its position and streamline its operations. This process began in the fall of 1958, when ICC leaders decided to call a conference of the heads of federal agencies and private organizations concerned with day care. The purpose was twofold: to determine what was being done in different quarters to promote day care and what direction future work should take; and to consider how to shape the ICC so that it could be most effective in that work. The organization stressed that it wanted "'policy-makers' to attend"; Laura Dale of the WB told her chief, Alice Leopold, that she would be "specifically invited."[109]

The conference provided the ICC's leaders with a reading of the salience of day care as an issue, and of its own organizational strength. The results, though sobering, served to galvanize the group. Neither Leopold nor Katharine Oettinger, her counterpart at the CB, attended the conference, which was held on January 8, 1959, but Dale and Clare Golden were there. They were, however, the sole representatives of federal agencies. The discussion was dominated by officials from children's and family agencies, including the CWLA, the Family Service Association, and the National Social Welfare Assembly (NSWA). Two educational organizations, the Association for Childhood Education International, and the National Association for Nursery Education, also made themselves heard.

Much to the disappointment of the ICC, the discussion indicated that the issue of child care was not high on the agenda of any of these organizations. The remarks of Robert Bondy of the NSWA suggested one possible explanation. While paying lip service to the importance of day care, he contended that because its principal advocates were not the parents who used the services but those who were solicitous of "the welfare of the children and . . . the welfare of the mothers," the issue had little "emotional steam." Thus it would not help fill the NSWA's coffers. "People give money where there is strong emotional appeal," he said.[110] In the field of voluntary social agencies, such considerations at least partially dictated the agenda. Bondy's comments, though perhaps somewhat cynical in their portrayal of the nature of support for charity, revealed something about public perceptions of child care. Because it encouraged maternal employment, child care was apparently viewed as a form of aid that *empowered* women, unlike counseling or other forms of assistance (even cash), which simply perpetuated their status as dependents or victims and, in turn, evoked an emotional response from contributors.

Asked by Guggenheimer where her group should locate itself in the field of voluntary and advocacy organizations, Bondy and other participants, including Joseph Reid of the CWLA, advised her that they might be more effective if they became affiliated with the CWLA. When pressed, however, Reid conceded that "day care is not more important than half a dozen other projects to the League. It would not receive priority over and above other areas."[111] As the meeting continued, it became increasingly apparent, at least to members of the ICC, that its fledgling group should not seek affiliation or absorption by any of these organizations; on the contrary, the cause of day care would best be served by an independent national entity. Thus ICC leaders ultimately resolved that their organization should not only continue to exist but should "expand its activities to include national participation."[112] Although the meeting did not produce the level of enthusiasm and support from colleagues that the ICC might have wished, it did serve to sharpen the organization's sense of its own purpose and raison d'être.

It is not clear whether Guggenheimer would have agreed to dissolve the ICC, had that been the sense of the meeting. She certainly would not have done so without a firm commitment from at least one of the other associations to give priority to the day care issue—and none was forthcoming. So although Guggenheimer may have taken a risk by putting her own organization on the line, she—and, more important, day care—would have won either way.

The goal of the ICC, as it became clear to its members, should not be to involve itself in running specific programs but rather to act as "a prod to other agencies," both national and local, urging them to focus on child care and take appropriate actions.[113] The organization hoped to develop and disseminate "a national view-point" to help generate discussions about child care among parents, labor, management, and professional disciplines. Members wanted to clarify the debate over whether women should be in the home or have a right to work. "Parents should have a choice,—which they do not have at present,—to work or not to work," the organization asserted.[114] By this it appeared that they were not reiterating Guggenheimer's earlier position, much influenced by the CWLA, that child care should not be used to compel low-income mothers to work as an alternative to welfare, but rather asserting the opposite—universal—principle that no mother should be *prevented* from working by a lack of day care.[115]

Moreover, the ICC wanted child care to receive more prominence as a necessary form of social policy. "None of the Federal departments or the national organizations concerned with children has been able to place sufficient emphasis on day care services," it pointed out, "nor is day care generally considered essential in the network of community services for children."[116] The ICC frequently referred to itself as the first national organization devoted wholly to the child care issue. Apparently both it and the CWLA suffered from institutional amnesia, but no one bothered to correct them by reciting the history of the National Federation of Day Nurseries or its successor, the National Association of Day Nurseries (which the CWLA had absorbed in 1942).

By mid-1959, the ICC was operating on a number of fronts simultaneously. During one two-day period in Washington, D.C., in late April, the ICC Executive Committee held extended meetings and also met with several key government officials. An appointment with CB Chief Oettinger went especially well. Oettinger asked whether the ICC planned to become a national organization, and Guggenheimer (after the decisive January meeting with other major welfare organizations) was able to assure her on that score. Both Oettinger and the ICC agreed that day care was "not totally a welfare program for deprived families"; day care combined a number of services and offered more than a nursery school could.[117] In private, Oettinger seemed to be confirming the ICC's commitment to the principle of universal, not income-based, provisions, but her public position was somewhat more circumscribed.

Oettinger and the ICC also consulted on strategies to ensure the place of day care on the White House Conference agenda. Oettinger urged the ICC to have materials sent to the WHC executive committee and also suggested that holding a day care conference in advance of the WHC would help focus attention on the issue and generate information to be fed into the WHC.[118] In particular, Oettinger felt that more data was needed "on the reasons *why* women go to work."[119] Summarizing the sense of the meeting, Marion Butler, an ICC member who headed the Associated Day Care Services of Boston, noted, "Most legislators assume that women belong at home. Day care as a necessity needs to be highlighted." The WHC could perform this function.[120]

The ICC's whirlwind tour of Washington (which Acting Secretary Cornelia Goldsmith described somewhat modestly as "two busy, memorable days") allowed the group to try out its self-appointed role as a "prod" to other important organizations and agencies. This role not only advanced the ICC's own purposes but allowed government officials to maintain a relatively neutral position on controversial issues while acknowledging pressure from the outside. A few days after the ICC left town, the CB and the WB responded by reminding the public that they were in the midst of conducting a joint survey "to measure the interest and activity of national voluntary and public organizations in stimulating community development of day care services" (this referred to *Child Care Arrangements of Full-Time Working Mothers*).

Although the announcement signaled renewed federal interest in child care, Oettinger and Leopold took care to delimit their position. They did not, for example, want to imply that they unconditionally endorsed maternal employment. Thus, while noting that the survey was being undertaken out of concern for the needs of "children whose mothers work," they assured the public that mothers with small children were "much less likely to be employed."[121] By the same token, they did not want to give the appearance that federal support for day care was forthcoming; hence the emphasis on what *voluntary* groups were doing in local communities. But this left open the possibility that the survey would show that local efforts were insufficient to meet growing needs.

Meanwhile, both the ICC and the WB began to carry forward plans for a national day care conference. It would be "inter-governmental," and Guggenheimer stressed the urgency of holding it by early fall 1959, "well in advance of the 1960 Spring White House Conference."[122] In July 1959 the WB announced that the conference would be scheduled to coincide with the publication of the joint CB-WB bulletin, which would present information concerning existing day care services and projected needs.[123]

SHAPING THE WHITE HOUSE CONFERENCE

At the same time, the now-incorporated ICC was making strenuous efforts to ensure that day care appeared on the agenda for the "Golden Anniversary" White House Conference on Children and Youth, scheduled to begin in late March 1960.[124] In attempting to use this major event as a vehicle for promoting the cause of day care, the ICC and other advocates were forced to swim against the tide of conservative opinion regarding maternal employment. President Dwight D. Eisenhower had already set the tone at the first meeting of the conference's national planning committee in Washington on December 16, 1958:

> Today there are 22 million working women. Of that 22 million, 7 and a half million are working mothers, and unquestionably a great number of [them] are working because they have to keep the wolf from the door. They work because they have to work. But if there is only a tiny percentage doing this because they prefer a career to an active career of real motherhood and care for the little child, I should think they would have to consider what is the price they are paying in terms of the opportunity

that child has been denied. Certainly no one can do quite as much in molding the child's habit of thinking and implanting certain standards as can the mother.[125]

From Eisenhower's perspective, only financial necessity justified maternal employment; this view was consistent with the Republican position on the child care tax deduction. The ICC, the WB, and the CB were, however, attempting to gain broader acceptance for maternal employment and, as a corollary, to expand the rationale for public child care provision. Their move, though extremely cautious, still represented a departure from the administration's position.

To their dismay, day care advocates quickly discovered that Eisenhower's views extended down through the ranks of state-level conference planners, who consisted primarily of civic leaders, state officials, and professionals in various child-related fields. When state committees were asked to prioritize their concerns, day care was low on their lists, behind services for handicapped children, prevention of juvenile delinquency, expanded employment opportunities and vocational counseling for adolescents, and education. Day care was seldom singled out for attention but was instead usually included in a group of programs to be extended or improved, along with homemaking, counseling services, and adoption and foster care procedures.[126] Linking day care with welfare services in this way dimmed prospects for its normalization.

Conference officials reinforced this linkage in the topic guide it distributed in February 1959 to state committees, national organizations, and others involved in preparing for the WHC. Maternal employment and day care were presented as a problematic: panels were to consider the factors determining maternal employment, weigh the advantages and disadvantages for both mothers and children, and compare the attitudes and problems of working mothers with those receiving public assistance. Absent from the proposed agenda were questions pertaining to the availability and quality of day care provisions or their relation to women's right to work.[127]

The ICC was determined to redirect the discourse of the conference. During their highly productive trip to Washington in April 1959, Guggenheimer and several other members of the group met with Ephraim Gomberg, director of the WHC, presenting him with a detailed set of program recommendations.[128] Prominent on the list were the quality and availability of day care, items which had been omitted from the topic guide. The ICC leaders told Gomberg they hoped that at least one conference session would be devoted to the topic "Day Care Services for Young Children, A Front Line of Defense in Today's Community," and that it would describe services being provided to children whose mothers were working, ill, or absent from home, whose living conditions were poor, or who had "particular problems, or needs" that could "best be solved by care away from home during the day." The session should also address the issue of federal, state, and local responsibility.[129]

According to members of the ICC who were present at the meeting, Gomberg and his associates "reacted favorably" to the ICC's suggestions; Gomberg "felt that [the] report had 'wonderful program ideas.'" Guggenheimer pushed her advantage, seeking assurance that the ICC would be included in the group of recognized national agencies to be invited to the conference (the number of such organizations would be limited to 1,700). Gomberg was noncommittal on this point, referring Guggenheimer to the appropriate committee, but he did ask the ICC to send in suggestions for panelists and speakers. When other members of the ICC emphasized the value of day care as a preventive measure, one of Gomberg's associates "agreed that concern for young children 'is a crying need.'" Gomberg conceded that "the breadth of interest in Day Care was impressive" and, an associate added, "quite evident."[130]

After this meeting, the ICC moved quickly. Guggenheimer sent the WB a memo proposing that day care materials "be included in all sessions [of the conference] where the discussion deals with programs for children living in their own homes, or with the total spectrum of health, education, and welfare services for children." She provided a detailed outline of specific topics to be covered and offered to set up a resource center with information and material. "It is our urgent hope," the memo stated, "that there will be an opportunity to present day care in the proper place as an essential service for children. . . . Our failure to recognize the importance of an adequate national program constitutes a very large problem. This is particularly true when we consider that in so many other countries the problem has been recognized and dealt with. At a time when the eyes of the nation will be focused on our children, we feel that it is vital to focus attention on their care during the day." One of the ICC's concerns was the persistent marginality of child care, not only within American society as a whole but even within the field of child welfare. Thus the organization urged conference organizers to invite "as many people as possible" from the day care field, in order to increase its visibility and respectability.[131]

In August the ICC sent a report to the Council of National Organizations on Children and Youth, the gatekeeper for the 1,700 conference invitations allotted to nongovernmental groups.[132] Finessing its status as a newcomer, the report claimed that the ICC's expertise was based "not from experience as an organization, but from the combined experience of those who felt the need to establish it."[133] The leaders of the ICC felt confident that their application would be accepted, because the council was chaired by Robert Bondy of the National Social Welfare Assembly.

To stress the importance of having a day care organization represented at the conference, the ICC dramatized the issue: "Without adequate daytime care during the most crucial formative years, many children today are being exposed to grave physical dangers, to forces detrimental to their emotional, intellectual and moral development, and even to the possibility of separation from their families."[134] Moreover, day care would be needed to cope with the needs of families in the coming decade. As a result of changing social and economic conditions, parents were confused about their own responsibilities, and family ties were becoming attenuated, leading to "feelings of personal and social insecurity" among children. The ICC pointed out, "Although the importance of the mother's role in the emotional development of her child is generally accepted as a fact, more and more mothers of young children are seeking employment."[135]

Emphasizing that the situation had reached crisis proportions, the ICC painted a bleak picture of the consequences of having no day care. Citing the CB's statistics on the numbers of working women with children of preschool and school age, the ICC noted that "children in every stratum of society [were] being adversely affected."[136] This was as close as they were willing to come to articulating a universalist stance; the meetings with federal officials seem to have tempered their earlier boldness on this point.

The WB also wanted the White House Conference to address the issue of day care but sought to tread carefully. The trick was to find a way to support child care without giving quarter to opponents of maternal employment. At a meeting in early March 1960, staff members discussed the kinds of data they wanted to assemble for the WHC. When one statistician asked if she should compile "working expectancy tables" (presumably, data on the likelihood that nonworking women would take up employment at some point), the others rushed to warn her that "this subject was taboo since it was not pertinent to day care services. The mothers staying at home were naturally not concerned with day care for their children." Alice Morrison, chief of the WB's Division of Labor Law and Civil and Political Status, thought that "even getting into the subject at all was rather dangerous." Whereas WB officials did not feel free to issue an unqualified call for government-supported child care, they could at least downplay the persistence of stay-at-home mothers, whose numbers might have undercut rationales for increasing services. It was more important to stress the growing number of children who needed day care, "rather than the fact that the women had a pattern of staying at home."[137] Though cautious, they were still evidently committed to child care for wage-earning mothers.

PLANNING THE NATIONAL DAY CARE CONFERENCE

While the ICC was jockeying for position at the White House Conference, the CB and the WB moved ahead with plans to hold a separate event devoted entirely to day care: the National Conference on the Day Care of Children. In November 1959 the two agencies convened an ad hoc advisory committee, which decided to schedule the day care conference in November 1960, after the WHC (instead of before, as proposed earlier), so as to implement and carry forward any recommendations on child care that might emerge from the WHC. When Dale and Golden asked ICC members for suggestions of "ideas, dreams, or problem areas" to be considered at the day care conference, Cornelia Goldsmith replied, "Day Care is no longer to be considered an emergency problem. It is here to stay and must be so recognized and dealt with."[138] In contrast to the views expressed by the Eisenhower administration and reflected in many of the WHC materials, Goldsmith's remarks signaled that the ICC was intent on using the day care conference to bring child care into the American mainstream.

Most participants at the planning meeting concurred. The ICC was joined by Christine Heinig, who had been involved in running the WPA nursery schools and was now affiliated with the American Association of University Women; Esther Peterson of the AFL-CIO; and representatives of the National Association for Nursery Education and several women's organizations, including the General Federal of Women's Clubs, United Church Women, and the Parent-Teacher Association. The National Conference of Catholic Women took a more qualified position; their "primary aim" was to remove "the need for day care through such measures as an adequate wage for the father so that the mother will not have to work."[139] Peterson did not agree; she condoned day care, although she did voice concern about the quality of services. Moreover, she stressed, day care "should be available without regard to the motives of the consumer. Persons in the lower income brackets should not be subjected to any more scrutiny . . . than those with higher incomes."[140]

Peterson's remarks were somewhat surprising, for they indicated that unions—at least those represented by the AFL-CIO—were coming to accept the presence of women, including mothers, in the workplace.[141] In place of their traditional insistence on the family wage (to which the Catholic women still clung), they seemed to be acknowledging mothers' growing contribution to household incomes. Peterson also rejected efforts to trivialize working mothers as "materialistic" or to stigmatize child care by linking it with welfare.[142] If maternal employment was becoming a normal part of American life, then so too must child care.

The theme of the "consumer" cropped up again at another planning meeting a few months later. Alice Morrison of the WB mentioned the importance of hearing from "day care consumers." Though most would be unable to attend owing to the pressure of their jobs and lack of finances, she suggested that community organizations or centers might sponsor a few mothers so they could participate.[143] In the absence of groups like the UPA, however, this would prove difficult to arrange. The gap between elite day care advocates and consumers was clearly a problem.

At subsequent meetings the debate over how to frame day care continued. Planners decided to emphasize "the significance of day care in a Democratic Society."[144] As this was later defined (in terms closely echoing an earlier ICC pronouncement), "mothers should have a choice of working or not working and this is not true at the present time."[145] In other words, without available child care, mothers could not exercise their *right* to work. In an effort to universalize the image of maternal employment, conference materials were to state that families' social needs had changed, partly because of the economy and increased employment of mothers, but also in response to "broad cultural changes affecting women and their families."[146]

Yet planners also felt that, given the complicated gender politics of the period, they must proceed with caution. They agreed that they "should avoid any urge to [encourage] the mushrooming of day care programs and that the use of the words 'to promote' might well be misunderstood."[147] Day care consultant Winifred Moore, a former official of both the CWLA and the CB who was now with the ICC, backpedaled even further. Departing from the ICC's more progressive position, she advised planners not to dwell on the link between day care and maternal employment but to stress instead the idea of "day care as a service which strengthens family life," a form of child welfare "to children living in their own homes" that obviated the need to break up families.[148] In other words, the conference should present day care as a substitute for Aid to Dependent Children.

Underlying the discussion were conflicting assessments of public opinion. The pessimistic view, expressed by Moore, was that Americans were unwilling to condone the use of day care unless it was cast as a form of child welfare, while the optimists, including other members of the ICC and many of the other voluntary organizations, believed that the country was gradually beginning to accept day care as part of a new vision of women's roles and rights. They acknowledged, however, that this shift did not really improve prospects for universal provisions. There seemed to be a shared understanding that when child care was linked to welfare, it had a stronger claim on public support.

Although some government officials may have privately favored the idea of providing child care to uphold women's right to work, they regarded this position as politically risky and in public took a modified pessimistic stance, stressing financial need as the primary motive for maternal employment and hedging on the question of how child care should be supported. In a pamphlet entitled "Who Are the Working Mothers?" prepared specifically for distribution around the time of the day care conference, the WB presented a carefully delimited description of working mothers. Using a question-and-answer format, the text pointed out that whereas more mothers were working than ever before, they were less likely to do so if they had husbands present in the home, were rearing small children, or enjoyed a high family income. Women with young children were more likely to go out to work if another female relative was available for child care. Discussion of women's reasons for seeking employment was reduced to demographic and economic factors, and the implication that maternal employment might be altering the gender division of labor was tempered by assurances that most women would rather rely on male breadwinners and, if they had to work, preferred to have their children cared for by female relatives (in a more "natural" or "homelike" setting) than by "strangers" in an institution such as a child care center.[149]

Government officials' constraints limited the potential scope of the conference in other ways. Although they generally favored the expansion of day care facilities, they sought to avoid enmeshing the federal government in any commitments by way of either financial aid or even administration. Moreover, they seemed to prefer that the *possibility* of federal aid not even be mentioned, so that they would not be put in the awkward position of having to deny requests for support that they appeared to encourage. Their repeated emphasis on the partnership between the voluntary sector and the government acknowledged the importance of groups like the ICC in creating momentum on the issue of day care, but it also served to relieve the federal government of some of the political onus. By the same token, government officials wanted the conference to prompt "community acceptance of responsibility" for day care."[150] Thus, although the occasion of a national day care conference sponsored by two federal agencies represented an important breakthrough for the day care movement and especially for the efforts of the still-young ICC, its agenda was tempered by the entrenched values as well as the political considerations of the planners, both within and outside of government. While asserting mothers' rights with the one hand, they seemed to be taking them away with the other. The CB and the WB allowed the committee's discussions to range freely but consistently followed their own line in official publications. Still, the two agencies had pledged to let conference debates take their course.[151]

UNEXPECTED GAINS AT THE WHITE HOUSE CONFERENCE

The White House Conference was held between March 27 and April 2, 1960, with the ICC, among other nongovernmental organizations, in attendance. Soon after it was over, the Inter-City Committee, now renamed the National Committee on the Day Care of Children (NCDCC), compiled a series of excerpts pertaining to child care from presentations and materials distributed at the conference.[152] These were to be used in preparing for the national conference on day care, now scheduled for the following November, and they were assembled in such a way that they provided a progressive gloss on the otherwise rather conservatively designed conference.

The excerpts emphasized the social and particularly the economic conditions that were pushing large numbers of women, including many mothers with small children, into the workforce. Out-of-wedlock births were increasing (there were more than two hundred thousand in 1957), and a growing proportion of ADC children came from families where the father was "'absent'—separated, estranged, divorced, or never married to the mother." Migrant workers continued to suffer from poor working conditions and deep insecurity, and in general mobility was high—a quarter of American children moved and changed schools in 1958. There was, moreover, widespread financial insecurity. In 1957, 13 million children were living in families with incomes below $3,000, 8 million in families earning less than $2,000 (the median family income for that year was $4,971); nearly half the 2 million children receiving ADC in 1958 received less than the minimum cost-of-living allowance, $38 per month. The absence of male breadwinners and low family incomes were placing increasing responsibility for family support on mothers. Nearly one-third of the labor force in 1958 was female (compared with 16 percent in 1890), and half of married women were employed (14 percent in 1890). Yet the incomes of female-headed families were only slightly more than half of those of families headed by men.[153]

At the same time, the NCDCC's selections showed, child care provisions were scarce. Many communities had none; others had only private facilities whose fees put them out of the range of low-income families. Among their proposals for action, some of the state committees recommended expanding day care services as a means of keeping families together; however, they passed the burden on to communities: "If the mother works, the States recommend that the community as well as the family should exercise responsibility for minimizing the possible detrimental effects on the children. [This would occur] through: Expansion of nursery school and day-care centers. Foster family day care for children under three." After-school programs, including planned recreation, were specifically recommended as "delinquency-prevention measures."[154]

The WHC participants debated the best way to respond to the situation. According to one CWLA representative, "Opinions differ as to whether pressure should be brought to increase the number of facilities or to try in some way to reverse the trend of mothers working, or both. . . . Some seem to fear that [making] more resources available for the care of children will encourage more mothers to work. The community has not as yet fully decided whether it is within the realm of its responsibility to make care available to the children of all working mothers."[155] There was, however, a growing consensus that the trend toward maternal employment was irreversible and that support for day care had to come from the government—at the federal level as well as the state and municipal levels. The National Association for Nursery Education called for an allocation of federal funds to the states, while the CWLA supported a combination of tax funds and voluntary contributions. Many organizations also endorsed the use of government funds to balance the uneven distribution of facilities throughout American society and address the needs of migrant women. The NCDCC cautioned that day care centers "must not be limited to the college campus, working mothers, or private facilities."[156]

The resolutions emerging from the WHC revealed that some progress had been made on the day care issue. One stated that because mobility due to economic conditions had become common among Americans, they needed to be "protected from its harmful effects by the right constellation of services at the right time"; all people had a right to work, and "every child [had the right] to be wanted wherever he is."[157] Although the need for day care provision was only implied in this resolution, it was made explicit in the category of child care and protective services for children and youth and was also singled out for specific mention with regard to working mothers. All of these measures, conferees believed, deserved support from federal, state, and local governments.[158]

Although the resolutions seemed to be condoning day care as both a social welfare measure *and* a program for "normal" families with working mothers, they also called for counseling "to help parents decide wisely whether [the mother's] employment will contribute more to family welfare than her presence in the home."[159] At the same time, they seemed to accept the *fact* of working mothers, urging industries to accommodate them by working with labor organizations and professional planning groups to tailor hours and work assignments to their needs and even establishing maternity leave.[160]

The recurrent issue of child care for the "under-threes" once again came up for debate. NANE took a flexible stance, advocating "the provision of group day care services for those children *of any age* for whom such a program is indicated."[161] But most conferees were reluctant to condone day care for the youngest group of children, resolving that "to maintain the important relationship of infant and mother, children under 3 [are to] remain in their own homes unless there are pressing social or economic reasons for care away from home."[162] Reservations about placing children under three in child care expressed the elitism and unreality that persisted among many children's advocates as well as in the CB. As day care veteran Ethel Beer had pointed out several years earlier, "Common sense tells us that the mother who must work cannot wait until her children are two or three years old."[163] But many within the child care field, even those who used financial rationales, refused to acknowledge the pressing needs of certain groups of mothers. Nevertheless, the WHC resolutions did indicate some movement away from this position. In prescribing appropriate care for children of various ages, they specified that the "under-threes" should receive either homemaker care or family day care. Implicitly, then, conferees seemed to be accepting the use of limited nonmaternal care for toddlers, even outside the home, as long as it was not in formal groups.

The ICC had not gone into the White House Conference with a set of specific policy positions; rather, its primary purpose was to carve out an organizational niche for itself by "coordinating the efforts of the many individuals and groups now working under so many auspices."[164] Through careful planning and strategizing, both on its own and in cooperation with the CB and the WB, it managed to reach this goal. One sign of the ICC's growing influence was the prominence of day care in both the agenda and the final resolutions of an omnibus conference on children and youth. Although the child care resolutions were relatively conservative, the issue received more space and attention than its placement on the initial list of proposed topics might have predicted. Moreover, the discussions tended to treat child care less as an anomaly than as an established element of American social provision.

DAY CARE'S HOUR

The National Conference on the Day Care of Children, held in Washington eight months later, had only a fraction of the attendance of the WHC—just four hundred people were invited. But its purpose was different, and it did allow for a fuller exploration of the single issue of day care, in all its multifarious dimensions.

It was evident from the outset that at least one question had already been resolved: the trend toward maternal employment was irreversible. Sketching the current demographic and economic picture, the first keynote speaker, Ewan Clague, commissioner of labor statistics for the U.S. Department of Labor, predicted that by 1970, not only would "fully half of all women in the population, between the ages of 35 and 55 . . . be in the labor force," but more mothers would be working than ever before.[165]

Clague's approach to working mothers was perhaps more blunt than the conference planners would have liked; he did not bother to qualify his description with the usual references to women's financial needs, much less their preferences or psychological motivation. Rather, he stressed the supply and demand for labor. Because of low birth rates during the Depression, the number of male workers between the ages of twenty-five and forty-four would level off or even decrease over the next ten years. At the same time, positions for women would open up in expanding white-collar occupations and service industries, and there would be more part-time jobs. If his projections were correct, Clague reasoned, "the day care problem can be much more serious than it is today."[166]

In contrast to Clague's matter-of-fact style, Elinor Guggenheimer, another keynote speaker, felt obliged to defend the rise of maternal employment and rationalize the need for more child care. At what was undoubtedly the pinnacle of her career in child care advocacy until that point, she used the occasion to make a reflective speech entitled "Why Day Care?"[167] As she addressed numerous objections to day care, her speech traversed the various discursive terrains on which maternal employment and child care had been examined since the late 1940s. In subtle ways, she "pushed the envelope," revealing how both she and the day care movement had progressed since the end of the war. But some of her arguments also reinforced the cultural and political biases that continued to hobble the movement, and the result was a rather contradictory message.

Beginning with first principles, Guggenheimer linked child care to citizenship. "As citizens of a free country," she reasoned, "we have the right and obligation to insure that health, welfare and education services are available for all who need or are entitled to them. . . . Therefore, quite simply the test of whether day care should be a community concern is related to whether it is a truly needed service. If it is, the question then is not whether, but how to supply it and how to insure its quality."[168] Although Guggenheimer fell far short of establishing child care as a universal right, she did move in the direction of establishing it as an entitlement, at least for a limited sector of the populace. But while the reference to a right to service invoked a social democratic concept of social citizenship, the insistence that rights be grounded in *needs* again immersed Guggenheimer in the charity-based view of social provision that had for so long retarded development of the American welfare state.

Moreover, Guggenheimer was still obliged to define need, and in so doing, she reverted to the twin rationales of poverty and pathology. Drawing on the 1959 study conducted by the CB and the Census Bureau, she cited statistics on children with working mothers who cared for themselves or were cared for by other children, and mentioned the high proportion who came from "broken homes"—almost 50 percent of those in New York City's public day care centers.[169] Other youngsters required outside care because the mother or another family member was ill, either mentally or physically, or because they lived in dangerous neighborhoods or were having "adjustment problems."

Finally, there were cases in which day care for children served as therapy for an adult:

> It is very unpopular to raise the possibility that all mothers are not warm and loving and yet we are well aware that some of our young parents themselves are the products of unloved childhoods—that having never had warm and affectionate parents themselves, they need a great deal of help in learning how to give to their children what they have never themselves received. In some instances it may be better for the mother to work and the child to relate to a warm and loving adult in a day care center.

Such an arrangement keeps the home from breaking up entirely and gives us an opportunity to work with the mother so that her own attitude may be changed.[170]

While seeking to avoid blaming women directly if they turned out to be inadequate mothers (they themselves were "unloved"), Guggenheimer nevertheless wanted to challenge the notion that "mother care" was a universal blessing. This was a roundabout way of signaling approbation for working mothers, and at the same time it provided an opening (as Eleanor Maccoby had done previously) for those who might want to engage in a bit of social engineering by remanding "unfit" mothers to work and placing their children in care.

In depicting a broad range of situations in which families might seek services outside the home, Guggenheimer did not completely decouple day care and maternal employment, but she succeeded in putting some distance between them. She did not deny that maternal employment was a factor in generating the need for child care but presented it as only one among several. At no point, however, did she claim that all mothers had a right to work and therefore a right to publicly provided child care.

Hewing to a moderate position, Guggenheimer appeared to be anticipating the mainstream tenor of the conference. Many of the participants still disapproved of mothers of young children entering the labor force, no matter what the circumstances. For example, when HEW Secretary Arthur Flemming, speaking at the final luncheon, referred to the growing demand for labor in the American economy, members of the audience expressed fear "that an inference might be drawn [from his remarks] that mothers of young children should be encouraged to work."[171] "By and large," according to observers from the Day Care Council of New York, conference participants believed that there was no justification for pressuring women to work. "On the contrary, whenever it is possible to avoid having children in a day care program for long hours, social agencies and departments of welfare should make every effort to do so."[172] Katherine Oettinger of the CB tried to find common ground: "All of us may have some ambivalence about whether mothers should work, [but] none of us can have any ambivalence about the need for the care of their children."[173]

Such remarks on the part of day care's supposed advocates suggested that many in the field had not moved much beyond the Victorian rhetoric of the National Federation of Day Nurseries, and this made it difficult for leaders to rationalize increasing public support for child care.[174] Guggenheimer, however, chose not to challenge them head on. Instead she explained the problems inherent in "apologizing" for child care: "Too often in discussing day care, we feel impelled to explain it as a service that should be used only when all else fails. This is a poor way to sell a product. Comparing day care for a child with care in his own home is confusing and makes it appear that there is a choice."[175]

Guggenheimer also pointed to the hypocrisy of a society that virtually "invited women to leave the home" by highlighting the material and social rewards of pursuing a career, on the one hand, and implicitly devalued motherhood, on the other. "We have an astonishing ambivalence about the role of modern women," she asserted. The same culture that urged women to attend college, pursue careers, and enjoy the benefits of consumerism also constructed a program of Aid to Dependent Children that offered "subsistence at the lowest level, no prestige, no hope for advancement." Many community leaders paid lip service to the value and virtues of motherhood but offered little in the way of tangible support that might induce mothers to stay at home. At the same time, they refused to endorse day care or support paying for quality care, on the premise that it would prompt more women to go out to work. "The fact is that mothers work whether good care is available or not. It is the child that suffers when the care is poor."[176]

In addition to the ideological entanglements of child care, Guggenheimer argued, its embeddedness in the nexus of welfare and charity also impeded its growth. Inadequate financing compelled some centers to set fees so high that few families could afford them; this led to underutilization, which, in turn, convinced Community Chest or other funding agencies that services were not needed. Funding agencies, Guggenheimer suggested, seemed to be looking for reasons not to support child care, instead of simply assuming that the need was there and trying to find the best ways to meet it.

By the same token, she conceded (taking her cue from Robert Bondy) that the relatively mundane nature of day care made it less attractive as a magnet for funding, whether through charitable donations or government appropriations, than services that appeared to address critical situations: "If a child is found half starved and abandoned, the community must provide care . . . but if he is being cared for by a neighbor who hasn't time to give him, who leaves him unsupervised during a good part of the day, who perhaps is even moderately cruel—his plight will go unnoticed. After all, if he's being fed and not getting into real trouble, it doesn't seem urgent to spend $15 a week of community funds that are so desperately needed in crisis programs."[177] Day care advocates must inform the public that their programs are designed to prevent crises from occurring in the first place.

One of the documents prepared for the conference was a report on the March 1959 Women's Bureau–Children's Bureau survey of the resources for day care currently being offered by national organizations. The report concluded, "To voluntary organizations, especially women's and civic groups, belongs much of the credit for the establishment of on-going social and welfare groups which contribute so much to the well-being of our country. . . . The . . . survey . . . supplies new evidence that provision of good day care facilities for children is a matter of concern to such organizations in all sections of the country."[178] The leaders of these organizations were no doubt gratified by the federal agencies' recognition of their efforts, but this in itself did not necessarily aid the expansion of child care. Many leaders, including Guggenheimer, believed that private and voluntary agencies had come to the end of their rope and could extend themselves no further in order to meet the growing need for services. It was now up to the federal government.

Yet the WB and the CB refused to take the lead in seeking federal assistance. Their report simply stated that the WB "shares the interest of women's organizations and other voluntary groups in the development of adequate day-care facilities and looks forward to continued cooperation with them at the national, State, and community levels."[179] But private funds, Guggenheimer insisted, would "never be able to meet the current national need." She told conferees, "We [of the NCDCC] believe that parents' fees, based on a realistic sliding scale, [community] chest or private donations and *government support* from local, state and federal sources must *together* create the financial structure necessary to support good services."[180] With this subtle rephrasing, Guggenheimer implicitly challenged the CB and the WB to move beyond their stated position and help fight for public funding.

MORE THAN A CENTURY OF DAY CARE ADVOCACY

With the staging of a national conference co-sponsored by the federal government and a young but vital advocacy organization, the issue of child care had gained new prominence. But policy itself seemed to have reached an impasse. Although the need for services clearly outstripped the capacity of the voluntary sector, the CB and the WB (perhaps not by their own choice) continued to insist that that was where the solution to the child care crisis lay. In fact, the success of the day care movement itself may have inadvertently shored up this position. Building a countrywide network, honing sophisticated techniques for fact-gathering and lobbying, gaining the ear of influential members of Congress, secretaries, and other government officials, and then organizing a conference—these were, to be sure, impressive achievements for an organization that was less than a decade old. But the growing prominence of the NCDCC may have falsely given the impression that such a movement could also mobilize the voluntary sector to provide child care on a mass scale. Political visibility was necessary but not sufficient to fund and carry out a national child care policy. Nor could it substitute for concrete action on the part of government, including financial support and practical administration.

Guggenheimer herself seemed to be at a loss about how to proceed. Although it was she who had been largely responsible for building a national movement, she seemed incapable of articulating a political vision or a viable strategy that could move child care to the next phase. Casting about for direction, she dramatically recounted how Mrs. Cornelius Du Bois founded the first (or so Guggenheimer thought) "crèche or day care center in this country" in 1854.[181] When this young New York City socialite learned that many impoverished mothers were forced to leave their children alone at home while they went out to work, she decided to do something about it. According to Guggenheimer, "In what has become the most effective method of getting things done, she proceeded to go home and nag her husband and her friends—and her friends' husbands until they responded from sheer exhaustion. . . ." and the crèche was established.[182]

Guggenheimer told this anecdote not merely to exploit its pathos but to demonstrate that "fanaticism" could eventually achieve results. She might have drawn similar anecdotes from her own reform career, for she was a modern exemplar of the kind of politics Mary Du Bois had practiced. In New York City, such politics had met with substantial success, but they seemed less well suited for making gains at the federal level. Perhaps sensing that sentimental imagery was no longer appropriate, Guggenheimer somewhat lamely proposed that the movement turn to advertising to promote its cause. As she herself conceded, however, selling day care was not like selling "Whizzo." Slogans and anecdotes alone were not strong enough to sway the tide of public opinion or mobilize the political forces necessary to create national, government-based support for the kind of child care system that was so desperately needed. Although the movement had succeeded in putting child care on the nation's political agenda, the issue now seemed to be stranded there.

At the height of its powers, the movement appeared to have already fallen behind the times. As part of her speech, Guggenheimer read from a letter she had received from President-Elect John F. Kennedy:

We must have provision for day care centers for children whose mothers are unavailable during the day. Without adequate day time care during their most formative years the children of the nation risk permanent damage to their emotional and moral character. . . . I believe we must take further steps to encourage day care programs that will protect our children and provide them with a basis for a full life in later years. The suggestion of a program of research, financing, and development to serve the children of working mothers and of parents who for one reason or another cannot provide adequate care during the day deserves our full support.[183]

Full of the promise so characteristic of his presidency, Kennedy's letter seemed to invite the child care movement to take an active part in his administration and at the same time to envision child care more broadly as a social provision for all Americans. But it was not clear whether the NCDCC and other organizations and agencies, including the CB and the WB, would be capable of articulating a vision that would take them beyond the ideology that had hobbled child care so greatly in the past, or of mobilizing the kind of political support required to carry legislation through Congress. Nor, despite Kennedy's optimism, was it apparent that the American polity was truly receptive to a broader vision of public policy toward wage-earning mothers.

Chapter 7 A Divided
Constituency

Between 1960 and 1990, American society underwent a major transformation. As economist Ewan Clague predicted in 1960, the proportion of mothers with children under the age of six in the paid labor force rose dramatically, from 30 percent in 1960 to nearly 60 percent in 1991.[1] The number of child care "slots" also grew, but the total supply of child care did not keep pace with the rapid growth in maternal employment. In 1990, only 38 percent of children under five with wage-earning mothers attended child care centers, while another 20 percent went to family day care homes and 33 percent were cared for by relatives or unrelated caregivers at home.[2] Regulation of both child care centers and family day care homes was erratic, and accepted standards, such as maintaining a high ratio of caregivers to children, were often ignored. The best child care—indeed, much child care—was very costly.

Child care provisions, such as they were, became divided into distinct sectors according to mode of organization, sponsorship, and clientele. Services might be "custodial" or "developmental" in emphasis. They might be offered by child care centers, family home providers, or either relatives or nonrelatives within the home. They might take the form of proprietary or for-profit, voluntary, church-based, employer-supported, or government-supported programs. Providers might be credentialed professionals; teachers, aides or nannies with some training; or individuals whose main qualification was personal experience and "love of children."

These numerous differences among types and providers of child care were, in turn, reflected among their clienteles; certain groups of parents became identified with specific provisions. For example, poor and low-income mothers were associated with publicly supported care, while middle-class parents often chose developmental child care centers, and many upper-class parents exercised a preference for in-home caregivers.[3] As a result of these many internal divisions, no coherent or unified constituency emerged to call for a universal system of public care offering a full range of high-quality, affordable resources to all families desiring services. In the absence of such a constituency, the potential political power of any child care lobby was fragmented and weak.

One of the major lines of cleavage in the child care constituency was already becoming apparent during the 1950s (if not before), namely, that of class and, by extension, race. The principal form of federal support for child care, the 1954 income tax deduction, targeted low-income families and was cast as a poverty prevention measure. This pattern continued during the 1960s with passage of federal anti-poverty measures that included funds for child care. Policy formulations increasingly spoke of allowing, encouraging, or, eventually, mandating low-income mothers to work so as to prevent or reduce dependency on public assistance, with public child care provision being used as a lever to achieve these goals.

These anti-poverty measures did little to address the child care needs of the nonpoor mothers who were also entering the paid labor force in growing numbers from the 1960s on, but attempts to legislate universal federal child care provisions were repeatedly blocked. As federal child care assistance became inextricably associated with poverty and its remediation, nonpoor parents chose or were compelled to turn to private alternatives. It was at this point that the various other types of child care—employer-sponsored, voluntary, for-profit, family-based, and private in-home services—began to proliferate. From the mid-1970s through the mid-1980s, a broadening of tax relief to individual parents through the child care credit, along with failed attempts to enforce federal child care regulations, fostered the growth of these alternatives but at the same time widened the gap between public and private provisions and their constituencies.

As background to this complicated yet familiar American pattern of public-private policy making, we must understand the political forces (and absences) at play. One of the most important was the New Right, whose remarkable growth, beginning in the early 1970s, derived in part from its opposition to universal child care. The women's liberation movement, confronting the New Right on this as well as many other issues, endorsed universal child care but lacked the Right's political strength and organization. Out of a principled aversion to "mainstream" and "establishment" politics, feminists tended to eschew conventional politicking in favor of local action and grassroots, community-controlled (and community-funded) provisions. They were, as a result, no match for the highly mobilized and politically sophisticated lobbying machinery of their conservative opponents. Congressional liberals, while positioned to be more effective, were increasingly caught up in the discourse of welfare reform. They thus saw child care primarily as a means of effecting the shift from welfare to "workfare" and, with only momentary exceptions, refrained from proposing more universal applications.

GLIMMERS OF UNIVERSALISM

The 1950s ended on a note of uncertainty with regard to child care policy. Although the national child care movement had gained the ear of federal officials, its message was ambiguous; sometimes it called for child care for all working mothers, while at other times it focused more narrowly on the needs of low-income families. Congressional politicians tended to favor the second course, as was evident in debates surrounding the 1954 child care tax deduction. But rising employment rates for mothers at all income levels meant that a narrowly delimited child care policy would no longer be adequate. Thus the politics of child care continued to oscillate between universalistic and targeted programs and policies.

Early in the 1960s there were signs that at the federal level the pendulum was swinging toward universalism and normalization of maternal employment, the first being President-Elect Kennedy's letter to Elinor Guggenheimer. Soon after JFK took office, Guggenheimer met with Arthur Goldberg and Abraham Ribicoff, the new secretaries of labor and of health, education, and welfare, respectively; both agreed to include child care provisions among proposed amendments to the Social Security Act (eventually passed as the Public Welfare Amendments of 1962).[4] Although most of these amendments were concerned with "rehabilitation of the poor,"[5] child care funding was to be noncontingent.

The goals of the legislation were twofold: to encourage mothers receiving public assistance to take paid employment and to address the problem of the many children of nonpoor mothers who were reportedly in self-care or inadequate care.[6] Child care, in this context, was both a component of anti-poverty policy and a developmental boon to children.

JFK's message to Congress concerning the legislation expressed this dual purpose: "Many women now on assistance rolls could obtain jobs and become self-supporting if local day care programs . . . were available. The need for such programs . . . has been increasing rapidly. . . . [About 3 million working women] have children under 6, and another 4 1/2 million have school-age children. . . . Adequate care for these children in their most formative years is essential to their proper growth and training."[7] Kennedy went on to recommend $5 million in block grants to states for 1963, and $10 million for each of the next two years. The bill passed, but less than $6 million total was eventually appropriated.[8] Although its child care provisions did not exclusively target low-income families or families on welfare, their inclusion in public welfare amendments meant that this new phase of federally supported child care inevitably became associated with efforts to reduce poverty.

Elinor Guggenheimer believed that the bill, however limited, was valuable because at the very least it provided a vehicle for putting child care on the federal agenda and gaining public funding for it.[9] Guggenheimer was appointed to the Home and Community Committee of the President's Commission on the Status of Women (PCSW) set up by JFK soon after he took office, and she no doubt had a strong hand in formulating its position on child care.[10] Referring to the 1962 legislation in its report to the president, the commission asserted, "Recent Federal legislation offering assistance to communities establishing day care is a first step in raising its provision to the level of national policy."[11]

The PCSW's overall position on maternal employment wavered, however. First it argued that because changes in the economy were placing new demands on women, they could no longer shoulder exclusive responsibility for family life. "If the family is to continue to be the core institution of society . . . new and expanded community services [including child care] are necessary." Moreover, "child care facilities are essential for women *in many different circumstances,* whether they work outside the home or not. . . . Those who decide to work should have child care services available." But the traditional maternalist position was also invoked: "It is regrettable when women with children are forced by economic necessity or by the regulations of welfare agencies to seek employment while their children are young."[12]

Apparently seeking to sidestep the issue of how child care affected women's right to work, the PCSW instead focused on potential social, cognitive, and developmental benefits to children. Notably, the commission argued that group care could advance the cause of social and racial integration: "Where group programs serve children from a cross section of a city, they provide training grounds for democratic social development. Their educational possibilities range from preparing underprivileged children for school, to providing constructive activities for normal youngsters, to offering especially gifted children additional means of development."[13]

Moving somewhat beyond official policies of the late 1950s, the PCSW recommended sliding-scale fees and a mix of funding: "For the benefit of children, mothers, and society, child care services should be available for children of families at all economic levels. . . . Costs should be met by fees scaled to parents' ability to pay, contributions from voluntary agencies, and *public appropriations*."[14] And finally, it called for an expansion of the child care tax deduction to cover dual-worker families earning a "median income."[15] In other words, the tax deduction should be used to underwrite employment for moderate-income as well as poor mothers. Though generally favorable toward child care, the PCSW's message was too guarded and equivocal to provide a mandate for a fully funded universal program for child care.

TRADITION CRUMBLES

The PCSW apparently felt obliged to make a gesture toward maternalist views of child care, but in the more traditionally minded sectors of the child welfare movement the trend was actually moving rapidly toward normalization. In 1964 Florence Ruderman of the Child Welfare League of America declared, "There is no evidence that the majority of working-mother families are in any way abnormal, that there is an absence of parental love or responsibility, or that indeed there is any problem other than the need for a good form of supplementary care. In our definition . . . this is a normal, not a pathological need."[16] In a few sentences, Ruderman swept away her organization's many decades of vacillation over maternal employment, its dozens of articles and speeches explaining why child care services should *not* be made available to the millions of working mothers who needed them. Reporting on the findings of a large-scale study being conducted by the CWLA, she pointed out that between 1948 and 1958 the number of employed mothers had increased by 80 percent, and they now constituted almost half of all female workers. In 1962, 8 million working mothers had children under eighteen (a total of 15 million children). This shift was important not only because of sheer numbers but also because working mothers now represented a cross-section of American society. Women were working because they had to and also because they *chose* to. In contrast to earlier decades, when the bulk of wage-earning mothers had husbands earning below-average incomes, now "the greatest rise was among women whose husbands earn over $5,000—i.e. in families with 'middle' or 'lower-middle' class incomes. . . . The rise has been particularly sharp," Ruderman noted, "among women whose husbands earn $7–9,999."[17]

The CWLA day care project was set up to "deproblematize" or "depathologize" child care and maternal employment. Instead of studying only low-income families, for example, it sampled a cross-section of families with small children. This, according to Ruderman, enabled researchers "to see what patterns of supplementary daytime care occur in *all* families, what social and economic circumstances are associated with *all* arrangements, how families feel about them. . . . We were not predetermining the relevant population (the population for whom it *is* or *should be* a child welfare service), as is done when studies focus on ADC families, low income groups, broken homes, etc."[18] Defining day care broadly to include "all daytime care of children by persons other than their mothers," the CWLA surveyed not only formal day care centers and homes but a range of services and facilities including nursery schools and after-school recreation programs.

With access to a mixed population of families, the researchers uncovered an interesting phenomenon: "Just as women work because they must, so others *stay home* because they must: i.e., they would like to work, but feel they cannot do so because they are unable to make satisfactory child-care arrangements."[19] Some had even given up jobs when child care became a problem. This observation had the effect of normalizing maternal employment and denaturalizing, or problematizing, "stay-at-home" motherhood. Instead of assuming that remaining at home was the "normal state of affairs," Ruderman's report showed that it was not always women's choice but was sometimes compelled by circumstances.

New trends in female employment created child care problems not only because they increased demand but also because a number of traditional care-givers, like grandmothers, were also in the labor force and no longer automatically available. According to the CWLA, "Today's younger, healthier grandmother seems to be less willing than the grandmother of an earlier era to be the 'taken-for-granted,' 'built-in' child care resource for her children. Like her

daughters and daughters-in-law (the mothers of young children), she too has
. . . greater independence and broader horizons."[20] In many instances,
mothers now depended on nonrelated teenaged babysitters for child care but
found them to be less reliable than the female relatives or live-in domestic help
(housekeepers, nursemaids) who had performed this task in earlier periods.

The CWLA study revealed that only about 1 percent of all American children with working mothers were in organized day care. The remaining youngsters were cared for in a variety of informal arrangements, ranging from relatives
and neighbors both in and outside of the children's own homes to self-care.
Families did not always prefer these alternatives, nor were they entirely satisfied
with them, but in many instances they were either unaware of other possibilities or unable to find group care facilities that were convenient and affordable. Moreover, many parents did not know how to assess or weigh alternatives.
According to Ruderman, "mothers sometimes feel unsure of the criteria for
evaluating day care arrangements."[21] They had little knowledge of what impact
their employment would have on their children, or whether care that seemed
less than optimal would really affect them negatively.

Finally, the CWLA's study showed that in the minds of many parents, group
care remained stigmatized, associated with poverty, relief, and welfare, and with
minority segments of the population. "This class-and-caste character, of individual facilities, and to a great extent of the entire institution of organized day
care, tends to be self-perpetuating. Many families who might like group care,
and for whom it may be appropriate, associate it with the very poor . . . and are
reluctant to use it."[22] In Ruderman's view, community officials and leaders were
at least partly responsible for the prevalence of such attitudes. Researchers
found that they continued "to see day care problems as affecting only the
underprivileged and inadequate, and to feel that day care planning should
therefore be restricted to these groups."[23] Ruderman believed that the shift in
the social profile of working mothers called for a new conception of the
purposes and provision of day care.

Other experts in the field of social welfare responded to Ruderman's call to
destigmatize child care. Writing in the journal *Child Welfare* in 1965, Milton
Willner, a New York City child care researcher, pointed out that "because of
unnecessary and false fears about the effect of separation on children, a sense of
guilt weighs heavily on the field of day care." Instead of apologizing for child
care or making it contingent on extraneous factors, Willner wanted leaders to
present it as a good in itself, emphasizing its proven benefits. These included
"providing a variety of everyday experiences that form a basis for wider learning

and expression and . . . fostering a child's capacity for later learning."[24] His arguments were reminiscent of some of those made by Eleanor Maccoby in the 1950s.

CHILD CARE AS POLICY LEVER

The public pronouncements of experts like Ruderman and Willner, in conjunction with the report of the President's Commission on the Status of Women, suggested that normalization of maternal employment and child care was in the wind. But there were also strong policy currents flowing in the opposite direction, toward targeted programs. Many politicians maintained that federal support for child care was legitimate only to facilitate employment among poor mothers and thus reduce the welfare rolls. The issue was still somewhat open in 1962, when the Public Welfare Amendments were passed. The bill stipulated that "a child should not be in day care unless his need for the service is real"; "real need" was broadly construed to mean having a mother who worked, no matter what her income level, and employment was still optional for recipients of ADC (now Aid to Families with Dependent Children, or AFDC). In the Work Incentive Program (WIN) legislation of 1967, however, the link between public child care provisions and poverty reduction became more explicit, as Congress shifted from "encouraging" low-income mothers to find work to mandating participation in job training or work program for AFDC mothers, even those with small children.[25]

Both these laws followed a trajectory in federal policy toward low-income mothers that had begun with passage of the child care income tax deduction in 1954. This trajectory moved away from the principle established with mothers' pensions in the Progressive Era that mothers—at least *some* mothers—belonged at home taking care of their children and, in the absence of a male breadwinner, that the government should support them.[26] Now, employment for poor mothers—or workfare—was articulated as a policy goal.

On the face of it, the legislation was not race-specific, but there are strong indications that its passage was racially motivated.[27] The immediate precipitants of the shift to workfare policy were twofold: a marked expansion of public assistance, and changes in the racial composition of those receiving aid. Between 1940 and 1960, the number of ADC recipients had grown by nearly 1 million per decade (from 1.2 million in 1940 to 3.1 million in 1960), and the cost had increased more than sevenfold (from just over $100 million in 1940 to nearly a billion in 1960).[28] A number of states, primarily those in the South, had systematically used questionable and quasi-legal means to keep welfare rolls low and bar black recipients in particular. A favorite ploy was to claim that illegitimacy (which was higher among blacks than whites) was prima facie evidence that the applicant was not providing a "suitable home" for her children.[29] In 1960 the Social Security Administration ruled that illegitimacy could no longer be considered grounds for rejection of AFDC applicants, opening the way for more blacks to receive benefits. Between 1960 and 1967 the proportions shifted from 86 percent white to 46 percent nonwhite, with 95 percent of the nonwhites being African American.[30]

Seeking other ways to bar blacks and unmarried mothers (who were closely linked in the minds of many legislators) from receiving benefits, Congress hit upon the policy of workfare. In 1961 Representative Jamie Whitten, a conservative Democrat from Mississippi, introduced a bill requiring welfare recipients to work. Although this initial measure went nowhere, it signaled a definite shift in congressional mood, and the following year the first set of work requirements for AFDC recipients was passed in the form of the Community Work and Training Program title of the Public Welfare Amendments of 1962.[31]

At hearings on the bill, Abraham Ribicoff stressed that the measure would help welfare recipients achieve "self-sufficiency" by offering them "rehabilitation instead of relief" (the catchwords of the day).[32] Other welfare officials, in contrast, expressed the fear that the existence of day care services might be used to pressure ADC mothers to take jobs. The second group proved to be the more prescient: instead of opening the way to universal child care, the 1962 amendments put federal welfare policy on the slippery slope toward workfare.

Lawmakers claimed that the 1962 bill would reduce dependency by making recipients self-sufficient. Between 1961 and 1965, however, 1.3 million *new* recipients came on the rolls, doubling the rate of growth. Congress responded by tightening the work requirements, passing the WIN bill of 1967, which, among other things, gave states the option of requiring mothers of children under six (or even under three if they chose) to be "referred" for job training or immediate employment, *provided that child care was available.* Child care had to meet standards set by the Department of Health, Education, and Welfare (HEW); child care centers were also to be used as a source of employment for recipients.[33]

Responses to these new measures were mixed. At hearings on WIN, both liberal and conservative social welfare advocates expressed deep reservations about proposals for increasing work requirements for mothers. Conservative representatives from Catholic Charities objected that the measure would undermine the male-headed family, while liberals argued that compulsory employment was unfair when no jobs were available and criticized efforts to save money at the expense of the well-being of families, especially children. Ruth Atkins of the National Council of Negro Women opposed mandatory employment and predicted that families would be forced into using second-rate child care arrangements. She pointed to the irony that, under the terms of the bill, a woman who refused to leave her children in unsatisfactory conditions to enter a training program could then be labeled an unfit or unsuitable mother and penalized.[34]

Members of Congress insisted that there were safeguards: the work requirement for mothers was discretionary, and states were prohibited from implementing it without providing adequate child care. Support for the bill came from both liberal and conservative legislators who, for different reasons, shared a belief that dire measures were needed to avert a perceived crisis in American social policy. Conservatives claimed that only punitive measures would reduce illegitimacy and alleged "welfare fraud," while liberals continued to argue that employment training and work programs would ultimately lead to self-sufficiency and an end to welfare.

Problematic as these 1960s bills were, they did in theory contain provisions that, properly implemented, might have allowed some AFDC recipients to participate in training and find jobs with the assurance that their children were receiving adequate care. In practice, however, the WIN program did not deliver. Part of the problem had to do with erratic administration and funding. Many states dragged their feet in establishing training programs and were even slower in setting up the child care that was necessary before women could be "referred."[35] Unless a state had some sort of child care advocacy organization or bureaucracy in place, there was little impetus to apply for federal funding.[36] But even in those states that already had child care services, local welfare officials were often reluctant to refer applicants to training programs, for the employment of mothers did not sit well with their maternalist/paternalist views of gender roles.[37]

Such views reflected the attitudes toward gender that predominated in liberal circles in Washington in the mid-1960s. Following publication of Daniel Patrick Moynihan's *The Negro Family: The Case for National Action* (the so-called Moynihan Report,[38] which claimed that the ascent of a "black matriarchy" had caused black families to erode), many policy makers began to argue that employment programs should focus on black men, not women. This line of thinking, in turn, set up a competition between HEW, which was charged with implementing the various jobs programs for women, and the Department of Labor, which was administering the Manpower Development and Training Act, also passed in 1962. At least one member of Congress, Representative Martha Griffiths (Democrat–Michigan) protested against what she saw as blatant discrimination against low-income women in employment programs at both the federal and state levels. In a 1968 hearing on Income Maintenance Programs, Griffiths contended, "If you do not say anything about mothers working, then [the Labor Department is] going to see to it that none work. . . . And in my opinion, this is wrong. . . . If you give the welfare officials the chance, and the Labor Department, you are going to consign the women to welfare. I just do not think that is fair."[39]

Not only were federal employment programs for women discriminatory, but they also foundered because the child care being made available was low in quality. This was the result of conflicts over how federally funded services should be regulated. The 1962 legislation required federally funded child care programs to be licensed by the state, but the drafters of the 1967 bill sought to shift regulation to Washington by setting federal standards. The task of defining these standards was delegated to HEW, which created the Federal Panel on Early Childhood, chaired by Jule Sugarman, the founding director of Head Start. The panel was hobbled from the beginning by philosophical divisions among its members about the content and purposes of federally sponsored child care.[40] On one side were the developmentalists—representatives of the Children's Bureau, the Women's Bureau, and Head Start—who believed that quality should not be sacrificed even (or especially) in programs for poor children. On the other were representatives of the Department of Labor's Manpower Administration and the Bureau of the Budget, who took a more instrumentalist position, calling for provisions that were safe but simple and would keep costs to a minimum.[41] That way, more money could be channeled into training, and more of the poor would receive assistance.

The developmentalists took as their model the still relatively new but already successful Head Start program. Ultimately the most enduring component of the War on Poverty, Head Start was based on the principle that early intervention into the lives of disadvantaged children through an enriched and comprehensive curriculum of early childhood education, nutrition, and health monitoring could enhance their development and reverse or at least mitigate the effects of poverty and cultural deprivation.[42] Though costly at the outset, programs like Head Start, developmentalists argued, would reduce maladjustment, delinquency, and educational failure, and thus ultimately prove to be cost-effective. Assuming that there was little or no difference between the children who were eligible for Head Start and those who would be attending the WIN-related child care centers, they believed that the same developmental, comprehensive principles should apply.

Given his background, Sugarman was expected to side with the developmentalists, but he bent over backward to avoid being identified with this position so as not to antagonize the more pragmatic, cost-conscious members of his committee. Developmentalists composed the majority of the working committee assigned to come up with a first draft for the standards, but Sugarman allowed the pragmatists to have their say in the final version, which came to be known as the Federal Inter-Agency Day Care Requirements (FIDCR). Not only were child-to-staff ratios higher than those initially defined by the developmentalists, but the regulations allowed both clerical and housekeeping workers, as well as unpaid volunteers, to be counted in determining ratios. Although facilities, safety, curricula, and nutrition were all required to be "adequate," the regulations contained no specifications. Finally, and probably most significantly, no agency was designated or empowered to enforce the requirements.[43] This last fact expressed the committee's consensus that the FIDCR were to be thought of as goals, not binding regulations.[44]

The price of consensus was quality, but this sacrifice, according to some observers, was actually the means to a different end: deterring potential recipients from seeking public assistance in the first place.[45] This, at least, was the conservative agenda. Senate liberals, by contrast, saw in the FIDCR the means of ensuring at least a modicum of quality in federally sponsored child care services. Beneath this goal was the faint hope that if quality child care proved too costly, Congress might be willing to abandon programs like WIN and continue support for needy mothers who remained outside the labor force.

Either way, poor and low-income women who *wanted* to find a way into employment would lose out. The combination of the threat of benefit loss on the one hand and paternalist attitudes on the other left AFDC mothers at the mercy of both local and federal authorities. Neither the punitive nor the so-called protective aspects of the 1960s legislation were conducive to giving these women the choice or the wherewithal to establish themselves in a labor force that was in any case inhospitable toward them.

TOWARD A UNIVERSAL POLICY?

While most federal policy makers were still focusing on child care that was linked in some way to welfare reform, some began to address women's child care needs in a more positive—and universal—way. In 1969 and 1970, Congress held its first hearings on measures to expand and improve services that were *not* coupled to welfare.[46] These measures, which called for federal funding to expand the supply of day care centers and enhance their educational benefits, ultimately formed the basis of the Comprehensive Child Development Act of 1971 (CCDA). Under the terms of the bill, low-income families would have access to free child care, while other families would pay on a sliding scale. Supporters of the bill—who included feminists, labor leaders, civil rights activists, and early childhood educators—cited its positive impact on child development as well as its potential for combating racism by integrating children of all races at an early age. Sponsored by two Democrats, Senator Walter Mondale (Minnesota), and Representative John Brademas (Indiana), the CCDA passed both houses of Congress but was vetoed by President Richard M. Nixon.[47]

Nixon's veto was by no means a foregone conclusion; in the early days of his administration he had indicated a strong interest in childhood development.[48] His own Task Force on Women's Rights and Responsibilities cited the lack of child care as an impediment for women at all income levels and recommended establishing "a system of well-run child care centers available to all pre-school children" as well as after-school provisions for older children. Although priority should be given to low-income working mothers, the Task Force said, there should also be consideration of middle-income mothers.[49] Interpreting such statements as favorable to their cause, proponents of comprehensive federal policies toward children expected Nixon to sign the bill. Thus his eventual veto—expressed in rather harsh terms—came as something of a surprise.

Two factors account for the bill's early progress. First, the growing success of Head Start had made the public aware of the importance of fostering child development; this was also a major theme at the 1970 White House Conference on Children. Mondale and Brademas were astute legislators who delayed introduction of the bill until they felt that support for the principles of child development, both inside and outside Congress, was strong, and then they paved the way for the legislation with a series of hearings.[50] They also knew they could count on the support of a strong coalition made up of feminists; civil rights, welfare, and child care activists; early childhood educators; labor; and mayors. One of the leading figures in the coalition was Marian Wright Edelman, a veteran of the civil rights movement in Mississippi who had moved onto the Washington stage.

Second, the bill progressed because it initially caught the Nixon administration somewhat off guard. The attention of HEW, now headed by Elliot Richardson, was focused on welfare policy. With rolls increasing at a rate of about 200,000 cases per month, Nixon declared in his 1971 State of the Union address that the welfare system was a "'monstrous and consuming outrage' for both the taxpayer and the welfare recipient."[51] At the urging of his social policy adviser, Daniel P. Moynihan, and a preinaugural task force on welfare, Nixon sought to make dramatic changes in the welfare system by passing the Family Assistance Plan (FAP).[52]

This plan had two basic components: a guaranteed annual income (which, in the course of debate, ranged from $1,600 to $2,400) and a tightened work requirement for welfare mothers, which was, in turn, linked to expanded day care provisions. The bill that comprised FAP, H.R. 1, also raised both the deductible and income ceiling for the child care tax deduction.[53] The inclusion of child care provisions in H.R. 1 eventually provided Nixon with one rationale for vetoing the CCDA (that is, child care was already covered), even though, as his task force on women pointed out, families not eligible for the FAP *also* needed federal assistance for child care.[54]

Although Richardson was preoccupied with FAP, he found time to engage in contretemps with the architects of the CCDA over two issues: the income criteria for families receiving free child care, and the size of units permitted to become "prime sponsors" of federally funded child care centers. The measures initially passed by the House and Senate set the income cutoff at $6,960, a figure that would have extended eligibility to some 6.8 million preschool children at a cost of $17 billion—far exceeding the $1.2 billion in funding initially approved by Richardson. An amendment lowering the cutoff point to $4,320 reduced the number of eligible preschoolers to 3.6 million at a cost of $4.5 billion, but this was still too high for Richardson.[55] He made it clear that the Nixon administration had no intention of moving in the direction of universal child care by extending eligibility for government provisions more broadly.

The definition of prime sponsorship was even more politically charged. At issue was who would control federally supported child care: existing state educational bureaucracies or smaller local and nongovernmental groups. Pushing for the smaller groups were Edelman and Representative Carl Perkins (Democrat–Kentucky). To Edelman, high-quality child care was not just an end in itself but could serve as a force for social change—provided that it was controlled by parents and the local community. Vivid in her mind was the memory of trying to set up Head Start programs in small Mississippi towns controlled by racist school boards—an experience she had no wish to repeat.[56]

Perkins, responsive to his activist Appalachian constituency, shared Edelman's aversion to the entrenched bureaucracies where Richardson and many congressional Republicans believed responsibility for federal child care should be lodged. While the liberals called for prime sponsoring units as small as ten thousand, which would have permitted community control, conservatives tried to keep the requirement at five hundred thousand, which in many areas would have pushed it up to the state level. The two sides compromised at one hundred thousand, a number that still would have created an "administrative nightmare" for HEW, with thousands of prime sponsors as grantees.[57] But Perkins was still not satisfied, and he took it upon himself to pass an amendment pushing the population requirement back down to ten thousand. This move created tensions within the child care coalition, many of whose members believed that the central purpose of the bill should be child development, not community change. It also drove away many of the bill's Republican sponsors and handed Nixon a further reason to veto.

Race was undoubtedly one of the subtexts of Nixon's objections to the bill. In the wake of pressure to achieve school integration through busing, there was widespread fear about creating a public service that would mix the races at an even earlier age.[58] This blatantly racist motivation was masked in Nixon's veto message, which drew on more acceptable Cold War rhetoric about the need to preserve the American family as well as on latent conservative opposition to increasing government services in general. Nixon claimed that whereas his welfare reform policy was designed to enhance family togetherness, "this child development program appears to move in precisely the opposite direction." It would diminish "both parental authority and parental involvement with children—particularly in those decisive early years when social attitudes and a conscience are formed and religious and moral principles are first inculcated." And finally, it would commit the federal government "to the side of communal approaches to child rearing over against the family-centered approach."[59]

Such language accorded smoothly with the lexicon of the radical right, which had besieged first Congress and then the White House with objections to the bill. For months, right-wing magazines like *Human Events* had railed against the CCDA, depicting it as a form of Orwellian social engineering that was reminiscent of Nazi or Communist efforts at "thought control." The family, not the government, should serve as a bastion against Communism, conservatives argued.[60] Replacing the family with government would lead to familial breakdown and train children for lifelong dependency on the state—the first steps toward totalitarianism. Right-wing magazines also criticized the measure's universalistic thrust, which, they claimed, would produce a "class-less society" that would "Sovietize" American youth. The right's reaction was undoubtedly fueled by the feminist rhetoric surrounding child care, which managed to touch a number of sensitive conservative nerves all at once. By the early 1970s, "free 24-hour day care centers" had become one of the rallying cries of the women's movement.[61] It was bad enough that socialist feminists framed such demands in terms of women's right to economic independence, but radical feminists went even further, asserting that child care would help dissolve the nuclear family by redistributing responsibility for children.[62] Even the more moderate National Organization for Women called for the establishment of child care facilities by law, "on the same basis as parks, libraries and public schools, adequate to the needs of children from the preschool years to through adolescence, as a community resource to be used by citizens from all income levels."[63] Such demands confirmed conservative fears about feminist designs on traditional female roles and also raised the twin specters of expanded bureaucracies and government intervention into family life.

Nixon's veto message, with its praise for family togetherness and critique of "communal approaches to child rearing," was carefully crafted to cosset right-wing, anti-Communist, anti-feminist sentiment. Nixon succeeded in tainting the concept of universal child care to such an extent that for years to come, few Republicans dared to support it. Moreover, Nixon's message cast the Edelman-Perkins insistence on community control in a new (and unfavorable) light. Thus in 1972, when Mondale and Brademas proposed a modified version of the CCDA that omitted the controversial provisions for prime sponsorship and offered less free child care, they still could not garner bipartisan support, and subsequent efforts throughout the 1970s to legislate universal child care met with similar rebuffs from Republicans.[64]

By contrast, neither Nixon nor the right objected to using child care to push welfare mothers into employment; social engineering was clearly acceptable when directed at the poor. As a result, bills linking child care to the poor gained momentum. One of the most important of these, Nixon's FAP, was ultimately defeated, but two others were passed: Title XX of the Social Security Act, which targeted child care to workfare and "at-risk" populations, in 1974; and in 1976, the Aid to Day Care Centers Act (ADCC), which increased funding in order to raise standards in public day care centers (while deferring implementation of those standards) and encouraged the creation of child care jobs for low-income women. Both bills funneled sorely needed resources to child care centers serving low-income populations. Many of these centers had been started in the

1960s with anti-poverty funds (mostly through the Office of Economic Opportunity) that dried up under the Nixon administration. Title XX came just in time to save some of these valuable community facilities from extinction, and the ADCC brought in additional funding for some.[65]

But at the same time, both bills effectively limited child care subsidies to only the neediest families. Title XX allowed the federal government to match state funds on a three-to-one basis with the aim of providing services to low- and moderate-income families to "achieve or maintain economic self-support to prevent, reduce, or eliminate dependency." States were required to dedicate half the services "to individuals in welfare-related categories," but the other 50 percent could go to families earning as much as 115 percent of the state median (states could opt for a lower maximum), who would pay for a service such as child care on a sliding scale. In practice, most states set their maxima lower—at or below 80 percent of the median—thus excluding families who, though above the poverty line, could still ill afford to pay the full cost of child care. This either forced families to place children in cheaper but probably lower-quality child care or discouraged them from increasing their incomes unless the gains were great enough to offset lost eligibility for subsidized services. In many two-parent families, this served as a disincentive to wives' employment.[66]

Title XX also denied parents a choice of child care provisions. Most states contracted with specific providers for Title XX slots, usually concentrating on either center-based or family-based care. Eligible families had to take what was available, regardless of their preferences regarding the type of care they wanted for their children; only a few states allowed parents to choose freely.[67] Low-income mothers who did not feel comfortable with the available choices—whether they were centers or family providers—were reluctant to place their children in care. They could not, however, make use of their preferred type of care if subsidized slots were not available.[68]

The ADCC, signed reluctantly by President Ford after he had vetoed a more comprehensive bill, increased Title XX funding to allow states to improve child care services and come into compliance with the Federal Interagency Day Care Requirements. Implementation of the FIDCR, which had engendered much controversy and resistance from conservatives, had been postponed several times since they were first introduced in the late 1960s.[69] In the compromise that allowed final passage of the ADCC, implementation was postponed once again, although the extra funds became available immediately. Congress neglected, however, to include a "maintenance of effort" clause, with the result that "states . . . simply substituted new money for old," diverting matching funds previously used for child care to other social services.[70] Thus the new funding did little or nothing to expand or improve the supply of child care.

Child care funded by Title XX was, nevertheless, an important component of the growing federal effort to move welfare mothers into employment. Both the WIN program, which was specifically targeted at AFDC recipients, and the Comprehensive Employment and Training Act (CETA), passed in 1973, permitted a portion of the funds earmarked for support services to be used for child care. Some administrators chose to use funds for that purpose, but others did not, even though regulations barred mothers from entering work or training if child care arrangements were not in place. Many states relied on provisions funded by Title XX to take up the slack.

In 1979 CETA regulations were tightened in an effort to compel local sponsors to provide child care, the rationale being that without it, women were denied equal opportunity in the program. Local sponsors, however, took advantage of the program's inherent flexibility to circumvent these regulations, either by failing to make provision, refusing to accept applicants who required child care, or, at best, providing only limited services that would be cut off soon after a mother entered paid employment.[71] These mothers were generally still eligible for Title XX slots, if available, but they often had to compete with other women who were at an even greater disadvantage—namely, those who were still in training programs and had not yet gotten jobs. The problem was exacerbated by an increase in the proportion of black households headed by solo mothers (39 percent by 1978), most of whom preferred to work rather than rely on public assistance but needed subsidized child care to do so.[72]

In the early 1980s, already scarce child care resources for low-income women shrank still further as a result of funding cuts made by the Reagan administration, and the quality of these provisions was severely compromised. Under the Omnibus Budget Reconciliation Act of 1981 (OBRA), Title XX was transformed into a block grant and funding was cut by 20 percent. Total funding was reduced still further by elimination of the state matching requirement. At the same time, the amount of child care expenses that AFDC recipients could deduct from their income was capped at $160 per month.[73] The following year, CETA was replaced by the Job Training Partnership Act, which authorized less funding for support services, including child care.[74] Between 1980 and 1986, these cuts produced major reductions in almost all categories of federal spending for child care for low-income families (table 7.1).[75]

To make matters worse, transformation of Title XX into a block grant automatically abrogated the FIDCR for child care providers who had previ-

Table 7.1

Federal Expenditures for Child Care, Fiscal Years 1980 and 1986

Program	Expenditure (Millions of Dollars)	
	1980	1986
Title XX (SSBG)	600[a]	387[a]
Head Start	766[b]	1,040
AFDC Disregarded (Title IV-A)	120[a]	35
Child Care Food Program	239[a]	501[a]
Title IV-C (WIN)	115[d]	—
ARC (Appalachian Regional Commission) Child Dev.	11[b]	1
Employer-provided child care	—	110[c]
Dependent care tax credit	956[a]	3,410[a]
Total	2,807	5,484
Total without tax credit	1,851	2,074[f]

Source: Alfred Kahn and Sheila B. Kamerman, *Child Care: Facing the Hard Choices.* Copyright © 1987 by Auburn House. Reproduced with permission of Greenwood Publishing Group, Inc., Westport, Conn.

Note: State and local education and social service expenditures are not included in this table.

[a] Estimate from the American Council for Young Children, provided by Patricia Divine Hawkins.

[b] Testimony, Jo Ann Gasper, Deputy Assistant Secretary for Social Services *Child Care: Beginning a National Initiative* (Washington, D.C.: GPO, 1984).

[c] E. Duval, et al., "AFDC: Characteristics of Recipients in 1979," *Social Security Bulletin* 45, no. 4:4–19.

[d] Data from the Congressional Budget Office (CBO).

[e] CBO data, based on Joint Tax Committee estimates.

[f] Because the inflation rate was 31 percent between 1980 and 1985, according to the CBO, this total would have had to be $2,425 to sustain the 1980 direct expenditure level.

ously been mandated to comply as a condition of receiving federal funding. After years of wrangling, these requirements had finally been put into effect in 1980. Because they had been under discussion for so long, however, they had already begun to take hold; a 1981 government report found that most states were, in fact, meeting or close to meeting the standards for their Title XX facilities. Moreover, many private facilities not funded by Title XX were also adhering to the standards because they were "emerging as the preferred norm."[76] With the elimination of the FIDCR, pressure to conform dissipated rapidly.

This trend, coupled with funding decreases, reduced both the supply and quality of child care for low-income families while raising its cost to all consumers. According to a Children's Defense Fund study of changes between 1981 and 1983:

• Thirty-two states provided less Title XX child care in 1983 than in 1981, some cutting more than the federal expenditure cutback.
• In a significant number of states (10) there was a decrease in eligibility for low-income working families.
• Some states (20) made eligibility for child care more difficult for low-income mothers in training.
• Many low-income AFDC mothers were cut from the rolls by the new policy, and in some states they became ineligible for publicly supported child care.
• Some states imposed fees or raised fees for Title XX day care.
• States were compelled to choose between child care for child protection cases and . . . for children of working mothers.
• Many states cut child care staffs (32), lowered standards (33), or decreased training programs (24) in order to conserve funds.
• Some states shifted Title XX child care cases to AFDC child care disregard (IV-A), a less costly and therefore lower-quality alternative.
• Thirty-three states lowered standards and reduced enforcement staff.[77]

As these data indicate, the overall impact of Reagan-era cuts in spending for public child care was devastating. For low-income and welfare mothers, inadequate child care, coupled with erratic and poorly paying job opportunities and discrimination in job training programs, meant that it was extremely difficult for them to become or remain self-sufficient. Already at a disadvantage, they now had to compete with an increasing number of middle-class women for both jobs *and* child care slots. These conditions, in turn, caused welfare rolls and expenditures to swell. Critics pointed to the folly of such a policy. In August 1982, Arthur Y. Webb, New York State acting commissioner of social services, pointed out, "In fact, it is day care that keeps thousands of households from joining welfare ranks."[78] But the Reagan administration could not be deterred from its course. Nevertheless, Congress blamed AFDC, rather than the lack of child care, for the growth of poverty among female-headed households.

A SPUR TO THE PRIVATE SECTOR

At the same time that he was slashing support for child care for the poor, President Ronald Reagan was increasing federal outlays for child care for middle-class families. Under the Dependent Care Assistance Plan provisions of the 1981 Economic Recovery Tax Act, individuals were permitted to exclude the value of employer-provided child care services from their gross income.[79] The law also allowed employers to accelerate depreciation for the cost of constructing on-site or nearby child care facilities. By 1986, the annual value of taxes foregone under these provisions amounted to $110 million (see table 7.1). Simultaneously, the amount of the child care tax credit was increased (mainly to the advantage of lower-income families), and the Internal Revenue Code was modified to permit taxpayers to shelter pretax dollars for child care and other personal and dependent care services under "flexible spending plans" (families had to choose between flexible spending or the tax credit).[80] The total value of these foregone taxes more than tripled between 1980 and 1986, constituting by far the greatest single expenditure for child care in both of those years.

The nature of these policies—tax cuts for individuals and tax breaks for employers and proprietors—were intended to facilitate parent choice and spur child care initiatives in the private sector. To a large extent, they appear to have achieved the desired effect. Moreover, a sizable increase in the labor force participation rates of middle-class mothers made such policies especially timely.[81] This group of women both needed child care and was reasonably well positioned to take advantage of financial assistance in the form of tax credits or flexible spending accounts, which require advance planning and some leeway in household cash flow.

Simultaneously, the private sector, responding as predicted to the government's financial incentives, took steps to meet the increased demand for child care. Between 1980 and 1990 the capacity of employer-sponsored child care programs increased dramatically (fig. 7.1). Operators of for-profit centers gravitated toward lucrative markets such as suburbs that were underserved by nonprofits, and regions that had looser regulations, mainly in the South and Southwest.[82] In 1977, 41 percent of American child care centers were being run for profit (7,500 out of 18,310); most of these were independent "mom and pop" outfits.[83] Over the next few years, however, child care became big business, as the chains and franchisers took over the industry. From 1980 to 1985, Kinder-Care, the largest chain of proprietary child care centers, more than doubled in size, expanding from 510 centers serving 53,000 children to 1,040 centers serving 100,000, while from 1980 to 1986, Children's World, the third-largest chain, grew from 84 centers in seven states to 240 centers in thirteen states.[84]

Many nonprofit child care facilities were also set up during this period.

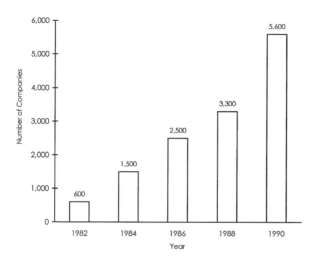

Fig. 7.1. Employer-supported child care services expanded rapidly from the late 1970s through the 1980s. Data from D. E. Friedman, Families and Work Institute, "Update on Employer-Supported Child Care," distributed memo, 1991.

Among the sponsors were educational institutions and voluntary organizations such as the YWCA and the Salvation Army, which made child care a national priority, along with hundreds of local groups, both independent and affiliated. Churches and synagogues started child care centers or converted existing part-day nursery schools into all-day programs, and feminist groups opened dozens of day care cooperatives in urban storefronts and similar locales.[85] The availability of these new services facilitated a shift from family-based to center-based care; between 1958 and 1982 the proportion of families using child care centers of all types more than quadrupled (table 7.2).

Family-based child care (outside the child's home) by both relatives and nonrelatives increased from 1958 through 1982 but fell off somewhat from 1982 to 1994. Throughout these years, the use of family providers still exceeded the use of center-based care, although the margin shrank over time. In 1982, more than 46 percent of wage-earning mothers used family-based care (25.5 percent by nonrelatives, including family day care providers; 20.8 percent by relatives), as opposed to 19.9 percent who used center-based care. By 1994, those figures had changed markedly: only 33 percent used family-based care (20 percent by nonrelatives, 13 percent by relatives), as opposed to 28 percent

Table 7.2

Child-Care Arrangements Used by Families with Employed Mothers, 1958–82

Child-Care Arrangement	1958[a]	1965	1977	1982
Mother Employed Full Time				
Care in child's home	56.6	47.2	28.6	27.2
By father	14.7	10.3	10.6	10.9
By other relative	27.7	18.4	11.4	10.9
By nonrelative	14.2	18.5	6.6	5.4
Care in another home	27.1	37.3	47.4	46.3
By relative	14.5	17.6	20.8	20.8
By nonrelative	12.7	19.6	26.6	25.5
Child-care center	4.5	8.2	14.6	19.9
Child cares for self	0.6	0.3	0.3	—[b]
Mother cares for child while working	—[b]	6.7	8.2	6.6
All other arrangements	11.2	0.4	0.8	0.3
Total	100.0	100.0	100.0	100.0
Mother Employed Part Time				
Care in child's home		47.0	42.7	41.2
By father		22.9	23.1	21.3
By other relative		15.6	11.2	13.3
By nonrelative		8.6	8.4	6.6
Care in another home		17.0	28.8	35.7
By relative		9.1	13.2	16.4
By nonrelative		7.9	15.6	19.3
Child-care center		2.7	9.1	7.9
Child cares for self		0.9	0.5	—[b]
Mother cares for child while working		32.3	18.5	15.1
All other arrangements		—	0.4	0.1
Total		100.0	100.0	100.0

Source: U.S. Bureau of the Census, Current Population Reports, *Trends in Child Care Arrangements of Working Mothers,* series P-23, no. 117 (Washington, D.C.: GPO, 1982), 6; and Current Population Reports, *Child Care Arrangements of Working Mothers: June 1982,* series P-23, no. 129 (Washington, D.C.: GPO, 1983), 4.

Note: All figures are percentages. Data prior to 1982 are restricted to children of ever-married mothers. Data for 1965 and 1958 are for children under six; for 1977 and 1982 data are for children under five.

[a]Data are not available for mothers employed part time in 1958.

[b]Included with "all other arrangements."

who used centers. Much of the shift appears to have been from care by relatives to center-based care;[86] a core of parents, however, continued to prefer family-based care by nonrelatives.

Between 1958 and 1990 the proportion of families with employed mothers using in-home care by nonrelatives declined significantly,[87] though it remained an important source of care for middle- and high-income families. For various reasons, many of those in a financial position to do so preferred to avoid group care situations, athough for older preschool children they often arranged a combination of part-day nursery school and in-home care. A number of families found nannies and caretakers among the growing influx of female workers from Mexico and other Latin American countries. Driven by the dire economic circumstances and the needs of children and other family members left behind and often undocumented, these "transnational mothers" were willing to work long hours at low wages.[88] By paying salaries that frequently fell below minimum wage, more American families than ever before could afford live-in child care.

As a result of these various arrangements, a multi-tiered system emerged during the 1980s: publicly funded centers or family caregivers struggling, with declining resources, to provide child care for poor and low-income children; family child care with a primarily working-class and lower-middle-class clientele; voluntary or proprietary centers for middle-class families; and in-home caregiving by nonrelatives, supplemented by nursery schools, for the well-to-do.

THE ECONOMICS OF CHILD CARE PROVISION

From the early 1980s on, providers of all types of care responded to the perception that the need—or market demand—for child care was growing. But their motivations, goals, and methods, as well as the quality of care offered, differed considerably. One of the most significant contrasts was between proprietary and voluntary child care. Most observers concurred that, with a few notable exceptions, the level of care in nonprofits generally exceeded that at proprietary centers.[89] With the exception of Children's World centers, which were considered high in quality, most for-profits sought to keep standards low and, if part of a chain, standardized equipment and curricula to the detriment of cultural variations and preferences among clienteles.[90] The profit motive clearly affected the atmosphere of child care facilities. Whereas the environments and curricula of voluntary centers took many forms, often reflecting the countercultural tastes of their founders, for-profits maintained a modicum of quality that tended to remain only at the surface. As one study put it, "while all centers met licensing requirements, none exceeded minimum standards. Centers were clean and bright, but unimaginative."[91]

Educator Joseph Featherstone was one of the first social critics to sound the alarm about the deleterious effects of for-profit child care. In a famously entitled 1970 article, "The Day Care Problem: Kentucky Fried Children," Featherstone offered snapshots of some of the D.C.-area proprietaries he had toured. In one he saw forty or more preschoolers "huddled in even rows of chairs in the darkness, watching television."[92] Elsewhere he found children playing in a busy parking lot and proprietors who offered a lunch of junk food (or, in one case, apparently nothing at all). Sadly, Featherstone observed, it was almost impossible to shut down such low-quality centers because the regulatory apparatus in most places was either overburdened or lacked teeth.[93]

Most of the proprietary centers Featherstone described were independently run; in the early 1970s, the chains and franchises were just being established. Featherstone deplored the idea of marketing child care franchises "the way others have sold franchises for root beer and fried chicken," and he remarked (rather mildly, considering the powerful images he had invoked), "I don't think the franchisers will be able to make money running good programs."[94]

Whether voluntary, independent for-profits, or chains, all child care centers tended to operate with extremely tight budgets. Chains were able to achieve certain economies of scale by purchasing supplies and equipment in bulk and constructing multiple facilities simultaneously, but this kind of savings was seldom available to independent centers. The major expense—and therefore the major site for realizing a profit, if that was the goal—was (and is) in salaries; thus profits could be achieved only by maintaining the lowest possible salaries and caregiver-to-child ratios that the local labor market and the law would allow. According to one study performed in the mid-1970s, the salary ranges in nonprofits were generally about 5–10 percent higher than those in for-profits, even though caregiver-to-child ratios were higher in nonprofits.[95] Another study found that in 1982 for-profit centers spent only 63 percent of their budgets on salaries, while nonprofits spent 73 percent.[96] Staff turnover, not surprisingly, was greater at for-profits than at voluntary centers. To cover the cost of higher salaries and better staffing ratios and to ensure continuity of personnel, fees at nonprofits sometimes ran higher than at commercial facilities.

Contemporary research pointed to a strong relationship between compensation and child care quality. "The most important predictor of the quality of care children receive . . . is staff wages," according to the 1989 National Child Care Staffing Study.[97] The study also found that staff salaries in child care centers were "abysmally low" compared to salaries of employees with similar levels of education and training in other occupations; that between 1977 and 1988, "staff turnover has nearly tripled, . . . jumping from 15% . . . to 41%; and that "children attending lower-quality centers [those with lower staff salaries and lower provider-to-child ratios] were less competent in language and social development."[98] Because salaries tended to be lower in proprietary than voluntary child care centers, children attending for-profits during the 1980s were more likely to suffer the consequences of their caretakers' poor pay.

Whereas voluntary child care centers struggled to offer the best possible care while still keeping fees down, proprietary child care center operators sought to maintain or, preferably, raise profit margins by minimizing standards and regulation, even if this meant (as it inevitably did) compromising quality. A 1977 study showed that because the proprietaries spent so little on wages, compliance with regulations such as those set out in the 1968 FIDCR would increase their labor costs by 25 to 51 percent (whereas labor costs for the nonprofits would have to go up by only 4 to 20 percent).[99] Not surprisingly, whenever legislators and children's advocates called for tougher requirements at both the federal and state levels, the proprietaries rose to challenge them. By the early 1980s, the National Association of Child Care Management, with a membership of owners and managers of proprietary centers, had become "a strong lobby on Capitol Hill."[100] Their chief concern was to block federal standards that would raise either staffing levels or salary requirements, and they rejoiced when the 1981 OBRA converted Title XX into block grants, effectively depriving Washington of its regulatory power over child care.

OUTSIDE THE CENTERS

During this same period, more informal arrangements, such as family child care and in-home caregiving, were also expanding. The proportion of mothers using family care doubled between 1958 and 1982, with the bulk coming from working-class or lower-middle-class backgrounds. As Caroline Zinsser's ethnography of family child care reveals, much of the growth in family child care arose from a generational shift in work patterns among women in these economic strata. Those in the older cohort had stayed at home with their children unless forced by economic need (usually owing to divorce or widowhood) to seek employment, but their daughters began taking jobs outside the home as a matter of course. In the absence of other forms of affordable and desirable child care (such as group care, which most of these families disdained), daughters turned to their mothers or, less frequently, mothers-in-law, to help care for their children. Many women moved from caring for their own grandchildren to taking in other children.[101]

Family caregivers tended to attract clients from their own social class who expressed a preference for an environment that was "warmer" and "more homelike" than what was available at child care centers—a feature parents judged to be particularly important in finding care for infants and young toddlers. In addition, family child care was often, though not always, more affordable than center-based care. Informal methods of referral and intake allowed both parents and caregivers to be highly selective and thus, if desired, avoid the social and racial integration they might encounter in centers (although many centers were also de facto segregated, depending on their sources of support).

It is difficult to document patterns of growth in this sector of care because most providers operated independently in a kind of occupational "gray market."[102] They did not regard themselves as professional or even employed in any usual sense. Adopting the identifier "babysitter" rather than "child care provider" or "caregiver," they saw their activities as an extension of their domestic duties that required no particular training or qualifications other than a "love of children."[103] Some family providers were young mothers who took in a few extra children in order to afford staying home with their own offspring while they were young; in their minds, they were merely "temporary providers" for whom family day care was an expedient. This group also tended to eschew professionalism with regard to child care, although they might not have done so with regard to an occupation outside the home.

It is also difficult to track family care because only a small proportion of the providers were licensed—some because state laws did not require it, others because they did not want to report their income, their homes did not meet regulatory standards, or they wished to avoid oversight for other reasons, such as maintaining ethnic or racial homogeneity. Nevertheless, in the 1970s, several organizations of or for family child care providers emerged, attracting those who wished to enhance their own visibility and status or obtain access to government benefits such as food assistance, which might not be available to small-scale providers operating independently.

At least one of these organizations was not created by child care providers but arose from the needs and self-help efforts of child care consumers. This was BANANAS, a parent-generated resource and referral agency started by a collective of feminist mothers in Berkeley, California, in the early 1970s. It began as an informal information network, offering referrals to members seeking family child care, and eventually evolved into a de facto regulatory agency, responding to complaints and keeping track of negative reports and their outcomes. BANANAS helped draw out family providers by offering them a registration system that was less cumbersome and off-putting than the state's licensing procedures but could still serve as a selling point by offering parents a modicum of protection.[104]

More mainstream was Quality Child Care, a network begun in Minnesota in 1978 to take advantage of U.S. Department of Agriculture surpluses, which later began to offer assistance to providers dealing with licensing and regulation and also branched into training. By 1984, the network extended into seven other states.[105] In the mid-1980s a national organization was finally formed, called the National Association for Family Day Care. This group held conferences that emphasized the business and professional aspects of family day care, stressing content and curriculum, and generally sought to combat the image that family day care providers were "just babysitters."[106]

In spite of efforts from various quarters to mobilize, family day care organization remained relatively static. A 1994 study reported that 25 percent of the providers in the field knew no other providers, 42 percent had no weekly contact with other providers, and 54 percent had no contact with organized groups of any type.[107] Moreover, an unknown (but apparently large) proportion of family providers remained unlicensed, and there was evidence that care in the gray market continued to be low in quality. In 1994 researchers found that a lack of professional involvement and regulation correlated with inferior care.[108] But many providers remained underground to avoid licensing and taxation (despite tax benefits that were available specifically to them) and retain control over the selection of clients, which they feared losing under government supervision.

Although the proportion of families using care in their own homes by either relatives or nonrelatives had declined since 1958, this mode of care remained important for upper-income families. Many professional and managerial couples chose such arrangements in the belief that they were superior to center or family care. One study suggested, however, that this was not always the case because of inherent contradictions between the expectations of the employers and the qualifications of the caregivers and the conditions under which they worked. Problems included a lack of communication between employers and nannies, unreasonable expectations (not calibrated to the qualifications of the caregivers) on the part of parents, and poor remuneration and benefits.[109] The "Nannygate" scandals of the early Clinton administration also spotlighted some of the risks inherent in hiring undocumented workers as caregivers.[110]

EMPLOYER-SPONSORED CHILD CARE

An increasingly important category of private-sector provisions was employer-sponsored child care; this is worth examining in some depth, for it displays both the advantages and disadvantages of private-sector initiatives. From the 1960s through the 1990s, the number of employer-supported child care programs rose from fewer than 200, serving about 6,000 children, to 5,600, serving perhaps 500,000 youngsters (see fig. 7.1).[111] By offering a new kind of employee benefit to selected groups of workers, this undertaking effectively expanded the scope of the American welfare state (broadly defined to include both public and private social provision).

Before the 1960s, there were a few experiments in employer-sponsored child care, the most notable being the Kaiser Child Service Centers established at the Kaiser Shipyards in Portland, Oregon, during World War II.[112] Privately run but funded by the federal government, these centers set high standards for child care in any era, but they did not serve as precedents for future child care policy, either public or private. The more immediate precedent for employer-supported services can be found in the early 1950s, when hospitals across the nation, faced with a severe shortage of nurses, began to set up on-site child care facilities. Surveys by hospital managers revealed that although nurses were being trained in substantial numbers, many abandoned the profession after they married and had children. Nursing administrators eventually realized that these women were forced to drop out because they could not find adequate care for their children.[113] The obvious solution was for hospitals themselves to provide services.[114] Hospital-based child care, enjoying its "start-up" advantage and sustained by the ongoing need for skilled nurses, became (and has remained) the predominant form of employer-sponsored care.[115]

Outside of hospitals, employer-supported child care programs developed in two phases. In the late 1960s and early 1970s, they went through an experimental or exploratory period that fizzled rather quickly. After a brief hiatus, a more sustained and expansive phase started up in the early 1980s, continuing to the present. A number of major firms were involved in the first phase, including Control Data Corporation in Minneapolis; Polaroid and KLH in Cambridge, Massachusetts; AT&T and Singer in Washington, D.C.; Levi Strauss in San Francisco; Whirlpool in Benton Harbor, Michigan; TRW in Texas; and Bell Telephone in several locations. Nearly three hundred colleges and universities also offered some form of child care.[116] Although educational institutions gave preference to the children of students rather than staff, commercial firms focused on the needs of female employees, an increasing proportion of whom were mothers of young children.[117] Federal agencies such as the Women's Bureau, the Departments of Labor and Agriculture, and the National Institutes of Health also set up centers for their employees.[118]

By 1970, women composed nearly 40 percent of the labor force, twice their proportion in 1940. Of the 31 million women at work, 12.2 million had children, nearly half of them under the age of six.[119] Recruitment of women, including mothers, was especially intense in such growth industries as service, electronics, and light manufacturing. Once hired, however, these new workers came to be perceived as problematic, with high rates of absenteeism and turnover. Employers were quick to attribute these trends to women's difficulties in combining work with domestic responsibilities. In earlier periods, employers had avoided this problem simply by insisting that potential hirees have child care arrangements well in hand or by refusing to hire mothers in the first place.[120] Now, many employers did not have that choice; in certain economic sectors and geographic areas, labor shortages compelled employers to hire women no matter what their family status. But there was also a severe shortage of child care slots; according to one survey, existing centers had a capacity for only 625,000 children—slightly more than 10 percent of those with working mothers.[121]

To address this issue, business leaders held several national conferences in the early 1970s.[122] At one of these, consultants offered "Seventeen Ways in Which Business Can Become Involved in Child Care" (appendix D). Opening a corporate child care center was only one of the suggestions, which also included encouraging the development of community facilities and lobbying for new day care legislation (Nixon had just vetoed the Comprehensive Child Development Act of 1971). Like the hospital administrators, however, many commercial employers came to believe that setting up their own facilities was the most direct and practical solution.

Federal incentives were also nudging employers in this direction. Through Title IV-A of the Social Security Act (one of the Public Welfare Amendments of 1962), firms could obtain funds for child care for employees who were low-income mothers or welfare recipients. This source was quite lucrative, for the government matched employer dollars on a three-to-one basis. One of the best-known projects based on this type of funding was located in Minneapolis, where a firm called Control Data joined with five other companies to form Northside Child Development. Control Data had originally planned to run a private on-site center for its own employees, but a sharp drop in business curtailed hiring and the project became financially untenable. At that point, the company turned to other firms in the area and started a consortium supported partly by Title IV-A funding. The large Northside center gave preference to employees of the participating companies but also accepted children from outside. According to one report, within a short time "the center had evolved from a private facility to a quasi-public one."[123] With a capacity for 120 children, it became the largest employer-supported facility in the United States in the early 1970s.

Employers who were not in a position to hire low-income women, most of whom had few skills, could take advantage of a tax write-off for child care expenses. A landmark 1973 Internal Revenue Service ruling stipulated that the expense was justified if the purpose of a center or program was "(1) to provide an employee with a place to send his or her child while at work knowing that the child is receiving proper care, (2) to reduce absenteeism, increase productivity, and reduce company training costs, and (3) to reduce employee turnover."[124] Given such broad parameters, many businesses could take advantage of the deduction. In addition, the Small Business Administration offered loans to cover start-up costs and lease guarantees, and the Department of Agriculture provided funding for lunches.[125]

By the early 1970s, the annual cost of full-time center-based care was running from $1,100 to $2,000 per child. At employer-sponsored facilities, parent fees usually covered only a portion of the cost, with employers absorbing the rest. When making their calculations, employers also figured in other expenses. Where there was heavy investment in plant and equipment as well as tight production schedules, for example, employee turnover could be very costly; a modest investment in child care could lower turnover and increase productivity. Government subsidies could ease the financial burden considerably.[126]

Because of the way government aid was set up, the initiative was all on the side of the employer; each firm could decide whether it wanted to create some sort of child care program—a decision that was, in turn, based on whether it wanted to attract female employees. Businesses were under no compunction to offer universal care or to offer any services at all. When they did so, it was often to enhance public relations. Businesses would opt for highly visible, architect-designed facilities that served as emblems of corporate enlightenment (fig. 7.2).[127]

Although on-site centers attracted a good deal of attention (partly because of their novelty, partly because of the efforts of corporate public relations departments), they were by no means the only or even the most common form of employer-supported child care. Many companies maintained that although it was incumbent upon them to support child care, operating a center, even with trained professionals on staff, lay outside their realm of expertise. Such companies preferred to take an indirect approach. This could range from setting up "resource and referral" (R&R) services—sometimes nothing more than a list of local providers—to arranging for group discounts at a nearby independent facility. Other firms preferred to reserve slots for their employees in off-site facilities, which they subsidized either individually or as part of a corporate consortium. Subsidies might take the form of expert services (such as accounting) as well as cash.

Some forms of indirect support, like R&R services or cooperative arrangements, cost the company very little. Others, however, might be just as expensive as setting up an on-site facility. Polaroid, for example, offered child care vouchers whose value depended on the employee's salary and total household income, the size of her family, and the cost of the child care. Employees could choose where to send their children, but each facility had to be licensed and company-approved, with certified teachers. According to Polaroid's community-relations administrator, "We require quality centers—not just baby warehouses."[128] Polaroid had, in effect, become a surrogate for the state with regard to both financial support and regulation of child care.

By the mid-1970s, the economic downturn, coupled with certain practical problems, dampened the initial wave of enthusiasm for employer-supported services, and management undertook a more sober assessment of its policies. Few companies turned out to be as committed to child care, especially for low-income workers, as Control Data, or as flexible and resourceful in finding new ways to pursue their goals when initial plans fell through. As a result, many on-site programs were terminated or converted into public services no longer supported by business. Some small on-site centers, such as those run by Stride Rite in Boston and Connecticut General Life Insurance in Hartford, along with the Polaroid voucher program, remained in operation, while Control Data's center continued in its new, government-subsidized form. As of 1976, it was estimated, the number of employer-supported programs, including centers,

Fig. 7.2. Warner Bros. was the first film production company to build an on-site child care facility. Their award-winning Children's Center, designed by Rios Associates (a Los Angeles architectural firm) and located in a corner of their back lot in Burbank, California, in the early 1990s, has a capacity for more than 100 children, from infants through preschoolers. Images of Bugs Bunny, Daffy Duck, and other signature Warner Bros. cartoon characters are laminated onto the center's windows. Photograph by David Hewitt and Anne Garrison.

had stabilized at about 150–200, still serving only about 6,000 children (see fig. 7.1). More than half of these programs were sponsored by hospitals or other health care or nonprofit institutions.[129]

In spite of much fanfare and substantial investment in plant, equipment, and personnel on the companies' part, many of the new on-site facilities simply failed to attract substantial numbers of families. There were several reasons for this: cost, a preference for facilities closer to home or for a different type of facility (for instance, family child care), and the demographics of the employees themselves. Underutilization not only disappointed corporate planners but also created financial problems. Although most companies were willing to subsidize services to some extent (often with the help of the government), they expected parents to pick up at least part of the expense. Fewer children meant less outside revenue, both from parents and from the government, and this shortfall, in combination with continuing absenteeism and turnover, convinced many employers that supporting child care was not cost-effective after all.[130]

Some of the resistance might have been predicted, had managers bothered to conduct inquiries before embarking on their various programs. Most, however, simply assumed that child care was what their female employees needed and, without bothering to assess their preferences or practices, plunged ahead to create it. Employees had little voice in the process. For one thing, they could not find appropriate channels for expressing their views. Most mothers targeted by first-phase corporate-based services were blue-collar, clerical, and service workers who, for the most part, lacked union representation and were not mobilized in any other way.[131]

Workers who belonged to unions were not much better off, for labor's leadership did not begin to bargain consistently for child care until the 1980s (fig. 7.3). One female-dominated union, the Amalgamated Clothing and Textile Workers' Union (ACTWU), had won employer support to set up its own centers, first in Virginia in 1968 and then in Maryland, Pennsylvania, and Illinois. By the early 1970s, ACTWU's child care centers, with a capacity for some 1,600 children, had become one of the largest providers in the country.[132] Two ACTWU staff members, Joyce Miller and Connie Kopelov, insisted on making child care one of the central issues of the Coalition of Labor Union Women (CLUW), a women's labor organization they helped found in 1974. As a result, CLUW pushed unions to negotiate for employer-sponsored child care benefits for members, but the organization found unions unresponsive and employers even less so. The overwhelming majority of blue-collar women workers continued to lack access to formal, affordable child care.[133]

All told, by the mid-1970s, employer-supported services could accommodate only a tiny proportion of more than 6 million children who had working mothers. In its initial phase, corporate child care was hampered by a relatively low level of employer initiative as well as resistance on the part of its potential clientele. To a certain degree, corporate policy was determined by state objectives, although government incentives to corporations were effective only insofar as they coincided with corporations' own business goals—that is, when it was in their interest to hire women. This was particularly true when it came to tapping the pool of low-income women targeted by workfare subsidies under Title IV-A.

THE SECOND PHASE OF EMPLOYER-SPONSORED CARE

The second phase of corporate child care development, which began in the early 1980s, was marked by greater congruity between government aims and private-sector policies. At the same time that the Reagan administration was

Fig. 7.3. Unionized workers increasingly made an issue of child care in the 1980s. In 1988, members of the American Federation of State, County and Municipal Employees demonstrated (unsuccessfully) for child care at the University of Illinois at Urbana-Champaign. The two sign holders are twin brothers Bobby and Jimmy Schnitzlein, children of staff members. Courtesy of Sari Schnitzlein.

reducing support for public child care for low-income families, Congress was coming up with additional incentives for the creation of employer-sponsored provisions. In addition to the tax breaks already in place for firms offering various types of services (with on-site facilities being the most lucrative in tax terms), Congress determined that as of 1982, child or dependent care would no longer be considered taxable fringe benefits; instead, their value could be *excluded* from an employee's gross income.[134] This more favorable tax situation conveniently coincided with corporate efforts to focus on the needs and de-mands of upper-level employees such as management and skilled technicians.

The resurgence of corporate interest in child care had multiple sources. In part it arose from the women's liberation movement, which, more than ever before, framed child care as a feminist issue and claimed to speak for working mothers.[135] Although the women's movement undoubtedly broke the ice, it was *individual* women in high-level positions who ultimately brought the issue home to employers. By 1980 the efforts of the Equal Employment Oppor-tunity Commission were beginning to show results, and the gender profile of the American labor force was changing. Occupational segregation and the concentration of women in the service sector were declining, while the proportion of women in the professions, management, and sales was on the up-swing.[136] According to the *Wall Street Journal,* "Far more career-minded women have joined the work force, and day-care demand is stronger than ever."[137] Few women had risen high enough in the corporate ranks to begin worrying about hitting the "glass ceiling," but many felt sufficiently confident of their market value to seek special benefits such as maternity leave and child care without fear of being stigmatized, marginalized, or dismissed outright. As one Harvard Business School graduate expressed it to a recruiter from Corning Glass Works, "What's your company going to do about my two-year-old daughter?"

This woman was probably not overestimating her worth in the corporate world. In sectors that were experiencing severe labor shortages, such as high technology, employers were more than willing to accommodate women's de-mands. A spokesman for Wang Laboratories in Lowell, Massachusetts, con-ceded, "We have women in highly-skilled positions. These are one-of-a-kind people."[138] To retain such employees, in 1981 Wang invested $150,000 in an on-site child care center—three-fifths of the program's annual budget. Parent fees made up the remainder of the cost (twenty-five dollars per week for Wang employees, fifty dollars for non-Wang personnel). In general, women made the most gains in personnel-intensive industries, particularly where their talents or skills were perceived as unique. Hospitals continued to view on-site child care as the best means of retaining nurses.[139]

Employers' renewed interest in sponsoring child care was based on a simple calculation: it was cheaper to support child care than to train fresh cohorts of new employees for high-level managerial and technical positions. In 1979 Union Fidelity Insurance, a Pennsylvania firm, started an on-site child care center when it was threatened with the departure of five key executives who had all become pregnant simultaneously.[140] With training for some positions run-ning as high $100,000 per employee, executives readily concluded that it was less expensive to provide child care and allow innovations such as flexible hours and job sharing than to risk turnover by rigidly adhering to work rules and conditions that had been codified in the days when managers were nearly all male and depended on non-wage-earning wives to shoulder most family re-sponsibilities.

Some observers attributed the spread of enlightened personnel policies to a new generation of managers—many of them veterans of the 1960s countercul-ture—who used a more people-oriented approach.[141] Whereas benevolence and humanitarian concern may have motivated some employers to offer child care and other family-related services, most were simply pragmatic, recognizing that it was necessary to offer attractive benefits packages in order to recruit and retain the most desirable personnel. Many of those same "enlightened" managers were simultaneously rebuffing trade union initiatives to win child care benefits for lower-skilled, nonprofessional, and nonmanagerial employees, who were generally regarded as interchangeable.

While denying union demands, management sometimes went overboard in trying to accommodate upper-level personnel. Some companies even used complicated "sensing" techniques to determine what employees actually wanted, thus relieving them of the burden of making demands on their own behalf (and thus reducing the risk of employee mobilization at the middle level).[142] In the competition for recruitment prizes, however, managers sometimes made serious errors of judgment and ended up offering benefits that were inappropriate, untenable, or wasteful. In 1982, child care consultant Jacquelyn McCroskey cautioned, "Far too many employers make the decision to invest in a family-oriented benefits program just because someone else is doing it."[143] McCroskey advised companies to spend time surveying employees' needs and developing a comprehensive framework for relating proposed benefits to overall policies, before proceeding to the point of actually offering specific programs.

Consultants like McCroskey were much in demand during the early 1980s, as companies sought guidance in planning and setting up benefits and services for their employees. More than two hundred representatives of hospitals, government agencies, and major corporations flocked to a conference titled "New Management Initiatives for Working Parents," held at Wheelock College in Boston in 1981.[144] Hundreds of other companies invited consultants, usually accompanied by their research teams or "groups," to come into their firms, conduct on-site surveys, and design customized solutions. Most in demand were consultants who could offer unique "products" such as "cafeteria-style benefits," an array devised to compensate employees who would not make use of services such as child care, which were meaningful primarily to the parents of young children.[145] Cafeteria plans ensured fairness across the board by allowing employees to pick and choose among a range of benefits that might include discount tickets to ball games or membership in a health club as well as child care. (It is worth pondering whether companies would have felt compelled to compensate for benefits that accrued only, or mainly, to men.) Consultants were available to guide personnel departments through the administrative complexities involved in setting up such plans.[146]

Consultants and research groups were only one type of spin-off from the benefits bonanza. Day care brokers offered to locate slots and providers to suit particular clients, whereas firms like "Wheezles and Sneezles" in Minneapolis specialized in lining up caretakers for sick children on short notice.[147] For companies that still preferred to provide their own services, commercial day care vendors pitched proposals for setting up and operating on-site centers. Such vendors could oversee every aspect of the service, ranging from design and construction of the building to curriculum development, menu planning, and the hiring, training, and supervision of personnel.

By extricating the functions of planning and operating child care from corporate personnel divisions, repackaging them, and then marketing them back, consultants and suppliers allowed companies to reap the benefits of enlightened employerhood while avoiding the headaches involved in setting up a new operation or division. To companies accustomed to purchasing parts and equipment (or, closer to home, health insurance and pension plans) from outside vendors, it seemed only logical to contract for child care. At the same time the creativity and momentum generated by spin-offs helped to channel and maintain energy around the idea of corporate child care, making it more feasible for employers to "install" as well as more attractive to employees.

But employer-sponsored child care could not, on its own, resolve the child care problem. Most corporate programs, designed for instrumental rather than altruistic purposes, offered convenience and reliability but ignored cost issues, replicating the larger child care market, in which access to quality services was linked to ability to pay. Such policies implicitly favored mid- to upper-level employees but left lower-paid workers on their own. Only a few companies, which were highly dependent on low-wage workers, came up with plans that actually provided subsidies for child care.[148]

Even leaving aside the problems of low-wage employees, employer-sponsored programs fell short of meeting the growing needs of working families; issues of supply and quality continued to plague both employers and employees. In 1992, some corporate leaders became convinced that the question of child care was too broad to be addressed through the efforts of individual companies and decided to develop a collective approach. A group of twenty-one major corporations, self-identified as Champions, formed the American Business Collaboration for Quality Dependent Care (ABC), putting together a multimillion-dollar fund to support the development of community-level programs to care for preschoolers as well as school-age children and elders. Administered through Work/Family Directions, an independent contractor, ABC distributed more than $27 million between 1992 and 1995, with another $100 million committed for the years 1995–2000.[149] Also in 1992 a group of Champions in Texas joined other businesses to form a smaller local version of ABC, the Houston Area Network for Dependent Services (HANDS); by 1996, the annual budget of this organization had reached $750,000.[150]

Although ABC and HANDS aimed at offering one-time funding to establish services or upgrade quality, they did not address the issue of maintaining quality on an ongoing basis, which would have required continuing financial assistance to reduce operating costs, either through direct grants to centers or indirect subsidies to parents. Instead, the quality of the programs they had assisted depended upon the affluence of their clienteles. This meant that, once again, the market would determine which parents had access to high-quality, well-regulated services.

Where they were available, employer-supported services raised employee expectations and consolidated a clientele for one form of privatized child care. However, only a tiny proportion of American employees had access to such provisions, and many of those eligible could not take advantage of the facilities because of high costs. Nevertheless, a small, select constituency arose around this benefit, serving to hive off one group of articulate consumers who might otherwise have played an active role in a united child care constituency.

A DIVIDED CONSTITUENCY

In spite of its fragmentation, child care, throughout the 1980s, was becoming a more normal part of everyday life in the United States, with parents of all stripes dropping off their children at centers dotting the urban and suburban landscape or handing them off to family or in-home providers. The Child Care Media Action Campaign, started by Elinor Guggenheimer in 1983, played up the energy and variety of these new services. The image of child care also benefited from the endorsement of leading early childhood educators, experts, and organizations. These included longtime opponents of child care such as the pediatrician T. Berry Brazelton, who, in his 1985 book *Working and Caring*, abandoned his usual stance urging mothers to stay at home with their children and instead offered advice about how to find good child care and make the adjustment to it.[151]

One of the most important voices favoring normalization was that of early childhood educator Bettye Caldwell, who deplored the disciplinary barriers and jurisdictional competition among the many fields dealing with children and families, which, she felt, prevented cooperation and instead led to incoherent policies and low-quality provisions. Caldwell had testified at the 1969 hearings on comprehensive preschool education about the need to incorporate learning experiences into all programs for young children, and from 1969 to 1978, she directed a project combining child care and early education in Little Rock, Arkansas.[152] Based on her success there, she began to promote a concept called "educare" as a way of overcoming what she saw as a counterproductive split between child care and early childhood education. In the absence of federal regulation of child care programs, Caldwell also endorsed efforts on the part of the National Association for the Education of Young Children to develop an interdisciplinary accreditation system involving both self-study and on-site observation.[153]

But even support from prominent children's experts like Brazelton and Caldwell could not fend off the perception that the child care system was in crisis. As the demand for services increased, especially among the middle class, the shortcomings of America's provisions became more visible. The media routinely deplored the lack of adequate facilities, the high costs, and the questionable standards. To make matters worse, right-wing ideologues such as Phyllis Schlafly seized on every tale of abuse and mismanagement as evidence for her assertion that maternal employment and child care were simply bad ideas.[154]

The perception of crisis had a distressing effect on parents. At a time when their need for child care was greater than ever, their confidence about deciding to place their children in care, and about the quality of the services themselves, was wavering. As one scholar has put it, the situation was one of "dependence overshadowed by doubt."[155] The situation came to a head when child care providers across the country were subjected to a series of allegations of sexual abuse.[156] These changes thrust child care into the headlines and, throughout the 1980s, placed it in the worst possible light. Notably, however, because of the prevailing political inertia and antigovernment sentiment, such allegations did not immediately lead directly to calls for more regulation and better oversight, and quality remained uncertain.[157]

The self-doubt of middle-class parents, coupled with the tensions between and among the consumers and providers of different types of care, created a divided constituency for child care. The most obvious lines of cleavage were those of class and race, but the differences among various kinds of providers also created friction. For example, family day care providers (many of them still "underground") and their clients came to disdain publicly funded child care centers as havens for teenage welfare moms and their children. Family providers, who did not see child care as work and preferred to stay home, also sniffed at the professionalism of trained staff at both public and private centers. At the same time, they were critical of "yuppie" mothers (but not fathers) for neglecting their children and focusing on their careers.[158]

The middle-class clientele of child care centers were equally disdainful of family providers, whose services, they said, consisted mainly of parking kids in front of television sets and feeding them junk food while they talked on the phone and puffed on cigarettes. Middle-class parents tended to discount the advantages of a homelike setting, a small group, and continuous care from one adult. Nevertheless, these same parents were sometimes compelled to turn to family providers when they failed to find affordable slots for their children in child care centers.

Meanwhile, upper-income parents (the yuppies derided by family providers) were using corporate child care when it was available or hiring in-home caregivers such as au pairs, legal and illegal immigrants with only informal experience, babysitters of all ages, and trained nannies, thus creating more or less satisfactory webs of care that might also include nursery schools and myriad lessons of all sorts, sometimes linked by paid transportation services. Families who made such arrangements often mentally exempted themselves from the child care constituency altogether.[159]

These divisions helped shape, and were in turn reproduced by, the politics of child care in the late 1980s, as Congress once again considered a series of bills based on competing visions of child care and rationales for government support. At this point the federal government was, as it had been throughout the decade, actually spending more on child care subsidies for families with moderate incomes and above than it was for poor and low-income families. The legislation being considered addressed this discrepancy in various ways. The Family Support Act (FSA), a new version of workfare, offered additional funding for child care services for the poor in conjunction with its mandatory work requirements, whereas the Act for Better Child Care (ABCC) was intended to improve the supply and quality of child care across the board.[160] The FSA passed in 1988, while the ABCC was watered down and transformed into the more limited Child Care and Development Block Grant, which passed in 1990.

The reasons for this outcome were complicated. The Republicans wanted welfare reform to address the continuing increase in welfare dependency (a phenomenon that should have come as no surprise, given the cutbacks in child care services to the poor imposed by the 1981 OBRA). Many Democrats were also uneasy with the existing welfare system and responded to a bipartisan effort to pass the FSA led by Senator Daniel P. Moynihan. By contrast, the ABCC was just one of some 100 bills introduced in the 1980s to address the growing perception of a child care crisis. With the rapid increase in the number of working mothers, nearly every member of Congress felt compelled to "do something" about child care, and turf battles broke out; in addition to various Democratic bills, Republican Senator Orrin Hatch of Utah submitted his own. Meanwhile, President George Bush, under pressure from Phyllis Schlafly and other New Right forces to oppose the growing trend toward maternal employment, weighed in with his "toddler allowance"—a blanket allotment to all families with children, regardless of the income level and employment status of the parents.[161]

Even without all this competition, the ABCC bill would probably have foundered over an internal issue: the question of church-based care. When Marian Wright Edelman, now head of the prominent Children's Defense Fund, decided to accede to Republican demands that church-run facilities be allowed to receive federal funding, the compromise tore Democrats apart. Some believed that it was worth making a concession to gain support for child care, while others clung strictly to the principle of church-state separation. Congress' only alternative was to come up with a much-weakened bill that could garner enough Republican support to pass and win Bush's signature. Whereas the original ABCC bill would have authorized some $2.5 billion to improve child care across the board, the Child Care and Development Block Grant that finally passed contained only $825 million, most of which was targeted to low-income groups.[162] Thus the 1980s came to an end without bringing the United States much closer to a system of universal child care.[163]

During the Clinton administration, nearly all discussion of child care has occurred within the context of welfare reform. Before signing the Personal Responsibility and Work Opportunity Act of 1996 (PRWOA), President Bill Clinton vetoed two bills on the grounds that they contained inadequate funding for child care. According to the Congressional Budget Office, however, the monies appropriated by the PRWOA would still be insufficient to support the amount of child care required if all the states were to meet their mandatory goals for moving welfare recipients into work. The architects of the bill perhaps assumed that the child care issue would simply take care of itself; they identified child care as a promising occupation for former AFDC mothers—the *only* occupation to be singled out in this way. Such a suggestion was dismaying for many reasons, not the least of which was that there was no indication that welfare mothers were any more suited to providing child care than any other group of women (or men for that matter).[164] One highly regarded study of family day care specifically cautioned that because motivation and engagement are closely correlated to the quality of care, "no public policies at the federal or state level should push or require people to care for children if they do not want to be providers."[165] Yet many state and local welfare officials have advocated such programs as an inexpensive and efficient means of meeting job placement quotas *and* addressing child care needs simultaneously.[166]

Although child care policy received considerable attention at the federal level for nearly four decades, little progress was made toward developing a system of universal care. Rifts between public and private provision, and among the clients and advocates of different types of care, created a divided constituency that was, in turn, perpetuated by congressional vacillation between targeted and universal policies. The most powerful political forces were advocates of welfare reform seeking to use child care provisions as an instrument of their own policy aims, not as an end in itself. Also vocal were lobbyists for commercial operators such as the National Association of Child Care Management, who generally succeeded in keeping standards low and regulatory bodies weak.

Their opponents, nongovernmental groups such as the Children's Defense Fund, the Child Care Action Campaign, and the National Black Child Development Institute, lobbied long and hard with minimal resources and eager but intermittent support from a number of other children's advocacy groups for whom child care was only one of many concerns. Middle- and upper-class parent-consumers, well supplied with tax credits and other concessions, tended to act as individuals, seeking to maximize their purchasing power to find quality care for their children but reluctant to join parent coalitions or engage in long-term legislative campaigns.[167] Feminists, surprisingly, played a relatively minor role in the struggle for child care, although *feminism* served as a red flag to right-wing groups seeking to oppose all government support for child care except when it targeted welfare recipients. Weakest of all were the poor and low-income beneficiaries of federally sponsored provisions, who were seldom able to make themselves heard as Congress tightened work regulations while slashing funding for child care and other needed services.

Ironically, the rationale for public child care near the end of the twentieth century has advanced little beyond that which motivated the benevolent women of Philadelphia to found their day nursery more than two centuries ago:

to help indigent women help themselves. In seeking to explain the failure of the United States to establish a universal system of public child care, I have examined a range of factors, including the initial stigmatizing link between child care and philanthropy, which was reinforced by the unfortunate split between "custodial" and "developmental" programs. Opposition to state expansion and to the intervention of the state into what is cast as "private" life has also been decisive; with regard to child care, it has meant that Americans have been reluctant to call upon the state and expect little from it in the way of direct public provision except under extreme circumstances such as economic depression and war or, more recently, under pressure to reduce perceived high levels of welfare dependency. The lack of public services, coupled with strategic tax incentives to both individuals and corporations, has had the effect of building up the supply of child care in the private sector, creating a constituency for this type of provision and deflecting demands upon the state for universal services.

Such patterns are the hallmark of a liberal or "public-private" welfare state regime.[168] What is important to note here is that the United States did not suddenly emerge as a full-blown liberal regime. Rather, this system was produced and reproduced over time, with child care provision as one of its key constituents. A typology of welfare-state regimes does not, however, fully explain the specific and consistent opposition to maternal employment and, by extension, to child care that this book has documented. We must also consider the challenge posed by wage-earning mothers to the prevailing ideal of motherhood: full-time care by a stay-at-home mother supported by a male breadwinner-father.[169] Except when interrupted temporarily by World War II (and, to a lesser extent, by the Great Depression), the persistent formulation of maternal employment and child care as exceptional, pathological, or anomalous left that ideal virtually untouched until the emergence of feminism in the 1960s.

Although the women's movement challenged the prevailing prescription for motherhood, it failed to mobilize a viable campaign for public child care. The rights-based orientation of the most visible branch of second-wave feminism—liberal organizations such as the National Organization for Women and the Women's Political Caucus—focused on formal aspects of gender equity such as access to education and employment but generally ignored the implications of women's lack of social citizenship epitomized by the absence of public child care.[170] The more radical branch of the movement—Marxist or socialist feminists—made sweeping demands that might have reconfigured social citizenship for women but it went too far beyond the political pale to be able to mobilize a unified constituency. Without focused feminist leadership and propelled by a policy that persistently linked public provisions to welfare-related goals, wage-earning mothers divided along class and racial lines instead of joining together.

As welfare reform takes hold, American child care policy appears to have reached a temporary stalemate, with the country further than ever from establishing universal provisions. At a time when poor and low-income women are being offered only minimal services, it might appear unseemly even to raise the issue of universal entitlements. Yet it is precisely because the discourses surrounding child care have become so fractured by race and class that this deeply flawed policy has been allowed to develop in the first place. By unifying the constituency for child care, it may be possible to change the terms of provision. State governments, with federal support, must increase funding and expand existing facilities to accommodate not only families moving from welfare to work under the terms of the Personal Responsibility and Work Opportunity Act but *all* low-income families.[171] In addition, parents of every class, along with feminists, children's advocates, the labor movement, and all those committed to social justice, must join to insist that these services be high in quality and made available as long as need persists. America's poor and low-income families deserve nothing less.

Such developments have the potential for serving as the foundation for a strong, positive system of public child care. Although such a system would initially be restricted in terms of class, it could, with the introduction of sliding-scale fees, eventually be expanded to include children from families at all income levels, and the United States could finally write a universal coda to its long, sad history of child care. Americans as a nation must recognize the social value of child rearing, whether it is performed by parents or nonparental caregivers.[172] They must also grant every woman the right to choose between caregiving and wage-earning by offering *paid* parental leave as well as public child care.[173] Until then, children cannot be guaranteed adequate resources for nurturance, security, and development, and true social citizenship will remain beyond the grasp of American women.

Epilogue: American Child Care in Comparative Perspective

In 1989, the French-American Foundation initiated a nationwide effort to introduce Americans to the wonders of the French child care system in the hopes that it would provide a model for child care reform in the United States. The foundation invited scholars, civic leaders, professionals, and politicians to a series of regional symposia and distributed a polished, highly laudatory report, *A Welcome for Every Child: How France Achieves Quality in Child Care: Practical Ideas for the United States*.[1] After attending one of those presentations, I came away duly impressed by the images of contented children interacting with attentive caretakers in bright, well-designed crèches and cozy day care homes, by descriptions of thoughtful, sensible arrangements of hours and fees, and, above all, by statistics measuring the government's generous public support for child care. But I was also left wondering, Why in France and not here?

A few years later, as a Fulbright scholar in Stockholm, I had the opportunity to observe some of the justly famous child care centers that are the pride of the Nordic countries. In Sweden and also in Finland, I was charmed by visits to tiny "house corners" furnished with miniature versions of classic Scandinavian modern furniture, and I found myself envying the many mothers I spoke to who, no matter what their income level, knew that their children were receiving care of the highest quality. Again, the question arose, Why there and not here?

It is no simple matter to pluck a policy from one country and introduce it into another, for no matter how practical or appealing it may seem, there are likely to be numerous barriers to its acceptance and implantation. A policy such as public child care, whether universal or targeted, evolves through a chain of specific historical events and is deeply embedded in a broader national context or political culture, of which it is a constituent element (fig. E.1). Given the halting, piecemeal development of child care in the United States, one would not expect our political culture to be particularly hospitable to a French or Swedish social import.

To understand why certain societies have produced successful child care programs while the United States has largely failed to do so, some comparative analysis is in order. Such an analysis will allow us to pinpoint the factors that have been conducive to the development of public provisions in other societies—factors that may have been weaker or entirely missing in the American context.

A COMPARATIVE FRAMEWORK

To begin our comparison, we might sort the "successful" cases not by the child care systems themselves but according to the political environments in which they have emerged.[2] Comparative scholars use different sets of categories for this purpose; one of the most prevalent is "welfare-state regime," the term coined by the comparative historical sociologist Gøsta Esping-Andersen to refer to the type of complex but systematic relationship between social policy, employment, and "general social structure" that has developed in a given society.[3] Though not static, each type of regime produces a certain political logic that generally determines the overall direction, if not the specific details, of social welfare policy.

While abjuring the use of strict categories, Esping-Andersen argues that modern democratic market societies tend to "cluster" around three major regime types: liberal, conservative corporatist, and social democratic.[4] The United States, Canada, and Australia, with their characteristic emphasis on free competition within an unfettered marketplace and reluctance to commit public resources to social goals, are examples of the liberal type.[5] In such regimes,

Fig. E.1. Since the 1980s, architectural journals have featured
distinctively designed child care facilities from around the world.
This Parisian crèche was built in an industrial area in the late
1980s. Designed by architects Olivier Brénac and Xavier Gonzalez,
it is run by the municipality and has a capacity for sixty children.
Attached to it are a shop where crèche furniture from around the
city is taken for repair, and an apartment for the crèche's director.
From "Paris 20è crèche," *Le moniteur architecture–AMC,* no. 64
(September 1995): 22; photograph by Hervé Abbadie.

social assistance is usually modest and often means-tested, and many services
are offered through the private sector with the encouragement of the state.[6]
France, Germany, Austria, and Italy are most often classified as conservative-
corporatist regimes. Charged with upholding class, occupational, religious,
and, most important for our concerns, gender distinctions, they tend to allow
the state "to displace the market as a provider of welfare" but, given their
traditional values, are not strongly redistributive.[7] The Scandinavian states,
embracing the principles of universalism, full employment, and equality, typify
the social democratic regime. Committed to reducing both class and gender
inequality, such regimes are most likely to deploy generous social programs to
compensate for the workings of the market.

To evaluate the impact of these different types of regimes, Esping-Andersen
measures the level of "decommodification" produced by each one—that is,
"the degree to which [it] permit[s] people to make their living standards
independent of pure market forces."[8] On this scale, social democratic regimes
appear to be the most decommodifying, liberal ones the least. As feminist
sociologists Ann Shola Orloff and Julia S. O'Connor point out, however, the
concept of decommodification cannot fully capture the impact of welfare states
on women's social citizenship. Because this concept is based on the needs of the
(male) citizen-worker, it is implicitly gender biased. What women need is,

precisely, to *become commodified*—that is, to gain access to the labor market, a move that requires specific services as well as benefits and entitlements. For this reason Orloff proposes a substitute measure for a regime's impact on women: the extent to which it enhances women's autonomy and capacity to form independent households.[9]

Because a different logic is at play with regard to policies directed at women, we might expect to find that levels of autonomy enhancement and decommodification do not always match.[10] As sociologist Jan Windebank points out, provisions such as child care implicitly challenge "the dominant ideology of mothering," evoking resistances or requiring justifications that policies directed at men, such as unemployment insurance or workmen's compensation, would not.[11] This observation should give us pause when we encounter studies that claim to show a close correlation between child care systems and welfare-state regimes categorized according to levels of decommodification alone. For example, economist Siv Gustafsson, comparing the United States, Sweden, and the Netherlands, expects to—and does—find similarities between child care provision and levels of decommodification in general (both measures are high in social democratic regimes, low in liberal and conservative-corporatist regimes).[12] But her argument is flawed by a skewed selection of cases. For each type of welfare-state regime, she uses a country whose child care system and maternal employment patterns have developed in the predictable direction. It is possible, however, to find cases for each regime type in which policies and patterns have developed in the opposite or unexpected direction. A more complex comparative framework that takes gender into account is needed to explain these cases as well as the more predictable ones.

Indeed, the societies where the most comprehensive systems of child care may currently be found (France, most of the Scandinavian countries, Australia, and Japan) do not fit into any single regime category. In each of these societies, nationally supported provisions have been in place at least since the 1970s. (The near-universal systems of the Soviet Union and countries of the Eastern bloc, which were established as part of Communist regimes, have been more or less dismantled since 1989.)[13] Canada, which had a fairly strong system in the 1970s and 1980s, has now reverted to an intermittent and localized pattern resembling that of the United States.[14] Using a modified comparative welfare-state regime framework, the following accounts, necessarily condensed and schematic, trace the evolution of child care policy in Sweden, France, Japan, Australia, and Canada, pointing out the factors that either fostered or hindered its development in each country.

SWEDEN: GENDER EQUALITY IN THE
"PEOPLE'S HOME"

Much of the support for Sweden's generous and comprehensive child care system may be attributed to the social democratic hegemony that, with only brief interruptions, has prevailed in the country since the 1930s. But it is also important to credit the role of the nation's feminists, who, at critical moments, intervened into policy debates to insist on policies that were both woman-friendly and universal. The social democratic state had its roots in the concept of the "people's home," a vision that was developed, in part, as a response to concerns about declining population and low marriage rates. Although such concerns might have easily militated against maternal employment, a cross-class, cross-party alliance of women strategically linked pronatalist concerns to married women's right to work, arguing that if they were barred from employment, women might refrain from marriage and childbearing.[15] Thus support for gender equity, as expressed through women's right to work (though not specifically supported by child care services), was inscribed in Swedish social democracy from the outset.

Through the 1950s, the country's growing prosperity worked against employment for married women. In the 1960s, however, the demand for labor increased as a result of rapid industrial expansion, and the labor federation (LO) decided to mobilize Swedish housewives rather than bring in immigrants to fill the need. In the policy debates that ensued, Social Democratic women demanded universal state-sponsored child care, while the conservative and center parties proposed care allowances that could be used either for child care or as a subsidy to mothers caring for their own children. Left-wing women pointed out that even with care allowances, single mothers could not really afford to stay at home; moreover, they feared that the allowances would encourage the growth of privatized services while undermining the quality of the existing system of public child care.[16]

The women's arguments resonated with other Social Democratic concerns: population decline and the goal of reducing class inequality through early socialization and education.[17] The result was a dramatic increase in publicly supported child care. In 1965, Sweden's public child care centers could accommodate fewer than 12,000 children; by 1980, they had spaces for more than 136,000. During the same period, family day care slots increased from 19,000 to 88,500.[18]

Striking as these gains in child care were, modifications of Swedish social policy over time have tended to downplay incentives to full-time maternal employment and instead attempted to modulate women's life cycles so as to permit a combination of child-rearing and labor-force activity. Most Swedish mothers provide full-time care for their own children through the first year or so, and then part-time care until they reach school age, first turning to paid parental leave and then using a combination of group child care and the "short hours" option, which allows them to work only about thirty hours per week.

The explicit purpose of these policies is to allow parents to reconcile work and family and to encourage parent-child bonding at crucial stages of development. But it also saves the state some of the expense of child care, particularly for infants, which is the most costly. At the same time, these policies perpetuate women's primary association with motherhood. For financial as well as physiological reasons, mothers have been far more likely than fathers to take advantage of parental leave, resulting in patterns of intermittent employment for women.[19] Thus, according to political scientist Rianne Mahon, despite the general availability of affordable, high-quality child care, "instead of the egalitarian family with two earners (and two active parents), the 'one and three-quarters' wage earner family has become the norm, leaving many women economically dependent on their men and on the state."[20]

In the 1990s, Swedish feminists have fended off repeated attacks on the child care system from across the political spectrum, including the left. The Social Democrats have, for example, sought to balance feminist calls for increased child care against LO demands for purportedly gender-neutral benefits such as extended vacations. But Social Democratic governments could also be relied upon to reverse attempts by the center and right-wing parties to reduce funding for public child care services by substituting care allowances and allowing for-profit companies to set up shop (under the guise of offering "choice").[21] Keeping up pressure from both inside and outside the party, feminists have shored up the Social Democrats' commitment to child care, although concessions to both labor and anti-feminist forces have created a situation in which child care alone cannot guarantee either Swedish women's equality in the labor force or the complete realization of the ideal of "worker-mother."

FRANCE: THE POWER OF PRONATALISM

Although France is usually cited as a prototypical conservative-corporatist regime, it has provided public child care for nearly a century and a half. Services, currently organized at the municipal level, are offered within the context of a comprehensive family policy that also includes generous maternity leave and children's allowances. Child care falls under the aegis of two divisions of the state. For children aged two and three, the emphasis is developmental, and child care is considered part of family policy. Overseen by the Ministry of Health and organized and financed by municipalities, this stage of child care takes the form of both crèches (similar to American child care centers) and family home providers who belong to networks that, through a variety of incentive and enrichment plans, supervise and regulate them.[22] For older children (three to six), the stress is on education, and facilities are run through the Ministry of Education.

As political scientist Jane Jenson explains, since the late nineteenth century, French social policy has been driven by pronatalist concerns. But the demand for more children had to be reconciled with a distinct and persistent pattern of female participation in the labor force, first on farms and in small family-owned businesses and shops, later in factories. Beginning in the mid-nineteenth century, French mothers placed their very young children in charitable crèches;[23] by the turn of the century, many of these (unlike American day nurseries) were receiving municipal support. Also in place were écoles maternelles (similar to nursery schools but with longer hours) for children too old for crèches but too young for schools; these were funded by a combination of public and charitable funds.[24] During World War I, French factories set up nursing rooms on their premises to ensure that the infants of wage-earning mothers would receive proper nourishment without causing major interruptions to the work schedule.[25]

Pronatalist concerns took on new momentum following World War II, as conservative social Catholics pressed for "familist" policies designed to keep mothers out of the labor force. They emphasized the value of family care for children and actively opposed increasing the number of crèches. They also criticized the use of family policy to manipulate the rate of female labor force participation.[26] Starting in the 1950s, however, the direction of French policy changed. Although the center-right Gaullists were in power, they were less responsive than might be expected to the influence of the social Catholics when it came to crafting family policy. The growth of the service sector of the economy was creating a fresh demand for female labor; moreover, pressure from the Socialists as well as their own nationalist aspirations led the Gaullists to engage in a wave of state building.[27] Child care was one of the beneficiaries of this tendency; from the mid-1960s on, hundreds of new crèches and écoles maternelles were founded. State authorities presented the crèches as developmental; they would, it was claimed, make children more sociable and better adjusted. This, in turn, imbued public child care with universal appeal. At the same time, feminists, whose influence within both the Socialist and Communist parties was on the rise, claimed that family policy must be an arm of equality policy, with child care crucial to the reconciliation of work and family.

By the mid-1970s, with the joint support of feminists and the left, public child care had gained a solid foothold in French society. But contestation for power between the center right and the Socialists brought with it a neo-liberal program for economic restructuring and government reduction. From the late 1970s on, public child care came under attack, and only the persistence of pronatalism protected it from complete collapse. Crèches continued to be established, but at a much slower rate. At this point, the opposition to child care was motivated less by familism than by cost-cutting.

In the mid-1980s, the Socialists implemented a new policy of parent allowances, which encouraged mothers to stay at home with their children (although these allowances could also be used to pay for in-home caregivers). In the spirit of neo-liberalism, the stated intention of the new policy was to give parents "choice," and it served to initiate a trend toward privatized or individualized, rather than collective, forms of care.[28] Pronatalist goals were once again invoked to justify public expenditure, but there were indications that the new policy was also motivated by economic concerns. The allowances were too low to keep better-paid women out of the labor force, but they did discourage many lower-paid mothers from seeking jobs, thus reducing the pressure of unemployment. There was no pretense of using the combined policy to create either class or gender equity. On the one hand, caretakers were presumed to be women, but on the other hand, mothers remained invisible in debates over child care, which spoke instead of "parents" or even "consumers."[29]

As Jenson's account demonstrates, the persistence of pronatalism as a theme in French family policy has had important but mixed implications. It has led not only to the endorsement of reproduction but also to a recognition of the value of caring for children, serving to legitimize state expenditures for that purpose. What form expenditures would take depended, however, on the political climate. At certain times there has been a preference for family allowances and privatized forms of care (preferably by mothers themselves), while at other times support for public, collective forms of care has increased. These policy shifts cannot easily be reduced to categories of left and right, as center-right governments engaged in state building while Socialists pursued neo-liberal policies. But each of these policy trajectories had, of course, a different impact on women's economic and social status and labor force participation.

No matter what the emphasis, it is clear that some form of governmental support for motherhood has become an entitlement, one that cannot be easily dislodged from French notions of social citizenship. That is, French women are conceived of as mother-*worker*-citizens. Thus, even when women are barred from the labor force because of a lack of child care, they can expect to receive compensation from the state.[30] It is also important to note that although funding for child care appears to be public, French employers, in keeping with the corporatist structure of the state, actually underwrite a considerable proportion of the expense through mandatory payments to the *Caisse d'allocations familiales*.[31] However, the centralization and redistribution of these funds through the state neutralizes employers' ability to use support for child care as a management tool (as they do in the United States).[32]

JAPAN: CHILD CARE IN THE INTEREST OF THE STATE

Japan, normally considered one of the least gender-egalitarian of modern industrial societies, has, since the early twentieth century, supported a robust system of child care.[33] "Paupers' kindergartens" appeared in Japan as early as 1900. Like Western day nurseries, these were established by private charities, but they also received substantial subsidies from the government's Home Ministry, which saw them as a vehicle for moral reform as well as an antidote to poverty. The nurseries also came to fill an important need for the growing population of urban working-class families that depended on the wages of two earners in order to survive. Between 1926 and 1937, the number of such institutions increased from 273 to almost 1,000.[34]

As in most of the other belligerent nations, government support for child care increased exponentially in Japan during World War II. The state was interested not only in increasing women's productivity but also in guarding children's health and welfare. After the war, however, Japanese policy moved in a different direction. While the other belligerents were, in one way or another, engaged in campaigns to return working mothers to the home, Japan (with the support of U.S. occupation forces)[35] encouraged mothers to remain in the labor force by increasing the supply of public child care. Every hand, including female ones, was deemed vital to the country's economic recovery and rapid expansion.[36]

The Japanese government continued to support public child care even through the 1960s and 1970s, when the female labor force dipped and female domesticity was promoted as a cultural ideal. By the mid-1980s, however, government support was reduced as part of an effort by both liberal and conservative administrations to lower social expenditures. At the same time, there was a trend away from child care centers toward kindergartens, which parents believed offered children greater educational benefits. Kindergartens, which were open only part of the day, could accommodate the needs of a growing number of mothers who worked part time, but not those of full-time employees.[37] Despite an economic recession and an end to expansion in the system, as of 1993 Japan still had more than 22,000 licensed day care centers with a capacity for nearly 1.7 million children. Almost 60 percent of these centers were publicly run.

Historian Sheldon Garon has identified a range of factors that explain the phenomenon of more or less consistent state support for child care in Japan's supposedly male-dominated society. The earliest institutions were established as a means of addressing poverty but also spurred productivity by caring for the children of two-earner, nuclear urban working-class families, which lacked the built-in child care resources of extended rural families. From the outset, the state also regarded public child care as an important vehicle for the education, moral training, and socialization of the lower classes. This view enhanced the role not only of child care centers but also of the government, leading to "growing acceptance of the state as an equal partner with, if nor a superior caregiver to, lower-income parents in matters concerning the health, welfare, and socialization of preschool children." Garon also emphasizes the importance of "technocratic" factors—the bureaucratic momentum created by social welfare experts, professionals, and upper-level government officials to expand and perpetuate the services in which they were involved.[38]

On the whole, according to Garon, the Japanese state has presented an image of child care as centering on the child rather than serving women's interests or upholding their right to work. So cast, child care policy leaves women virtually invisible rather than raising their status. There is no pretense of portraying Japanese women as exemplary mother-worker-citizens. Any benefits that accrue to women appear to be secondary effects of a policy that is designed primarily to advance the specific political and economic goals of the state.[39]

AUSTRALIA: AN OPENING FOR "FEMOCRATS"

The distinctive pattern of Australia, a "liberal" welfare-state regime, is perhaps best encapsulated in the subtitle of Deborah Brennan's history, "From Philanthropy to Feminism."[40] Australian child care began, as in many of the other countries, with charitable day nurseries established in the late nineteenth and early twentieth centuries.[41] In the 1930s and 1940s, the Australian government offered support for child care, but unlike the United States, which created its own institutions (the Emergency Nursery Schools), the commonwealth sought to shore up existing privately sponsored nurseries. The universalistic tone of public support, which emphasized the health benefits of child care in the 1930s and then its essential role in freeing mothers for the war effort in the 1940s, served to destigmatize child care and inscribe a role for the state in this policy arena. During the same period, a leftist feminist discourse also began to form around the universal right to public provisions.[42]

In the immediate postwar period, debates over child care policy were dominated by professional preschool educators and bureaucrats, but in the 1960s, feminists began to challenge their hegemony, demanding greater parental control over the delivery of services. Feminists were thus poised to take advantage of the openness of Labor's Gough Whitlam, who came to power in 1972, inviting dissidents and outsiders to participate in his government.[43] As a result of this process, according to Brennan, "the hegemonic position of [the professionals] was seriously undermined . . . and has never been entirely recovered."[44] Under Labor, a universal, community-based, nonprofit child care system was established, which set fees on a sliding scale and created mechanisms for continual parental input.

The Whitlam government, emphasizing the developmental aspects of child care, took the position that it should be part of educational policy. In the 1980s, this focus was replaced by concerns about worker productivity and labor market shortages, and the government increasingly called on the private sector for funding, but overall support for the principles of maternal employment and some form of collective child care did not flag.[45] Feminist vigilance, first outside and then within government, ensured that it would not. Although commonwealth funding was sharply reduced under succeeding governments, the basic features of the system remained undisturbed owing to the efforts of a newly formed coalition of female government officials occupying key positions (the so-called femocrats), organized child care workers (aided by the Australian Council of Trade Unions), and parents. By the 1980s, Brennan argues, child care "had come to be regarded as an important component of the social wage."[46]

Nevertheless, in the 1990s, under the pressure of globalization, Australia, like so many other states, has begun to drift toward privatization in the matter of child care. Since 1996, this tendency has gained momentum under the Liberal-National Party Howard government, whose weak support for women-friendly measures coincides with efforts to reduce government regulation and encourage the growth of small business. An inquiry undertaken by the Senate has elicited considerable testimony about the harm being done to children and families as a result of cutbacks in public services, and the Labor Party has pledged to restore funding if it returns to power.[47]

CANADA: POVERTY PREVENTION VERSUS WOMEN'S RIGHTS

For much of its history, liberal Canada's approach to child care closely resembled that of the United States. Like its neighbor to the south, from the mid-nineteenth to the early twentieth centuries Canada developed a network of voluntary day nurseries based on maternalist anti-poverty principles, which, until World War II, constituted almost the whole of the country's child care provisions.[48] (Canada also passed a family allowance, not as generous as Sweden's, in 1944.) During the war, the federal government gave child care a tremendous boost by offering universal provisions, only to withdraw them at the war's end. In at least one province, Ontario, militant parent groups, many of them Communist-led, fought to keep public child care centers open to all comers, but as in the United States, they lost out to a coalition of public officials and social work professionals who insisted on targeting needy and "abnormal" families.[49] As historian Susan Prentice shows, Canadian professionals, influenced by American social workers, viewed with suspicion "non-needy" parents who requested care for their children.[50]

The trend toward targeting child care services continued into the 1960s and early 1970s, when the Canadian government expanded child care provisions as part of its "war on poverty." Under the terms of the Canada Assistance Plan (CAP), the cost of child care for low-income families was evenly divided between the federal government and the provinces. As in the United States, this development appears to have been independent of the advent of feminism. At the same time, however, provincial activists were calling for a more progressive approach to child care. In Ontario, for example, a day care movement formed in the early 1970s to pressure the provincial government into maintaining support for public services and, when these proved insufficient to meet growing needs, established many community-based centers. In 1980 the movement succeeded in convincing the Ontario Federation of Labor to support its drive for universal child care,[51] creating a powerful alliance called Action Day Care.

In Quebec, a growing feminist movement joined community groups work-ing on urban anti-poverty projects in calling for public child care in the mid-1970s. The *Parti québecois* (PQ), which depended on feminist support, was initially quite responsive to their demands but, once in power, backtracked as it also tried to satisfy "more traditional wings of the electorate concerned with the upholding of 'family values.'"[52] Despite the PQ's vacillation, Quebec was able to build a progressive child care program that included before- and after-school services and provided opportunities for meaningful parent partici-pation in running centers.

In the early 1980s feminists and child care activists, including such groups as Action Day Care, formed the National Action Committee on the Status of Women, with the aim of bringing work and family issues, including child care, to the national level.[53] Pushing the Liberal government, they won paid mater-nity leave but failed to universalize targeted child care provisions before the Tories came to power in 1985. The Tories' strategy, like that of their conserva-tive American counterparts, was to offer more "choice" to middle-class families through care allowances (tax credits) to parents, including nonworking mothers, and through a proposed Child Care Act, which, among other things, would have subsidized for-profit child care centers. Feminists, working in coalition, were able to block the Child Care Act, although the care allowances went through.[54] In the mid-1990s, over the objections of a feminist coalition that included activists and sympathetic bureaucrats within the government, the CAP was converted into block grants with the power of allocation given over to the provinces. This not only yielded a shrinking pool of funds for all social programs, including child care, but also gave provinces the option of eliminat-ing child care programs altogether. Many of these programs have, as a result, been greatly eroded and in some places disappeared.[55]

LESSONS FOR AMERICANS

Although these national child care systems are similar in certain ways, each also bears the markings of the political culture and institutions from which it evolved and which it continues to inform. We must now ask how much of each national history can be explained by Esping-Andersen's typology of welfare-state regimes and how much by other factors, such as those suggested by Esping-Andersen's feminist critics.

Siv Gustafsson argues that child care systems hew closely to regime type. Thus, in the liberal United States, with a high rate of maternal employment (and the highest rate of *full-time* maternal employment), mothers must rely heavily on the market for child care, gaining access to state-sponsored provisions only in instances of personal or national crisis or dire need. Mothers in social democratic Sweden also have high rates of employment but, in contrast to the United States, enjoy universal access to publicly run and publicly supported child care. The Netherlands, Gustafsson's example of a conservative-corporatist regime, has for decades "protected" mothers (including solo mothers) from the need to enter the labor market, with the result that it has had one of the lowest rates of maternal employment. Only belatedly, as part of an effort to move solo mothers into the labor force, has the state called on municipalities to provide subsidies to *employers* to set up child care.[56]

But the cases I have just examined reveal significant exceptions to this pattern. Most obvious is France, one of the preeminent conservative-corporatist regimes, which has one of the more generous and comprehensive systems of child care.[57] Japan, also arguably a conservative-corporatist regime, has offered at least partial provisions since the beginning of the twentieth century. The factors that appear to have overcome the logic of conservative corporatism, at least in these two cases, include pronatalism and social eugenics, labor shortages, and a strong sense of nationalism. In France, feminist and socialist politics also served as catalysts at crucial moments.

Although child care systems in the social democratic countries tend to conform more closely to regime type, a detailed analysis of the Swedish case reveals that most mothers of preschool children work only part time, and those with children under one year tend to take parental leave rather than use child care services.[58] "Family values" have clearly tempered the social democratic version of gender equality.[59] Moreover, in several other social democratic countries, economic restructuring has led to cutbacks in public provisions, including child care, in the 1990s.[60]

Esping-Andersen's conceptualization of liberal welfare-state regimes does appear to explain a good deal of the development of American child care policy I have presented in this book: the gap between formal gender equality and women's social citizenship; the reluctance of both children's and family advocates and government officials to call upon the state to support or expand state capacity and responsibility for child care (as well as other types of social policy that would promote gender equality, such as paid parental and dependent-care leave); and the residual or crisis-oriented (as opposed to universal) rationale for child care provisions, accompanied by means-testing and a lack of generosity in the services offered.

There have also been exceptions to the liberal pattern, however. Canada had fairly extensive child care provisions in the 1970s and 1980s, while Australia has had a universal system in place since the early 1970s. These cases demonstrate that the logic of liberal welfare-state regimes may also be overcome under certain conditions. Once again the question arises, Why not in the United States? Until the 1970s, the history of child care in both Canada and Australia roughly paralleled that in the United States, with charitable provisions aimed at the poor shifting to a state-supported system in the 1930s in Australia and during World War II in Canada. One small but significant difference is that in Australia the split between child care and early childhood education was not as marked as in the other two countries, so child care never became as thoroughly stigmatized. This in turn led to earlier and more sustained governmental support for universal provisions.

The divergences that appeared in the 1970s and 1980s resulted from positive forces and conditions in Australia and Canada that were absent from the United States during the same period: strong movements of child care advocates, parents, and feminists, supported by labor, who were committed to the principle of universal child care, and the conjuncture of these movements with a sustained period of left-liberal (or social democratic) political hegemony. By contrast, American social policy at this time was decisively shaped by Republicans Nixon and Ford (presidents whose politics were considered fairly conservative at the time but appear moderate in the wake of Reagan and Bush), and it changed little during the weak Democratic administration of Jimmy Carter. Moreover, racial tensions, though a factor in all three societies, were handled more adroitly in Australia and Canada, and thus never became as divisive as they did in the United States.[61] Child care policy became one of the key terrains on which racial conflict was played out in the American case; this did not occur in Canada or Australia.

Although the American women's movement was also at its height in these years, feminists never made child care a national priority and would have found little receptivity in Washington had they done so. Nor were they interested in forming a coalition with early childhood educators, who were more narrowly focused on child development, or with psychological professionals, who viewed child care as a form of "family policy." Meanwhile the labor movement was turning its attention to the growing proportion of female workers in its ranks, but union leaders stopped short of putting child care on the bargaining table or lending support to universal child care legislation. Thus the conjuncture of a hospitable left-liberal government and a strong feminist child care movement, such as occurred in Australia, or a Canadian-style coalition of feminists, labor, and child care professionals, never materialized in the United States.

In each cluster of welfare-state regimes, then, it appears that the reigning logic may at times be mitigated by certain factors—both progressive (feminist) and conservative—which shift the expected direction of policies like child care that enhance women's autonomy (that is, divert such policies from the pattern predicted by decommodifying policies). In all these cases, child care originated as a form of charity or benevolence that was taken over or displaced by the state (either at the municipal or national level) at some point. France was the first to do so, as early as the mid-nineteenth century, followed by Japan around the turn of the century, Australia and the United States in the 1930s, Canada during World War II, and finally Sweden in the 1960s. The fact that one of the strongest public systems, Sweden's, is also the most recent, suggests that longevity is not in itself a key to sustaining provisions, whereas timing and the strength and persistence of mitigating factors are essential to establishing and maintaining momentum.

Some observers have predicted that with the pressures of global competition and the consolidation of political-economic alliances such as the North American Free Trade Association and the European Union, all democratic market societies, regardless of regime type or extraneous factors, will follow America's lead in restructuring their welfare states. To be sure, the 1990s have witnessed widespread cutbacks in social spending, but, with the possible exception of Britain,[62] not one has been as drastic as those in the United States. With regard to child care policy in the cases we have been examining, since the mid-1980s, Canada has drawn closer to the United States, but Sweden and France, despite certain changes and compromises, have retained the basic infrastructure of their systems. Similarly, parent involvement and feminist support are combining to resist the tide of change in Australia, and Japan, with its continuing emphasis on state-assisted child rearing, also appears to be holding its own.

The political cultures, institutions, and interest groups spawned by extensive public child care provision in these societies seem to have "inoculated" them against the complete collapse of their systems.[63] The United States, unfortunately, has not been vaccinated. Never having enjoyed the benefits of universal child care outside wartime, Americans appear to have become inured by the constant struggle to find adequate services in a fragmented system based on competition and inequality. Thus there has been little resistance to the deployment of targeted public child care as a means of ending welfare "dependency" and mandating employment for the poor—a perverse and tragic misuse of a form of social provision that in other societies is regarded as a boon to both children and mothers.[64] The United States is perhaps the "purest" example of a liberal welfare-state regime. Exceptional in this as in so many other areas, it now bears the dubious distinction of being the only democratic market society to take welfare-state devolution to such an extreme.

Appendix A: Early Childhood and Parent Education Movement Professionals in the Emergency Education Program

Name	Professional Position	Organizational Affiliation	Emergency Education Program Position
Rose Alschuler	Director, Franklin Park Nursery School, Chicago	National Commission for Young Children	Chicago Regional Advisor (RA)
Dr. Harold Anderson	Research Asst. Prof., Iowa Child Welfare Research Station	American Psychological Association	Midwest RA
Dr. Ruth Andrus	N.Y. State Bureau of Mental Hygiene	NANE	N.Y. RA
Winifred Bain	Teachers College, Columbia	Association for Childhood Education (ACE)	South RA
Edna Dean Baker	President, ACE	ACE	NAC member; lower midwest RA

(*continued*)

Appendix A (*continued*)

Name	Professional Position	Organizational Affiliation	Emergency Education Program Position
Muriel Brown	Faculty, Smith College School of Social Work; Research Assoc., NCPE	National Council of Parent Education (NCPE)	Parent Education Specialist
Mary Dabney Davis	U.S. Office of Education	NANE	ENS Specialist
Abigail Eliot	Director, Nursery Training School of Boston	NANE	NAC member; New England RA
Amy Hostler	Faculty, Western Reserve Univ.	ACE	Southern States RA
Dr. George Stoddard	Director, Child Welfare Research Station, U. Iowa	ACE	Midwest RA
Lois Meek (Stolz)	Education Secretary, American Association of University Women	NANE	Conn., Virgin Islands RA
Lovisa Wagoner	Faculty, Mills College	Am. Psychol Assn.	Nevada RA
Edna Noble White	Director, Merrill-Palmer School, Detroit; Chair, NCPE	NCPE	Chair, NAC; Mich., Ohio, W. VA. RA

Note: Other RAs for whom no further data were available include Margaret Holmes (New York City) and Emma Johnson (Penn., Del., Md., and N.J.).

Appendix B: Participation in WPA Programs by State

Number of Employees, Schools, and Enrollees Reported in Nursery Schools Conducted by the Division of Education Projects in 48 States, the District of Columbia, and New York City, November 1937

State	Number of employees				Number of schools	Number attending classes	
	Total	Teachers	Supervisors	Other		Enrollees	Other
Alabama	164	91	1	72	—	—	—
Arizona	82	48	2	32	21	659	—
Arkansas	50	37	1	12	12	336	359
California	343	191	7	145	71	2,176	—
Colorado	111	52	3	56	25	541	704
Connecticut	129	69	2	58	24	703	115
Delaware	23	5	3	15	5	170	—
District of Columbia	45	29	2	14	10	278	35
Florida	231	153	2	76	49	1,469	351
Georgia	142	71	3	68	34	878	554
Idaho	59	29	1	29	15	328	—
Illinois	296	143	9	144	60	1,452	448
Indiana	84	60	2	22	27	600	747
Iowa	44	23	1	20	13	439	—
Kansas	51	49	2	—	28	900	—
Kentucky	165	101	2	62	53	1,713	319
Louisiana	54	26	1	27	13	345	—
Maine	20	5	1	14	5	150	51
Maryland	74	51	3	20	21	629	19
Massachusetts	433	306	13	114	167	5,146	—
Michigan	183	89	9	85	37	1,088	2,920
Minnesota	75	59	5	11	30	966	—
Mississippi	73	41	1	31	16	482	—
Missouri	124	70	2	52	23	774	45

State						
Montana	56	35	1	20	18	468	—
Nebraska	59	36	3	20	17	341	39
Nevada	17	8	1	8	4	108	96
New Hampshire	52	32	1	19	16	469	—
New Jersey	124	82	2	40	30	747	185
New Mexico	56	20	1	39	20	648	—
New York City	148	47	10	91	14	579	—
New York State	189	105	8	76	52	1,266	—
North Carolina	54	50	1	3	17	540	86
North Dakota	85	38	1	46	15	444	47
Ohio	219	148	5	66	72	1,986	—
Oklahoma	78	46	1	31	18	677	—
Oregon	57	38	1	18	18	386	273
Pennsylvania	305	181	12	112	71	1,935	—
Rhode Island	108	61	1	46	27	669	161
South Carolina	26	25	1	—	9	263	25
South Dakota	32	32	—	—	7	221	—
Tennessee	95	54	1	40	27	809	—
Texas	144	55	31	58	28	1,374	—
Utah	68	40	7	21	8	180	—
Vermont	40	25	2	13	13	296	—
Virginia	81	57	1	23	26	711	219
Washington	51	23	1	27	72	302	—
West Virginia	184	116	10	58	38	1,627	536
Wisconsin	68	44	1	23	16	456	—
Wyoming	27	15	1	11	60	149	89
Total	5,482	3,211	183	2,088	1,472	39,873	8,450

Source: Doak Campbell et al., *Educational Activities of the Works Progress Administration*, Staff Study 14 (Washington: GPO, 1939), 110.

Appendix C: Attendees at the Conference on Day Care of Children of Working Mothers, Washington, D.C., July 31–August 1, 1941

Edith Abbott, Dean, School of Social Service Administration, University of Chicago

C. Anderson Aldrich, Professor of Pediatrics, Northwestern University Medical School

Mary Anderson, Director, U.S. Women's Bureau

Mary Irene Atkinson, Director, Child Welfare Division, U.S. Children's Bureau

Katherine M. Bain, M.D., Director, Division of Research in Child Development, U.S. Children's Bureau

Margaret Batjer, Chief, Home Economics Projects Section, Works Progress Administration

Paul L. Benjamin, Executive Secretary, Council of Social Agencies, Buffalo, N.Y.

Mary L. Bogue, Madison, Conn.

H.E. Chamberlain, M.D., Consulting Psychiatrist and Chief of Division of Child Welfare Services, California State Department of Welfare

Elisabeth Christman, Secretary, National Women's Trade Union League

Ewan Clague, Director, U.S. Bureau of Employment Security

Elizabeth Woodruff Clark, Executive Director, National Association of Day Nurseries

Source: Proceedings of the Conference on Day Care of Children of Working Mothers, Children's Bureau Publication No. 28 (Washington, D.C.: GPO, 1942).

Martha L. Clifford, M.D., Bureau of Child Hygiene, Connecticut State Department of Health

Abigail A. Eliot, Director, Nursery Training School, Boston

Martha A. Eliot, M.D., Associate Chief, U.S. Children's Bureau

Anita J. Fatz, Assistant Director, Maryland State Department of Welfare

Arnold Gesell, M.D., Director, Clinic of Child Development, Yale University Medical School

Christine Glass, Secretary and Treasurer, National Association for Nursery Education

Bess Goodykoonz, Assistant Commissioner, U.S. Office of Education

Agnes E. Hanna, Director, Social Service Division, U.S. Children's Bureau

Elsie Harper, Executive Secretary, National Board of the YWCA

Jane Hoey, Director, Bureau of Public Assistance, Social Security Board, Federal Security Agency

Anne Sarachon Hooley, Administrator in Charge of Women's Division, National Catholic Community Service

Howard Hopkirk, Executive Director, Child Welfare League of America

Helen Jeter, Secretary, Family Security Advisory Committee, Office of Coordinator of Health, Welfare, and Related Defense Activities

Marie Dresden Lane, Chief, Service Projects Section, National Youth Administration

Grace Langdon, Specialist, Family Life Education, Works Progress Administration

Katherine M. Lenroot, Chief, U.S. Children's Bureau

N. S. Light, Director, Bureau of Supervision, Connecticut State Board of Education

Emma O. Lundberg, Child Welfare Consultant, U.S. Children's Bureau

Beatrice McConnell, Director, Industrial Division, U.S. Children's Bureau

Col. Frank McSherry, Chief, Defense Training Branch, Labor Division, Office of Production Management

Frieda S. Miller, Industrial Commissioner, New York State Department of Labor

Louise Moore, Special Agent for Women and Girls in Trade and Industrial Education, U.S. Office of Education

Eleanor Neustaedter, Secretary, Chelsea-Lowell District, (New York) Community Service Society

Ellen C. Potter, M.D., Director of Medicine, New Jersey State Department of Institutions and Agencies

Leroy A. Ramsdell, Executive Secretary, Hartford Council of Social Agencies

Charles I. Schottland, Assistant to the Chief, U.S. Children's Bureau

Louise Stanley, Chief, U.S. Bureau of Home Economics

Louise Stitt, Director, Division of Minimum Wage, U.S. Women's Bureau

Charles P. Taft, Assistant Coordinator of Health, Welfare, and Related Defense Activities

Ethel Verry, Executive Director, Chicago Orphan Asylum

Edna Noble White, Director, Merrill-Palmer School

Appendix D: The Seventeen Ways in Which Business Can Become Involved in Child Care

Just as people commonly think of day care in terms of "the day care center," companies considering becoming involved in day care often think only in terms of opening their own day care center. Opening a day care center is a costly and difficult venture, and it is far from the only (or best) option available to a company. In fact, there are many different ways in which a company can become involved in day care, some of which are listed below:

1. Open your own center.
2. Develop a coalition of businesses to start a center.
3. Develop a coalition of businesses and community groups to sponsor a center.
4. Develop a company-union day care center partnership.
5. Develop a company program which involves training and licensing of family day care homes.
6. Donate money to a community center.
7. Donate expertise—your lawyers, architects, public relations department— to a community center.
8. Donate services—make repairs, do the accounting—to a community center.

Source: Industry and Day Care II: Proceedings of the Second National Conference on Industry and Day Care, ed. Eunice Schatz and Thea K. Flaum (Chicago: Urban Research Corporation, 1973), 12.

9. Donate space and facilities for a day care center.
10. Start a company child-care service to help employees find day care for their children.
11. Subsidize employees' day care costs with a tuition-aid program.
12. Encourage new day care centers by guaranteeing a local entrepreneur that employees' children will fill a specified number of spaces.
13. Develop training programs for paraprofessionals and professionals in cooperation with your community college or university.
14. Pay the salary or consulting fee of an expert—in learning disabilities, child psychology, cost efficiency—whose services your local center needs but can't afford.
15. Underwrite day care research.
16. Join—or initiate—a group to push for more day care in your community.
17. Lobby—for new day care legislation, a higher level of funding, more help for low- and middle-income families, etc.

Notes

In the notes, the names of archives and libraries have been identified by the following abbreviations:

AHS   Atlanta Historical Society
CHS   Chicago Historical Society
HSP   Historical Society of Pennsylvania, Philadelphia
LC   Library of Congress, Washington, D.C.
LCP   Library Company of Philadelphia
MHS   Massachusetts Historical Society, Boston
NA   National Archives, Silver Spring, Maryland
NYPL   New York Public Library
PJAC   Philadelphia Jewish Archives Center, Balch Institute, Philadelphia
QC   Quaker Collection, Haverford College Library, Haverford, Pennsylvania
RSC   Russell Sage Collection, City College Library, New York City
SC   Special Collections, University of Illinois-Chicago Library
SL   Schlesinger Library, Radcliffe College, Cambridge, Massachusetts
SWHA   Social Welfare History Archives, University of Minnesota, Minneapolis
UA   Urban Archives, Temple University, Philadelphia

INTRODUCTION

1. U.S. Bureau of the Census, *Statistical Abstract of the United States, 1994* (Washington, D.C.: GPO, 1994).

2. On provisions in other advanced industrial societies, see Janet C. Gornick, Marcia K. Meyers, and Katherin E. Ross, "Supporting the Employment of Mothers: Policy Variation across Fourteen Welfare States," *Journal of European Social Policy* 7 (1997): 45–70.

3. Studies have shown, however, that the provision of child care alone does not guarantee women labor equity, for other deterrents persist, both inside and outside the workplace. These include explicit and subtle forms of discrimination with regard to opportunities for education and training, hiring, promotion, compensation, job assignments, membership in unions and professional organizations, and workplace environments; as well as inadequate maternity and dependent care leave. See Barbara Bergmann, *The Economic Emergence of Women* (New York: Basic Books, 1986); Barbara F. Reskin with Patricia A. Roos, *Job Queues, Gender Queues: Explaining Women's Inroads into Male Occupations* (Philadelphia: Temple University Press, 1990); and Francine D. Blau, Marianne A. Ferber, and Anne E. Winkler, *The Economics of Women, Men, and Work,* 3rd ed. (Englewood Cliffs, N.J.: Prentice-Hall, 1998).

4. See Julia O'Connor, "Gender, Class and Citizenship in the Comparative Analysis of Welfare State Regimes: Theoretical and Methodological Issues," *British Journal of Sociology* 44 (1993): 301–18; and Ann Shola Orloff, "Gender and the Social Rights of Citizenship: The Comparative Analysis of Gender Relations and Welfare States," *American Sociological Review* 58 (1993): 303–28.

5. T. H. Marshall, *Citizenship and Social Class* (Cambridge: Cambridge University Press, 1950; reprint, London: Pluto Press, 1992).

6. Carole Pateman, "The Patriarchal Welfare State," in *Democracy and the Welfare State,* ed. Amy Gutmann (Princeton: Princeton University Press, 1989), 235.

7. Marshall, *Citizenship and Social Class,* chap. 4. According to Pateman, it was the mandate to compensate for the risks and dangers of the market that constituted "the moral basis of 'the 'social rights' of democratic citizenship"; "Patriarchal Welfare State," 235. Gøsta Esping-Andersen calls this function of the state "decommodification"; see *The Three Worlds of Welfare Capitalism* (Princeton: Princeton University Press, 1990).

8. Nor, for that matter, did he consider race in relation to these issues. See, for example, Jennifer Hochschild, "Race, Class, Power, and the American Welfare State," in Gutmann, *Democracy and the Welfare State,* chap. 7.

9. Pateman explores the political implications of motherhood most fully in the essay "Equality, Difference, Subordination: The Politics of Motherhood and Women's Citizenship," in *Beyond Equality and Difference: Citizenship, Feminist Politics and Female Subjectivity,* ed. Gisela Bock and Susan James (London: Routledge, 1992), 17–31.

10. Rich's phrase, "compulsory heterosexuality," is itself a variation on Gayle Rubin's "obligatory heterosexuality." See Rich, "Compulsory Heterosexuality and Lesbian Existence," in *Powers of Desire: The Politics of Sexuality,* ed. Ann Snitow et al. (New York: Monthly Review Press, 1983), 177–205; and Rubin, "The Traffic in Women: Notes on the

Political Economy of Sex," in *Toward an Anthropology of Women,* ed. Rayna Reiter (New York: Monthly Review Press, 1975), 157–210.

11. There are, of course, many other arguments to be made for universal child care. As feminist economist Nancy Folbre, for example, points out, "All citizens of the United States enjoy significant claims upon the earnings of future working-age adults through Social Security and public debt. But not all citizens contribute equally to the care of these future adults. Individuals who devote relatively little time or energy to child-rearing are free-riding on parental labor." "Children as Public Goods," *American Economic Review* 84, no. 2 (1994): 86.

12. I am aware that some feminist scholars have argued that motherhood is a form of work, and therefore nearly all mothers are "working mothers." Such scholars therefore prefer to use the term "wage-earning mothers" for those who are gainfully employed. This term is not, however, strictly accurate for women in all the periods I discuss. For example, in the late eighteenth and early nineteenth centuries, women were engaged in market work that did not bring in wages but contributed to household incomes or produced surplus goods to be bartered. I refer to these and similar women as "working mothers," and I use the term "wage-earning mothers" where it is appropriate.

13. Evelyn Nakano Glenn makes this point in "Social Constructions of Mothering: A Thematic Overview," in *Mothering: Ideology, Experience, and Agency,* ed. Evelyn Nakano Glenn, Grace Chang, and Linda Rennie Forcey (New York: Routledge, 1994), 16. Several historians of American women workers have made a similar observation; see, for example, Leslie Woodcock Tentler, *Wage-Earning Women: Women, Industrial Work and Family Life in the United States, 1900–1930* (New York: Oxford University Press, 1982), and Winifred Wandersee, *Women's Work and Family Values, 1920–1940* (Cambridge: Harvard University Press, 1981).

14. Some women's historians have perpetuated the notion of irreconcilability between women's work and family roles by conceptualizing them as parts of two separate realms, operating on very different ideologies. Carl Degler, for example, claims that "the great values for which the family stands are at odds not only with the women's movement, but also with those of today's world [democracy, individualism, and meritocracy]"; *At Odds: Women and the Family from the Revolution to the Present* (New York: Oxford University Press, 1980), 471. Such interpretations rest on sociological theories of modernization that themselves require further interrogation; see Rita Felski, *The Gender of Modernity* (Cambridge: Harvard University Press, 1995), chap. 3. The studies cited in the previous note suggest that working mothers themselves do not tend to see employment as belonging to a separate realm.

15. Mary Frances Berry, *The Politics of Parenthood: Child Care, Women's Rights, and the Myth of the Good Mother* (New York: Viking, 1993).

16. Maternalism is the label given by a number of scholars, myself included, to a politics that claims a position of authority for women in their "natural" roles as wives and mothers and seeks to protect the health and welfare of women and children. This politics, growing out of nineteenth-century Victorian ideology, has been identified in many advanced industrial societies, including the United States around the turn of the century.

See *Mothers of a New World: Maternalist Politics and the Origins of Welfare States,* ed. Seth Koven and Sonya Michel (New York: Routledge, 1993); Theda Skocpol, *Protecting Soldiers and Mothers: The Political Origins of Social Policy in the United States* (Cambridge: Harvard University Press, 1995); and Molly Ladd-Taylor, *Mother-Work: Women, Child Welfare, and the State, 1890–1930* (Urbana: University of Illinois Press, 1994). Linda Gordon makes a similar point about the unpredictable politics of female professionals in *Pitied but Not Entitled: Single Mothers and the History of Welfare* (New York: Free Press, 1994), 8. However, she includes under the rubric of "feminism" all the women (and sometimes men) who were concerned with women's oppression, no matter what solutions they proposed. Although I agree that feminism is not monolithic, I believe that broadening its definition to comprise maternalism confuses the issue. Feminists sometimes used maternalist arguments (in arguing why women should have the vote, for example), but were (and are) fundamentally opposed to the social structures that lead to women's subordination and dependency, while maternalists tended to *affirm* those structures even while calling for women's rights—e.g., to state support for motherhood—within them. Maternalists' refusal to challenge women's assignment to the family and their de facto exclusion from the workforce limited women's choices and served to reinscribe them in the social order as mothers. See Nancy Fraser, "After the Family Wage: A Postindustrial Thought Experiment," in *Justice Interruptus: Critical Reflections on the "Postsocialist" Condition* (New York: Routledge, 1997), 41–66; see also Gwendolyn Mink, *The Wages of Motherhood: Inequality in the Welfare State, 1917–1942* (Ithaca: Cornell University Press, 1995), pt. 1.

17. See Eileen Boris, *Home to Work: Motherhood and the Politics of Industrial Homework in the United States* (New York: Cambridge University Press, 1994).

18. See Katherine Jellison, *Entitled to Power: Farm Women and Technology, 1913–1963* (Chapel Hill: University of North Carolina Press, 1993).

19. See Robyn Muncy, *Creating a Female Dominion in American Reform, 1890–1935* (New York: Oxford University Press, 1989); Skocpol, *Protecting Soldiers and Mothers;* and Michael Katz, *In the Shadow of the Poorhouse: A Social History of Welfare in America* (New York: Basic Books, 1986), pt. 2.

20. Some states and municipalities continued to offer services; see chapter 5 of this book.

21. In the novel *Benefits* (London: Virago, 1979), the British feminist writer Zoë Fairbairns projected a similar dystopian vision of a welfare state run amok.

22. One study that has undertaken such an exploration is Barbara Beatty, *Preschool Education in America: The Culture of Young Children from the Colonial Era to the Present* (New Haven: Yale University Press, 1995).

23. Katz's *In the Shadow of the Poorhouse* would be one exception.

24. See, for example, Skocpol, *Protecting Soldiers and Mothers;* and Gordon, *Pitied but Not Entitled.*

25. The term "residual" has been used by Richard Titmuss, whereas Gøsta Esping-Andersen has included the United States in the category "liberal," and also characterizes it as "public-private." Contrasting types would be social democratic states (such as the Scandinavian societies) and such conservative-corporatist states as France and Germany. See Titmuss, *Essays on the Welfare State* (New Haven: Yale University Press, 1959); and

Esping-Andersen, *Three Worlds.* For an expanded discussion of these issues, see the comparative note that concludes this book.

26. According to Esping-Andersen, in public-private regimes, "the state encourages the market, either passively—by guaranteeing only a minimum—or actively, by subsidizing private welfare schemes," to offer benefits that would likely be provided by the state itself in other types of welfare-state regimes; *Three Worlds,* 26–27. In the United States, health care, pensions, and dozens of other provisions and services, in addition to child care, are offered primarily through the private rather than the public sector.

27. See, for example, Gornick et al., "Supporting the Employment of Mothers." In addition to child care, they examine such policies as paid maternity and parental leave, after-school care, and daily and annual public school schedules. Although they rely on data from 1984–97, the trends they analyze have more or less held steady, with the United States still ranked at or near the bottom in terms of universal subsidized provisions. The increases in funding for child care that accompanied the welfare "reforms" of 1996 will not alter but only deepen this pattern.

28. See Caroline Zinsser, *Raised in East Urban: Child Care Changes in a Working-Class Community* (New York: Teachers College Press, 1991).

CHAPTER 1: THE MULTIPLE ORIGINS OF AMERICAN CHILD CARE

1. Most later accounts use the founding of the New York Nursery for the Children of Poor Women (later the New York Nursery and Child's Hospital) in 1854 as the starting point of American day care. Part of the confusion comes from the fact that the First Day Nursery of Philadelphia served as the model for other American nurseries, and the Troy Day Home, undoubtedly one of the oldest, continued to operate well into the twentieth century. See Margaret O'Brien Steinfels, *Who's Minding the Children: The History and Politics of Day Care in America* (New York: Simon and Schuster, 1973), chap. 2; Ethel S. Beer, *The Day Nursery* (New York: Dutton, 1938), chap. 2; Edward F. Zigler and Mary E. Lang, *Child Care Choices: Balancing the Needs of Children, Families, and Society* (New York: Free Press, 1991), 31–33. Lynn Y. Weiner, *From Working Girl to Working Mother: The Female Labor Force in the United States, 1820–1980* (Chapel Hill: University of North Carolina Press, 1985), chap. 6; and Emily D. Cahan, *Past Caring: A History of U.S. Pre-school Care and Education for the Poor, 1820–1965* (New York: National Center for Children in Poverty, Columbia University, 1989), 3–16; argue that the earliest form of child care in the United States was not the day nursery but the infant school, the first of which was founded in Boston in 1828 (Weiner [p. 124] confuses matters by referring to this as a day nursery, which it was not). For reasons that will become clear in the course of this chapter, I accept this argument, with qualifications.

2. History of Virginia Day Nursery (N.Y.C.), n.d., typed on [National] Federation of Day Nurseries letterhead, found in the records of the Child Welfare League of America, SWHA, box 21, folder 9. Internal evidence indicates that it was written around 1909. An account of the founding of the Colored Orphans' Asylum of New York, written much later (c. 1956), has a similar tone:

For a child to lose his parents has always seemed as great a misfortune as life could deal him, but for a Negro child to become an orphan in New York City before the year of 1836 was an almost hopeless disaster. . . .

That was the situation until one chilly spring day in 1836 when two Quaker ladies, Miss Anna M. Shotwell and her niece, Miss Mary Murray, found two wistful little Negro children sitting on the steps of an old house in lower New York. They learned that the children were orphans, and that they were soon to go to the Almshouse. It seemed too cruel a fate for the poor children, so the ladies emptied their purses to a kindly woman who promised to care for the children until some more hopeful solution could be found. When Miss Shotwell and Miss Murray returned a few days later, four more little waifs were waiting for them. The problem had tripled in just a few days.

The two ladies discovered that neither the Long Island Farms, the public nursery for white orphans, nor the three existing orphanages in New York would accept Negro children. So the indomitable Quaker women began what would prove for Miss Shotwell, at least, a life's work. The doors of the Colored Orphans' Asylum were opened for the first time in November 1836. They have never closed.

Riverdale Children's Association (hereafter RCA), "The Story of the First 120 Years," Riverdale Children's Association papers, SL (hereafter RCAP), box 62, folder 2, n.p. (1). Another history of the RCA claims that the New York Colored Orphans' Asylum was the first of its kind in the United States (see RCA, "A History of the Riverdale Children's Association, RCAP, box 62, folder 1), but in fact one was founded in Philadelphia in 1822.

3. Mrs. Randolph [Elinor] Guggenheimer, "Why Day Care," speech presented at the National Conference on Day Care for Children, Washington, D.C., November 17–18, 1960, WB records, NA, RG 86, box 366, folder: National Conference on the Day Care of Children Pre, 12–13.

4. The term is Molly Ladd-Taylor's, in her study *Mother-Work: Women, Child Welfare, and the State, 1890–1930* (Urbana: University of Illinois Press, 1994), 7. Ladd-Taylor uses the term to identify an ideology that emerged most markedly in the late nineteenth and early twentieth centuries, when most of these accounts were actually written, although they refer to an earlier period. But similar language can be found in many contemporary accounts as well.

5. For the distinction between, and yet conflation of, these two impulses, see Seth Koven, "Philanthropic Tourism and the Spectacle of Poverty in Victorian London," paper presented to the American Historical Association, San Francisco, December 1993.

6. See Ladd-Taylor, *Mother-Work,* chaps. 2 and 3; and Seth Koven and Sonya Michel, "Mother Worlds," introduction to *Mothers of a New World: Maternalist Politics and the Origins of Welfare States,* ed. Seth Koven and Sonya Michel (New York: Routledge, 1993), 1–42.

7. For her own account of the founding of the Nursery and Child's Hospital, see Mrs. Mary A. Du Bois, "Thirty Years' Experience in Nursery and Child Hospital Work," *Proceedings, Twelfth Annual Conference of Charities and Corrections* (1885): 181–91. For a detailed discussion of the early history of this institution, see Virginia A. Metaxas Quiroga, *Poor Mothers and Babies: A Social History of Childbirth and Child Care Hospitals in Nineteenth-Century New York City* (New York: Garland, 1989), chap. 4.

8. For example, Olwen Hufton and Frank Tallett describe the "crèche-type services for working mothers" provided by *béates,* lay sisters, in the lace-making regions of seventeenth-century France. Béates kept small children and girls up to the age of twelve in their own houses, where they were given religious instruction and taught the rudiments of lace making. "The service was partly . . . to keep the fingers of the prying toddler away from the mother's lace bobbins." Hufton and Tallett, "Communities of Women, the Religious Life, and Public Service in Eighteenth-Century France," in *Connecting Spheres: Women in the Western World, 1500 to the Present,* ed. Marilyn J. Boxer and Jean H. Quataert (New York: Oxford University Press, 1987), 79, 83.

9. Karin Calvert, *Children in the House: The Material Culture of Early Childhood, 1600– 1900* (Boston: Northeastern University Press, 1992), 23–24. Calvert explains that the primary purpose of swaddling was to ensure the straight development of the infant's torso and limbs; it also served to keep the baby warm during cold seasons.

10. Ibid., 33–36. On standing stools, see also Alice Earle, *Child Life in Colonial Days* (1899; reprint, Williamstown, Mass.: Corner House Publishers, 1989), 24–29. A cradle settee was a long bench with a rail running along the front of half the seat; this enabled the sitter to place an infant on the seat while working, without fear that the child would roll off (some cradle settees had rockers). Most extant cradle settees date from the early nineteenth century, but it is possible that they were used earlier as well; see Ralph and Terry Kovel, *American Country Furniture, 1780–1875* (New York: Crown, 1965), 39.

11. Calvert, *Children in the House,* 36.

12. Walter Herbert Small, *Early New England Schools* (Boston: Ginn, 1914), chap. 6. Some dame schools did receive public support during the eighteenth century; see "Dame Schools—America," in *Encyclopedia of Education,* ed. Paul Monroe (New York: Macmillan, 1911–1913), vol. 2, 248.

13. Small, *Early New England Schools,* 162–63.

14. George Emery Littlefield, *Early Schools and School-Books of New England* (Boston: Club of Odd Volumes, 1904), 81–82.

15. Lucy Larcom, "A Dame School in Beverly, Massachusetts (c. 1830)," from *A New England Girlhood* (Boston, 1889); excerpted in *Education in the United States: A Documentary History,* ed. Sol Cohen (New York: Random House, 1974), vol. 3, 1290.

16. Mrs. [Mary] Livermore, quoted in Small, *Early New England Schools,* 185.

17. Larcom, "A Dame School," 1290.

18. In the putting-out system, a "middleman" would purchase raw materials (such as cotton or straw) and distribute them to home manufacturers who would produce finished goods (such as cloth or hats), which the middleman would then market. Home manufacturers were usually paid by the piece or in kind, if the middleman was also a local merchant.

19. For the impact of the market on agricultural production and women's relation to it, see Joan M. Jensen, *Loosening the Bonds: Mid-Atlantic Farm Women, 1750–1850* (New Haven: Yale University Press, 1986), esp. chap. 5; and Nancy Grey Osterud, *Bonds of Community: The Lives of Farm Women in Nineteenth-Century New York* (Ithaca: Cornell University Press, 1991), chap. 9. Osterud argues that although the market devalued women's work, they did not necessarily perceive this as a loss of status, because they

"espoused standards of value and notions of social relations which were opposed to the pecuniary and impersonal standards of the capitalist marketplace" (12). On the impact of the market on rural life in general, see Steven Hahn and Jonathan Prude, eds., *The Countryside in the Age of Capitalist Transformation: Essays in the Social History of Rural America* (Chapel Hill: University of North Carolina Press, 1985). Unfortunately, none of these studies—not even those dealing specifically with women—explore the impact of changing production on patterns of child care. Although admittedly it is easier to deal with young children in a rural setting where home and workplace are not separate, the pressures of meeting quotas for the market, whether self-imposed or external, must have increased pressure on mothers. Did they expect more child care from servants, indentured or otherwise? From older siblings? Did they limit their families? Jensen suggests not; see *Loosening the Bonds*, 20–21.

20. Mary H. Blewett, *Men, Women, and Work: Class, Gender, and Protest in the New England Shoe Industry, 1780–1910* (Urbana: University of Illinois Press, 1988), 11–12.

21. Ibid., 18.

22. Pregnancy also interfered with the work, as the existing technology required the shoe binder to hold a metal clamp in her lap while she sewed; ibid., 16–17, 54.

23. Blewett explains that because the task of sewing uppers had initially belonged to women, it was less well paid than most other tasks, and other workers, especially skilled artisans, refused to do it. This meant, however, that women who worked at it also earned substantially less than men engaged in other aspects of shoemaking; ibid., 24–25 and chap. 3.

24. See Ruth Bloch, "American Feminine Ideals in Transition: The Rise of the Moral Mother, 1785–1815," *Feminist Studies* 4 (June 1978): 101–27; and Linda K. Kerber, *Women of the Republic: Intellect and Ideology in Revolutionary America* (Chapel Hill: University of North Carolina Press, 1990), 189–288. For continuations of these ideologies into the nineteenth century, see Sylvia Hoffert, *Private Matters: American Attitudes toward Childrearing and Infant Nurture in the Urban North, 1800–1860* (Urbana: University of Illinois Press, 1989), chap. 4; and Mary P. Ryan, *The Empire of the Mother: American Writing about Domesticity, 1830–1860* (New York: Harrington Park Press, 1985).

25. Faye Dudden examines this set of beliefs from the perspective of servants. Although "experts," painting grim pictures of the evils that might result, advised middle-class mothers not to "delegate the sacred offices of motherhood" to their domestics, "the economy and practical appeal of this service was compelling," and in fact early nineteenth-century servants performed many of duties of child rearing; Dudden, *Serving Women: Household Service in Nineteenth-Century America* (Middletown, Conn.: Wesleyan University Press, 1983), 148–49. Jane Censer analyzes the complicated relationships between white Southern women, their children, and slave nurses or mammies. She claims that although white women used slaves to care for their children, they "also showed an ongoing interest in their young children's activities. . . . It is unlikely," according to Censer, "that many [mammies] supplanted mothers in either affection or authority" unless a mother died. Censer, *North Carolina Planters and Their Children, 1800–1860* (Baton Rouge: Louisiana State University Press, 1984), 36–37.

26. Billy G. Smith reports one instance in which a three-year-old girl was bound out, simply because her pregnant mother was found deserted and destitute; *The "Lower Sort": Philadelphia's Laboring People, 1750–1800* (Ithaca: Cornell University Press, 1990), 167.

27. Two excellent discussions of changing methods of poor relief and their impact on the poor are Priscilla Ferguson Clement, *Welfare and the Poor in the Nineteenth-Century City: Philadelphia, 1800–1854* (Rutherford, N.J.: Associated University Presses, 1985); and Robert E. Cray, Jr., *Paupers and Poor Relief in New York City and Its Rural Environs, 1700–1830* (Philadelphia: Temple University Press, 1988). On children and welfare, see Clement, chap. 5.

28. M. Carey, "To the Printer of the Delaware Advertisements," pamphlet, February 9, 1830, Mathew Carey Pamphlet Collection, LCP.

29. Blewett has an excellent discussion of the evolution of the gendered division of labor in shoemaking and its effects on wage differentials in *Men, Women, and Work*, chap. 1. See also Jeanne Boydston's discussions of the cash value of men's and women's work in *Home and Work: Housework, Wages, and the Ideology of Labor in the Early Republic* (New York: Oxford University Press, 1990), chaps. 2 and 3; and Smith's discussion of the wages of women and children, *"Lower Sort,"* 124.

30. Carey, "To the Printer."

31. "The Dying Grandmother," interview conducted by Mrs. Sarah J. Hale, *Ladies' Magazine* 3 (November 1830): 494.

32. Claudia Goldin, *Understanding the Gender Gap: An Economic History of American Women* (New York: Oxford University Press, 1990), 60.

33. When widows took over their husbands' trades, they could usually earn the same income, but most wage-paying jobs were gender-differentiated and paid accordingly. See Goldin, *Understanding the Gender Gap*, 49 and chap. 4.

34. Boydston, *Home and Work*, 92; Christine Stansell, *City of Women: Sex and Class in New York, 1789–1860* (Urbana: University of Illinois Press, 1987), chaps. 3, 10.

35. Smith, *"Lower Sort,"* 160.

36. Boydston, *Home and Work*, 92.

37. On the Quaker women of Philadelphia, see Margaret Hope Bacon, *Mothers of Feminism: The Story of Quaker Women in America* (New York: Harper and Row, 1986), chap. 5.

38. The Female Society for the Relief and Employment of the Poor (hereafter FSREP), *120th Annual Report* (1915), n.p. Also in response to the epidemic, female philanthropists in New York City, under the leadership of Mrs. Isabella Graham, set up a similar charity, the Society for the Relief of Poor Widows with Small Children, in 1797. This society brought needlework to women in their homes and ran a Ladies' School for Poor Children, but it does not seem to have set up a workroom or nursery. See Joanna Bethune, comp., *The Power of Faith Exemplified in the Life and Writings of the Late Mrs. Isabella Graham* (New York: American Tract Society, 1843), chaps. 6–8; and *The Life of Mrs. Isabella Graham* by her daughter, Joanna Bethune (New York: M. W. Dodd, 1842).

39. Elizabeth Marshall, "An Account of Anna Parrish" (n.d.), holograph, QC, 31.

40. Gary B. Nash, *Urban Crucible: Social Change, Political Consciousness, and the Origins of the American Revolution* (Cambridge: Harvard University Press, 1979), 192–93.

41. "Rules to Be Observed by the Women Employed at the House of Industry" (n.d.), FSREP papers, QC.

42. This may have had the effect of imposing a schedule on breastfeeding, which otherwise was probably done "on demand."

43. See Clement, *Welfare and the Poor,* 46.

44. See Bloch, "American Feminine Ideals." The managers had abandoned the Calvinist notion of innate corruption in favor of the more Lockean conception of tabula rasa but had not yet embraced a concept of childhood as a state of purity and innocence; that would emerge a few decades later, around the 1830s and 1840s; see Anne L. Kuhn, *The Mother's Role in Childhood Education: New England Concepts, 1830–1860* (New Haven: Yale University Press, 1947), 18; also Hoffert, *Private Matters,* 184–86; and Ryan, *Empire of the Mother,* 103.

45. "Thoughts for the House," pt. 1 (n.d.), FSREP papers.

46. Minutebook no. 1, FSREP papers, 49–50.

47. On Pestalozzi, see Barbara Beatty, *Preschool Education in America: The Culture of Young Children from the Colonial Era to the Present* (New Haven: Yale University Press, 1995). The first kindergarten in the United States, founded on Pestalozzian principles, was set up in Philadelphia in 1806 by William McClure, a Scottish reformer and self-appointed disseminator of Pestalozzi's ideas. See Will S. Monroe, *History of the Pestalozzian Movement in the United States* (Syracuse, N.Y.: C. W. Bardeen, 1907; reprint, New York: Arno Press, 1969), chaps. 2 and 5. Unless they had read the works of Friedrich Froebel, founder of the modern kindergarten system, in German, it is unlikely that the managers of the House of Industry would have known about his ideas so early, for their philosophical shift occurred five years before Margarethe Schurz set up the first American Froebelian kindergarten in Watertown, Wisconsin, in 1856; see Michael Steven Shapiro, *A Child's Garden: The Kindergarten Movement from Froebel to Dewey* (University Park: Pennsylvania State University Press, 1983), chap. 2; and Elizabeth Dale Ross, *The Kindergarten Crusade* (Athens: Ohio University Press, 1976), chap. 1. For an excellent overview of the European origins of many American ideas about early childhood education, see Beatty, *Preschool Education,* chap. 1.

48. FSREP, *Annual Report* (1851).

49. The female proportion of the almshouse population rose from 50 percent to 65 percent between 1811 and 1814, then declined steadily, to about 35 percent, in 1845; see Clement, *Welfare and the Poor,* 76.

50. Because the practice of indenturing the children of destitute widows and single mothers had become so common during the early decades of the nineteenth century, many women avoided charitable organizations of all sorts because they feared having their children removed; see "Dying Grandmother," 494.

51. "Rules To Be Observed by the Women Employed at the House of Industry": "they shall be satisfied with the work allotted them and the price paid them." (n.d.), FSREP papers.

52. Clement, *Welfare and the Poor,* chap. 4.

53. This comparison is rough at best, because the cost of living in 1836 was about 13 per

cent *higher* than in 1840; see Series E 183–186: "Cost of Living Indexes: 1820–1926," in U.S. Bureau of the Census, *Historical Statistics of the United States, Colonial Times to 1870,* Bicentennial Edition, pt. 1 (Washington, D.C.: GPO, 1975), 212.

54. A Citizen of Philadelphia [Mathew Carey], *Plea for the Poor* (Philadelphia, December 18, 1836), 6.

55. "Dying Grandmother," 494. Delicacy no doubt prevented the magazine from mentioning another likely alternative: prostitution.

56. *Constitution and By-Laws of the Infant School Society* (Boston, 1828), n.p., quoted in Steinfels, *Who's Minding the Children,* 36.

57. William Russell, *Address on Infant Schools,* speech delivered at the request of the Managers of the Infant School Society (Boston: Hiram Tupper, 1829), 9.

58. Robert Owen, *A New View of Society* (1813), quoted in Dean May and Maris Vinovskis, "A Ray of Millennial Light: Early Education and Social Reform in the Infant School Movement in Massachusetts, 1826–1840," in *Family and Kin in Urban Communities, 1700–1930,* ed. Tamara K. Hareven (New York: New Viewpoints, 1977), 66.

59. Owen, "An Address to the Inhabitants of New Lanark," in *Socialist Thought: A Documentary History,* ed. Albert Fried and Ronald Sanders (Garden City, N.Y.: Doubleday Anchor, 1964), 159; quoted in Steinfels, *Who's Minding the Children,* 35.

60. "An Exposition of the Principles on Which the System of Infant Education Is Conducted" (orig. British pamphlet), 2nd Philadelphia ed. (Philadelphia, 1827), excerpted in *American Journal of Education* (hereafter *AJE*) 3 (1828): 413.

61. Dolores Hayden, *The Grand Domestic Revolution: A History of Feminist Designs for American Homes, Neighborhoods, and Cities* (Cambridge: MIT Press, 1981), 33. According to Barbara Taylor, the Owenites' actual treatment of women fell far short of its rhetoric; see *Eve and the New Jerusalem: Socialism and Feminism in the Nineteenth Century* (New York: Pantheon, 1983), chap. 4.

62. On the incorporation of the infant school into the British governmental education system, see Anna Davin, *Growing Up Poor: Home, School and Street in London, 1870–1914* (London: Rivers Oram Press, 1996), chap. 7.

63. For a comprehensive discussion of infant schools in the United States, see Beatty, *Preschool Education,* chap. 2.

64. See Hayden, *Grand Domestic Revolution,* 33. For other utopian child care schemes, see Hayden, *Seven American Utopias: The Architecture of Communitarian Socialism, 1790–1978* (Cambridge: MIT Press, 1976); and Steven Mintz and Susan Kellogg, *Domestic Revolutions: A Social History of American Family Life* (New York: Free Press, 1988), "Childrearing in a Utopian Community," photograph between pp. 140 and 141. The caption notes that in this particular community, Zoar, in Ohio, "because women were expected to share in fieldwork, childrearing responsibilities fell on older girls."

65. *The Christian Observer,* August 1824; quoted in "Account of the System of Infant Schools," *AJE* 1 (1826): 10.

66. "Account of the System," 10–11.

67. Ibid., 11.

68. Ibid., 13.

69. Ibid., 18.

70. Davin, *Growing Up Poor,* 116–17.

71. "Progress of Education during the Year 1826," *AJE* 1 (1826): 753. There is some confusion about whether infant schools were actually in operation by the end of 1826; in fact, Russell's congratulations may have been premature. In April 1827, the *AJE* printed an excerpt from the *Hartford Observer* on plans to establish what would be the *first* infant school on this side of the Atlantic. Russell demurred that his earlier statements were based on "printed intelligence from New-York and Philadelphia—places so distant that no other source of information, than that of the press, is easily accessible" (the *AJE* was published in Boston). Although Russell seemed willing to concede an error on his part, it is equally plausible that the editors of the Hartford newspaper were unaware of developments in the other cities. The Hartford reformers had, apparently, been inspired not by articles in the *AJE* but by trips that two of their number, one a Yale professor, had taken to observe infant schools in Edinburgh and London; note to "Infant Schools in Hartford," *AJE* 2 (1827): 254.

72. The anonymous author of the article "Infant Schools in Philadelphia" (reprinted from the *Philadelphia Album* in *AJE* 3 [1828]: 122) noted that the managers of the Chester Street Infant School saw the need for "a school for coloured children."

73. "Education of Infant Children," transcribed from the preface by the American editor to the British pamphlet "An Exposition of the Principles on Which the System of Infant Education Is Conducted," 2nd Philadelphia ed. (Philadelphia, 1827), *AJE* 3 (1828): 412.

74. As historian Anne Kuhn has pointed out, "this humanitarian appeal was reinforced by the argument that women know, better than men do, 'how much may be done towards forming the mental and especially the moral character, during the first years of a child's life'"; "Infant Schools," *Ladies' Magazine* 5 (April 1832): 182; quoted in Kuhn, *Mother's Role,* 27. Although she did not use the term *maternalist* in her analysis, Kuhn was certainly sensitive to the importance of this type of politics for women.

75. See "Education of Infant Children," *AJE* 3 (1828): 455.

76. Review of "Infant Education, etc.," comp. Mrs. [Joanna] Bethune, *AJE* 2 (1827): 575.

77. "Infant Schools," *AJE* 3 (1828): 383.

78. May and Vinovskis, "Ray of Millennial Light," 93.

79. Only one other organization, the Western Society for the Relief and Employment of Women, founded in 1847, also in Philadelphia, followed the House of Industry's pattern of workroom cum industry.

80. Barbara Berg, *The Remembered Gate: Origins of American Feminism* (New York: Oxford University Press, 1978), 236.

81. See Kenneth Cmiel, *A Home of Another Kind: One Chicago Orphanage and the Tangle of Child Welfare* (Chicago: University of Chicago Press, 1995), chap. 1.

82. *The Little Wanderer* 1, no. 4 (March 1868): 18 (published by the Home for little Wanderers, Philadelphia).

83. John Visher, *Handbook of Charities,* 3rd edition (Chicago: Charles W. Kerr, 1897), 94.

84. Day Nursery for Children, *Fourth Annual Report* (1867), 6.

85. Day Nursery for Children, *Eleventh Annual Report* (1874), n.p.

86. See Michael R. Haines, "Poverty, Economic Stress, and the Family in a Late Nineteenth-

Century American City: Whites in Philadelphia, 1880"; and Claudia Goldin, "Family Strategies and the Family Economy in the Late Nineteenth Century: The Role of Secondary Workers," both in *Philadelphia: Work, Space, Family, and Group Experience in the Nineteenth Century,* ed. Theodore Hershberg (New York: Oxford University Press, 1981), 240–310; and Carol Groneman, "'She Earns as a Child; She Pays as a Man': Women Workers in a Mid-Nineteenth-Century New York Community," in *Class, Sex, and the Woman Worker,* ed. Milton Cantor and Bruce Laurie (Westport, Conn.: Greenwood Press, 1977), 83–100.

87. In Fanny Fern's 1855 novel *Ruth Hall* (reprint, New Brunswick, N.J.: Rutgers University Press, 1986), the eponymous heroine, struggling to make a living as a writer, must work steadily yet feels torn when her daughter becomes bored and weary of waiting for her attention (134–35). See also Franklin Day Nursery, "President's Report," *Sixth Annual Report* (Philadelphia, 1912), 4. For a comprehensive discussion of the history of women and industrial homework, see Eileen Boris, *Home to Work: Motherhood and the Politics of Industrial Homework in the United States* (New York: Cambridge University Press, 1994).

88. "Margaret Etter Crèche," in Visher, *Handbook,* 94.

89. Morton Street Day Nursery (Philadelphia), *First Annual Report* (1885), 1.

90. M. H. Burgess, "The Evolution of 'The Children's House,'" *Kindergarten Review* 12 (1901–2), 401.

91. Ibid. See also Lizzie W. Collings, "Cottage Place Kindergarten and Day Nursery"; Lavinia I. Dodge, "The North Bennett Street Day Nursery"; C. E. Soper, "Ruggles Street Neighborhood House," and "Mothers' Meetings at the Cambridgeport Neighborhood House," all in *Kindergarten Review* 12 (1901–2): 404ff.

92. Dodge, "North Bennett Street," 406.

93. "Rules as Revised," (1910), typescript, North Bennett Street Industrial School papers, SL, series 2, box 4, folder 51, 1. There is evidence that this practice existed earlier than 1910; see Dodge, "North Bennett Street," 406.

94. Quoted in Ruth Bordin, *Woman and Temperance: The Quest for Power and Liberty, 1873–1900* (New Brunswick, N.J.: Rutgers University Press, 1990), 102.

95. On the Hamilton Crèche, see Larry Prochner, "A Brief History of Daycare in Canada: The Early Years," *Canadian Children* 19, no. 2 (1994): 14–15.

96. "Department of Day Nurseries," letter from Helen L. Hood, superintendent, *Union Signal* 12, no. 9 (March 4, 1886): 12.

97. Ibid., 103. The Department of Day Nurseries seems to have lasted for only a few years; during its brief existence it was listed under the category "Preventive" rather than "Education"; *Union Signal* 13, no. 9 (March 3, 1887): 11.

98. N. S. Rosenau, "Day Nurseries," *Twenty-First National Conference of Charities: Official Proceedings* (Boston, 1894): 336. For a sensitive discussion of women's responses to these routines, see Weiner, *Working Girl to Working Mother,* 121–35.

99. Rosenau, "Day Nurseries," 337.

100. For example, Fannie Barrier Williams explained that in the early days of black women's organizations (from 1890 to 1895, when they became affiliated under the National Association of Colored Women), "those who, in the proper sense, may be called the

best women in the communities . . . became interested and joined in the work of helpfulness"; "Club Movement among Negro Women," in *The Colored American from Slavery to Honorable Citizenship,* ed. J. W. Gibson and W. H. Crogman (Atlanta: J. L. Nichols, 1906), 206.

101. On African American women and social reform, see Lynda F. Dickson, "Toward a Broader Angle of Vision in Uncovering Women's History: Black Women's Clubs Revisited," *Frontiers* 9, no. 2 (1987): 62–68; Dorothy Salem, *To Better Our World: Black Women in Organized Reform, 1890–1920,* vol. 14 of *Black Women in American History,* ed. Darlene Clark Hine (Brooklyn: Carlson, 1990); Kathleen C. Berkeley, "'Colored Ladies Also Contributed': Black Women's Activities from Benevolence to Social Welfare," in *The Web of Southern Social Relations: Women, Family, and Education,* ed. Walter J. Fraser, Jr., et al. (Athens: University of Georgia Press, 1985), 181–203; and Cynthia Neverdon-Morton, *Afro-American Women of the South and the Advancement of the Race, 1895–1925* (Knoxville: University of Tennessee Press, 1989). On differences between white and African American women's visions of reform and social welfare, see Eileen Boris, "The Power of Motherhood: Black and White Activist Women Redefine the 'Political,'" *Yale Journal of Law and Feminism* 2, no. 1 (Fall 1989): 25–49, reprinted in Koven and Michel, *Mothers of a New World;* and Linda Gordon, "Black and White Visions of Welfare: Women's Welfare Activism, 1890–1945," *Journal of American History* 788 (September 1991): 559–90.

102. On general patterns, see George Rawick, ed., *The American Slave: A Composite Autobiography,* ser. 1 and 2 (Westport, Conn: Greenwood Press, 1977 and 1979), passim; and Wilma King, "'Suffer with Them Till Death': Slave Women and Their Children in Nineteenth-Century America," in *More Than Chattel: Black Women and Slavery in the Americas,* ed. David Barry Gaspar and Darlene Clark Hine (Bloomington: Indiana University Press, 1996), 152–53.

103. See Charles Joyner, *Down by the Riverside: A South Carolina Slave Community* (Urbana: University of Illinois Press, 1984), 70. Joyner compiled his list of occupations by surveying the records and probate inventories of a number of rice plantations. Richard Dunn found similar patterns at plantations in Jamaica and Virginia, although in Jamaica, children as young as five were put to work; Dunn, "A Tale of Two Plantations: Slave Life at Mesopotamia in Jamaica and Mount Airy in Virginia, 1799 to 1828," *William and Mary Quarterly* 34 (1977): 47.

104. Dorothy Sterling, ed., *We Are Your Sisters: Black Women in the Nineteenth Century* (New York: Norton, 1984), 5.

105. Ibid., 6.

106. Some infants were apparently left alone in the quarters while their parents were at work; see narrative of Rose Holman in Rawick, *American Slave,* supplement, ser. 1, vol. 8, 1038.

107. Dunn, "Tale of Two Plantations," 47, 51.

108. Sterling, *We Are Your Sisters,* 6. This statement suggests a certain level of rational benevolence on the part of slaveholders, but according to other sources, such attitudes were not universal. In *Them Dark Days: Slavery in the American Rice Swamps* (New York: Oxford University Press, 1996), William Dusinberre analyzes British actress

Fanny Kemble's interviews with female slaves on the Georgian rice plantation she visited in 1838–39. Kemble's writings, along with other data, show that while birth rates among slave women on cotton and rice plantations were high (about 7.2 live births per woman), on average only 2.6 of those children lived to age twenty-one. Cumulative child mortality rates indicate that 33.9 percent of children on the cotton plantation, and 45.9 percent of those on the rice plantation, died before age six (239, 243).

109. King, "'Suffer with Them,'" 153.

110. Narrative of Ellen Betts in Rawick, *American Slave,* ser. 2, vol. 2, 267.

111. Sterling, *We Are Your Sisters,* 6.

112. Narrative of Annie Little in Rawick, *American Slave,* supplement, ser. 2, vol. 6, 2393–94.

113. King, "'Suffer with Them,'" 153.

114. Narrative of Charlie Davenport in Rawick, *American Slave,* ser. 1, vol. 7, 34. See also narrative of Lucy Donald, ser. 1, vol. 7, 636.

115. Censer (*North Carolina Planters,* chap. 2) argues that white planter mothers in North Carolina relied less on black mammies than the stereotype suggests, but other historians indicate that the practice was prevalent throughout the rest of the antebellum South; see, for example, Jacqueline Jones, *Labor of Love, Labor of Sorrow: Black Women, Work, and the Family from Slavery to the Present* (New York: Basic Books, 1985), 22–27.

116. The proportion of African American women in domestic service peaked at 53.5 percent in 1930, declining slowly until 1980, when it finally fell to 5 percent. See Teresa L. Amott and Julie A. Matthaei, *Race, Gender, and Work: A Multicultural Economic History of Women in the United States* (Boston: South End Press, 1991), 125, 158. On the child care duties of black domestic servants during the interwar period, see Phyllis Palmer, *Domesticity and Dirt: Housewives and Domestic Service in the United States, 1920–1945* (Philadelphia: Temple University Press, 1989), chap. 3.

117. Rev. Joseph E. Smith, "The Care of Neglected Children," in *Social and Physical Condition of Negroes in Cities,* Atlanta University Publications no. 2 (Atlanta: Atlanta University Press, 1897), 41–42.

118. "The Black Mother," *The Crisis* (December 1912): 78.

119. See Elizabeth Lindsay Davis, *Lifting as They Climb* (Washington, D.C.: National Association of Colored Women, 1933).

120. Reports from state chapters in Davis, *Lifting,* indicate day nursery activity in Indiana, Chicago and downstate Illinois, Denver, Tampa, Oakland, Lexington, and at various sites in New Jersey and Pennsylvania. On day nurseries in Denver, see Lynda Faye Dickson, "The Early Club Movement among Black Women in Denver, 1890–1925," Ph.d. diss., University of Colorado at Boulder, 1982; for Atlanta, see Louie D. Shivery, "The Neighborhood Union: A Survey of the Beginnings of Social Welfare Movements Among Negroes in Atlanta," in "The History of Organized Social Work Among Atlanta Negroes," M.A. thesis, Atlanta University, 1936, excerpted in *The Black Heritage in Social Welfare, 1860–1930,* comp. and ed. Edyth L. Ross (Metuchen, N.J.: Scarecrow Press, 1978), 263–81. For Indiana, see Earline Rae Ferguson, "A Commu-

nity Affair: African-American Women's Club Work in Indianapolis, 1879–1917," Ph.D. diss., Indiana University, 1997.

121. See Orville Vernon Burton, "The Rise and Fall of Afro-American Town Life: Town and Country in Reconstruction Edgefield, South Carolina," in *Toward a New South? Studies in Post-Civil War Southern Communities,* ed. Orville Vernon Burton and Robert C. McMath, Jr. (Westport, Conn.: Greenwood Press, 1982), 152–92.

122. See Theodore Hershberg, "Free Blacks in Antebellum Philadelphia: A Study of Ex-Slaves, Freeborn, and Socioeconomic Decline"; Hershberg and Henry Williams, "Mulattoes and Blacks: Intragroup Color Differences and Social Stratification in Nineteenth-Century Philadelphia"; and Frank F. Furstenberg, Jr., Theodore Hershberg, and John Modell, "The Origins of the Black Female-Headed Family: The Impact of the Urban Experience," all in Hershberg, *Philadelphia.* See also Elizabeth Rauh Bethel, *Promiseland: A Century of Life in a Negro Community* (Philadelphia: Temple University Press, 1981), chaps. 6–7; and Elizabeth Clark-Lewis, "'This Work Had a End': African-American Domestic Workers in Washington, D.C., 1910–1940," in *"To Toil the Livelong Day": America's Women at Work, 1780–1980,* ed. Carol Groneman and Mary Beth Norton (Ithaca: Cornell University Press, 1987), 196–212.

123. On options for African American children in Philadelphia, see Clement, *Welfare and the Poor,* 120, 124–25, 129, 136, 162.

124. Association for the Care of Colored Orphans (Philadelphia), *Second Annual Report* (1836), 4. This report refers to the founding of the shelter in 1822.

125. Homer Folks, *The Care of Destitute, Neglected, and Delinquent Children* (New York: Macmillan, 1902), 52–53. The New York institution, founded in 1836 as the Colored Orphans' Asylum, later became known as the Riverdale Children's Association; see RCA, "Story of the First 120 Years."

126. Leonard P. Curry, *The Free Black in Urban America, 1800–1850* (Chicago: University of Chicago Press, 1981), 133–35.

127. See Davis, *Lifting,* passim; also Neverdon-Morton, *Afro-American Women.* On the Carrie Steele Home, see Ross, *Black Heritage,* 144–46.

128. In light of Speaker Newt Gingrich's proposal to remove the children of poor mothers who are deemed "unfit" and place them in orphanages, it should be noted that, in contrast, the decisions of nineteenth-century parents to place their children in orphanages were, within certain constraints, voluntary. I am merely describing the practice here, not condoning it.

129. RCA, "History of the Riverdale Children's Association," 11.

130. Home for Destitute Colored Children (Philadelphia), *Second Annual Report* (1857), 6–7.

131. [Sidney Andrews], "Children's Homes and Orphan Asylums," pt. 8 of the *13th Annual Report of the Secretary of the [Massachusetts] Board of State Charities,* October 1876 (Boston, 1877), 5–30.

132. M. W. Shinn, "Charities for Children in San Francisco," *Overland Monthly* 15 (January 1890): 78–101. See also Timothy A. Hacsi, *Second Home: Orphan Asylums and Poor Families in America* (Cambridge: Harvard University Press, 1997), chaps. 4 and 7.

133. Four was the minimum at most boarding institutions.

134. See Quiroga, *Poor Mothers and Babies,* 66–68; and Du Bois, "Thirty Years' Experience."

135. Du Bois, "Thirty Years' Experience," 181.

136. Ibid.

137. Quiroga, *Poor Mothers and Babies,* 68.

138. Mary Bunting Wolff, "Historical Sketch of the Philadelphia Home for Infants," 1919, typescript, Children's Aid Society Collection, HSP, 1. See also Philadelphia Home for Infants, Board Minutes, 1873–94, HSP, passim.

139. See Janet Golden, "Trouble in the Nursery: Physicians, Families, and Wet Nurses at the End of the Nineteenth Century," in Groneman and Norton, *"To Toil the Livelong Day,"* 125–40. See also Quiroga, *Poor Mothers and Babies.*

140. In some cases, public support was restricted only to "true orphans"; see, for example, the Colored Orphans' Asylum of New York (RCA, "History," 16).

141. Priscilla Ferguson Clement, "Children and Charity: Orphanages in New Orleans, 1817–1914," *Louisiana History* 27 (1986): 347.

142. Ibid.

143. Ibid., 345. It may be that widowers had an easier time of remarrying, or at any rate were more likely to receive offers of assistance from female neighbors or kin and thus did not as often require the services of orphanages for their children.

144. Priscilla Ferguson Clement, "Families and Foster Care: Philadelphia in the Late Nineteenth Century," *Social Service Review* 53 (1979): 413.

145. On indenturing practices in late eighteenth- and early nineteenth-century Philadelphia, see Clement, *Welfare and the Poor,* chap. 3. In *In the Shadow of the Poorhouse: A Social History of Welfare in America* (New York: Basic Books, 1986), Michael B. Katz claims that Brace was "the first major reformer to formulate an anti-institutional strategy of child rescue" (106), yet there are continuities between Brace's thinking and that of the earlier advocates of indenture. The principal difference between them seems to be the distance they were willing to put between children and their families of origin.

146. "A writer in 1830," quoted in Homer Folks, *The Care of Destitute, Neglected, and Delinquent Children* (New York: Macmillan, 1902), 24.

147. Folks, *Care of Destitute,* 39.

148. Katz, *In the Shadow,* 106. For Brace's views on children and child rescue, see *The Dangerous Classes of New York and Twenty Years' Work among Them* (New York: Wynkoop and Hallenbeck, 1872). Brace's scheme was unsatisfactory for many reasons, not the least of which was that because few of these children were actually orphans, they suffered prolonged, often involuntary separations from their families.

149. Folks, *Care of Destitute,* 80–81.

150. Andrews, "Children's Homes," 29.

151. Quoted in Shinn, "Charities for Children," 85.

152. Folks, *Care of Destitute,* 41.

153. See, for example, Home Missionary Society of Philadelphia, *Fiftieth Annual Report* (1885), 9.

154. Home for Destitute Colored Children (Philadelphia), *Annual Reports,* 1865–95 (HSP).

155. Franziska Children's Home, *Annual Reports,* 1893–94 and 1894–95 (HSP).

156. See Sonya Michel, "Children, Institutions and Community: The Jewish Orphanage of Rhode Island, 1909–1942," *Rhode Island Jewish Historical Notes* 8 (1977): 193–221.

157. Records of the Chicago Nursery and Half-Orphan Society, Chapin Hall Collection, CHS, boxes 1–3. For a full account of the many lives of this institution, see Cmiel, *Home of Another Kind.*

158. Shinn, "Charities for Children," 85.

159. See also Rosenau, "Day Nurseries."

160. See Sherri Broder, "Child Care or Child Neglect? Baby Farming in Late-Nineteenth-Century Philadelphia," *Gender and Society* 2, no. 2 (June 1988): 128–48. The Juvenile Protective Agency of Chicago also ran a major investigation of baby farms in 1916; see chapter 2 of this book.

161. In "Child Care or Child Neglect?" Broder notes that by the end of the century, in Philadelphia at least, the SPCC had come to terms with the prevalence of such informal care and campaigned to institute regulation and supervision of all home-based providers.

162. See Linda Gordon, *Heroes of Their Own Lives: The Politics and History of Family Violence: Boston 1880–1960* (New York: Penguin, 1988), chap. 2.

163. Consider, for example, the views of one nursery philanthropist, Lucy Bainbridge of New York City. Addressing the maternalist National Congress of Mothers in 1897, she referred to the clientele of day nurseries as the "mothers of the submerged world," who were plagued by a series of "D's": Darkness, Dirt, Disease, Dress (extravagance of), Debt, Distress, Drink, the Disaster, and Death. See Mrs. Lucy S. Bainbridge, "Mothers of the Submerged World—Day Nurseries," *Report of the Proceedings of the First National Congress of Mothers* (Washington, D.C., 1897): 47–55. The Boston nurseries of Pauline Agassiz Shaw were exceptional in their mixing of children from different classes.

164. Similarly, middle-class reformers who sought to aid working-class women through organizations like the New York Working Woman's Protective Union were mainly intent on moving them out of the labor market and back into the home, often over the objections of wage-earning women. See Alice Kessler-Harris, *Out to Work: A History of Wage-Earning Women in the United States* (New York: Oxford University Press, 1982), 91–93.

165. See Boris, *Home to Work,* pt. 1.

166. See Michael B. Katz, *The Irony of Early School Reform* (Cambridge: Harvard University Press, 1968). Katz shows that public schools (like day nurseries) were first presented as a method of preventing social pathology. See also Ira Katznelson and Margaret Weir, *Schooling for All: Class, Race, and the Decline of the Democratic Ideal* (New York: Basic Books, 1985), which emphasizes the role of the working class in the struggle for public education.

CHAPTER 2: THE ROAD NOT TAKEN

1. "The Children's Building of the World's Columbian Exposition," pamphlet, n.p., 1893, World's Columbian Exposition collection, CHS, 23.

2. Ibid.

3. On the campaign to include a day nursery, see Jeanne Madeline Weimann, *The Fair Women: The Story of the Woman's Building, World's Columbian Exposition, Chicago, 1893* (Chicago: Academy Chicago, 1981), 344–46. As Gail Bederman points out, the male managers of the exposition were also bent on obscuring women's contributions to civilization through work; this no doubt fueled their opposition to establishing a day nursery, insofar as its chief raison d'être was to permit women to undertake paid labor. See *Manliness and Civilization: A Cultural History of Gender and Race in the United States, 1880–1917* (Chicago: University of Chicago Press, 1995), 33.

4. For a detailed description of the daily operation of the nursery, see Weimann, *Fair Women*, 346–52. According to her account, the nursery was not without its problems. The staff was exhausted from running day after day at full capacity, and inevitably, children became inconsolable when they realized they were in a roomful of strangers and their parents were nowhere to be seen. In addition, the nursery became a favorite target for popular jokes and newspaper stories ridiculing the idea of "checking the baby." Nonetheless, the nursery did run for six months without major mishap.

5. J. B. Campbell, *Campbell's Illustrated History of the World's Columbian Exposition* (Chicago: J. B. Campbell, 1894), vol. 2, 578.

6. "Children's Building," 23.

7. The Chicago Exposition, with its Congress of Representative Women and its Women's and Children's Buildings, served as a focal point for existing national women's organizations and galvanized the formation of others. Along with the NFDN, the National Association of Colored Women, the National Council of Jewish Women, and the General Federation of Women's Clubs, among others, were also organized at this time. See Anne Firor Scott, "Women's Voluntary Associations: From Charity to Reform," in *Lady Bountiful Revisited: Women, Philanthropy, and Power,* ed. Kathleen D. McCarthy (New Brunswick, N.J.: Rutgers University Press, 1990), 43–44.

8. Lynn Y. Weiner, *From Working Girl to Working Mother: The Female Labor Force in the United States, 1820–1890* (Chapel Hill: University of North Carolina Press, 1985), 86. See also Winifred D. Wandersee, *Women's Work and Family Values, 1920–1940* (Cambridge: Harvard University Press, 1981). Both Wandersee and Weiner tend to date this shift at around 1920, but there are signs of it in earlier decades.

9. On the regulation of homework during this period, see Eileen Boris, *Home to Work: Motherhood and the Politics of Industrial Homework in the United States* (New York: Cambridge University Press, 1994), pts. 1 and 2.

10. From 1890 to 1920, the birth rate for women aged 15–44 fell from about 138 per thousand to 115 per thousand; see Susan Householder Van Horn, *Women, Work, and Fertility, 1900–1986* (New York: New York University Press, 1988), 6.

11. See Weiner, *From Working Girl to Working Mother,* 6–7; and Wandersee, *Women's Work,* 68. Before 1940, maternal employment rates were not calculated separately on a nationwide basis; for earlier decades, therefore, they must be inferred. Local studies and anecdotal evidence suggest that many of the married and once-married women in the labor force were also mothers. For example, a U.S. Women's Bureau analysis of 1920 census data from four geographically diverse cities (Jacksonville, Florida; Wilkes-Barre

and Hanover Township, Pennsylvania; Butte, Montana; and Passaic, New Jersey) found that 53 percent of married and once-married women workers had children, 40 percent of them under age five; U.S. Women's Bureau, *Family Status of Breadwinning Women in Four Selected Cities,* Bulletin of the Women's Bureau, no. 41 (Washington: GPO, 1925), 10. See also Gwendolyn Hughes, *Mothers in Industry: Wage-Earning Mothers in Philadelphia* (New York: New Republic, 1925), 9; and Claudia Goldin, *Understanding the Gender Gap: An Economic History of American Women* (New York: Oxford, 1990), 143–48.

12. Anne Durst, "Day Nurseries and Wage-Earning Mothers in the United States, 1890–1930," Ph.D. diss., University of Wisconsin-Madison, 1989, 6–7. See also Linda Rosenbaum Goldmintz, "The Growth of Day Care Services, 1890–1946," D.S.W. diss., Yeshiva University, 1987, 533–34. Because these numbers are culled from the NFDN's annual reports, they may underestimate the actual number of nurseries, some of which may have been unknown to the organization. At the same time, part of the increase may be an artifact of reports of hitherto unknown but pre-existing day nurseries.

13. As Josephine Shaw Lowell, another luminary of New York charities, put it, "the Roosevelts and the Dodges . . . you can depend on every time,—they are most satisfactory wherever you meet them; being all rich, too, they have time to work, which is decidedly a good thing." Letter from Lowell to Mrs. Robert Gould [Annie] Shaw [her sister-in-law], May 23, 1882, in *The Philanthropic Work of Josephine Shaw Lowell,* comp. William Rhinelander Stewart (New York: Macmillan, 1911), 129. One of the most notable members of the family was Josephine Dodge's niece by marriage, Grace Hoadley Dodge, whose lifelong philanthropic works included setting up clubs for young working girls, founding the Teachers College of Columbia University, and serving as national president of the Young Women's Christian Association. See "Grace Hoadley Dodge," in *Notable American Women, 1607–1950* (Cambridge: Belknap Press of Harvard University Press, 1971), vol. 1, 489–92; and Lori D. Ginzberg, *Women and the Work of Benevolence: Morality, Politics, and Class in the Nineteenth-Century United States* (New Haven: Yale University Press, 1990), 199–200.

14. Mrs. Arthur Dodge, "Woman Suffrage Opposed to Woman's Rights," *Annals of the American Academy of Political and Social Science* 14 (November 1914): 100. Dodge's views were close to those of another conservative maternalist and anti-suffragist of this period, Elizabeth Lowell Putnam of Boston. Putnam, whose area of concern was maternal and child health, organized clinics and also lobbied for pure milk laws in her home state, but she later opposed federally supported measures like the Sheppard-Towner Act and tried to bring down the U.S. Children's Bureau. See Sonya Michel and Robyn Rosen, "The Paradox of Maternalism: Elizabeth Lowell Putnam and the American Welfare State," *Gender and History* 4 (1992): 364–86.

15. Officials of the COS criticized governmental methods of distributing relief on the grounds that they pauperized recipients by failing to change their habits and thus perpetuated dependency; see Daniel Levine, *Poverty and Society: The Growth of the American Welfare State in International Comparison* (New Brunswick, N.J.: Rutgers University Press, 1988), 29–30. Nevertheless, once mothers' pensions were passed, COS workers often became involved in their administration.

16. Molly Ladd-Taylor, *Mother-Work: Women, Child Welfare, and the State, 1890–1930* (Urbana: University of Illinois Press, 1993), 7–8.

17. National Federation of Day Nurseries, *Report of the Conference* (hereafter NFDN, *Report*), 1905, 11.

18. See NFDN, *Report,* 1912: Edward Bunnell Phelps, "Some Possibilities of New Life and Broader Usefulness for the Day Nursery Movement in this Country," 50–51; and Mrs. Arthur Dodge, "Address of the President of the Federation," 1912, 17.

19. John Spargo, *The Bitter Cry of the Children* (1906; reprint, New York: Johnson Reprint, 1969), 232.

20. Day nursery philanthropists were no doubt familiar with the influential book *A Study of Nine Hundred and Eighty-Five Widows,* by Mary Richmond and Fred S. Hall, published by the Russell Sage Foundation in 1913. Resisting calls for statistical measures of agency treatment, Hall and Richmond insisted that each case be examined individually, "for the thing to be measured is care . . . and this cannot be expressed in figures" (9). They also opposed the idea that a single policy could meet the needs of all families. For a detailed discussion of this text, see Sonya Michel, "Rationalization and Resistance: Child Care and Family Policy in the Early U.S. Welfare State," paper presented at a conference titled "The Politics of Social Welfare and the Rationalization of Everyday Life: The United States and Germany during the Interwar Years," Werner Reimers Foundation, Bad Homburg, Germany, February 1995.

21. Phelps noted that the city of Los Angeles had established a day nursery near a public school in an immigrant neighborhood, although this had been done not at the urging of the NFDN but at the behest of the Board of Education to prevent truancy on the part of girls compelled to stay at home and play "little mother" to younger siblings. See Phelps, "Some Possibilities," 50. California was by far the most progressive state in the union when it came to child care, and continued to be so throughout the twentieth century. See Frances Cahn and Valeska Bary, *Welfare Activities of Federal, State, and Local Governments in California, 1850–1934* (Berkeley: University of California Press, 1936), 34–37.

22. See, for example, Mrs. Arthur Dodge, "Address of the President of the Federation," in NFDN, *Report,* 1906, 7–9.

23. According to Margaret O'Brien Steinfels, only one nursery was ever dropped from membership for noncompliance; *Who's Minding the Children: The History and Politics of Day Care in America* (New York: Simon and Schuster, 1973), 54.

24. See NFDN, *Report,* 1916: Mrs. Arthur M. Dodge, "Address of the President of the Federation," 24; Mrs. R. R. Bradford, "Standardization of Day Nurseries," 60; and "Report of the Philadelphia Association of Day Nurseries," 106; also Cahn and Bary, *Welfare Activities,* 35–37; and Goldmintz, "Growth of Day Care," 230–32.

25. For example, when the Cleveland Welfare Federation instituted day nursery regulations in 1918, it acknowledged New York and Chicago as models; see "Mushroom Day Nurseries Checked," *Survey* 41 (November 23, 1918): 229–30.

26. Dr. S. Josephine Baker, "Day Nursery Standards," in U.S. Children's Bureau, *Standards of Child Welfare,* Bulletin No. 60 (Washington, D.C.: GPO, 1919), 220.

27. "Boarding and Sale Homes for Babies," *Survey* 39 (January 5, 1918): 403. See also

Arthur Alden Guild, *Baby Farms in Chicago: An Investigation Made for the Juvenile Protective Association* (n.p., 1917), CHS.

28. "Boarding and Sale Homes," 404. Chicago had been concerned with baby farming for some time. In early 1903 Nellie Campbell, a notorious "baby farm keeper," was acquitted on a charge of infanticide after a sensational trial. The Chicago reform community stood by helplessly as she went free because of a lack of specific evidence concerning the child who had died. A few months later, a measure intended to regulate the "surrender, placing, and transfer of children," which was specifically aimed at baby farms, was submitted to the Illinois General Assembly but failed to pass. See "Methods of a Baby Farm," *Charities* 10 (1903): 79; and "A Blow at Baby Farms," *Charities* 10 (1903): 464.

29. By contrast, some traditional organizations demonstrated that they could change when necessary; during the campaign for mothers' pensions, for example, both the National Congress of Mothers and the General Federation of Women's Clubs adapted themselves quite effectively as vehicles for lobbying. See Ladd-Taylor, *Mother-Work,* chap. 2, and Theda Skocpol, *Protecting Soldiers and Mothers: The Political Origins of Social Policy in the United States* (Cambridge: Harvard University Press, 1992), chaps. 6 and 8.

30. See Barbara Beatty, *Preschool Education in America: The Culture of Young Children from the Colonial Era to the Present* (New Haven: Yale University Press, 1995), chaps. 4–6.

31. Mrs. A. Dodge, "The Development of the Day Nursery," *Outlook* 56 (1897): 62.

32. One exception was the network of day nurseries and charitable kindergartens founded in Boston by philanthropist Pauline Agassiz Shaw; see chapter 1 of this book.

33. Marjory Hall, "Concerning the Administration of the Day Nursery," *Charities* 8 (1902): 544.

34. Young Women's Union of Philadelphia, "The History of the Young Women's Union" (1910), typescript, Young Women's Union collection, PJAC, 3.

35. Elizabeth H. Rose, "Americanizing the Family: Class, Gender, and Ethnicity in a Jewish Settlement House," paper delivered to the Eighth Berkshire Conference on the History of Women, Rutgers University, New Brunswick, N.J., 1990. See also Rose, "Maternal Work: Day Care in Philadelphia, 1890–1960," Ph.D. diss., Rutgers University, 1994, chap. 1. It should be noted that, in dictating standards to the newcomers, the German Jewish women were clearly affirming their own status as Americans. On tensions between German Jewish and East European Jewish women, see Charlotte Baum, Paula Hyman, and Sonya Michel, *The Jewish Woman in America* (New York: Dial, 1974), chap. 2.

36. Training for nursery personnel was always a problem. Beginning in the late nineteenth century, the Fitch Crèche of Buffalo offered a training program for nursery maids, in which an attempt was made to "dignify labor," but nursery managers always complained about the difficulty of attracting "the higher type of girl" into day nursery work. See comments by Miss Love of the Fitch Crèche, NFDN, *Report,* 1914, 9. For details on qualifications and wages for staff, see Durst, "Day Nurseries," chap. 4.

37. For a more detailed discussion of this problem, see Sonya Michel, "The Challenge to Educate: Day Nurseries and Early Childhood Education in the Progressive Era," paper delivered to the History of Education Society, Chicago, 1989.

38. Mrs. Arthur M. Dodge, "Address of the President of the Federation," NFDN, *Report,* 1906, 10.

39. The following discussion is based on data drawn from NFDN, *Reports* of 1916, 1919, 1922, 1925, and 1929. On the child health movement, see Richard Meckel, *Save the Babies: American Public Health Reform and the Prevention of Infant Mortality, 1850–1929* (Baltimore: Johns Hopkins University Press, 1990).

40. See Meckel, *Save the Babies,* chap. 4, for a discussion of maternal education as part of the child health movement.

41. Mrs. William Conger and Miss Ward, "District Nursing in Relation to Day Nurseries," in NFDN, *Report,* 1905, 53–55.

42. Philadelphia Association of Day Nurseries, "History of the Philadelphia Association of Day Nurseries," *Annual Report* 1915, UA, 8–9.

43. See Michael B. Katz, *In the Shadow of the Poorhouse: A Social History of Welfare in America* (New York: Basic Books, 1986), 118–21.

44. Edward T. Devine, *The Principles of Relief* (New York: Macmillan, 1904), 339.

45. Mrs. Arthur M. Dodge, "Recognition—Co-Operation," in NFDN, *Report,* 1905, 10. (Possibly because of Dodge's long-term ties by marriage to the COS, she was particularly sensitive to its opinion of the NFDN.) At the same conference, Rev. Harris E. Adriance, another New York COS official, also praised day nurseries for preserving families; see "The Day Nursery as a Conserver of the Home," in NFDN, *Report,* 1905, 18–21. Josephine Shaw Lowell consistently supported the use of day nurseries for widows with children; in 1902 she wrote to the editor of *Charities* calling for Mills Hotels (a kind of inexpensive hotel that catered to low-income transients) that would include day nurseries, kindergartens, restaurants, and laundries; *Charities* 8 (May 3, 1902): 389. Ironically, Lowell's proposal was not dissimilar from Charlotte Perkins Gilman's 1904 scheme for "feminist apartment hotels." The main difference was that Gilman's plan was designed for middle-class professional women and their children. See Dolores Hayden, *The Grand Domestic Revolution: A History of Feminist Designs for American Homes, Neighborhoods, and Cities* (Cambridge: MIT Press, 1981), 194–95.

46. Edward T. Devine, "The Need of Co-Operation between Day Nurseries and Other Organizations," in NFDN, *Report,* 1905, 17.

47. Dodge, "Address of the President," in NFDN, *Report,* 1906, 7.

48. Devine, *Principles,* 339.

49. Dodge, "Address of the President," in NFDN, *Report,* 1906, 8.

50. Even trained social workers were not immune to handling cases improperly. In their 1910 study of widows, Richmond and Hall found that social workers were responsible for many cases of overwork because, in the interest of preventing pauperization, they encouraged women to take jobs instead of permitting them to apply for (or simply offering them) additional allowances. See *Nine Hundred and Eighty-Five Widows,* 8–9.

51. Goldmintz, "Growth of Day Care," 244. Another solution was for a group of nurseries that could not afford to hire their own investigators to "share" such professionals. The ADNNYC considered such a proposal in 1918.

52. Bradford, "Standardization," 56.

53. Lillie Hamilton French, "While the Mother Works: A Look at the Day Nurseries of New York," *Century Illustrated Monthly Magazine* (December 1902): 174.

54. The quoted phrase is Susan Porter Benson's, in *Counter Cultures: Saleswomen, Managers, and Customers in American Department Stores, 1890–1940* (Urbana: University of Illinois Press, 1986), 82–91. Benson notes, in fact, that many department stores included day nurseries among the amenities they offered customers (85–86).

55. In Veblen's terms, these women were combining "conspicuous leisure" with "conspicuous consumption." See *The Theory of the Leisure Class* (New York: Macmillan, 1899), chaps. 3, 4, and 7. On the relation between class and public culture, see Lawrence Levine, *Highbrow/Lowbrow: The Emergence of Cultural Hierarchy in the United States* (Cambridge: Harvard University Press, 1988).

56. Scott, "Women's Voluntary Associations," 48.

57. See Durst, "Day Nurseries," 140.

58. French, "While the Mother Works," 174.

59. A matron named Miss Olyphant did speak at the 1892 conference of day nursery philanthropists held in New York City before the formation of the NFDN or ADN-NYC. Her appearance, however, did not set a precedent, possibly because she presumed to tell board members what their duties were (these included attending meetings regularly, informing themselves about the workings of the nursery, visiting often enough to become acquainted with mothers and children as well as staff members, and committing themselves to fundraising for the institution); see *Proceedings of the 1892 Conference on Day Nurseries* (New York: J. J. O'Brien and Son, 1893), 58–60, cited in Goldmintz, "Growth of Day Care," 151.

60. Katharine S. Anthony, *Mothers Who Must Earn* (New York: Survey Associates, 1914), 152. It should be noted that Anthony still seemed to be privileging bourgeois child care practices and standards. The mothers she considered worthy of committee membership were those whose experience had brought them into contact with upper-class households; she did not seem to think that any would be qualified on the basis of their own class experience alone.

61. Ibid.

62. Scott, "Women's Voluntary Associations," 48.

63. Virginia A. Metaxas Quiroga, *Poor Mothers and Babies: A Social History of Childbirth and Child Care Hospitals in Nineteenth-Century New York* (New York: Garland, 1989), 69. "The Nursery's managers set high standards for the care of the house and its children, reflecting their notions of domestic order." Mothers were assigned to perform many housekeeping tasks as well as care for the children, as was common in many nineteenth-century residential institutions, including hospitals.

64. Ethel Beer, *The Day Nursery* (New York: Dutton, 1938), 100; quoted in Goldmintz, "Growth of Day Care," 149. Beer, a supporter of day nurseries who could also be rather tart in her assessment of them, added that matrons were typically untrained and had no understanding of modern approaches to young children. According to Beer, "their care if adequate was due to good luck rather than good management."

65. See Dodge, "Address of the President," in NFDN, *Report,* 1906, 8; and comments, in

NFDN, *Report,* 1914, 11. The main similarity between nursery matrons and settlement workers was that both lived where they worked.

66. The managers of the Model Day Nursery at the World's Columbian Exposition ran a training school for nursery maids in conjunction with their exhibit, but this project was short-lived; see "Children's Building," 23.

67. See Roy Lubove, *The Professional Altruist: The Emergence of Social Work as a Career, 1880–1930* (Cambridge: Harvard University Press, 1965).

68. Durst, "Day Nurseries," esp. chap. 4.

69. See Hamilton Cravens, *Before Head Start: The Iowa Station and America's Children* (Chapel Hill: University of North Carolina Press, 1993), introduction and chaps. 1–3.

70. Address by Dr. Caroline Hedger, in NFDN, *Report,* 1912, 28–30.

71. Address by Mrs. Arthur Dodge, in NFDN, *Report,* 1916, 19. For a full account of this controversy, see Goldmintz, "Growth of Day Care," 226–28.

72. Myrn Brockett, discussion following a paper by S. Josephine Baker, in CB, *Standards,* 226–27.

73. See Katharine Anthony, ed., *The Endowment of Motherhood* (New York: B. W. Huebsch, 1920); for discussions of this policy in the American context, see Ladd-Taylor, *Mother-Work,* 117–18; and Gordon, *Pitied but Not Entitled,* 57–59.

74. Mary Church Terrell, "Club Work of Colored Women," *Southern Workman* 30 (August 1901): 436–37.

75. See Rev. Joseph E. Smith, "The Care of Neglected Children," in *Social and Physical Condition of Negroes in Cities,* Atlanta University Publications No. 2 (Atlanta: Atlanta University Press, 1897), 41–42. On racial differences among maternalists generally, see Eileen Boris, "The Power of Motherhood: Black and White Activist Women Redefine the 'Political,'" in *Mothers of a New World: Maternalist Politics and the Origins of Welfare States,* ed. Seth Koven and Sonya Michel (New York: Routledge, 1993); and Linda Gordon, "Black and White Visions of Welfare: Women's Welfare Activism, 1890–1945," *Journal of American History* 78 (1991): 559–90.

76. According to Tullia Brown Hamilton, 73 percent of NACW members had been employed at some point during their lives; see "The National Association of Colored Women, 1896–1920," Ph.D. diss., Emory University, 1978, 45; cited in Durst, "Day Nurseries," 179 n. 18.

77. The conferences were directed by W. E. B. DuBois. See Louie D. Shivery, "The History of Organized Social Work among Atlanta Negroes, M.A. thesis, Atlanta University, 1936, excerpted in *Black Heritage in Social Welfare,* ed. and comp. Edyth L. Ross (Metuchen, N.J.: Scarecrow Press, 1978), 259; and Elisabeth Lasch-Quinn, *Black Neighbors: Race and the Limits of Reform in the American Settlement House Movement, 1890–1945* (Chapel Hill: University of North Carolina Press, 1993), 122.

78. Shivery, "Organized Social Work," 260. The president of the Neighborhood Union was Lugenia Burns Hope, wife of John Hope, the first black president of Morehouse University. See her biography by Jacqueline Rouse, *Lugenia Burns Hope, Black Southern Reformer* (Athens: University of Georgia Press, 1989). Louie Shivery was secretary of the organization from 1910 to 1930; thus her thesis doubles as a kind of memoir.

79. Similar patterns have been found for other types of community projects and elsewhere in the country; see, for example, the support for the black-run Provident Hospital in Chicago described by Susan Lynn Smith, "'Sick and Tired of Being Sick and Tired': Black Women and the National Negro Health Movement, 1915–1950," Ph.D. diss., University of Wisconsin-Madison, 1991.

80. Shivery, "Organized Social Work," 262.

81. Sheltering Arms [of Atlanta], *Annual Report* 1909–10, AHS, 14.

82. Shivery, "Organized Social Work," 263.

83. Ibid., 262.

84. Ross, *Black Heritage,* 263–64.

85. See Lasch-Quinn, *Black Neighbors,* 128–31.

86. Ross, *Black Heritage,* 263–64.

87. Shivery, "Organized Social Work," 262.

88. "The Day Nursery Discussed by Miss Addams," *Charities and the Commons* 15 (December 30, 1905): 412.

89. Ibid., 411. The "results" she had in mind were reports of encounters between these children and the police, sometimes leading to arrests for loitering, petty theft, and similar offenses.

90. Jane Addams, "Greetings from National Conference of Charities and Correction," in *Proceedings of the Sixth National Conference of Jewish Charities,* St. Louis, Missouri, 1910 (Baltimore: Kohn and Pollock, 1910), 40; for a slightly different version of this anecdote, see Addams, *Twenty Years at Hull-House* (1910; reprint, New York: Signet, 1960), 130–31.

91. Florence Kelley, "The Family and the Woman's Wage," *Proceedings of the National Conference of Social Work* (1909): 121.

92. Florence Kelley, *Modern Industry in Relation to the Family, Health, Education, Morality* (New York: Longmans, Green, 1914), 16.

93. Sophonisba Breckinridge and Edith Abbott, *The Delinquent Child and the Home: A Study of the Delinquent Wards of the Juvenile Court of Chicago* (New York: Russell Sage Foundation, 1917). For an extended discussion of their views, see Joanne L. Goodwin, "An American Experiment in Paid Motherhood: The Implementation of Mothers' Pensions in Early Twentieth Century Chicago," *Gender and History* 4 (1992): 323–42.

94. In fact, day nurseries never achieved the level of popularity that NFDN leaders had envisioned; in the social welfare literature from about 1900 to 1920, the number of articles, conference addresses, and studies on day nurseries was far smaller than those concerning mothers' and widows' pensions. At a conference held in conjunction with the 1911 Chicago Child Welfare Exhibit, day nurseries were never mentioned, even though prominent activists involved with child care, such as Jane Addams and Julia Lathrop, participated; nor was the NFDN represented. See Cyrus Hall McCormick, *The Child in the City* (Chicago: Department of Social Investigation, Chicago School of Civics and Philanthropy, 1911).

95. NFDN, *Report,* 1905, 36. Frankel seems to have had no compunction about denouncing the day nursery to a conference of its principal supporters, which speaks volumes

about the weakness of the child care movement during this period. (It may well also say something about Frankel's male arrogance, although the day nursery also took a drubbing from its female critics during this conference.)

96. Lee R. Frankel, quoted in "National Conference on Day Nurseries: A Report," *Charities* 14 (1905): 777.

97. Julia C. Lathrop, "The Day Nursery Child and His Future," in NFDN, *Report,* 1905: 30.

98. Robyn Muncy, *Creating a Female Dominion in American Reform, 1890–1935* (New York: Oxford, 1991), chaps. 2, 4, and 5.

99. On this campaign, see Muncy, *Female Dominion,* chap. 4; Skocpol, *Protecting Soldiers and Mothers,* chap. 9; and Ladd-Taylor, *Mother-Work,* chap. 6.

100. Spargo, *Bitter Cry,* 39.

101. Anthony, *Mothers Who Must Earn,* passim; see also Ladd-Taylor, *Mother-Work,* 30.

102. On the origins of Rathbone's idea, see Susan Pedersen, "Social Science and Social Feminism," paper delivered to the Social Science History Association, New Orleans, 1996.

103. In California, for example, a state court decision in 1888 allowed funds allocated for orphans and half-orphans to be given to counties for support of children outside institutions; by 1899, nearly 30 percent of the more than eight thousand children receiving county support were living in their own homes or in foster homes; Cahn and Bary, *Welfare Activities,* 20–21.

104. Megan McClintock, "Shoring Up the Family: Civil War Pensions and the Crisis of American Domesticity," paper delivered to the American Historical Association, Chicago, 1991; and Amy E. Holmes, "'Such is the Price We Pay': American Widows and the Civil War Pension System," in *Toward a Social History of the American Civil War: Exploratory Essays,* ed. Maris Vinovskis (New York: Cambridge University Press, 1990), 171–95. Only the dependents of Union soldiers were eligible for federal benefits; after the war, some Southern states passed pension legislation for Confederate veterans and their dependents.

105. See McClintock, "Shoring Up the Family."

106. Anna Garlin Spencer, "What the State and Society Owe to All Children," address before the New England Conference of Charities, October 1894, reprinted in *Lend a Hand* 14, no. 1 (January 1895): 27–28. Spencer's speech anticipated President Theodore Roosevelt's well-known concern with race suicide.

107. "The Needy Mother and the Neglected Child," *Outlook* 104 (June 7, 1913); reprinted in *Selected Articles on Mothers' Pensions,* comp. Edna Bullock (White Plains, N.Y.: H. W. Wilson, 1916), 25.

108. Quoted in F. C. Howe and Marie Jenney Howe, "Pensioning the Widowed and the Fatherless," *Good Housekeeping* 57 (September, 1913); reprinted in Bullock, *Mothers' Pensions,* 119–20.

109. Mary Conyngton, *How to Help* (New York: Macmillan, 1909), 186, quoted in Mark Leff, "Consensus for Reform: The Mothers'-Pension Movement in the Progressive Era," *Social Service Review* 47, no. 3 (September 1973): 398.

110. Roosevelt, quoted in U.S. Congress, Senate, *Conference on Care of Dependent Children: Proceedings,* 60th Cong., 2d sess., 1909, S. Doc. 721, p. 36.

111. For a detailed discussion of the groups involved and the political differentiations among them, see Leff, "Consensus for Reform."

112. Ibid., 402–13.

113. Skocpol, *Protecting Soldiers and Mothers,* chap. 8. One exception to this pattern was Illinois, where such individual reformers as Julia Lathrop, Edith Abbott, and Sophonisba Breckinridge played key roles in formulating legislation, but where grassroots women's organizations were less important; see Joanne Goodwin, *Gender and the Politics of Welfare Reform: Mothers' Pensions in Chicago, 1911–1929* (Chicago: University of Chicago Press, 1997), chaps. 3–4.

114. One of the best discussions of the corruption of the system, which was largely due to political patronage, is Ann Shola Orloff, "The Political Origins of America's Belated Welfare State," in *The Politics of Social Policy in the United States,* ed. Margaret Weir, Ann Shola Orloff, and Theda Skocpol (Princeton: Princeton University Press, 1988), 45–52.

115. Leff, "Consensus for Reform," 399. He notes that Oklahoma and Michigan used public funds to pay "school scholarships" to the children of indigent widows. In California, the practice began after the San Francisco fire of 1906, when public funds were used to board children who could not be accommodated in the city's overcrowded institutions, at first in foster homes and then with their own mothers. Other counties soon followed suit. See Cahn and Bary, *Welfare Activities,* 21.

116. In a certain sense, these organizations were only as good as their state connections allowed them to be. The GFWC had affiliates in all forty-eight states by 1912, while the NCM had branches in only twenty-two states by 1911 and thirty-six by 1919; see Skocpol, *Protecting Mothers and Soldiers,* chap. 8.

117. Ibid., 456–65. The establishment of the CB in 1912 gave maternalists a beachhead in Washington, but its clout remained minimal for some time, and its early chiefs, first Julia Lathrop and then Grace Abbott, continued to work through lines of power that traced down through state and local agencies and organizations. The CB worked with existing organizations and encouraged the creation of state-level bases where there were none; for example, according to Robyn Muncy, Lathrop saw to it that agencies of maternal and child health were established in as many states as possible, usually headed by someone she had handpicked and with whom she remained in constant contact. See Muncy, *Female Dominion,* 100–101.

118. See Katz, *In the Shadow,* chap. 3. Not all charity officials saw this process as inevitable. Lee Frankel, for one, claimed that his organization, United Hebrew Charities, had demonstrated "that we can take care of widows and their children without pauperizing them. We have instances where women have been carried on our books for ten or twelve years, and we have invariably found that their self-respect has been preserved— even the children may not know that the mother receives a pension"; "Summary," in NFDN, *Report,* 1905, 7.

119. Frankel, "Summary," in NFDN, *Report,* 1905, 7.

120. The clubwomen anticipated, by many decades, more recent feminist discussions of

caring work; see Kari Waerness, "Caring as Women's Work in the Welfare State," in *Patriarchy in a Welfare Society,* ed. Harriet Holter (Oslo: Universitetsforlaget, 1984); Waerness, "The Invisible Welfare State: Women's Work in the Home," *Acta Sociologica* (1978), supp.: 193–207; Waerness, "On the Rationality of Caring," in *Women and the State,* ed. Anne Showstack Sassoon (New York and London: Hutchinson, 1987); Janet Finch and Dulcie Groves, eds., *Labour of Love: Women, Work and Caring* (London: Routledge, 1983); and Clare Ungerson, ed., *Gender and Caring: Work and Welfare in Britain and Scandinavia* (New York: Harvester Wheatsheaf, 1990).

121. Mary Wood, "The Legal Side of Industrial Betterment," in GFWC, *Official Report of the Eleventh Biennial Convention* (1912), 185; quoted in Skocpol, *Protecting Mothers and Soldiers,* 442. This claim that motherhood should be seen as the equivalent of soldiering was made in the strongest and most explicit terms by Australian feminists struggling for an endowment of motherhood during the same period; for example, they compared the physical risks of childbirth with those of battle. See Marilyn Lake, "A Revolution in the Family: The Challenge and Contradictions of Maternal Citizenship in Australia," in Koven and Michel, *Mothers of a New World,* 378–95.

122. L. T. Hobhouse, quoted in William Hard, "The Moral Necessity of 'State Funds to Mothers,'" *Survey* 29 (1913): 773. The influence between British and American policy movements was sometimes reciprocal; according to Jane Lewis, later in the decade British reformers pointed to the success of mothers' pension policies in the United States as an argument to extend them in their own country. See Lewis, "Models of Equality for Women: The Case of State Support for Children in Twentieth-Century Britain," in *Maternity and Gender Policies,* ed. Gisela Bock and Pat Thane (London: Routledge, 1991), 73–92.

123. Hard, "Moral Necessity," 773. On the implications for women of the concept of dependency, see Nancy Fraser and Linda Gordon, "'Dependency' Demystified: Inscriptions of Power in a Keyword of the Welfare State," *Social Politics* 1, no. 1 (Spring 1994): 4–31.

124. Both Hard and the clubwomen, however, drew a sharp distinction between widows and the wives of disabled workmen, on the one hand, and those who were victims of desertion. According to historian Anne R. Igra, reformers were reluctant to endorse public support for the families of deserters out of fear that it would encourage male irresponsibility and spendthriftiness. See Igra, "Male Providerhood and the Public Purse: Anti-Desertion Reform in the Progressive Era," in *The Sex of Things: Gender and Consumption in Historical Perspective,* ed. Victoria de Grazia with Ellen Furlough (Berkeley: University of California Press, 1996), 188–211.

125. Ann Shola Orloff and others contend that *conceptually,* mothers' pensions did succeed in raising pensions above the level of relief, but it was only *in practice* that they became discriminatory; see Orloff, "Gender in Early U.S. Social Policy," *Journal of Policy History* 3 (1991): 249–81. I have argued elsewhere that many of the flaws in the policy appear to have been inherent from the outset; see Sonya Michel, "The Limits of Maternalism: Polices toward American Wage-Earning Mothers during the Progressive Era," in Koven and Michel, *Mothers of a New World,* 298–300. Historian Christopher Howard makes an argument similar to mine but draws a conclusion similar to Orloff's;

see "Sowing the Seeds of 'Welfare': The Transformation of Mothers' Pensions, 1900–1940," *Journal of Policy History* 4, no. 2 (1992): 188–227.

126. Katharine Anthony, "The Family," in *Civilization in the United States,* ed. H. E. Sterns (New York: Harcourt Brace, 1922), 329.

127. Goodwin, *Gender and the Politics of Welfare Reform,* 167. Of the applicants who were rejected between 1911 and 1927, 49 percent were denied on grounds of "economic sufficiency"; 8 percent for lack of cooperation; and 4 percent for lack of fitness or moral standards. The other 37 percent were deemed legally ineligible because of technicalities in the law concerning nativity, citizenship, and marital status (desertion was usually disqualified).

128. Although the COS and other social work organizations had initially opposed pensions—chiefly on the grounds that, like other forms of outdoor relief, they pauperized recipients—they now rushed to fill the administrative vacuum and put their own stamp on the policy through the use of casework. For social workers' opposition, see articles by Mary E. Richmond, Frederic Almy, C. C. Carstens, and Edward T. Devine in Bullock, *Mothers' Pensions.*

129. For a detailed description of the process in Chicago, see C. C. Carstens, "Public Pensions to Widows with Children," *Survey* 29 (1913); reprinted in Bullock, *Mothers' Pensions,* 161–64. For other locales, see A. E. Sheffield, "Administration of the Mothers' Aid Law in Massachusetts," *Survey* 31 (1914): 644–45; and Gertrude Vaile, "Administering Mothers' Pensions in Denver," *Survey* 31 (1914): 673–75; both reprinted in Bullock, *Mothers' Pensions.*

130. For example, in 1914, the board of Hamilton County, Ohio, included two businessmen, a vice-president of Associated Charities who was also a minister, a labor union officer and journalist, and two middle-class married women; see T. J. Edmonds and Maurice B. Hexter, "State Pensions to Mothers in Hamilton County, Ohio," *Survey* 32 (1914): 289–90; reprinted in Bullock, *Mothers' Pensions.* On general patterns see Howard, "Sowing the Seeds," 197–98.

131. For a detailed account of this process, see Goodwin, *Gender and the Politics of Welfare Reform,* chap. 4.

132. See Goodwin, "An American Experiment."

133. Edith Abbott, "The Experimental Period of Widows' Pension Legislation," *Proceedings of the National Conference of Social Work* (1917): 163–64.

134. See Libba Gaje Moore, "Mothers' Pensions: The Origins of the Relationship between Women and the Welfare State," Ph.D. diss., University of Massachusetts-Amherst, 1986, 148.

135. Moore calculates that in 1931, "about half of the black families aided nationwide were from counties in Ohio and Pennsylvania"; "Mothers' Pensions," 158. Goodwin shows that in Chicago from 1910 to 1930, the proportion of African American households receiving mothers' pensions was at least one percentage point, and usually two, less than their proportion of the population; "Gender, Welfare and Social Reform," 253. See also Leff, "Consensus for Reform," 414.

136. Moore, "Mothers' Pensions," 156.

137. Ibid., 145. On the surface, mothers' pensions appeared to grant women more autonomy in raising their children than did day nurseries, but because of the intense

surveillance to which they were subjected, pension recipients were in fact quite restricted.

138. "Statement of Miss Sophie Irene Loeb," *Mothers' Aid in the District of Columbia*, Hearings before the U.S. Senate, Subcommittee of the Committee on the District of Columbia, January 11, 1926, 10. My thanks to Caroline Waldron for drawing my attention to this document.

139. Ibid., 14.

140. In most states, the process was also time consuming and drawn out, adding to the anxieties and desperation of the applicants; see Barbara Nelson, "The Origins of the Two-Channel Welfare State: Workmen's Compensation and Mothers' Aid," in *Women, the State, and Welfare*, ed. Linda Gordon (Madison: University of Wisconsin Press, 1990), 123–51.

141. See Skocpol, *Protecting Mothers and Soldiers*, chap. 8. By 1927, mothers' aid laws had been passed in all but two states.

142. Pennsylvania was one of these states that lacked sufficient funds; see Emil Frankel, "Source of Income, Standards of Mothers' Work and of Children's Education in Families Aided by the Pennsylvania Mothers' Assistance Fund," *Proceedings of the National Conference of Social Work* (1927): 253–57. The 1927 study showed that $4 million was needed to fund all who were eligible, but that year the legislature appropriated only $2.75 million, which was still an increase of $1 million from the previous biennium (257). Edith Abbott and Sophonisba Breckinridge were also critical of county boards in Illinois that refused to allocate funds for mothers' pensions; in their view, unfunded statutes stood as "an official mockery of the needs of the poor"; Abbott and Breckinridge *The Administration of the Aid-to-Mothers Law in Illinois*, CB Publication No. 82 (Washington, D.C.: GPO, 1921), 171.

143. Mrs. Arthur Dodge, "Neighborhood Work and Day Nurseries," *Proceedings of the National Conference of Charities and Corrections*, 1912, 113.

144. Allotments were calculated on a per-child basis; there was usually no funding for the support of the mother per se. See Davis, "Mothers' Pensions," 578–79; see also Moore, "Mothers' Pensions," 174–79. Moore calculates that in 1918, the minimum cost of living for a mother and three children was $1,000 per year, or $83 per month; yet the maximum grant in all states fell short of that, ranging from as low as $20 to only as high as $60 or $70 per month. Pensions for Civil War veterans' dependents, by contrast, had been relatively generous. See McClintock, "Shoring Up the Family"; and Holmes, "'Such Is the Price We Pay.'"

145. Frankel, "Source of Income," 256. These sources were considered "desirable"; undesirable sources included low-paid industrial homework, mother's full-time work outside the home that required leaving children without supervision, or any work on her part that detracted from fulfillment of her responsibilities to her children (254).

146. In the second decade of the century, these included Idaho, Illinois, Missouri, New Hampshire, Ohio, South Dakota, and Utah; see Martha May, "Home Life: Progressive Social Reformers' Prescriptions for Social Stability, 1890–1920," Ph.D. diss., State University of New York at Binghamton, 1984, 257.

147. Moore, "Mothers' Pensions," 182–83. Most states also prohibited women from taking

in boarders, a time-honored wage-earning strategy particularly among immigrant women, but one that supervisors frowned upon as immoral.

148. One of the original arguments for mothers' and widows' pensions was that they would cost the same as, or less than, what the state was paying to keep children in institutions. See Mary E. Shinnick, "Pensioning of Widows," *Second National Conference of Catholic Charities* (1912): 122–26; and David F. Tilley, "Review of the Legislation Relating to Mothers' Pensions," *Third National Conference of Catholic Charities* (1914): 129–40. See also Bullock, *Mothers' Pensions.*

149. Goodwin, *Gender and the Politics of Welfare Reform,* chap. 5; see also Goodwin, "An American Experiment."

150. Economist Paul H. Douglas opposed the idea of a family wage for men as well, on the grounds that it allowed single men to receive money they did not really need to support "phantom" wives and children, while the wages of working mothers were insufficient to support their real dependents. As an alternative, Douglas proposed a variable minimum wage that included a kind of family allowance based on the number of dependents, supported by "equalization funds" or pools created by conglomerates of industries. See Douglas, "The Living Wage and Family Allowance Systems," in *Proceedings of the National Conference of Social Work* 1926: 305–17; and Douglas, *Wages and the Family* (Chicago: University of Chicago Press, 1925), chap. 17.

151. Goodwin, "Gender, Politics, and Welfare Reform," 254.

152. In her foreword to Hughes's *Mothers in Industry,* Helen Glenn Tyson notes that "out of the 237 widows of this study, only 38 had applied for pensions, and only 9 were receiving them! Working mothers, as a group, are not applicants for public aid in any form" (xiv).

153. "Report of the New York Association," in NFDN, *Report,* 1916, 98.

154. According to Robyn Muncy, these contacts were crucial to establishing and maintaining the power of the "female dominion"; see *Female Dominion,* chaps. 2 and 4. Lathrop even remained in touch with individuals with whom she did not totally agree but whose work was relevant to the agenda she had set for the CB, such as the conservative maternal and infant health advocate Elizabeth Lowell Putnam; see Michel and Rosen, "Paradox of Maternalism," 372–75.

155. Charlotte Perkins Gilman, "Pensions for 'Mothers' and 'Widows,'" *Forerunner* 5 (January 1914): 7.

156. See Ann J. Lane, *To Herland and Beyond: The Life and Work of Charlotte Perkins Gilman* (New York: Pantheon, 1990), chap. 9.

157. Ibid., 262.

158. Benita Locke, "Mothers' Pensions: The Latest Capitalist Trap," *Woman Rebel* 1, no. 1 (March 1914), 4–5.

159. Mrs. Harvey Wiley, "The Work of the Woman's Party," *Equal Rights* 1, no. 3 (March 3, 1923): 21.

160. Conference of the New York Centre of Day Nursery Associations and Day Nurseries, *Proceedings* (1917): 11; cited in Goldmintz, "Growth of Day Care," 250. For a discussion of the factory crèches and nursing rooms (*chambres d'allaitement*) within the context of French women's labor history, see Laura Lee Downs, *Manufacturing Inequal-*

ity: Gender Division in the French and British Metalworking Industries, 1914–1939 (Ithaca: Cornell University Press, 1995), chap. 5.

161. Account given by Dodge in informal discussion, Session on Children, PNCCC, 1919, 49. The meeting between Dodge and Lathrop occurred in 1917.

162. Dodge, informal discussion, 49.

163. Connecticut Department of Labor, *Report on the Conditions of Wage-Earners in the State [1919–1920]* (Hartford: State of Connecticut, 1920), 48–49.

164. Dodge, informal discussion, 49.

165. Conn. Dept. of Labor, *Report,* 50.

166. See Alice Kessler Harris, *A Woman's Wage* (Louisville: University of Kentucky Press, 1990), chaps. 1 and 2.

167. On the meaning of pensions in the lives of women of this period, see Gordon, *Pitied but Not Entitled,* chap. 2.

168. For an expression of this sense of entitlement, see the Congressional testimony of Beulah Sanders, vice-chair of the National Welfare Rights Organization and chair of the New York Citywide Coordinating Committee of Welfare Groups; U.S. Congress, Joint Economic Committee, *Hearings on Income Maintenance Programs, June 1968* (Washington, D.C., 1968), vol. 1, 66–71. My thanks to Ben Donovan for bringing this document to my attention.

169. See Nancy Fraser, "Struggle over Needs: Outline of a Socialist-Feminist Critical Theory of Late-Capitalist Political Culture," in Gordon, *Women, the State, and Welfare,* esp. 221.

CHAPTER 3: STUDIED NEGLECT

1. The term is Michael Katz's; see *In the Shadow of the Poorhouse: A Social History of Welfare in America* (New York: Basic Books, 1986), pt. 2.

2. Ibid. Katz notes that between 1903 and 1928, public welfare expenditures increased by 168 percent, mostly owing to the expansion of mothers' pensions.

3. See Robyn Muncy, *Creating a Female Dominion in American Reform, 1890–1935* (New York: Oxford University Press, 1991), chaps. 4 and 5. Many of the women in the second generation were the protégées of, or had been trained by, members of the first; there was a direct line of influence from Hull House to the CB.

4. The phrase is Lynn Weiner's; see *From Working Girl to Working Mother: The Female Labor Force in the United States* (Chapel Hill: University of North Carolina Press, 1985).

5. See Winifred Wandersee, *Women's Work and Family Values, 1920–1940* (Cambridge: Harvard University Press, 1981), chaps. 3 and 4; and Leslie Woodcock Tentler, *Wage-Earning Women: Industrial Work and Family Life in the United States, 1900–1930* (New York: Oxford University Press, 1979), chap. 6.

6. As Eileen Boris shows, strikes, changes in manufacturing processes, and attempts at regulation affected opportunities for industrial homework in the 1920s, making it difficult for mothers to depend on it as a source of income; see *Home to Work: Motherhood and the Politics of Industrial Homework in the United States* (New York: Cambridge University Press, 1994), esp. 151–56.

7. The reasons for this assumption are explained in chap. 2., n. 11, above.

8. *Social Work Yearbook* (New York: Russell Sage Foundation, 1929), vol. 1., 118.

9. See Gwendolyn Salisbury Hughes, *Mothers in Industry: Wage-Earning by Mothers in Philadelphia* (New York: New Republic, 1925), 195.

10. Linda Goldmintz, "The Growth of Day Care Services, 1890–1946," D.S.W. diss., Yeshiva University, 1987, 534. Goldmintz's figures are primarily culled from the records of the NFDN; the 1931 figure, however, comes from a different source: White House Conference on Child Health and Protection, *Nursery Education: A Survey of Day Nurseries, Nursery Schools, and Private Kindergartens in the United States* (New York: Century, 1931), 7. This study may have used different criteria from the NFDN's, thus accounting for the sharp rise.

11. It is difficult to ascertain the precise number of mothers who were employed during the war years. According to Susan Hartmann, more than half a million *new* female workers—many of them mothers—took jobs between 1940 and 1944; *The Home Front and Beyond: American Women in the 1940s* (Boston: Twayne, 1982), 78. Those entering the work force would, presumably, increase the number of women workers who had children under age seventeen in 1940, estimated at 1.9 million by Ivan Nye and Lois Hoffman in *The Employed Mother in America* (Chicago: Rand McNally, 1963), 8. Because the birth rate increased sharply during the war, many of these workers' children would still be of preschool age by 1945 (Hartmann, *Home Front*, 170).

12. See Sonya Michel, "American Women and the Discourse of the Democratic Family in World War II," in *Behind the Lines: Gender and the Two World Wars*, ed. Margaret Higonnet, Jane Jenson, Sonya Michel, and Margaret Weitz (New Haven: Yale University Press, 1987), 154–67.

13. For an overview of the CB, see Kriste Lindenmeyer, *"A Right to Childhood": The U.S. Children's Bureau and Child Welfare, 1912–1946* (Urbana: University of Illinois Press, 1997).

14. The term *overfeminization* is Denise Riley's; see *Am I That Name? Femininity and the Category of Women in History* (Minneapolis: University of Minnesota Press, 1988). Margery Spring Rice, a British reformer of the 1930s, was in effect pointing out the implications of overfeminization for women's health when she noted that a program targeting maternal and child health offered women limited benefits because it was concerned with them—with their bodies—only insofar as they were bearing and nursing children. Under such a program, women's reproductive functions become fetishized while their nonperinatal health problems were ignored, leaving them without access to health care for much of their life cycle. See Spring Rice, *Working-Class Wives: Their Health and Condition* (1939; reprint, London: Virago, 1981), 27.

15. See Kathryn Kish Sklar, "Hull-House Maps and Papers: Social Science as Women's Work in the 1890s," in *The Social Survey in Historical Perspective, 1880–1940*, ed. Martin Bulmer, Kevin Bales, and Kathryn Kish Sklar (Cambridge: Cambridge University Press, 1991), 111–47; Muncy, *Female Dominion*, chap. 3; and Molly Ladd-Taylor, *Mother-Work: Women, Child Welfare, and the State, 1890–1930* (Urbana: University of Illinois Press, 1994), esp. chap. 6.

16. There was less child labor in areas dominated by heavy industry, such as the coal-mining

regions of West Virginia. But those areas, usually dominated by a single industry, also offered women fewer employment opportunities outside the home because of the traditional exclusion of women from the prevailing occupational sectors. Wages for men tended to be higher in those sectors, but many women still kept lodgers, did laundry, or cleaned by the day. See, for example, Nettie P. McGill, *The Welfare of Children in Bituminous Coal Mining Communities in West Virginia*, CB Publication No. 117 (Washington, D.C.: GPO, 1923), 32–46 and 70–71.

17. For a discussion of "feminized" occupations and the relation between wages and the gender of workers in specific sectors, see Alice Kessler-Harris, *Out to Work: A History of Wage-Earning Women in the United States* (New York: Oxford University Press, 1982), chap. 9; Teresa L. Amott and Julie A. Matthei, *Race, Gender and Work: A Multicultural Economic History of Women in the United States* (Boston: South End Press, 1991), esp. chap. 2; Claudia Goldin, *Understanding the Gender Gap: An Economic History of American Women* (New York: Oxford University Press, 1990); and Barbara R. Bergmann, *The Economic Emergence of Women* (New York: Basic Books, 1986), chaps. 4–6. On earnings for industrial homework, see Eileen Boris and Cynthia Daniels, eds., *Homework: Historical and Contemporary Perspectives on Paid Labor at Home* (Urbana: University of Illinois Press, 1989), sec. 1; and Boris, *Home to Work*. Excellent analyses of the process by which specific occupations became gendered may be found in Ava Baron, ed., *Work Engendered: Toward a New History of American Labor* (Ithaca: Cornell University Press, 1991).

18. The classic study of child labor reform is Walter L. Trattner, *Crusade for the Children: A History of the Child Labor Committee and Child Labor Reform in America* (Chicago: Quadrangle, 1970); on the issue of enforcement, see pp. 122–23.

19. On the question of "choice," see Boris and Daniels, *Homework*, 5–6.

20. Viola I. Paradise, *Child Labor and the Work of Mothers in Oyster and Shrimp Canning Communities on the Gulf Coast*, Children's Bureau Publication No. 98 (Washington, D.C.: GPO, 1922).

21. Florida enacted one in 1919, but it was not yet in effect at the time of the study.

22. Paradise, *Child Labor*, 14.

23. Ibid., 15.

24. A charity official in one of the communities told Paradise that "the laws are not applied to the Negroes as strictly as to the white people, and therefore more Negro children than white work"; ibid., 18.

25. Ibid., 17.

26. Ibid., 18.

27. Ibid., 64.

28. Ibid.

29. Both Josephine Dodge and Julia Lathrop disapproved of factory-provided nursing rooms because they encouraged mothers to bring nursing infants to work with them. But nursing rooms would obviously have been a vast improvement over the measures described here; they would have provided a safe place for keeping the infants and, by encouraging more mothers to bring their infants in, would have allowed for more frequent feedings.

30. Paradise, *Child Labor*, 65.

31. Ibid., 66.

32. Ibid.

33. Ibid.

34. Ibid., 35.

35. Ibid., 66.

36. Ibid., 35.

37. Ibid., 67.

38. Ibid., 58.

39. Ibid.

40. Alice Kessler-Harris has noted this shift in Southern textile mills, where, up through the early 1920s, women were permitted to leave production lines for brief intervals, passing their machines over to co-workers, while they went to nurse infants or deal with children's other needs. By the late 1920s, however, such practices were prohibited (personal communication, July 15, 1993).

41. Ellen Nathalie Matthews, *Children in Fruit and Vegetable Canneries: A Survey in Seven States,* CB Publication No. 198 (Washington, D.C.: GPO, 1930); the studies were conducted in 1923, 1925, and 1926.

42. Frances Cahn and Valeska Bary indicate that these measures had limited effectiveness. Although the Canners' League of California helped distribute copies of the guidelines, supervision of nurseries connected to seasonal plants remained "of an emergency character"; *Welfare Activities of Federal, State, and Local Governments in California, 1850–1934* (Berkeley: University of California Press, 1936), 36.

43. Matthews, *Children in Fruit and Vegetable Canneries,* 27.

44. Ellen Nathalie Matthews, *Child Labor and the Work of Mothers in the Beet Fields of Colorado and Michigan,* CB Publication No. 115 (Washington, D.C.: GPO, 1923), 59.

45. Ibid., 60.

46. Ibid., 85.

47. Ellen Nathalie Matthews and Ethel Maria Springer, *Child Labor and the Work of Mothers on Norfolk Truck Farms,* CB Publication No. 130 (Washington, D.C.: GPO, 1924), 4.

48. Ellen Nathalie Matthews and Helen Maretta Dart, *The Welfare of Children in Cotton-Growing Areas of Texas,* CB Publication No. 134 (Washington, D.C.: GPO, 1924), 13.

49. Nettie P. McGill, *Children in Agriculture,* CB Publication No. 187 (Washington, D.C.: GPO, 1929), 22.

50. See Boris, *Home to Work,* esp. 107–11.

51. Harry Viteles, Emma Duke, and Eloise Shellabarger, *Industrial Home Work of Children: A Study Made in Providence, Pawtucket, and Central Falls, R.I.,* CB Publication No. 100 (Washington, D.C.: GPO, 1922), 23.

52. Home Missions Council of North America, "Migrant Information for Workers," mimeo, June 1942, in J. F. Thaden Papers, Library of Michigan, Lansing, Michigan, box 227, folder 2, p. 1. My thanks to Kathleen Mapes for sharing this and other documents on Home Missions programs for migrants with me.

53. Ibid., 4.

54. For data on later programs, including child care, see surveys and reports in Thaden Papers, folders 2 and 4.

55. Charles S. Johnson, *Negro Housing*, Report of the Committee on Negro Housing, Nannie H. Burroughs, chair (Washington, D.C.: n.p., 1932; reprint, New York: Negro Universities Press, 1969), 239–48. The Dunbar Apartments were designed as a cooperative, although payment terms were flexible and tenants were carried during periods of unemployment (247). The Michigan Avenue Apartments were rental units, and the rents, unsubsidized, were "somewhat high" (240). Rosenwald believed, however, that the African American community of Chicago had evolved to the point where many of its members could afford such housing, and he was proved right. By the end of the first six months, the occupancy rate was 98 percent (241). My thanks to Barbara Mooney for drawing my attention to this information.

56. The bureau's concern with child labor predated passage of the bill; the issue had been prominent in the maternalist reform circles responsible for creating the CB in the first place. Members of the male-dominated National Child Labor Committee, irritated at some CB policies, claimed that the agency owed its very existence to the child labor issue (Trattner, *Crusade for the Children*, 133–34), but revisionist accounts suggest that this was not the only issue on the minds of the CB's founders (Muncy, *Female Dominion*, chap. 2).

57. Muncy, *Female Dominion*, 102–3.

58. On the CB and child labor legislation in the 1920s, see ibid., chaps. 2 and 4; and Trattner, *Crusade for the Children*, chap. 7.

59. On the politics of Abbott's appointment, see Lela B. Costin, *Two Sisters for Social Justice: A Biography of Grace and Edith Abbott* (Urbana: University of Illinois Press, 1983), chap. 5.

60. Anna Rochester, *Infant Mortality: Results of a Field Study in Baltimore, MD, Based on Births in One Year*, CB Publication No. 123 (Washington, D.C.: GPO, 1923), 130. The study showed that poverty and conditions related to it were also linked to these risks, but maternal employment produced "excessive" rates of pregnancy failure and infant mortality (178–79).

61. Ibid., 125. Rochester was being alarmist here, for by this time, as the CB's own studies revealed, adequate methods of artificial feeding had been developed and were becoming increasingly popular among mothers of all classes. Safety depended, of course, on the availability of pure milk and sanitary preparation of formulas, but by the 1920s, the milk supply in most cities was reliable, and information on "care of the bottle" had been widely disseminated, in part through distribution of the CB's popular pamphlet *Infant Care*. See Rima Apple, *Mothers and Medicine: A Social History of Infant Feeding, 1890–1950* (Madison: University of Wisconsin Press, 1987), chaps. 8 and 9.

62. Ibid., 130.

63. On the CB's approach to infant mortality in general, see Ladd-Taylor, *Mother-Work*, chap. 3; on the struggle over Sheppard-Towner, see Muncy, *Female Dominion*, chap. 4; and Ladd-Taylor, *Mother-Work*, chap. 6.

64. *Norfolk Truck Farms*, 27.

65. For example, three years before the publication of the Norfolk study (1924), the CB had issued a study of mothers' pensions that included a breakdown by race: Edith Abbott and Sophonisba Breckinridge, *The Administration of the Aid-to-Mothers Law in Illinois*, CB Bulletin No. 82 (Washington, D.C.: GPO, 1921).

66. The following discussion is based on Sonya Michel, "Children's Interests/Mothers' Rights: Women, Professionals, and the American Family, 1920–1945," Ph.D. diss., Brown University, 1986, chap. 2, "The Child Guidance Movement and the Transformation of Social Work." The therapeutic turn began shortly after Sigmund Freud's visit to the United States in 1909, when his work was becoming increasingly popular. I argue, however, that the main contours of early therapeutic thinking in the United States did not follow Freudian principles but in fact radically contradicted them.

67. For a history of this movement, see Margo Horn, *Before It's Too Late: The Child Guidance Movement in the United States, 1922–1945* (Philadelphia: Temple University Press, 1989).

68. Grace Caldwell, "Standards of Admission to Day Nurseries," NFDN, *Report of the Conference,* 1919, 54.

69. For an extended discussion of this shift, see Goldmintz, "Growth of Day Care," chap. 8.

70. On the philosophy of the Chicago School of Social Administration, see Costin, *Two Sisters,* chap. 8; Ellen Fitzpatrick, *Endless Crusade: Women Social Scientists and Progressive Reform* (New York: Oxford University Press, 1990), chap. 7; and Muncy, *Female Dominion,* chap. 3.

71. D. A. Thom, M.D., *Habit Clinics for the Child of Preschool Age: Their Organization and Practical Value,* CB Publication No. 135 (Washington, D.C.: GPO, 1924).

72. Ibid., 15.

73. Ibid.

74. Quoted in Katharine Anthony, "The Family," in *Civilization in the United States,* ed. H. E. Stern (New York: Harcourt Brace, 1922), 325.

75. See Weiner, *From Working Girl to Working Mother,* 7.

76. See Susan Porter Benson, "Living on the Margin: Working-Class Marriages and Family Survival Strategies in the United States, 1919–1941," in *The Sex of Things: Gender and Consumption in Historical Perspective,* ed. Victoria de Grazia with Ellen Furlough (Berkeley: University of California Press, 1996), 212–43.

77. Stock Yards Community Clearing House, "Report on the Community Study, 1918," Mary McDowell papers, CHS, folder 20; cited in James R. Barrett, *Work and Community in the Jungle: Chicago's Packinghouse Workers, 1894–1922* (Urbana: University of Illinois Press, 1987), 103. See also Dominic Pacyga, *Polish Immigrants and Industrial Chicago: Workers on the South Side, 1880–1922* (Columbus: Ohio State University Press, 1991), chap. 4.

78. According to Benson, "Between 1919 and 1941 . . . most American working-class families remained on the margins of the emerging world of consumption because their incomes were neither large enough nor steady enough to allow the wide range of discretionary spending usually associated with mass consumption"; "Living on the Margin," 212.

79. Hughes, *Mothers in Industry,* 8.

80. Ibid., 13.

81. Tentler, *Wage-Earning Women,* 154.

82. WB, *The Share of Wage-Earning Women in Family Support,* Bulletin No. 30 (Washington, D.C.: GPO, 1923), 145; and WB, *Family Status of Breadwinning Women,* Bulletin No. 23 (Washington, D.C.: GPO, 1922), 10.

83. Eva Whiting White, "The Day Nursery—Aim and Problems," *NFDN Bulletin* 6, no. 10 (October 1930): 4. White was president of the Women's Educational and Industrial Union.

84. Sadie Ginsberg, "The Child Care Center Chronicle," in *Early Childhood Education: Living History Interviews,* comp. James L. Hymes, Jr., book 2, *Care of the Children of Working Mothers* (Carmel, Calif.: Hacienda Press, 1978), 12.

85. See Michael Steven Shapiro, *Child's Garden: The Kindergarten Movement from Froebel to Dewey* (University Park: Pennsylvania State University, 1983); and Barbara Beatty, *Preschool Education in America: The Culture of Young Children from the Colonial Era to the Present* (New Haven: Yale University Press, 1995), chaps. 4–6.

86. McMillan, the leading advocate of early childhood education in Britain, was committed to offering an enriching experience to poor children. Eliot learned about her ideas in 1921, when she was sent by the Boston Women's Education Association to train at McMillan's Deptford Centre. On McMillan's ideas, see Carolyn Steedman, *Childhood, Culture and Class in Britain: Margaret McMillan, 1860–1931* (London: Virago Press, 1990), chap. 4, "Gardens"; on teacher training, 184–87. For Eliot's responses to her London experience and a detailed account of the Ruggles Street School, see Beatty, *Preschool Education,* 142–44. Eliot also ran a nursery school in Cambridge, Massachusetts, which served a more middle-class clientele; see Abigail Eliot, "America's First Nursery Schools," in *Early Childhood Education: Living History Interviews,* comp. James L. Hymes, Jr., book 1, *Beginnings* (Carmel, Calif.: Hacienda Press, 1978), 7–25.

87. For more on the early history of nursery schools, see Beatty, *Preschool Education,* chap. 7.

88. *Social Work Yearbook,* vol. 1: 119.

89. Mary E. Reed and E. Mae Raymond, "Day Nurseries, Nursery Schools, and Kindergartens in Six Settlements in New York City" [1929], typescript, National Federation of Settlements and Neighborhood Centers collection, supp. 1, box 109, folder 15, SWHA. The copy I consulted contained numerous irate marginal scrawls by an anonymous critic who, among other things, found the conflation of day nurseries with other programs regrettable.

90. Ibid., 6–8.

91. Ibid., 9–11. The standards of the New York Association of Day Nurseries (ADNNYC) had been vague on acceptable adult-child ratios and staff qualifications, simply stating, "Care should be taken that a sufficient number and the proper type of attendants be provided for infants and runabouts, so that they shall have adequate and skilled attention" (ADNNYC, *Annual Report,* 1928–29 [RSC], 61–62). As early as 1921, the New England Centre of Day Nurseries had decreed that proper ratios were one adult for every six "infants" under three, or for every ten children between three and eight (referred to in Harrison G. Wagner, "Child Welfare Needs of Lawrence, Methuen, Andover, and North Andover, Mass." [1921?], typescript, American Red Cross, New England Division papers, MHS, 14.

92. Reed and Raymond, "Day Nurseries," 23.

93. Ibid., 25.

94. Ibid., 32. Here, as elsewhere, the authors do not specify what type of institution this was, but one can readily surmise that it was one of the day nurseries in the survey, for it is

unlikely that a program would advertise itself as a nursery school or kindergarten without providing some sort of activity for the children, whereas a day nursery could minimally fulfill its function by providing only custodial care.

95. ADNNYC, *Annual Report,* 1931 (RSC), 8–9.

96. Philadelphia Association of Day Nurseries (PADN), Annual Reports for 1925, 1927, and 1930 (title varies), PADN collection, UA.

97. On Anderson's work, see Hamilton Cravens, *Before Head Start: The Iowa Station and America's Children* (Chapel Hill: University of North Carolina Press, 1993).

98. John E. Anderson, "The Infant and Preschool Child," in White House Conference on Child Health and Protection, *White House Conference 1930: Addresses and Abstracts of Committee Reports* (New York: Century, 1931), 162–63.

99. Ibid., 163.

100. Glenn Steele, *Care of Children in Day Nurseries,* CB publication "Separate from Publication No. 209" (Washington: GPO, 1932), 1.

CHAPTER 4: UNCLE SAM'S CRADLES

1. U.S. Work Projects Administration, *Final Report on the WPA Program, 1935–43* (Washington, D.C.: GPO, 1946), 60–61; for an analysis of the gendered aspects of these programs, see Susan Ware, *Beyond Suffrage: Women and the New Deal* (Cambridge: Harvard University Press, 1981), chap. 5; and Nancy E. Rose, *Put to Work: Relief Programs of the Great Depression* (New York: Monthly Review Press, 1994), 42. Scenes of the entire range of WPA projects in action may be found in the series of WPA films "A Better Massachusetts," "A Better West Virginia," etc., housed in Motion Picture, Sound and Video Branch, NA (hereafter MPSVB), RG 69.

2. Glenn Steele, *Care of Children in Day Nurseries,* CB publication "Separate from Publication No. 209" (Washington, D.C.: GPO, 1932), 4–5. Although most nurseries lost children, in a few cities their clientele increased as mothers went out to work to replace or supplement fathers' lost or reduced wages (5). It is possible that at least some fathers were at home and thus theoretically available—but unwilling—to provide child care, but the report offers no data on this point.

3. They fell from eight hundred to six hundred; see Linda Goldmintz, "The Growth of Day Care Services, 1890–1946," D.S.W. diss., Yeshiva University, 1987, 534.

4. White House Conference on Child Health and Protection, *Nursery Education: A Survey of Day Nurseries, Nursery Schools, and Private Kindergartens in the United States* (New York: Century, 1931), 7.

5. Grace Langdon, "The Facts about Emergency Nursery Schools," *Childhood Education* 11, no. 6 (March 1935): 255. Until 1935, the program was under the auspices of the FERA; after 1935, under the WPA.

6. Bernard Greenblatt, *Responsibility for Child Care* (San Francisco: Jossey-Bass, 1977), 280.

7. Langdon, "The Facts," 256.

8. Harry L. Hopkins, "Announcement of Emergency Nursery Schools," *Childhood Education* 10, no. 3 (December 1933): 155. The announcement itself was made on October 23, 1933.

9. Ibid.

10. These items were usually assembled by representatives of public service organizations, who often also constituted advisory boards for the schools. See Bess Goodykoonz, Mary Dabney Davis, and Hazel F. Gabbard, "Recent History and Present Status of Education for Young Children," *The Forty-Sixth Yearbook of the National Society for the Study of Education*, pt. 2, *Early Childhood Education* (Chicago: University of Chicago Press, 1947), 49.

11. Langdon, "The Facts," 256.

12. According to Goodykoonz et al., "Recent History," it was the U.S. Commissioner of Education who recommended the program.

13. Christine Heinig, "The Emergency Nursery Schools and the Wartime Child Care Centers: 1933–1946," in *Early Childhood Education: Living History Interviews*, comp. James L. Hymes, Jr., book 3, *Reaching Large Numbers of Children* (Carmel, Calif.: Hacienda Press, 1978), 13.

14. Mary Dabney Davis, note following "Announcement of Emergency Nursery Schools," *Childhood Education* 10, no. 3 (December 1933): 155. Members included Edna N. White, chair; Ruth Andrus (1936–38); Edna Dean Baker; Ralph B. Bridgman; Mary Dabney Davis (1933–36); Abigail Eliot; Bess Goodykoonz (1936–38); Lois Hayden Meek (later Lois Meek Stolz); and George D. Stoddard; see Rose H. Alschuler, *Children's Centers* (New York: Morrow, 1942), 10.

15. WPA, "Supplement No. 2 to Bulletin #19—Nursery School Projects," September 13, 1935, 2–3, mimeo, WPA records, NA, RG 69 (hereafter WPAR), box 40, folder 321.

16. WPA, "Working Procedure, Emergency Nursery Schools," n.d., 1, WPAR, box 40, folder 323.

17. This is not surprising, given the findings of the 1929 report on early childhood programs in New York City (Mary E. Reed and E. Mae Raymond, "Day Nurseries, Nursery Schools, and Kindergartens in Six Settlements in New York City" [1929], typescript, National Federation of Settlements and Neighborhood Centers collection, SWHA, supp. 1, box 109, folder 15), which was widely circulated among early childhood educators and child welfare specialists.

18. Grace Langdon, "General Statement on WPA Nursery Schools," October 20, 1938, WPAR, box 49, folder 323: N–R, 10.

19. Langdon, "The Facts," 257. The cost per trainee ranged from about sixty dollars to more than a hundred dollars; see "Memorandum on Teaching Training Plans Submitted by Various States" [1935?], WPAR, box 40, folder 323.

20. Langdon, "General Statement," 24–26.

21. Langdon, "Field Trip Report for Arizona," June 5–7, 1941, 3, WPAR, box 424, folder: Dr. Grace Langdon. This remark was not atypical.

22. See, for example, Grace Langdon, "Field Trip Report for Arkansas," February 9–14, 1942, 6–7, WPAR, box 425, folder 211.4: Dr. Grace Langdon.

23. For example, in December 1938, Florence Kerr, then regional director of education for the midwest, sent an alarmed telegram to Grace Langdon informing her that cuts in the Aid to Dependent Children program would affect about 30 percent of the personnel in nursery schools in Ohio, Illinois, and Nebraska. See Kerr to Langdon, telegram, Decem-

ber 22, 1938, WPAR, box 49, folder 323: G–K. As of November 1937, these three states had a total of 149 schools employing more than 500 people and serving nearly 4,000 students; see Doak Campbell, Frederick H. Bair, and Oswald L. Harvey, *Educational Activities of the Works Progress Administration,* Staff Study 14 (Washington, D.C.: GPO, 1939), 110.

24. Grace Langdon, memo to L. R. Alderman re: Visit to Ohio, March 21, 1941, WPAR, box 424, folder: Dr. Grace Langdon.

25. See, for example, Grace Langdon, "Field Trip Report for Alabama," January 19–22, 1942, 5, WPAR, box 425, folder 211.4: Dr. Grace Langdon. In Childersburg, she found staffing problems that she said were typical for defense areas: "The salary of one of the teachers is $83.40 [per month]. She pays $1.00 a day for room and $1.00 for food. The other commutes and transportation costs her $14 a month. Two unskilled 'B' workers on a salary of $33 a month have to pay $14 for transportation" (ibid). The WPA stipulated that each employee could earn only $800 per year; see William R. Brock, *Welfare, Democracy, and the New Deal* (Cambridge: Cambridge University Press, 1988), 271.

26. Goodykoonz et al., "Recent History," 46.

27. Grace Langdon, "Field Trip Report for Oklahoma," February 16–19, 1942, 4, WPAR, box 425, folder 211.4: Dr. Grace Langdon. By this time, Langdon's title had been changed to "Consultant, Child Protection Program."

28. Quoted in Goodykoonz et al., "Recent History," 60–61.

29. George D. Stoddard, "Emergency Nursery Schools on Trial," *Childhood Education* 11, no. 6 (March 1935): 261.

30. Goodykoonz et al., "Recent History," 49–50, 61.

31. Langdon, "General Statement," 7–9.

32. These films are found in MPSVB, RG 69.

33. See memo from Grace Langdon to L. H. Alderman, June 22, 1940, WPAR, box 429, folder 211.42: L–Z, p. 1.

34. Ibid., 2.

35. Ibid.

36. Letter from Elizabeth Woodruff Clark to Grace Langdon, July 16, 1940, WPAR, box 429, folder 211.42: L–Z; similar letter from Clark to Katharine Lenroot, July 11, 1940, WB Records, NA, RG 86 (hereafter WBR), box 699, file 4-9-10.

37. Letter from Lenroot to Clark, August 5, 1940, WBR, box 699, folder 4–9–10.

38. Grace Langdon, "A Tentative Plan Showing the Contribution the WPA Family Life Education Program Might Make to the Defense Preparations," August 6, 1940, 2, WPAR, box 429, folder 211.42: L–Z.

39. The WB published a series of bulletins and statements; see, for example, *Effective Industrial Use of Women in the Defense Program,* WB Special Bulletin No. 1 (Washington, D.C.: GPO, 1940).

40. See *Woman at Work,* the autobiography of Mary Anderson as told to Mary N. Winslow (Minneapolis: University of Minnesota Press, 1951), 96–101 and chap. 28.

41. On the CB's role in the campaign, see Linda Gordon, *Pitied but Not Entitled: Single Mothers and the History of Welfare* (New York: Free Press, 1994), esp. chap. 9.

42. See Sonya Michel, "American Women and the Discourse of the Family in World War II," in *Behind the Lines: Gender and the Two World Wars,* ed. Margaret Randolph Higonnet, Jane Jenson, Sonya Michel, and Margaret Collins Weitz (New Haven: Yale University Press, 1987).

43. The following discussion is based on *Proceedings of the Conference on Day Care of Children of Working Mothers,* CB Publication No. 281 (Washington, D.C.: GPO, 1942).

44. Ibid., 30–31.

45. Ibid.

46. Ibid., 32.

47. Both Clark and Lenroot appear to have modified at least somewhat the positions they took with regard to converting the WPA's Housekeeping Aide project into child care.

48. *Conference on Day Care,* 65.

49. Ibid., 6–7. For a critical discussion of British wartime child care, see Denise Riley, *War in the Nursery: Theories of the Child and Mother* (London: Virago, 1983).

50. *Conference on Day Care,* 66.

51. These regulations were the legacy of Josephine Dodge's campaign just after World War I; see chapter 2 of this book.

52. *Conference on Day Care,* 67.

53. "Program for the Care of Children of Working Mothers," *The Child* (the monthly publication of the CB) 6, no. 2 (August 1941): 31.

54. *Conference on Day Care,* 4–5.

55. See Langdon, Field Trip Reports from July 1941–March 1942, WPAR, box 425, folders: Dr. Grace Langdon and 211.4, Dr. Grace Langdon.

56. *Congressional Record,* 77th Cong., 2nd sess., House, June 10 and 11, 1942, 5106–8, 5160.

57. Commission members included John E. Anderson, Horton Casparis, Allison Davis, Lawrence K. Frank, Amy Hostler, Harriet A. Houdlette, Alice V. Keliher, Mary E. Murphy, Frederick L. Redefer, and Edna N. White.

58. Tentative Minutes of the Chicago Conference on Child Protection, July 6–8, 1942, WPAR, box 502, folder: Child Protection Conference, 1942, p. 3.

59. Ibid.

60. For a more detailed discussion of these arrangements, see Sonya Michel, "Children's Interests/Mothers' Rights: Women, Professionals and the American Family, 1920–1945," Ph.D. diss., Brown University, 1986, chap. 8.

61. The following section is based on testimony given in U.S. Congress, Senate, Committee on Education and Labor, *Wartime Care and Protection of Children of Employed Mothers,* Hearings on S. 876 and S. 1130, 78th Cong., 1st sess., 1943 (hereafter Thomas Bill Hearings), 29–44.

62. William Chafe contends that these figures are highly inflated. Eight months later, in February 1944, federally supported nurseries were caring for only slightly more than 65,000 children, and at the height of the program in the spring of 1945, no more than 100,000. See *The American Woman: Her Changing Social, Economic, and Political Role, 1920–1970* (New York: Oxford University Press, 1972), 170. Goodykoonz, Davis, and

Gabbard give similar figures: in October 1943 (only five months after the hearings), there were 1,180 centers enrolling 32,409 children, and by March 1945, 1,481 centers enrolling 51,229. Another 18,150 children attended centers that included both pre-school and school-age children. Even if these two groups are added together, the total is less than 70,000—and far less than the 250,000 that Kerr was claiming. See Good-ykoonz et al., "Recent History," 46.

63. See Chafe, *American Woman,* 170; and Eleanor F. Straub, "Government Policy toward Civilian Women during World War II," Ph.D. diss., Emory University, 1973, 280.

64. For a useful discussion of how this worked out in one state, see George N. Otey, "New Deal for Oklahoma's Children: Federal Day Care Centers, 1933–1946," *Chronicles of Oklahoma* 62 (Fall 1984): 296–311.

65. The following discussion is based on Michel, "Children's Interests," chap. 8.

66. The views of the two organizations had been similar for some time, and the merger took place at the request of the NADN. See Margaret S. Ijams, "Day Nurseries Turn to the League," *CWLA Bulletin* 21, no. 9 (November 1942): 9.

67. "Trends in Applications for Service," preliminary report of a study by Henrietta Gordon, *CWLA Bulletin* 21, no. 1 (January 1942): 9.

68. Ibid., 10.

69. For an excellent discussion of how three different communities (Baltimore, Detroit, and Seattle) went about establishing child care during the war, see Karen Anderson, *Wartime Women: Sex Roles, Family Relations, and the Status of Women during World War II* (Westport, Conn.: Greenwood Press, 1981), chap. 4.

70. Doris Campbell, "Counseling Services in the Day Nursery," *Family* (publication of the Family Welfare Association of America) 24, no. 1 (March 1943): 29.

71. Much of the following section is drawn from Michel, "American Women." Motherhood has been repeatedly politicized throughout American history; see, for example, Linda Kerber's discussion of the concept of Republican Motherhood in *Women of the Republic: Intellect and Ideology in Revolutionary America* (Chapel Hill: University of North Caro-lina Press, 1980), chap. 5.

72. Frances L. E. Ruegg, "Why Case Work Is Needed in Day Care for Children in This Emergency," *CWLA Bulletin* 21, no. 1 (January 1942): 7.

73. Ibid., 8.

74. CB, *Proceedings of the White House Conference on Children in a Democracy,* CB Publica-tion No. 266 (Washington, D.C.: GPO. 1940), 70.

75. Ibid., 10.

76. See Arnold Gesell and Catherine Amatruda, *Developmental Diagnosis* (New York: Har-per and Brothers, 1941), chap. 16; also Leo Kanner, *In Defense of Mothers* (New York: Dodd, Mead, 1941). Americans' receptivity to child-rearing advice grew out of anxieties fostered by movements like child guidance as well as a popular culture saturated with therapeutic discourse; women's magazines, daily newspapers, and radio were preferred sites for discussions of family problems and the like. (See Sonya Michel, " . . . And Counseling for Every Family: The Psychological Professions and American Radio, 1930–1950," paper presented to the Popular Culture Association, Louisville, Ky., 1982.) Through exposure to this discourse, American parents understood that while

their child-rearing practices were a matter for public concern, the functions of parenthood were not to be socialized (e.g., through services like public child care) but *supervised.* Surveillance, not provision, had been the catchword for decades.

77. See, for example, Winifred Holmes, "A British Mother to American Mothers," *Parents' Magazine* 17, no. 4 (April 1942): 26–28. A 1996 exhibit at the Imperial War Museum in London entitled "Evacuees" suggested that some children did suffer psychological damage, while for most, their experience was at best mixed.

78. The nursery was supported largely by American contributors. Freud and Burlingham's reports were later compiled and published as *Infants without Families: The Case for and against Residential Nurseries* (New York: International Universities Press, 1944).

79. Anna W. M. Wolf, *Our Children Face War* (Boston: Houghton Mifflin, 1942), 96.

80. Clifford Kirkpatrick, *Nazi Germany: Its Women and Family Life* (Indianapolis: Bobbs-Merrill, 1938), 288.

81. *Employment Security Review* (October 1942): 1.

82. Lewis B. Hershey, "The Impact of the Draft on the American Family," in *The Family in a World at War,* ed. Sidonie Matsner Gruenberg (New York: Child Study Association of America, 1942), 111.

83. Quoted (disapprovingly) in Susan B. Anthony II, *Out of the Kitchen and into the War: Women's Winning Role in the Nation's Drama* (New York: Stephen Daye, 1943), 130.

84. See, for example, the 1942 Office of War Information film "Manpower," which shows children being cared for in government-sponsored nurseries (probably one of the converted Emergency Nursery Schools); MPSVB, RG 208.

85. "Interviews with Martha May Eliot, M.D., December, 1973 through May, 1974," Jeannette B. Cheek, interviewer, Schlesinger-Rockefeller Oral History Project, SL, 104–18; see also Susan B. Hartmann, *The Home Front and Beyond: American Women in the 1940s* (Boston: Twayne, 1982), 175–76.

86. Anderson, *Wartime Women,* 125–26.

87. See William M. Tuttle, Jr., "Rosie the Riveter and Her Latchkey Children: What Americans Can Learn About Child Day Care from the Second World War," *Child Welfare* 74, no. 1 (January–February 1995), 92–114.

88. Rose H. Alschuler, *Children's Centers* (New York: William Morrow, 1942).

89. For a detailed description of provisions in several different locales, see Anderson, *Wartime Women,* chap. 4.

90. "Henry J. Kaiser," in *Current Biography 1961,* ed. Charles Moritz (New York: H.W. Wilson Co., 1961).

91. One is reminded of the cup of tea a mother might find on the other side of the passthrough in the front hall of a nineteenth-century day nursery (see chapter 1 of this book).

92. "Designed for 24-Hour Care," *Architectural Record* 95, no. 3 (March 1944): 84. See also Lois Meek Stolz, "The Kaiser Child Service Centers," in *Early Childhood Education: Living History Interviews,* comp. James L. Hymes, Jr., book 2, *Care of the Children of Working Mothers* (Carmel, Calif.: Hacienda Press, 1978), 26–56; and Amy Kesselman, *Fleeting Opportunities: Women Shipyard Workers in Portland and Vancouver during World War II and Reconversion* (Albany: State University of New York Press, 1990), chap. 3.

93. Stolz, "Kaiser Centers," 46–47. Note, however, that despite the honorific, child care was represented as a feminized occupation.

94. Donald Albrecht, ed., *World War II and the American Dream: How Wartime Building Changed a Nation* (Washington, D.C., and Cambridge: National Building Museum and MIT Press, 1995); on the Kaiser Centers, see Margaret Crawford, "Daily Life on the Home Front: Women, Blacks, and the Struggle for Public Housing," 90–143.

95. In 1972 a "Building Types Study" was devoted to child care centers; *Architectural Record* 151, no. 4 (April 1972): 130–42. American architectural journals did, however, occasionally show designs for child care facilities in other industrial societies throughout the postwar period.

96. See, for example, Agnes Meyer, *Journey Through Chaos* (New York: Harcourt, Brace, 1944), 206–8.

97. Much of the following is drawn from anecdotal material in Sherna Gluck, *Rosie the Riveter Revisited: Women, the War, and Social Change* (Boston: Twayne, 1987), passim; and in Gretchen Lemke-Santangelo, *Abiding Courage: African American Migrant Women and the East Bay Community* (Chapel Hill: University of North Carolina Press, 1996), 117–18, 125–26, and 145–49.

98. Lemke-Santangelo, *Abiding Courage,* 118.

99. Stolz, "Kaiser Centers," 49.

100. Documents pertaining to this case may be found in the NAACP Papers, 1940–45, Manuscript Division, LC, Legal File II B 62: Discrimination: Child Care, San Mateo, Calif., 1943–44. My thanks to Eileen Boris for sharing this material with me.

101. Rogers is best known for supporting the founding of the Women's Army Auxiliary Corps (WAAC).

102. *Congressional Record,* 77th Cong., 2nd sess., vol. 88, pt. 4 (1942), 5160. Norton's speeches recapitulated the entire history of twentieth-century child care to that point; she alluded to the role of day nurseries in staving off poverty in the families of war widows in World War I and also praised the achievements of the WPA nursery schools.

103. See Lois Scharf, *To Work and to Wed: Female Employment, Feminism, and the Great Depression* (Westport, Conn.: Greenwood Press, 1980), esp. chap. 3.

104. The National Women's Trade Union League, operating independently, backed working women's demands for child care but with little effect, because the organization no longer represented the vibrant coalition of the middle class and working class that it had two decades earlier. See Susan Hartmann, "Women's Organizations during World War II: The Interaction of Class, Race, and Feminism," in *Woman's Being, Woman's Place: Female Identity and Vocation in American History,* ed. Mary Kelley (Boston: G. K. Hall, 1980).

105. See Ruth Milkman, "Redefining 'Women's Work': The Sexual Division of Labor in the Auto Industry during World War II," *Feminist Studies* 8, no. 2 (Summer 1982): 365; and Milkman, "American Women and Industrial Unionism during World War II," in Higonnet et al., *Behind the Lines.* For continuing male opposition during the postwar period, see Nancy Gabin, "'They Have Placed a Penalty on Womanhood': The Protest Actions of Women Workers in Detroit-Area UAW Locals, 1945–1947," *Feminist Studies* 8, no. 2 (Summer 1982): 373–98.

106. Testimony of Eleanor Fowler, Thomas Bill Hearings, 106; testimony of Catherine Gelles, ibid., 91.

107. Howard Dratch, "The Politics of Child Care in the 1940s," *Science and Society* 38, no. 2 (Summer 1974): 175. "War-impact areas" was the term used in the Lanham Act for regions eligible for federal funding; the bill's author, Fritz Lanham, a conservative congressman from Texas, hoped that strict use of the designation would limit the growth of government provisions and services and prevent their extension into the postwar period.

108. I am not suggesting that feminists alone were responsible for the bill's failure; it collapsed for a tangled congeries of reasons. Moreover, given the wartime political context, passage of the Thomas Bill would have actually weakened the cause of child care. Nevertheless, I cite this testimony in favor of the bill as indication that a feminist alternative was articulated—however faintly—in the 1940s.

CHAPTER 5: SHOULD MOTHERS WORK?

1. Testimony of Mrs. Eleanor Vaughan, *Maternal and Child Welfare,* Hearings before the Committee on Education and Labor, U.S. Senate, 79th Cong., 2nd sess., June 21–22, 1946 (Washington, D.C.: GPO, 1946), 124–25. On the Congress of American Women, see Amy Swerdlow, "The Congress of American Women: Left-Feminist Peace Politics in the Cold War," in *U.S. History as Women's History: New Feminist Essays,* ed. Linda K. Kerber, Alice Kessler-Harris, and Kathryn Kish Sklar (Chapel Hill: University of North Carolina Press, 1995); and Harriet Alonso, "Mayhem and Moderation: Women Peace Activists during the McCarthy Era," in *Not June Cleaver: Women and Gender in the Postwar Era, 1945–1960* (Philadelphia: Temple University Press, 1994), 144–48.

2. Letter from the officers of St. John's Day Care Center, in *Maternal and Child Welfare,* 285.

3. Letter from George F. Addes, International Secretary-Treasurer, International Union, United Automobile, Aircraft, Agricultural Implement Workers of America (UAW-CIO), in ibid., 280. The disjuncture between the presumptive politics of the three organizations mentioned here and the positions they took on child care is striking: whereas the left-wing feminist organization seemed most concerned with keeping mothers off relief and the trade union sought to prevent juvenile delinquency, a group of church-based child care providers took the most universalistic, rights-based position. The National Women's Trade Union League, which might have been expected to weigh in on the child care issue, ignored that aspect of the bill and instead commented approvingly on its child health and welfare provisions.

4. U. S. Department of Labor, WB, "Working Mothers," typescript memo 12/20/48, NA, RG 86 (records of the Women's Bureau, hereafter WBR), box 828, file 246: Materials (hereafter cited as WB Materials).

5. The study was reported in "Day-Care Centers," *Child* 16 (August–September 1951): 13. The breakdown was as follows: Dallas, Tex., 20 percent; Jacksonville, Fla., 25 percent; Fort Wayne, Ind., 30 percent; Minneapolis, Minn., 50 percent; St. Petersburg, Fla., 80

percent; Denver, Colo., 100 percent; and Lowell, Mass., 166 percent. A 1948 survey of twenty-seven day nurseries and nursery schools in Boston found even worse conditions in Boston. Most programs had capacity enrollments and there were long waiting lists for all but three, which offered only part-day care. While total enrollment for all twenty-seven programs was only 845, there were 1,189 children on their waiting lists. Of the children awaiting admission, 77 percent were three and four years old, 23 percent two or younger. Parents gave three principal reasons for seeking admission for their children: maternal employment, relief from congested neighborhoods and living quarters, and desire for the benefits of nursery school education; in ten out of the twenty-seven schools, maternal employment was given as the sole or primary reason. See Florence R. Gootenberg, "A Survey of the Facilities of Twenty-Seven Philanthropic Day Nurseries and Nursery Schools in Boston," service paper, Boston University School of Education, 1948; my thanks to Paul Gootenberg for bringing this source to my attention.

6. See Dorothy Sue Cobble, "Recapturing Working-Class Feminism: Union Women in the Postwar Era," in Meyerowitz, *Not June Cleaver*, 71–72.

7. See the section "Activist Women and Their Organizations," esp. Susan Lynn, "Gender and Progressive Politics: A Bridge to Social Activism of the 1960s," in Meyerowitz, *Not June Cleaver*, 103–27; see also Leila J. Rupp and Verta Taylor, *Survival in the Doldrums: The American Women's Rights Movement, 1945–1960* (New York: Praeger, 1987). According to Amy Swerdlow, the Congress of American Women (which existed only from 1946 to 1950) initially made child care one of its priorities but later shifted its focus to international Cold War issues; see Swerdlow, "The Congress of American Women," 308–12.

8. The term "nesting" is Nancy Fraser's; in her discussion of the "politics of need interpretation," she argues that so-called needs claims "tend to be nested, connected to one another in ramified chains of 'in-order-to' relations." Within such chains, a simple assertion of need does not immediately materialize in satisfaction, for needs are always interpreted, and "need interpretations are politically contested." "Struggle Over Needs: Outline of a Socialist-Feminist Critical Theory of Late Capitalist Political Culture," in *Unruly Practices: Power, Discourse and Gender in Contemporary Social Theory* (Minneapolis: University of Minnesota Press, 1989), 163–64.

9. Both world wars brought new prestige to the psychological professions; on World War I, see Elizabeth Lunbeck, *The Psychiatric Persuasion: Knowledge, Gender, and Power in Modern America* (Princeton: Princeton University Press, 1994), 42–43; on World War II, see Rebecca Schwartz Greene, "The Role of the Psychiatrist in World War II," Ph.D. diss., Columbia University, 1977; and on the postwar era, see Ellen Herman, *The Romance of American Psychology: Political Culture in the Age of Experts* (Berkeley: University of California Press, 1995), chaps. 4–5.

10. The phrase is Betty Friedan's in *The Feminine Mystique* (New York: Norton, 1963).

11. Elaine Tyler May established the linkage between the Cold War and the ideology of "normal" families in *Homeward Bound: American Families in the Cold War Era* (New York: Basic Books, 1988).

12. These included John Bowlby, *Maternal Care and Mental Health*, WHO Monograph 2

(Geneva: World Health Organization, 1951); Dorothy T. Burlingham and Anna Freud, *Young Children in Wartime: A Year's Work in a War Nursery* (London: Allen and Unwin, 1942), and *Infants Without Mothers* (New York: International Universities Press, 1944); W. Goldfarb, "Psychological Privation and Subsequent Infancy Adjustment," *American Journal of Orthopsychiatry* 15, no. 2 (April 1945): 247–55; René Spitz, "Hospitalism: An Inquiry into the General Conditions of Early Childhood," in *Psychoanalytic Study of the Child*, vol. 1 (New York: International Universities Press, 1945); and René A. Spitz with Katherine M. Wolf, "Anaclitic Depression," in *Psychoanalytic Study of the Child*, vol. 2 (New York: International Universities Press, 1946). For a contemporary critique of these theories, see Margaret Mead, "Some Theoretical Considerations on the Problem of Mother-Child Separation," *American Journal of Orthopsychiatry* 24, no. 3 (July 1954): 471–83.

13. See the discussion of wartime nurseries in chapter 4 of this book.

14. Sheldon and Eleanor Glueck, *Unravelling Juvenile Delinquency* (Cambridge: Harvard University Press [for the Commonwealth Fund], 1951).

15. Mary Essig and D. H. Morgan, "Adjustment of Adolescent Daughters of Employed Women to Family Life," *Journal of Educational Psychology* 37 (1946): 228–29. This study reflected widespread concern about adolescent female sexuality during the 1950s; see Regina Kunzel, "White Neurosis, Black Pathology: Constructing Out-of-Wedlock Pregnancy in the Wartime and Postwar United States"; and Donna Penn, "The Sexualized Woman: The Lesbian, the Prostitute, and the Containment of Female Sexuality in Postwar America," both in Meyerowitz, *Not June Cleaver*. See also Rickie Solinger, *Wake Up, Little Susie: Single Pregnancy and Race before Roe v. Wade* (New York: Routledge, 1992), chap. 3.

16. Irving L. Berger, M.D., "Psychopathologic Attitudes of Frustrated Previously Employed Mothers toward Their Offspring," *Journal of Nervous and Mental Disease* 108 (1948): 241.

17. The quote is a paraphrase of Bruch by Mead in "Some Theoretical Considerations," 477, referring to Bruch's book, *Don't Be Afraid of Your Child* (New York: Farrar, Straus and Young, 1952).

18. Eleanor E. Maccoby, "Children with Working Mothers," *Children* 5 (May–June 1958): 83–89. Maccoby made similar points in her paper "Effects upon Children of Their Mothers' Outside Employment," published in a conference report by the NMC, *Work in the Lives of Married Women* (New York: Columbia University Press, 1959).

19. Maccoby, "Children with Working Mothers," 86. In "Effects upon Children," Maccoby also criticized the study by Essig and Morgan for failing to control for class and ignoring the relationship between daughters and fathers (154–56).

20. Maccoby, "Children with Working Mothers," 86.

21. In "Effects upon Children," Maccoby cited a study by Christoph Heinecke, "Some Effects of Separating Two-Year-Old Children from Their Parents," *Human Relations* 10 (1956), which compared children in a residential nursery with those who attended a day care center. The residential children exhibited far more desperation in their behavior, crying frequently for their parents, seeking attention "in a more intense way," and exhibiting increasing levels of hostility. Maccoby concluded from this study that most

young children could handle short-term separations quite well, while long-term separations were "much more disturbing" and had "repercussions which last for at least some period beyond the time when the child is reunited with his family" (167–68).

22. Maccoby, "Children with Working Mothers," 88.

23. W. Norton Grubb and Marvin Lazerson point to the dangers in this sort of argumentation; often class-biased, it inevitably implies that parental care is inferior and that children are better off receiving professional care. They compare this attitude to the more mutually reciprocal (and less class-differentiated) view that prevails between nursery school teachers and parents. See *Broken Promises: How Americans Fail Their Children* (New York: Basic Books, 1982), 211–12. For a discussion of such comparisons during the interwar period, see Elizabeth Rose, "Taking on a Mother's Job: Nursery Schools and Day Nurseries in Philadelphia," paper presented at the Tenth Berkshire Conference on the History of Women, University of North Carolina-Chapel Hill, June 1996.

24. Irene M. Josselyn, M.D., and Ruth Schley Goldman, "Should Mothers Work?" *Social Science Review* 23, no. 1 (1949): 80–81; emphasis added.

25. For discussions of this phenomenon, see Dorothy Sue Cobble, "'Drawing the Line': The Construction of a Gendered Work Force in the Food Service Industry," in *Work Engendered: Toward a New History of American Labor,* ed. Ava Baron (Ithaca: Cornell University Press, 1991), 230–31; and Dorothy Sue Cobble, "Recapturing Working-Class Feminism: Union Women in the Postwar Era," in Meyerowitz, *Not June Cleaver,* 70.

26. Josselyn and Goldman, "Should Mothers Work?" 80.

27. Ibid. The image evoked here might well have reminded contemporary readers of the mothers in such films as *Imitation of Life* (1934) and *Mildred Pierce* (1945). For discussions of the representations of mothers in these and other films, see Andrea Walsh, *Women's Film and Female Experience, 1940–1950* (New York: Praeger, 1984); E. Ann Kaplan, *Motherhood and Representation: The Mother in Popular Culture and Melodrama* (New York: Routledge, 1992); and Suzanna Danuta Walters, *Lives Together/Worlds Apart: Mothers and Daughters in Popular Culture* (Berkeley: University of California Press, 1992).

28. Josselyn and Goldman, "Should Mothers Work?" 81. Of course, if this were the case, mothers need not work full time; they might gain equal or greater benefits from part-time employment, or even social activities or volunteer work.

29. Ibid., 82.

30. Josselyn and Goldman extended their psychologically based analysis to all social policies affecting families. The test for any policy, they believed, was whether it considered individual family situations. The Aid to Dependent Children program failed to pass this test because of a basic tension in American society. On the one hand, Americans claimed to place great value on mothering, while on the other, they resisted paying higher taxes or making greater donations to local charities so that mothers of "fatherless children" could receive adequate support and remain at home with their children. Over the years, administrative practices had in effect pushed poor mothers toward employment, subverting the original intention of Aid to Dependent Children and its forerunner, mother's pensions, and "[cloaking] the application policy with duress"; ibid., 74–75.

31. Ibid.

32. Ibid., 87; emphasis added. Their position is reminiscent of that taken by Mary Richmond and Fred Hall in *A Study of Nine Hundred and Eighty-Five Widows* (New York: Russell Sage Foundation, 1913); see chapter 2 of this book.

33. Faye Higier von Mering, "Professional and Non-Professional Women as Mothers," *Journal of Social Psychology* 42 (1955): 31. She also observed that the formerly professional mothers scored very high on the scale for understanding, suggesting "that they tend to adopt the role of clinician toward their children, and in this sense . . . 'professionalize' the maternal role."

34. Ibid., 33. Although von Mering did not explicitly cite Irving Berger, her argument certainly would have applied to his findings.

35. Mead, "Some Theoretical Considerations," 477. More recently, this notion has been taken up and popularized by Hillary Rodham Clinton in her book *It Takes a Village, And Other Lessons Children Teach Us* (New York: Simon and Schuster, 1996).

36. Ethel Verry, "A Day Care Program to Meet Community Needs," *Child Welfare* 31 (April 1952): 7.

37. Ibid., 8.

38. See Herman, *Romance of American Psychology,* chap. 5.

39. Elizabeth Pope, "Is a Working Mother a Threat to the Home?" *McCall's* 82, no. 10 (July 1955): 29. Bartemeier's conservatism had become evident in other venues as well. He was, for example, a leading proponent of efforts to bar homosexuals from entering the military by subjecting them to psychiatric screening; see Alan Bérubé, *Coming Out under Fire: The History of Gay Men and Women in World War Two* (New York: Free Press, 1990), 15–16.

40. Pope, "Working Mother," 29.

41. Ibid., 72.

42. Ibid., 73.

43. Ibid.

44. Ibid. Jahoda's views reflected her many years as a member of Germany's Frankfurt School, a group of left-wing social theorists, many of whom had sought refuge in the United States during World War II. Overall, Jahoda felt ambivalent about the value of maternal employment because most of the women working out of financial need earned so little; the median wage for the factory and clerical jobs in which most found themselves was only about $1,400 a year. Jahoda called for raising minimum-wage standards "to a point where all able men can support their families and fewer mothers will be forced to work" (ibid.). Although Jahoda was concerned about the exploitation of female workers, her proposed solution—ensuring a family wage and returning, if possible, to the male breadwinner ideal—would have done nothing for the single mothers whose plight she most deplored.

45. Ibid.

46. Ibid.

47. Ibid., 73. Komarovsky's advice falls into the category of what Joanne Meyerowitz calls "the modern woman's life cycle"; "Beyond the Feminine Mystique," in Meyerowitz, *Not June Cleaver,* 239.

48. Nevitt Sanford, "Is College Education Wasted on Women?" *Ladies' Home Journal* 74,

no. 5 (May 1957): 198. Sanford's study anticipated by a decade Matina Horner's influential work on women's "fear of success," "Sex Differences in Achievement Motivation and Performance in Competitive and Non-Competitive Situations," Ph.D. diss., University of Michigan, 1968.

49. Sidonie Matsner Gruenberg and Hilda Sidney Krech, "The Modern Mother's Dilemma," Public Affairs Pamphlet No. 247 (New York: Public Affairs Committee, March 1957), 1.

50. Ibid., 2.

51. As the longtime president of the Child Study Association of America, Gruenberg should have included herself in that class. For her advice to parents in wartime, see Sidonie Matsner Gruenberg, ed., *The Family in a World at War* (New York: Child Study Association of America, 1942).

52. Gruenberg and Krech, "Modern Mother's Dilemma," 2.

53. Ibid., 14.

54. Ibid., 19–20.

55. Meyerowitz, "Beyond the Feminine Mystique," 251.

56. Ibid., 252.

57. See Barbara Bergmann, *The Economic Emergence of Women* (New York: Basic Books, 1986), chap. 5; and Claudia Goldin, *Understanding the Gender Gap: An Economic History of American Women* (New York: Oxford University Press, 1990), chap. 3.

58. See Susan Leighow, "'An Obligation to Participate': Married Nurses' Labor Force Participation in the 1950s," in Meyerowitz, *Not June Cleaver*, 37–56.

59. Susan Hartmann points to the self-contradiction inherent in Cold War ideology, which emphasized domesticity on the one hand while calling for a build-up of national strength on the other; see "Women's Employment and the Domestic Ideal in the Early Cold War Years" in Meyerowitz, *Not June Cleaver*, 86–87. See also May, *Homeward Bound*, passim. For a discussion of World War II parallels, see chapter 4 of this book.

60. The lack of unanimity was evident at the regional meetings and in the two volumes that emerged from the study: NMC, *Womanpower* (New York: Columbia University Press, 1958); and NMC, *Work in the Lives*.

61. World Health Organization publication, quoted in NMC, *Womanpower*, 54; emphasis added.

62. Frances Lomax Feldman, "Supplementary Income Earned by Married Women," in NMC, *Work in the Lives*, 93–115.

63. "Conference Discussion: Income Earned by Married Women," in NMC, *Work in the Lives*, 122.

64. Such concerns were reminiscent of nineteenth-century arguments that mothers who placed their children in day nurseries were working for wages only so that they could afford to buy frivolous items. See chapter 1 of this book.

65. Bartemeier conceded that a mother's work outside the home "is only one of many factors" affecting a child's development. "Certainly her physical presence in the home will not itself insure the healthy emotional development of the child." But he quickly restored the "proper" gender balance by asserting that mothers' attitudes toward their children "are conditioned considerably by their husbands"; "The Children of Working

Mothers: A Psychiatrist's View," in NMC, *Work in the Lives,* 181. Notably, Bartemeier was the only contributor to this volume who thought it necessary to invoke the authority of his profession in the title of his paper.

66. Maccoby, "Effects upon Children," 154.

67. Katherine Brownell Oettinger, "Maternal Employment and Children," in NMC, *Work in the Lives,* 135.

68. Ibid., 147.

69. Maccoby and Oettinger also addressed another argument frequently used against maternal employment, namely that it invariably upset the "normal" gender balance in the family. For one thing, Maccoby noted, mothers' prolonged absence from the home might leave room for fathers to develop more meaningful and sustained relationships with their children. For another, although mothers' earnings interfered with husbands' playing "a strongly dominant, autocratic role," this situation did not have to imply a reversal that put women in an unnatural position of power. Equally possible, Maccoby dared to suggest, "is an arrangement of shared authority—a 'democratic' relationship in which decisions are jointly made and mutual esteem exists—in which neither parent need be devalued in the eyes of the children when the mother goes to work"; ibid., 172. Oettinger concurred that such relationships constituted healthy models for children.

70. Oettinger, "Maternal Employment," 136.

71. Ibid., 139.

72. Ibid., 148.

73. "Conference Discussion," in NMC, *Work in the Lives,* 190–93.

74. On mothers' pensions, see chapter 2 of this book; for New Deal campaigns, see Linda Gordon, *Pitied but Not Entitled: Single Mothers and the History of Welfare* (New York: Free Press, 1994).

75. See Arthur A. Campbell and James D. Cowhig, "The Incidence of Illegitimacy in the United States," *Welfare in Review* 5, no. 5 (May 1967): 1–6. See also Solinger, *Wake Up, Little Susie,* 13–15.

76. Whereas widows had made up about three-quarters of those covered by state widows' and mothers' pensions, they numbered less than 10 percent of those on ADC; the remainder were divorced, deserted, and in some states, never-married mothers. See Gwendolyn Mink, *The Wages of Motherhood: Inequality in the Welfare State* (Ithaca: Cornell University Press, 1995), 136–39.

77. Winifred Bell, *Aid to Dependent Children* (New York: Columbia University Press, 1965), esp. pt. 2.

78. Ibid., 5.

79. In any case, the NMC's report, *Womanpower,* took a jaundiced view of the government's provisions during World War II. The report noted that at their height the Lanham Act child care facilities cared for only 130,000 children, hardly enough to meet the needs of the 1.5 million mothers in the workforce with children under six. In some war production areas, fewer than 11 percent of mothers placed their children in day care centers, relying instead on relatives and other household members. Mothers generally tended to be wary of public facilities, which seemed unfamiliar to them, and they feared that their children would not be cared for by "competent personnel" (p. 107).

80. For more on this, see Hartmann, "Women's Employment." The NMC did, however, endorse policies to enhance the employment status of *single* women workers; see Cynthia Harrison, *On Account of Sex: The Politics of Women's Issues, 1945–1968* (Berkeley: University of California Press, 1988), 48.

81. The CB was particularly weak during this period. It had been relocated twice since the war, first in 1946, from the Labor Department to the Federal Security Agency, and then again in 1953 to the Department of Health, Education, and Welfare. In each case its status was lowered, and requests for additional staff and funding were denied. The WB was slightly better off; see Harrison, *On Account of Sex*, passim.

82. On Oettinger, see *Current Biography* (1957): 418–19; on Leopold, see *Current Biography* (1955): 359–61; and Harrison, *On Account of Sex*, 34, 83; Harrison also includes an interesting comparison of the policies of Miller and Leopold.

83. "California—Women with Children," *Christian Science Monitor* (August 23, 1947).

84. Mary-Elizabeth Pidgeon, *Women Workers and Their Dependents*, WB Bulletin No. 239 (Washington, D.C.: GPO, 1952), 7–8.

85. Alice Kessler-Harris, *Out to Work: A History of Wage-Earning Women in the United States* (New York: Oxford University Press, 1982), 301.

86. On Miller see Barbara Sicherman et al., eds., *Notable American Women: The Modern Period* (Cambridge, Mass.: Belknap Press, 1980), 478–79; and Annelise Orleck, *Common Sense and a Little Fire: Women and Working-Class Politics in the United States, 1900–1965* (Chapel Hill: University of North Carolina Press, 1995), chap. 7.

87. Frieda S. Miller, "Women in the Labor Force," *Annals of the American Academy of Political and Social Science* 251 (May 1947): 41.

88. Ibid., 43; emphasis added.

89. Frieda Miller, "Why Do Women Work?" *National Parent-Teacher* (September 1952): 16–17.

90. Members included Hazel Gabbard, OE; Evelyn Smith, CB; Evelyn Murphy, Bureau of Employment Security; Elizabeth Long, Bureau of Public Assistance; and Mary-Elizabeth Pidgeon, WB.

91. Subcommittee of the Interdepartmental Committee on Children and Youth, "Planning Services for Children of Employed Mothers" (Washington, D.C.: U.S. Department of Labor, WB, May 1953).

92. Ibid., 5.

93. Ibid., 56.

94. Similarly, the number of children between the ages of five and nine was 24 percent higher in 1950 than in 1940.

95. Interdepartmental Committee, "Planning Services," 5.

96. Ibid., 57.

97. Ibid., 55.

98. Ibid., 11.

99. Ibid., 20. Although the Public Housing Administration provided the sites rent-free, it was not responsible for operating services; these were left up to local schools and welfare agencies. But such authorities were often either unwilling or unable to sponsor day care.

100. Ibid., 34.

101. "Women's Bureau Statement for Subcommittee on Children of Employed Mothers [of the Interdepartmental Committee on Children and Youth]," n.d. [1953?], WB Materials, 1–2; bracketed words were handwritten in the margins of the original typescript.
102. Interdepartmental Committee, "Planning Services," 39.
103. Many of these issues were the subjects of other studies and conferences sponsored by the WB under Frieda Miller. See Judith Sealander, *As Minority Becomes Majority: Federal Reaction to the Phenomenon of Women in the Workforce, 1920–1963* (Westport, Conn.: Greenwood Press, 1983), chap. 7; for a list of WB publications, see Sealander's appendix B.
104. WB, *Employed Mothers and Child Care,* WB Publication No. 246 (Washington, D.C.: GPO, 1953), 32–33.
105. Ibid., 45.
106. Ibid., 88.
107. On the critical demand for nurses, see Leighow, "'An Obligation to Participate,'" 37–56.
108. WB, *Employed Mothers,* 69.
109. Women were 41 percent of all non-agricultural workers in Hartford; ibid., 25, 33.
110. Ibid., 48 and 46. Licensed homes charged more if they offered planned programs.
111. Ibid., 33, 42.
112. Ibid., 54.
113. State support was made permanent in 1957.
114. San Diego centers charged $13.30 for a five-day week and $15.96 for six days. These were even higher than fees charged by some commercial nurseries, although public centers offered higher-quality programs; see WB, *Employed Mothers,* 86.
115. Yet women still comprised only 23 percent of the total labor force in San Diego, well below the national average.
116. WB, *Employed Mothers,* 85.
117. Female cannery workers were largely Mexican American; see Vicki Ruiz, *Cannery Women, Cannery Lives: Mexican Women, Unionization, and the California Food Processing Industry, 1939–1950* (Albuquerque: University of New Mexico Press, 1987).
118. Two such facilities were in Milwaukee, Wisconsin, and New Britain, Connecticut. See Leighow, "'An Obligation to Participate.'"
119. WB, *Employed Mothers,* 78.
120. Ibid.
121. National Education Association, "Trends in City School Organization, 1938–48," *NEA Research Bulletin* (February 1949); cited in WB, *Employed Mothers,* 12.
122. After visiting one hundred school systems in forty-three states during 1948–49, the Office of Education found that only fifty-four offered extended programs. Most ran extended hours during regular school days and a few offered weekend service; forty-two ran summer programs.
123. WB, *Employed Mothers,* 27.
124. Ibid., 74. Rates for *full-day* care for two children in both public and private nurseries in Idaho Falls were about $12.50 per week.

125. Ibid.
126. Ibid., 72.
127. This same woman reported that "some women offered jobs at the . . . plant could not take them because they had no place to leave their children"; ibid.
128. Ibid., 28.
129. Ibid., 29.
130. Ibid., 28.
131. Ibid., 30.
132. Interdepartmental Committee, "Planning Services," 3.
133. Ibid.
134. Ibid., 29.
135. On the political mood of this period, see Hartmann, "Women's Employment," 84–102.
136. Henry C. Lajewski, "Working Mothers and Their Arrangements for Care of Their Children," *Social Security Bulletin* (August 1959): 8. For complete data, see Henry C. Lajewski, *Child Care Arrangements of Full-Time Working Mothers,* CB Publication No. 378 (Washington, D.C.: GPO, 1959).
137. Lajewski, *Child Care Arrangements,* 11.
138. Ibid., 13.
139. Ibid., 6.
140. Ibid., 11.
141. An internal 1959 CB memo warned, "The 'lost' feeling a child experiences in coming to an 'empty' home after school may lead him to seek elsewhere security he misses in his family relationships. These children are apt to fall prey to accidents or harmful influences without proper adult supervision"; CB, "Day Care Services for Children Needing Day-Time Care," WBR, box 365, folder: Day Care 1958, 5 (a number of documents were found misfiled in WBR). This memo seemed to be expressing the same types of concerns that had been voiced by such psychologists as the Gluecks and Mary Essig and D. H. Morgan in their studies of the impact of maternal employment on adolescents.
142. CB, "Advance Release for Sunday, January 25, 1959," WBR, box 365, folder: Day Care 1958.
143. Draft of letter from Alice Leopold to Mrs. Katherine B. Oettinger [n.d.; sometime between January 25 and March 12, 1959], WBR, box 365, folder: Day Care 1958.
144. It is interesting that, after years of holding the line on this issue under the leadership of Democratic chiefs, the CB finally yielded under the leadership of the Republican Oettinger, whose background was in social work.
145. Lajewski, *Child Care Arrangements,* 4.

CHAPTER 6: MAKING AN ISSUE OF CHILD CARE

1. In this chapter I use the term "day care," rather than "child care," to reflect contemporary terminology. On women's political transformation, see Susan Ware, "American Women in

the 1950s: Nonpartisan Politics and Women's Politicization," in *Women, Politics, and Change,* ed. Louise A. Tilly and Patricia Gurin (New York: Russell Sage Foundation, 1990), 281–99; and essays in Joanne Meyerowitz, ed., *Not June Cleaver: Women and Gender in Postwar America, 1945–1960* (Philadelphia: Temple University Press, 1994), pt. 2.

2. Labor, as noted in the previous chapter, for the most part remained on the sidelines of this movement.

3. See, for example, Elizabeth Rose, "Maternal Work: Day Care in Philadelphia, 1890–1960, Ph.D. diss., Rutgers University, 1994, chap. 7; and Emilie Stolzfus, "Mother, Worker, Citizen: Public Provision of Child Care in the United States, 1945–1965," Ph.D. diss., Claremont Graduate University, 1998.

4. For federal lobbying, see *Maternal and Child Welfare,* Hearings before the Committee on Education and Labor, U.S. Senate, 79th Cong., 2nd sess., June 21–22, 1946 (Washington, D.C.: GPO, 1946).

5. On this sequence, see chapter 4 of this book.

6. The scenario occurred as follows: "On Dec. 30, 1942, FWA announced it would make direct grants to eligible child care facilities w/federal contributions for all costs not met by fees and local appropriations; in Feb. 1943, the formula was changed to make 'federal funds available for 50% of operating costs and 100% of the costs of equipment. Building renovation and rent, if necessary, became a federal charge.'" Ann Gussack Levine and Alice R. McCabe, "The Public-Voluntary Agency Sponsored Day Care Program for Children in New York City," mimeo, Department of Public Affairs, Community Service Society of New York, July 1965, 28.

7. Although the committee had been appointed by Mayor Fiorello LaGuardia, he was not a wholehearted champion of either day care or maternal employment. In fact, he was quoted as saying "The worst mother is better than the best institution," and he let it be known that he was reluctant to "make the State the father and mother of the child." For this reason he favored using voluntary agencies as liaisons between sponsoring agencies, local neighborhood groups, and parents (quotations in ibid., 36).

8. Cornelia Goldsmith, "The New York City Day Care Unit," in *Early Childhood Education: Living History Interviews,* comp. James L. Hymes, Jr., book 2, *Care of the Children of Working Mothers* (Carmel, Calif.: Hacienda Press, 1978), 65.

9. For details of the campaign to raise standards, see Yetta Bokhaut, R.N., "Day Care for a City's Children," *American Journal of Nursing* 46 (February 1946): 102–3; and "A City Improves Day Care for Its Children," *The Child* 11, no. 8 (February 1947): 138–40.

10. Concern with and prevention of juvenile delinquency was high on the postwar reform agenda. According to Levine and McCabe, "The Public-Voluntary Agency," however, this transfer indicated that New York State "had not really accepted the concept of any permanent responsibility for the day care of children" (30). Whether or not the move was intended to sound the death knell for the system, city officials and parents of children in day care protested the idea of applying the criteria of juvenile delinquency prevention to their day care centers.

11. Ibid., 29. In one year, $4 million had been spent to care for 5,000 children.

12. The planning and execution of this action may be followed through the clippings and

notes in the records of the Child Care Parents Association, SL (hereafter CCPAR), box 1, folder 4.

13. See Rose, "Maternal Work," 370; Stolzfus, "Mother, Worker, Citizen."

14. Day Care Council of New York City (DCC), "Report on the New York City Public-Private Day Care Program," September 13, 1950, CCPAR, box 1, folder 1.

15. Biographic resumé, Elinor Coleman Guggenheimer (Mrs. Randolph), Women's Bureau Records, NA RG 86 (hereafter WBR), box 17, folder: June 1 WHC Panelists/Speakers.

16. DCC, "Script of Day Care Center X," March 2, 1950, CCPAR, box 1, folder 1, p. 3.

17. In many ways DCC rhetoric was reminiscent of that of the nineteenth-century day nursery philanthropists; see chapter 1 of this book. Indeed, Guggenheimer consciously identified those women as her predecessors.

18. Janet Karlson, acting president of the Child Care Parents Association (part of the UPA coalition), quoted in "1,000 to Carry Child-Care Plea to Dewey Today," *Daily Mirror* (September 22, 1947).

19. This was a group of women who, like the middle-class mothers discussed in chapter 5 of this book, sought private solutions for their child care needs.

20. Leaders took advantage of the long train ride to plan strategies and distribute lobbying assignments to the parents (usually mothers) who came along. The organization frequently pointed out the sacrifices that these women made. In addition to giving up a day's wages, they often had to make supplementary child care arrangements. Other parents contributed to their train fares. See Bronx Day Care Parents Association, "Mrs. Working Mother Reports on Albany," [n.d.; winter 1948?], CCPAR, box 2, folder 14.

21. "Mothers and Children Protest," *New York Post* [n.d.; January 1948?], CCPAR, box 1, folder 4.

22. "Demonstrating for Continuance of Child Care Centers," *New York Times* (February 25, 1948).

23. Ibid.

24. "Background and Action," CCPAR, box 1, folder 4.

25. MacDonald also claimed that a number of the city's top child care administrators had been appointed without taking civil service examinations, and that at least one, Pearl Zimmerman, director of the Division of Day Care, Department of Welfare, had been exposed as the "backer of a Communist-front organization"; "Child Care Chiefs Got Jobs Without Exams," *New York World-Telegram* (March 1, 1948): 7.

26. Walter MacDonald, "Rich Parents Chiseling City on Child Care," *New York World Telegram* (February 28, 1948): 1.

27. Ibid., 1–2.

28. References and allusions to such activities occur throughout CCPA records.

29. The UPA continued its aggressive tactics, but at least one affiliate, the CCPA, also sought to gain respectability and legitimacy by assembling a board of advisers that included such well-known figures in the fields of early childhood education and child welfare as Ruth Andrus, Eduard Lindeman, and James L. Hymes, Jr.

30. Report on Mrs. Wallerstein's meeting with Day Care [Council], April 9, 1953, CCPAR, box 1, folder 7.

31. Ibid; emphasis added.

32. See Harriet Alonso, *Peace as a Women's Issue: A History of the U.S. Movement for World Peace and Women's Rights* (Syracuse: Syracuse University Press, 1993), chap. 6; and Amy Swerdlow, *Women Strike for Peace: Traditional Motherhood and Radical Politics in the 1960s* (Chicago: University of Chicago Press, 1993), chap. 2.

33. Bertha Reynolds, panel report, "Panel I: The Child's Needs in the Family," Bread and Butter Conference Report, [April 1950?], CCPAR, box 2, folder 12, p. 5. Reynolds, who chaired the panel, was a veteran social worker and activist in Social Work Today, a left-wing social workers' organization that was active in New York City in the late 1930s and early 1940s.

34. Women's groups that had formed independently before turning to left-wing politics, like the Women's International League for Peace and Freedom and the Congress of American Women, tended to take more feminist positions than women's caucuses or auxiliaries within the Communist Party; see Alonso, *Peace as a Women's Issue,* chap. 6; and Swerdlow, *Women Strike for Peace,* 37–38.

35. See Elsa Jane Dixler, "The Woman Question: Women and the American Communist Party, 1929–1941," Ph.D. diss., Yale University, 1974; and Swerdlow, *Women Strike for Peace,* 37. The Communist Party platform of 1948 did call for "an end to any and all political, social and economic inequalities practiced against women" (*New York Times,* August 7, 1948), but there was often a wide gap between rhetoric and practice within both the Communist Party and the organizations in which it played an influential role.

36. Helen Wortis, "Closing Remarks," Bread and Butter Conference Report, 28.

37. On the impact of McCarthyism on the women's movement generally, see Leila J. Rupp and Verta Taylor, *Survival in the Doldrums: The American Women's Rights Movement, 1945 to the 1960s* (Columbus: Ohio State University Press, 1990), chap. 7.

38. "Fact Sheet, Jan 31, 1951," WBR, box 828, folder 246: Materials (hereafter WBR Materials). See also Subcommittee of the Interdepartmental Committee on Children and Youth, "Planning Services for Children of Employed Mothers" (Washington, D.C.: U.S. Department of Labor, WB, May 1953), 31–32.

39. Interdepartmental Committee, "Planning Services," 32.

40. Minutes of the Legislative Committee, A Sub-Committee of the Day Care Committee (CWLA), September 6, 1951, SWHA, CWLA collection (hereafter CWLAC), box 42, folder 2, p. 4.

41. Ibid., 2.

42. It is unclear whether the designation of the CB as administering agency had anything to do with the CWLA. At the September 6 meeting, the committee delegated Guggenheimer and Spencer Crookes, another CWLA official, to meet with Oscar Ewing, chief of the Federal Security Agency (of which the CB was now a part), or his assistant, as soon as possible. Whether they did so is unknown, but the choice of the CB was announced at another meeting on September 17 (before the executive order was actually issued).

43. CWLA Legislative Committee minutes, September 6, 1951, 1.

44. Statement of Right Reverend John O'Grady, *Defense Housing Act: Hearings before the Committee on Banking and Currency on S. 349,* U.S. Senate, 82nd Cong., 1st sess., January 16, 17, 18, February 1, 2, 13, 14, 15, 16, 19, and 20, 1951, p. 150.

45. WB, Economic Studies Branch, Research Division, "Field Survey Guide: Community

Facilities with Relation to Utilization of Women in the Defense Program," October 22, 1951, WBR Materials, 1.

46. Ibid., 5.

47. Ibid., 6.

48. One result was the studies discussed in chapter 5 of this book.

49. The deduction also applied to care for dependents who were mentally or physically handicapped. For a head of household with one dependent, earning a net income of $3,000, the deduction would result in an annual tax savings of $120. *Internal Revenue Code of 1954: Hearings before the Committee on Finance on H. R. 8300,* U.S. Senate, 83rd Cong., 2nd sess., April 7–8, 1954, pt. 1, 136.

50. See, for example, "Statement of Mrs. Marie Jordan Munoz, Founder, Gold Star Wives of America, Inc.," *Internal Revenue Code,* pt. 2, 1069.

51. Extension of Remarks of Hon. Carl Elliott, *Congressional Record,* 83rd Cong., 1st sess., vol. 99 (1953), pt. 11, A3542.

52. "Representative Aimé J. Forand (Democrat, Rhode Island) Introduces a Bill Permitting Tax Deductions for Wages Paid for Child and Dependent Care (H.R. 4206)," *General Revenue Revision: Hearings before the U.S. Cong., House, Committee on Ways and Means,* 83rd Cong., 1st sess., June 16, 1953, pt. 1, 30.

53. Statement by Senator [Paul] Douglas, *Congressional Record,* 83rd Cong., 2nd sess., vol. 100 (1954), pt. 7, 9605.

54. "Statement of Miss Julia Thompson," *General Revenue Revision,* 50.

55. In 1952, according to the Federal Reserve Board's 1953 Survey of Consumer Finances, 59 percent of American households had annual pretax incomes of less than $4,000; 41 percent earned more than $4,000, but only 9 percent earned more than $7,000. At $4,000, according to Russ Nixon, the Washington representative of the United Electrical, Radio, and Machine Workers of America (UE), most families "do not have enough income to satisfy their many needs and to buy the mountain of goods our economy puts out. They are the ones who need tax relief to help make ends meet." "Statement of Russ Nixon," *Internal Revenue Code of 1954,* 646–47.

56. "Statement of Mrs. Nancy M. Henderson," *General Revenue Revision,* 62.

57. Thompson statement, 49–52. Thompson presented the following monthly budget as typical for a general-duty nurse with one preschool child working in a midwestern city: salary, $225; transportation, lunches, uniforms, $50; housekeeper or nursemaid, $135 (including lunches). This would leave $40 *before* deductions for taxes or Social Security. "This nurse's decision to accept a job in the hospital where she is urgently needed or to remain at home will be greatly influenced by whether or not she is allowed [the deduction]" (51). See also Susan Rimby Leighow, "An 'Obligation to Participate': Married Nurses' Labor Force Participation in the 1950s," in Meyerowitz, *Not June Cleaver,* 37–56.

58. "Statement of Ranice W. Davis," *Internal Revenue Code of 1954,* 1062; Davis' prepared statement was co-signed by five other individuals, including one physician, presumably all colleagues at Hopkins.

59. "Statement of Hon. J. K. Javits," *General Revenue Revision,* 55.

60. Sylvia Porter, "Working Mothers," *New York Post* (June 17, 1953), reprinted in *Congressional Record,* 83rd Cong., 1st sess., vol. 99 (1953), pt. 12, A4340. This and other articles

from the popular press were inserted into the record by Representative Kenneth Roberts (Democrat–Alabama).

61. Sylvia Porter, "Your Money's Worth: Wives Who Work Want Tax Exemption for Salaries Paid to Domestic Help" (n.p.), reprinted in *Congressional Record*, 83rd Cong., 1st sess., vol. 99 (1953), p. 12, A4341.

62. "Tax Laws Unfair to Working Wives," *Redbook* (February 1953), reprinted in *Congressional Record*, 83rd Cong., 1st sess., vol. 99 (1953), pt. 9, A752.

63. Porter, "Your Money's Worth."

64. Noah Mason, *General Revenue Revision*. Mason's remarks were interspersed in the question period following various statements. He also asserted that values had collapsed during World War II, when "the mother learned she could earn money . . . and now insists on doing it while the children are running loose and becoming a nuisance in the town" (27).

65. Ibid., 63.

66. John Byrnes, debate, ibid., 27.

67. "Statement of Hon. Leonore K. Sullivan," ibid., 32.

68. "Statement of Hon. Edna F. Kelly," ibid., 26. Kelly's and Sullivan's efforts were not made any easier by the rampant sexism that was taken for granted in mid-1950s congressional banter. At the end of Kelly's testimony, the following exchange occurred:

> MR. BOGGS [Hale Boggs, Democrat–Louisiana]: . . . I am not only very much impressed with what she has to say, but I am very much impressed with Mrs. Kelly as a witness. I think she is the most attractive witness we have heard in a long time.
>
> MRS. KELLY: Please do not embarrass me. [Kelly was forty-seven years old at the time.]
>
> THE CHAIRMAN [Daniel A. Reed, Republican–New York]: We can all agree with that, but I also know of another very attractive Congresswoman who is coming [Leonore Sullivan].
>
> MR. BOGGS: I meant up to this point (p. 31).

69. "Statement of Hon. Kenneth A. Roberts," ibid., 41.

70. Douglas statement.

71. Thompson statement, 49. Thompson also criticized that Tax Court for holding that "the cost of child care, even though necessarily incurred in order to permit the mother to work, was primarily personal and therefore not deductible." The case she was referring to was probably *Henry C. Smith vs. Commissioner of Internal Revenue* (40 BTA 1038), decided by the Board of Tax Appeals in 1939.

72. See, for example, "Statement of American Federation of Government Employees" and "Statement . . . by Stanley H. Ruttenberg, Congress of Industrial Organizations," *General Revenue Revision*, 68–69. For further discussion of labor's positions on the issue, see Mary Frances Berry, *The Politics of Parenthood: Child Care, Women's Rights, and the Myth of the Good Mother* (New York: Viking, 1993), 121.

73. Douglas statement.

74. As Elliott put it, "Should the Congress feel . . . that it cannot go all the way at this time and grant . . . deductions for all working mothers, then the least we can do is to provide such deductions for widows and widowers"; Elliott remarks.

75. According to Mary Frances Berry, President Eisenhower further underscored this position when he signed the bill. "He made clear his view that this new policy departure was the Republican way to deal with the child care issue. He insisted it provided mainly for widows, widowers, and wives whose husbands were incapacitated." Berry, *Politics of Parenthood,* 121–22.

76. In 1980, for example, Washington spent a total of $2.8 billion for child care, of which $956 million went to cover tax relief for child and dependent care; ibid., 155.

77. As the Maybank Bill was taking shape, Guggenheimer worked with the CWLA legislative subcommittee to draw up recommendations. They did this not out of idle fantasy but with some expectation that they would influence policy. The group also consulted with other CWLA officials, such as Mary Keeley, who had worked at the Office of War Services while the Lanham Act was being administered. She advised them to examine several reports, including her final report for the Office of War Services, to understand how cooperation between federal and state agencies might be set up.

78. Mrs. [Elinor] Guggenheimer, "A Proposal for Planning the Development of Good Group Programs for Young Children who Require Care Outside Their Homes during the Day," CWLAC, box 23, folder 1, p. 1.

79. Ibid.

80. See, for example, the discussion of similar views on the part of psychological experts Irene Josselyn and Ruth Schley Goldman in chapter 5 of this book.

81. Most early members were either personal acquaintances or political colleagues of Guggenheimer's. The group's membership grew rapidly; twelve individuals attended a meeting held in March 1958, and thirty-six came the following month; see minutes for ICC, March 3, 1958, and April 29, 1958, WBR, box 365, folder: Day Care 1959 (hereafter WBR Day Care 1959). Many of these records were misfiled, but they are cited here as they were found in the NA.

82. The conference on Work in the Lives of Married Women had been held just a month earlier (in October 1957), under the aegis of the National Manpower Council, with Guggenheimer, Leopold, and Oettinger all in attendance; see chapter 5 of this book.

83. Memo from Alice A. Morrison to Alice K. Leopold, November 29, 1957, WBR 365, folder: Day Care 1958 (hereafter WBR Day Care 1958).

84. Memos from Alice Morrison to Alice Leopold, January 13, 1958; and from Laura Dale to Alice Leopold and Alice Morrison, April 7, 1958; WBR Day Care 1958. At this same meeting, the CB and the WB agreed upon a division of labor: the CB would take the lead in "pointing out needs," and the two agencies would then decide jointly what actions to take; Leopold offered "to supplement the Children's Bureau's efforts with complementary projects" such as obtaining "information from industry about their day care activity"; CB, "Exploration on Day Care," [n.d.; sometime after November 22, 1957]; copy found in WBR Day Care 1959.

85. Henry J. Lajewski, *Child Care Arrangements of Full-Time Working Mothers,* CB Publication No. 378 (Washington, D.C.: GPO, 1959).

86. Memo from Oettinger to Guggenheimer, December 27, 1957, WBR Day Care 1959.

87. CB [Clare Golden, "Secretary for the Day,"], Inter-City Day Care Group Minutes, March 3, 1958, WBR Day Care 1959.

88. Minutes of ICC meeting, April 29, 1958, WBR Day Care 1959; the carbon copy of the typescript has the following handwritten note: "Received from Mrs. Guggenheimer, Day Care Council, N.Y.—5/16/58." It is noteworthy that Golden's report on the previous meeting was careful to record that she and Dale did not make any commitments to the ICC, whereas the ICC's own minutes of the subsequent meeting claim that Dale and Golden were not only offering the ICC valuable information but also encouraging them to pressure the government.

89. In its early days, the CB had also relied on support and mutual exchanges with outside groups; see Robyn Muncy, *Creating a Female Dominion in American Reform, 1890–1935* (New York: Oxford University Press, 1991), esp. chap. 3.

90. ICC minutes, April 29, 1958, 2.

91. "The Scope and Purpose of the Intercity Day Care Council," Tentative Committee Report, May 12, 1958, WBR Day Care 1959, 1.

92. Ibid; the WB's copy has the handwritten notation, "To be sent to nat'l org."

93. See Elaine Tyler May, *Homeward Bound: American Families in the Cold War Era* (New York: Basic Books, 1988), chaps. 6 and 8.

94. "Scope and Purpose," 1.

95. ICC minutes, May 28, 1958, WBR Day Care 1959. The points on which Schottland assured Guggenheimer and Ginsberg seemed to be identical to those that the ICC itself had framed, suggesting that he was "prepped" for the meeting, perhaps by Golden or Dale. If so, there appears to be no record of it.

96. Ibid.

97. See copy of letter from Oettinger to Guggenheimer, June 30, 1958, WBR Day Care 1959.

98. Guggenheimer to Witmer, October 21, 1958, WBR Day Care 1959. Guggenheimer also sent copies of her letter to other key officials at the CB and the WB.

99. Golden did, however, tell Dale that because the CB and the OE had not had many dealings of late, "preliminary negotiations would be needed before bringing them in on the program." Laura Dale to Alice Leopold and Alice Morrison, May 29, 1958, WBR Day Care 1959.

100. Neither Guggenheimer nor Javits allowed party loyalties to stand in the way of their common commitment to the cause of child care. In any case, Javits' generally moderate positions made him extremely popular with New York City Democrats, who repeatedly returned him to Congress.

101. Dale to Leopold and Morrison, May 29, 1958, WBR Day Care 1959, 2.

102. Ibid., 3.

103. ICC, "Afternoon Meeting on March 2, 1959," WBR Day Care 1959, 1.

104. Ibid.

105. ICC, Meeting of the Executive Committee Pro Tem, April 29–30, 1959, WBR Day Care 1959, 7.

106. Leopold expected hearings to be held by the Senate Labor and Welfare Committee and the House Committee on Education and Labor; Leopold to Guggenheimer, March 4, 1959, WBR Day Care 1959.

107. Memo from Guggenheimer to ICC, April 6, 1959, WBR Day Care 1959.

108. As a tax-exempt organization, the ICC was supposed to spend no more than 5 percent of its time on legislative matters (ICC, Minutes of Membership Committee Meeting, September 15, 1959, CWLAC, box 23, folder 1, p. 1). In order to stay within this limit, the organization seems to have made a distinction between lobbying for legislation and working with administrative agencies to improve child care.

109. Dale to Leopold and Morrison, memo on ICC meeting, September 26 and 27, dated September 29, 1958, WBR Day Care 1959.

110. ICC, Meeting with National Agencies, January 8, 1959, WBR Day Care 1959, 2. See also Meeting of the Inter-City Day Care Committee, January 8, 1959, CWLAC, box 23, folder 1.

111. ICC, Metting with National Agencies, 4.

112. Ibid., 6. Accordingly, they decided to set up a national office. Until this point, they had been operating out of the offices of the Day Care Council of New York, of which Elinor Guggenheimer had long been an officer. See Cornelia Goldsmith to Day Care Council, June 8, 1959, CWLAC box 23, folder 1.

113. ICC, "Relation of Inter-City Committee for Day Care of Children to Other National Agencies" [1959], CWLAC, box 23, folder 1, 1.

114. Ibid., 2.

115. See chapter 5 of this book.

116. ICC, "The Request" [1960], CWLAC, box 23, folder 1, 2.

117. ICC, Executive Committee Meeting, April 29–30, 1959, 4.

118. The idea of holding a day care conference was first mentioned in May 1958; see Dale to Leopold and Morrison, "Day Care Meeting, Children's Bureau, May 28, 1958," June 5, 1958, WBR Day Care 1958, 1–2.

119. Ibid., 5.

120. ICC, Executive Committee Meeting, April 29–30, 1959, 5.

121. U.S. Department of Labor, News Release, May 6, 1959, WBR Day Care 1959, 1–2.

122. ICC, Minutes of Executive Committee Meeting, April 29–30, 1959, 1.

123. Memo, Dale to Leopold and Morrison, July 11, 1958, WBR Day Care 1958.

124. The Golden Anniversary conference was to occur roughly fifty years after the first WHC, which was held in 1909.

125. *White House Conference on Children and Youth* (newsletter; hereafter cited as WHC newsletter) [no. 1] (February 1959): 7.

126. WHC newsletter, no. 6 (July 1959), 5. This list of priorities was based on responses from twenty-four states; seventeen ranked services to handicapped children first; only ten gave day care (along with other welfare programs) high priority.

127. WHC, "Topic Guide," February 13, 1959, WBR, box 366, folder: White House Conference. The guide was prepared by Mary Ellen Goodman, coordinator of conference studies. Goodman was present at several subsequent meetings between the ICC and federal officials, so she had an opportunity to hear the ICC's responses to the guide's presentation of the day care issue.

128. ICC, Executive Committee Meeting, April 29–30, 1959; Guggenheimer to Ephraim R. Gomberg, Director of 1960 WHC, April 30, 1959, WBR Day Care 1959.

129. ICC, "Recommendations for Programs," April 30, 1959, WBR Day Care 1959, 1–2.

130. Ibid., 7.

131. ICC, untitled memo, April 30, 1959 [noted: "Rec'd from Guggenheimer, 4/30/59"], WBR Day Care 1958, 5–6.

132. The total number of invitations to be issued was 7,000; of these, 2,900 were to go to state delegates, 600 to public officials (both federal and state), 500 to international guests, and the remainder to the press, the President's National Committee and its subcommittees, and various civic and voluntary organizations. WHC newsletter, no. 6, 1.

133. Memo from ICC to Council of National Organizations on Child and Youth, August 1959, WBR Day Care 1959, 1.

134. ICC to Council of National Organizations on Child and Youth, August 1959, 1.

135. Ibid., 2.

136. Ibid.

137. Morrison also wanted to emphasize that the women who were working and using day care were doing so out of financial need. See Draft Minutes of Day Care Statistical Meeting, March 8, 1960, WBR box 366, folder: National Conference on the Day Care of Children, Pre (hereafter cited as WBR NC Pre), 2.

138. Ibid., 5–6.

139. CB and WB, Minutes of Meeting of Ad Hoc Advisory Committee on a Day Care Conference, November 4, 1959, WBR NC Pre, 6.

140. Ibid.

141. See Ruth Milkman, "Union Responses to Workforce Feminization in the United States," in *The Challenge of Restructuring: North American Labor Movements Respond,* ed. Jane Jenson and Rianne Mahon (Philadelphia: Temple University Press, 1993), 226–50.

142. Peterson may have been referring to the discussions of women's motives that took place at the meetings of the NMC; see chapter 5 of this book.

143. Washington Meeting of Ad Hoc Advisory Committee on Day Care Conference, March 8, 1960, WBR NC Pre, 3.

144. Ibid., 2.

145. Memo, Moore to Leopold, April 6, 1960, WBR NC Pre, 2; for the ICC's earlier position, see "Relation of ICC to Other National Agencies," 2.

146. Minutes of Ad Hoc Advisory Committee for the Day Care Conference, June 16, 1960, WBR NC Pre, 2.

147. Ibid.

148. Winifred Moore to Staff Responsible for Day Care Conference, July 12, 1960, WBR NC Pre, 4–5.

149. WB, "Who Are the Working Mothers?" pamphlet, WBR, box 366, folder: National Conference on the Day Care of Children, November 17–18, 1960.

150. Draft Minutes of Day Care Statistical Meeting, WBR NC Pre, 1.

151. The sponsoring departments pledged that if discussion groups came up with recommendations that countered their own positions, they would still be free to express them. "Recommendations were the responsibility of the conference discussion groups. They would not reflect in any way the position of government agencies." Officials

believed, however, that "maximum benefit" would be gained by presenting findings "in the light of manpower shortage." WB and CB, Meeting on Day Care Conference Planning, September 21, 1960, WBR NC Pre, 1.

152. The abbreviation for the new organization was the same as that for the National Conference on the Day Care of Children, but I use it only to refer to the organization.

153. NCDCC, "Excerpts Related to the Day Care of Children" [n.d.; summer 1960?], WBR, box 366, folder: White House Conference, 4–6.

154. Ibid., 7.

155. Ibid., 9.

156. Ibid., 10–11.

157. Ibid., 17.

158. Ibid., 18.

159. Ibid., 18.

160. Ibid.

161. Ibid., 9–10.

162. Ibid.

163. Ethel Beer, "Providing for the Children of Working Mothers Here and Abroad," *Social Service Review* 26 (1952): 417.

164. ICC Minutes, September 15, 1959, 10.

165. Ewan Clague, "Economic Factors Affecting Day Care for Children," National Conference on the Day Care of Children, November 17, 1960, WBR NC Pre, 5–6. Clague was right on both counts; by 1970, nearly 50 percent of all women, and 40 percent of mothers, were employed.

166. Ibid., 7.

167. The choice of Guggenheimer as a keynote speaker was by no means automatic; WB and CB officials considered more than a dozen names before settling on her. See internal memos, WBR NC Pre.

168. Mrs. Randolph Guggenheimer, "Why Day Care?" National Conference on Day Care for Children, November 17–18, 1960, WBR NC Pre, 1.

169. Ibid., 2.

170. Ibid., 4.

171. "First National Conference Termed Successful," *Day Care Council [of New York] Newsletter* 2, no. 1 (January 1961): 3.

172. Ibid.

173. Abstract of remarks by Mrs. Katherine Oettinger, National Conference on Day Care of Children, November 18, 1960, WBR NC Pre.

174. Joseph Reid of the CWLA, who also attended the conference, emphasized, "The number one priority is to convince the public of the need for day care and gain its understanding"; Gertrude L. Hoffman, comp., *Day Care Services: Form and Substance*, CB Pub. No. 393 and WB Pub. No. 281 (Washington: GPO, 1961), 14.

175. Ibid., 5. Although Guggenheimer was criticizing her contemporaries, she might just as well have been chiding members of the NFDN who were expressing lukewarm support for their cause around the turn of the century.

176. Ibid., 6.

177. Ibid., 7–8.
178. WB and CB, "Day Care of Children under Twelve: Findings of a Survey on the Resources of National Organizations as Reported to the WB and CB, March 1959," October 1960, WB box 366, folder: National Conference on Day Care of Children, 7.
179. Ibid., 8.
180. Ibid., 10; emphasis added.
181. See the full anecdote in chapter 1 of this book.
182. Guggenheimer, "Why Day Care?" 12–13.
183. Hoffman, *Day Care Services*, 13–14. When Edythe Lutzker, former president of the Child Care Parents Association, heard about this, she could not resist writing to JFK to congratulate him; Lutzker to JFK, CCPAR, box 2, folder 16.

CHAPTER 7: A DIVIDED CONSTITUENCY

1. Children's Defense Fund, *The State of America's Children, 1992* (Washington, D.C.: Children's Defense Fund, 1992), 125.
2. Ibid., 17.
3. For a sensitive discussion of the differences among low-income, lower-middle-class, and middle-class clienteles, see Caroline Zinsser, *Raised in East Urban: Child Care Changes in a Working Class Community* (New York: Teachers College Press, 1991); on upper-class preferences for in-home caregivers, see Julia Wrigley, *Other People's Children* (New York: Basic Books, 1995).
4. Cynthia Harrison, *On Account of Sex: The Politics of Women's Issues, 1945–1968* (Berkeley: University of California Press, 1988), 157.
5. On this aspect of the legislation, see Gilbert Y. Steiner, *Social Insecurity: The Politics of Welfare* (Chicago: Rand McNally, 1965), esp. chap. 2; Joel Handler, *Reforming the Poor: Welfare Policy, Federalism, and Morality* (New York: Basic Books, 1972), chap. 4; and Richard K. Caputo, *Welfare and Freedom American Style, 2: The Role of the Federal Government, 1941–1980* (Lanham, Md.: University Press of America, 1994), chaps. 3 and 5.
6. This problem had been outlined in Henry C. Lajewski, *Child Care Arrangements of Full-Time Working Mothers,* Children's Bureau Publication No. 378 (Washington, D.C.: GPO, 1959); for a discussion of the origins of this publication, see chapter 5 of this book.
7. John F. Kennedy's Message to Congress, *Congressional Quarterly Almanac* (1962): 884.
8. Steiner, *Social Insecurity,* 44–45. Owing to technicalities, only $800,000 was appropriated in 1962 (for 1963); in subsequent years Congress proved reluctant to appropriate the full authorized amount, allocating only $3 million in 1963 and $2 million in 1964 (see *Congressional Quarterly Almanac* for those years). The low appropriations undermined the bill's child care provision, which was, at least theoretically, one of its more positive aspects.
9. Statement of Elinor Guggenheimer, U.S. Cong., House Committee on Ways and Means, *Public Welfare Amendments of 1962* (Washington, D.C.: GPO, 1962) (hereafter *1962 Hearings*), 416–19.
10. On the politics of the commission, see Harrison, *On Account of Sex,* pt. 3. The commis-

sion gave unprecedented national visibility to women not simply as mothers or defense workers but in their own right. Guggenheimer was appointed by Esther Peterson, an advocate for women's labor issues and child care, who succeeded Eleanor Roosevelt as head of the commission.

11. *American Women: Report of the President's Commission on the Status of Women* (Washington, D.C.: GPO, 1963), 19.

12. Ibid., 18–19; emphasis added.

13. Ibid., 19.

14. Ibid.; emphasis added.

15. Ibid., 21. The maximum joint income at which the deduction was allowable was, at that time, $5,100, but the median income for two-worker families had, by 1961, risen to $7,188.

16. Florence A. Ruderman, "Some Conclusions Drawn from the Child Welfare League Day Care Project," paper presented before the Maternal and Child Health Section of the American Public Health Association, October 6, 1964, CWLA collection, SWHA (hereafter CWLAC), box 23, folder 3, p. 4.

17. Florence A. Ruderman, "Day Care: A Challenge to Social Work," May 23, 1963, CWLAC, box 23, folder 3, p. 2.

18. Ibid., 2; emphasis added.

19. Ibid., 5; emphasis added.

20. Ibid., 5–6.

21. Ibid., 7.

22. Ibid., 9.

23. Ibid. In his foreword to the final report, CWLA Executive Director Joseph Reid distanced himself from some of these conclusions.

24. Milton Willner, "Day Care: A Reassessment," *Child Welfare* (March 1965): 129.

25. For detailed discussions of the jobs programs for women set up during this period, see Nancy E. Rose, *Workfare or Fair Work: Women, Welfare, and Government Work Programs* (New Brunswick, N.J.: Rutgers University Press, 1995), esp. chap. 4; and Sharon L. Harlan and Ronnie J. Steinberg, eds., *Job Training for Women: The Promise and Limits of Public Policies* (Philadelphia: Temple University Press, 1989), pt. 4.

26. This principle had become somewhat diluted in the 1930s, when mothers' and widows' pensions were incorporated into the Social Security Act and the pool of mothers was divided into an elite group that was eligible for non-means-tested survivors' benefits (a group that comprised mainly white women who had been married to wage earners in protected occupations) and a non-elite group that had to apply for Aid to Dependent Children, which required means testing and investigation and often rejected applicants on arbitrary and discriminatory grounds. See Winifred Bell, *Aid to Dependent Children* (New York: Columbia University Press, 1965), pt. 1.

27. See Joel Handler, "The Transformation of Aid to Families with Dependent Children: The Family Support Act in Historical Context," *New York University Review of Law and Social Change* 16 (1987–88): 489–91.

28. U.S. Department of Health, Education, and Welfare, *Social Security Programs in the United States* (Washington, D.C.: GPO, 1968), 96. After 1960 the number of recipients

rose even more steeply, from 3 million in 1960 to 9 million in 1970, 10 million in 1971, and more than 11 million by 1975. Thus the number tripled between 1960 and 1970; had the pace continued, there would have been 19 million recipients by 1980, but it actually began to level off in 1972 and even declined after 1975. See U.S. Department of Health and Human Services, *Social Security Bulletin* (Annual Statistical Supplement, 1977–79, September 1980): 248; cited in Mildred Rein, *Dilemmas of Welfare Policy: Why Work Strategies Haven't Worked* (New York: Praeger, 1982), 3.

29. Bell, *Aid to Dependent Children,* pt. 2.

30. Gwendolyn Mink, *The Wages of Motherhood: Inequality in the Welfare State, 1917–1942* (Ithaca: Cornell University Press, 1995), 182. The proportion of nonwhites included both African Americans and other people of color. Those who were still rebuffed now turned to the burgeoning civil rights movement for assistance with appeals and hearings, leading to a shift in the racial balance among recipients.

31. See Rose, *Workfare or Fair Work,* 89–90.

32. Statement of Abraham Ribicoff, *1962 Hearings,* 63ff. Ribicoff later conceded that he and his colleagues in the Kennedy administration were perhaps overly optimistic about the efficacy of rehabilitation programs; see Ribicoff, *America Can Make It!* (New York: Atheneum, 1972), chap. 6.

33. For an overview of the crafting of this legislation, see "Antipoverty Program Survives Assault, Gets $1.8 Billion," *Congressional Quarterly Almanac* (1967): 1058–86.

34. See *Social Security Amendments of 1967: Hearings before the Senate Committee on Finance,* 89th Cong., 1st sess. (Washington, D.C.: GPO, 1967), passim.

35. On the shortcomings of these programs with regard to women, see U.S. Civil Rights Commission, *Child Care and Equal Opportunity for Women,* Clearinghouse Publication No. 67 (June 1981), chap. 4; Rein, *Dilemmas of Welfare Policy,* chaps. 4 and 7; and Sharon Harlan, "Women and Federal Job Training Policy," and Judith Gueron, "Work Programs for Welfare Recipients," both in Harlan and Steinberg, *Job Training for Women.*

36. California, for example, with its long history of state-sponsored child care, was primed to make good use of federal funds, although local child care centers resisted at first, "fearing that federal money would change their character by restricting publicly subsidized child care to the poor, strengthening the welfare-oriented goals, and further downgrading the public's image of child care. But fiscal pressure was too great"; W. Norton Grubb and Marvin Lazerson, "Child Care, Government Financing, and the Public Schools: Lessons from the California Children's Centers," *School Review* 86, no. 1 (November 1977): 16. See also G. Brook DeVine, "Report on the California Children's Center Program: Its Needs, Resources, and Relation to Other Programs," prepared for the Department of Finance, State of California, August 1970; and "Children's Center Program Review: Interagency Contract between Department of Social Welfare and Department of Education," Program Assessment Branch, Department of Social Welfare, State of California, May 31, 1972. See also Monica Herk, "Helping the Hand That Rocks the Cradle: The Politics of Child Care at the State Level," Ph.D. diss., Princeton University, 1993, chap. 7. Herk also discusses the impact of this legislation more generally.

37. See Joel F. Handler and Ellen Jane Hollingsworth, "Work, Welfare, and the Nixon Reform Proposals," *Stanford Law Review* 22 (1970): 907–42.

38. Daniel Patrick Moynihan, *The Negro Family: The Case for National Action* (Washington, D.C.: Office of Policy Planning and Research, U.S. Department of Labor, March 1965). Except for a few feminists, most analysts of this report have ignored its blatant sexist assumptions; see, for example, Dona Cooper Hamilton and Charles V. Hamilton, *The Dual Agenda: The African-American Struggle for Civil and Economic Equality* (New York: Columbia University Press, 1997), 135–38. For an excellent feminist analysis, see Wahneema Lubiano, "Black Ladies, Welfare Queens, and State Minstrels: Ideological War by Narrative Means," in *Race-ing Justice, En-Gendering Power: Essays on Anita Hill, Clarence Thomas, and the Construction of Social Reality,* ed. Toni Morrison (New York: Pantheon, 1992), 323–63; also Margaret Cerullo and Marla Erlien, "Beyond the 'Normal Family': A Cultural Critique of Women's Poverty," in *For Crying Out Loud: Women's Poverty in the United States,* ed. Diane Dujon and Ann Withorn (Boston: South End Press, 1996), 369–78.

39. Martha Griffiths in U. S. Congress, Economic Committee, Subcommittee on Fiscal Policy, *Income Maintenance Programs* (Washington, D.C.: GPO, 1968), 77.

40. The following discussion draws on the excellent article by John R. Nelson, Jr., "The Politics of Federal Day Care Regulation," in *Day Care: Scientific and Social Policy Issues,* ed. Edward F. Zigler and Edmund W. Gordon (Boston: Auburn House, 1982), 267–306.

41. Although the pragmatists were probably unconscious of the continuities, their arguments echoed decades of rationales by philanthropists for providing "custodial" care for the children of the poor.

42. For one participant's richly detailed description of efforts to establish Head Start in one state, see Polly Greenberg, *The Devil Wears Slippery Shoes: A Biased Biography of the Child Development Group of Mississippi* (London: Macmillan, 1969).

43. According to Nelson, "Soon after the promulgation of FIDCR, informal assurances were passed . . . through HEW's regional offices to the states that the requirements would not be enforced" ("Politics of Regulation," 276). This meant that states could more or less continue to do what they wanted to; at least one, New Jersey, set up separate standards for child care for WIN children that were clearly *less stringent* than those for nonsubsidized care. See Herk, "Helping the Hand," 300.

44. Nelson, "Politics of Regulation," 278.

45. Sheila Rothman, "Other People's Children: The Day Care Experience in America," *Public Interest* (Winter 1973): 22.

46. See *Social Security and Welfare Proposals,* Hearings before the House Committee on Ways and Means, October and November 1969 (Washington, D.C.: GPO, 1970), pt. 4, Oct. 28, 30, 31; *Comprehensive Preschool Education and Child Day Care Act of 1969,* Hearings before the House Committee on Education and Labor, Select Subcommittee on Education, November and December 1969 and February and March 1970 (Washington, D.C.: GPO, 1970); and *Headstart Child Development Act,* Hearings before the Subcommittee on Employment, Manpower, and Poverty of the Senate Committee on Labor and Public Welfare (Washington, D.C.: GPO, 1970), pt. 1.

47. Nixon vetoed H.R. 10351, a bill to extend programs under the Office of Economic Opportunity (OEO), which included the provisions of the CCDA. Although he was generally hostile to the OEO, his veto message implied that he was aiming specifically at the child care and child development provisions.

48. Gilbert Y. Steiner, *The Children's Cause* (Washington, D.C.: Brookings Institution, 1976), 91.

49. U.S. President's Task Force on Women's Rights and Responsibilities (hereafter Task Force), *A Matter of Simple Justice* (Washington, D.C.: GPO, April 1970), 13.

50. See hearings listed in n. 46 above.

51. Quoted in *Congressional Quarterly* (March 19, 1971): 619.

52. The most comprehensive discussion of the career of this legislation may be found in Caputo, *Welfare and Freedom,* chap. 7.

53. The deduction would be raised to $750 for one child, $1,125 for two, and $1,500 for three or more, with a ceiling of $12,000 for adjusted gross income; under existing law, the amounts were $600 for one child, $900 for two or more, with a ceiling of $6,000. *Congressional Quarterly* (June 4, 1971): 1205.

54. Task Force, *A Matter,* 13–14. Nixon's use of FAP as a rationale was more than a bit disingenuous, because it was not actually a viable alternative at the time of the veto; the Nixon administration, brought up short by attacks on the plan from the left and especially the right, had basically abandoned it by then; see Caputo, *Welfare and Freedom,* 490–92; and Joan Hoff, *Nixon Reconsidered* (New York: Basic Books, 1994), chap. 4.

55. According to Gilbert Steiner, a contemporary policy analyst, "Every version of the . . . legislation promised more than the money it authorized could buy" and thus suffered from a lack of realism; *Children's Cause,* 112.

56. For a comprehensive discussion of Edelman's efforts, see Greenberg, *Devil Wears Slippery Shoes.*

57. Steiner, *Children's Cause,* 111.

58. Kimberly Morgan, "Race and the Politics of American Child Care," paper presented at the Comparative Research on Welfare States and Gender conference, University of Wisconsin-Madison, February 1, 1997.

59. "Excerpts from Nixon's Veto Message," *New York Times* (December 10, 1971): 20.

60. For a similar ideological stance in postwar West Germany, see Robert Moeller, *Protecting Motherhood: Women and the Family in the Politics of Postwar West Germany* (Berkeley: University of California Press, 1993).

61. In 1971, socialist feminists in Cambridge, Massachusetts, succeeded in passing a referendum calling for free, 24-hour, community-controlled child care, but the city never came up with the mandated services. See Vicki Breitbart, comp., *The Day Care Book: The Why, What and How of Community Day Care* (New York: Knopf, 1974).

62. For an overview of feminist positions on child care, see Lauri Umansky, *Motherhood Reconceived: Feminism and the Legacies of the Sixties* (New York: New York University Press, 1996), 46–50.

63. "NOW Bill of Rights," flyer in "NOW" file, n.d., Schlesinger Library, quoted in ibid., 46.

64. The 1972 bill passed the Senate but was blocked in the House, a still more diluted 1975 bill passed both houses but was vetoed by Ford, and a 1979 bill introduced by Senator Alan Cranston (Democrat–California) died in committee. For one participant's perspective on this campaign, see Edward F. Zigler and Jody Goodman, "The Battle for Day Care in America: A View from the Trenches," in Zigler and Gordon, *Day Care,* 338–50.

65. For detailed descriptions of some of these centers, see the case studies by Robert Ruopp, Sally Zeckhauser, and Brigid O'Farrell, in *A Study in Child Care,* sponsored by the Office of Economic Opportunity, vol. II-A (Washington, D.C.: U.S. Department of Health, Education, and Welfare/Office of Education National Center for Educational Communication, [1970?]).

66. In such cases, moving into a higher-paying job would result in either no gain or a loss, depending on how great the pay increase was in relation to child care costs. See discussion of this issue in Civil Rights Commission, *Child Care,* 19–20.

67. Ibid., 20.

68. A study of low-income black families in south central Los Angeles in the mid-1970s found that although there was generally a shortage of child care in the area, many day care slots went unfilled, even though parents preferred this type of care, because they were not subsidized and parents could not afford them. As a result, some high-cost centers with few or no subsidized slots had to close because of underenrollment, while subsidized family day care slots remained empty. See Karen Hill-Scott, "Child Care in the Black Community," *Journal of Black Studies* 10, no. 1 (September 1970): 78–97. It is likely that these parents relied on relatives instead. In "Day Care: A Black Perspective" (in Zigler and Gordon, *Day Care*), Evelyn Moore of the Black Child Development Institute points out that in the mid-1970s, this pattern persisted in black communities (425), much as it had in the 1940s and earlier (see chapter 4 of this book).

69. During the Nixon administration, HEW had appointed Yale child psychologist Edward Zigler to redraft the original FIDCR. In an attempt to make the requirements more "enforceable," he diluted them, but Nixon still objected to the idea of overriding state laws with federal regulations. Zigler's version, as a result, assumed the status of "guidelines"; see Nelson, "Politics of Regulation," 278.

70. Civil Rights Commission, *Child Care,* 20.

71. Ibid., 31.

72. See Moore, "Day Care," 427–28.

73. Alfred J. Kahn and Sheila B. Kamerman, *Child Care: Facing the Hard Choices* (Dover, Mass.: Auburn House, 1987), 19–22.

74. The Job Training Partnership Act was also less favorable to women than CETA in terms of its effectiveness in training them for "good" jobs (those that were well paying and carried benefits); see Harlan, "Women and Federal Job Training Policy," 73–82.

75. Exceptions were Head Start spending, which increased by about 50 percent, and the child care food program, which nearly doubled. Neither of these, however, affected the supply of affordable child care.

76. Kahn and Kamerman, *Child Care,* 106. It is important to distinguish here between voluntary and for-profit private child care providers; most proprietaries resisted higher standards because they cut into profit margins. See Sharon L. Kagan and Theresa

Glennon, "Considering Proprietary Child Care," in Zigler and Gordon, *Day Care,* 402–12.

77. Helen Blank, *Child Care and Federal Child Care Cuts* (Washington, D.C.: Children's Defense Fund, 1983), 5–7; summarized in Kahn and Kamerman, *Child Care,* 22.

78. Arthur Y. Webb, letter to the editor, *New York Times,* August 9, 1982, A14.

79. Such services were generally offered to mid- or upper-level (middle-class) employees; see the discussion of employer-supported child care later in this chapter.

80. Kahn and Kamerman, *Child Care,* 19–21; 195–96.

81. Although I realize that this is somewhat problematic, I am taking the category "married mothers, husbands present" as a surrogate for working class or middle class, that is, for families that were likely to have a stable income.

82. Kagan and Glennon, "Proprietary Care," 407.

83. Ibid., 403.

84. Kahn and Kamerman, *Child Care,* chap. 4. See also Kagan and Glennon, "Proprietary Care"; and Cheryl D. Hayes, John L. Palmer, and Martha J. Zaslow, eds., *Who Cares for America's Children? Child Care Policy for the 1990s* (Washington, D.C.: National Academy Press, 1990), 159–62.

85. Not all feminists agreed with this strategy. Some socialist feminists believed that it was more "revolutionary" to "struggle with the establishment" (businesses, universities, and the government) and "make demands on the system" for public services than to set up "counterinstitutions" that would necessarily exclude women who had no time to contribute and also let public institutions off the hook. See "The Nature of Change and Political Action—Reform vs. Revolution," in "Women's Liberation, Berkely, CA" file, Schlesinger Library, 2, quoted in Umansky, *Motherhood Reconceived,* 48.

86. In some instances, people who were initially willing to care for children of relatives branched out to take in nonrelated children, charging fees for services they had previously provided to kin for nothing; see Zinsser, *Raised in East Urban,* chaps. 1–3.

87. The proportion of families using this type of care peaked in 1965 at 18.5 percent; by 1990, it had fallen to 3 percent. See table 7.2 and Sandra Hofferth et al., *National Child Care Survey, 1990* (Washington, D.C.: Urban Institute Press, 1991).

88. The term is Pierrette Hondagneu-Sotelo's; see "I'm Here, but I'm There: The Meanings of Transnational Latina Motherhood," *Gender and Society* 11, no. 5 (October 1997): 548–71.

89. Hayes et al., *Who Cares for America's Children?* 160.

90. See Lynet Uttal, "Racial Safety and Cultural Maintenance: The Childcare Concerns of Employed Mothers of Color," in *Families, Kinship and Domestic Politics in the U.S.: Critical Feminist Perspectives,* ed. Anita Garey and Karen Hansen (Philadelphia: Temple University Press, 1998).

91. C. Avrin and G. Sassen, *Corporations and Child Care: Profitmaking Day Care; Workplace Day Care; and a Look at Alternatives* (Cambridge, Mass.: Women's Research Action Project, 1974); cited in Kagan and Glennon, "Proprietary Care," 408.

92. Television aside, the scene was reminiscent of the rigid, underfunded New York City day nurseries that Reed and Raymond had studied in the 1920s; see discussion of Mary E. Reed and E. Mae Raymond, "Day Nurseries, Nursery Schools, and Kinder

gartens in Six Settlements in New York City" [1929], in chapter 3 of this book.

93. Joseph Featherstone, "The Day Care Problem: Kentucky Fried Children," *New Republic* 163, nos. 10–11 (September 5 and 12, 1970): 12–16.

94. Ibid., 15.

95. J. Travers and R. Ruopp, *National Day Care Study: Preliminary Findings and Their Implications* (Cambridge, Mass.: Abt Associates, 1978).

96. Kagan and Glennon, "Proprietary Care," 406.

97. *Who Cares? Child Care Teachers and the Quality of Care in America,* Executive Summary of the National Child Care Staffing Study (Oakland, Calif.: Child Care Employee Project, 1989), 4.

98. Ibid.

99. Samuel Weiner, "The Child Care Market in Seattle and Denver," in *Child Care and Public Policy,* ed. P. Robin and S. Weiner (Lexington, Mass.: D. C. Heath, 1978).

100. Kagan and Glennon, "Proprietary Care," 410.

101. See Zinsser, *Raised in East Urban.*

102. Hayes et al., *Who Cares for America's Children?* 151–56.

103. In some cases this self-effacing stance allowed them to avoid the wrath of a spouse who opposed employment for women in general, or for his wife in particular.

104. Kahn and Kamerman, *Child Care,* 40–43.

105. Ibid., 226–29; the states were Connecticut, Illinois, Massachusetts, Minnesota, Nebraska, North Dakota, Texas, and Wisconsin.

106. Ibid., 230–31.

107. Ellen Galinsky, Carollee Howes, Susan Kontos, and Marybeth Shinn, *The Study of Children in Family Child Care and Relative Care: Highlights of Findings* (New York: Families and Work Institute, 1994), 45–46.

108. Ibid.

109. See Wrigley, *Other People's Children;* see also Hondagneu-Sotelo, "I'm Here, but I'm There."

110. Clinton attempted to appoint two different female lawyers as attorney general, Zoë Baird and Kimba Wood, both of whom were accused of violating Social Security laws regarding payments to their nannies; on the Baird case, see "Childlessness Equals Accountability," *Harvard Law Record* (February 26, 1993); on Wood, see Ronald J. Ostrow and David Lauter, "Kimba Wood Emerges as No. 1 Attorney General Candidate," *Los Angeles Times* (February 5, 1993): 2.

111. These programs included child care centers (both on- and off-site), voucher plans, after-school activities, and other schemes whose evolution will be discussed below. Because of the variety, it is difficult to calculate the total number of children being served at any one time. As late as 1990, employer-supported child care accounted for only a small proportion of the 10 million children receiving nonparental care: 38 percent in child care centers (some of them employer sponsored), 27 percent from relatives, 20 percent in family day care homes, 5.6 percent from an unrelated caregiver in their own homes, and 9.1 percent in other arrangements. Children's Defense Fund, *America's Children, 1992,* 17.

112. See chapter 4 of this book.

113. There was in general a scarcity of child care facilities during this period, and there was also a dearth of regulation and of trained personnel. See *Employed Mothers and Child Care,* U.S. Women's Bureau Publication No. 246 (Washington, D.C.: GPO, 1953).

114. Some of the earliest examples were in New Jersey, Ohio, and Tennessee. See Susan Rimby Leighow, "An 'Obligation to Participate': Married Nurses' Labor Force Participation in the 1950s," in *Not June Cleaver: Women and Gender in Postwar America, 1945–1960,* ed. Joanne Meyerowitz (Philadelphia: Temple University Press, 1994), 48–49.

115. By 1977, there were between 150 and 200 existing employer-supported facilities, more than half of them linked to hospitals, health care, or nonprofit organizations; see David Robison, "Working Parents Choose Home-Based Child Care Arrangements," *World of Work Report* 2, no. 2 (February 1977): 20. This trend continued; a 1984 survey of U.S. companies found that firms in the health care industry had the highest rate of involvement in providing child care, including the most on-site facilities; see Karen Krett, "Maternity, Paternity and Child Care Policies," *Personnel Administrator* 30 (June 1985): 136.

116. "Latest Benefit to Employees—Day Care for Their Children," *U.S. News and World Report,* December 11, 1972: 65.

117. Many university-based centers were also used as laboratories for educational research and teacher training.

118. Sadie Ginsberg, "The Child Care Center Chronicle," in *Early Childhood Education: Living History Interviews,* comp. James L. Hymes, Jr., book 2, *Care of the Children of Working Mothers* (Carmel, Calif.: Hacienda Press, 1978), 14–15.

119. "Latest Benefit," 64.

120. The 1953 WB study found, for example, that employers in Dallas insisted that mothers make arrangements with relatives or neighbors, not child care centers, because centers, with their strict health requirements, would refuse to accept children who were sick, compelling mothers to take an absence from work; see WB, *Employed Mothers and Child Care,* WB Publication No. 246 (Washington, D.C.: GPO, 1953), 78.

121. See Mary Keyserling, *Windows on Day Care* (New York: National Council of Jewish Women, 1972).

122. See *Industry and Day Care 2,* proceedings of the Second National Conference on Industry and Day Care, ed. Eunice Schatz and Thea K. Flaum (Chicago: Urban Research Corporation, 1973).

123. "Northside Child Care Center Prospers with Business Know-How," *World of Work Report* 2, no. 2 (February 1977): 15. The Northside project both reflected and contributed to an overall predisposition toward civic responsibility on the part of business firms in the Twin Cities that seemed to prevail throughout the 1970s and 1980s. "The most important things in this city have happened at the initiative of the business community, not because of government," Minneapolis mayor Donald M. Fraser told the *New York Times* (July 27, 1981): A1.

124. Quoted in Belle Canon, "Child Care Where You Work," *Ms.* (April 1978): 85.

125. See Women's Bureau, *Federal Funds for Day Care Projects* (Washington, D.C.: U.S. Department of Labor, 1969). During the 1960s different types of funding were also available through the Model Cities program and the Office of Economic Opportunity.

126. For instance, in 1972, the owner of a million-dollar paper-processing plant in Pennsylvania feared that his new factory would begin to molder unless he could secure a dependable labor force, but his low-wage female workers could not locate affordable child care. An on-site child care center proved so successful in lowering absenteeism and turnover that he decided he could provide *free* care for thirty-five children and still turn a profit. Anne Lorimer, "For Companies with Day Care, Big Dividends," *Philadelphia Inquirer* (January 31, 1982): 8-L.

127. Some sponsoring companies operated their centers directly, while others hired outside professionals or contracted with operators. No matter what the arrangement, publicity materials produced by the company touted the centers' emphasis on children's development, nutrition, and health.

128. "Latest Benefits," 66.

129. David Robison, "Working Parents Choose Home-Based Child Care Arrangements," *World of Work Report* 2, no. 2 (February 1977): 20.

130. Ibid.

131. Unions generally ignored female workers or failed to organize the sectors in which female workers predominated until the late 1970s and early 1980s; see Claudia Goldin, *Understanding the Gender Gap: An Economic History of American Women* (New York: Oxford, 1990), 210; and Teresa L. Amott and Julie A. Matthaei, *Race, Gender and Work: A Multicultural Economic History of Women in the United States* (Boston: South End Press, 1991), chap. 7.

132. "Clothing Union Opens Model Day Care Unit," *AFL-CIO News,* May 1, 1976, 8.

133. Joyce D. Miller, "The Urgency of Child Care," *AFL-CIO American Federationist,* June 1975, 1–8.

134. *Tax Incentives for Employer-Sponsored Day Care Programs,* Tax Angles and Tax Savings Series, CCH Editorial Staff Publication (Chicago: Commerce Clearing House, 1980), 21.

135. Feminists addressed demands toward the federal government and also began to criticize labor unions for failing to take up the issue. According to Muriel Tuteur, director of ACTWU's Chicago child care center and a member of the Coalition of Labor Union Women (CLUW), child care was not a "gut issue" for male union leaders. "Until women take hold of that issue," Tuteur told a *New York Times* reporter, "we are not going to see a heck of a lot happen"; "Better Child Care Urged as a Support to Family," *New York Times* (November 20, 1979): B11.

136. Goldin, *Understanding the Gender Gap,* 74–75.

137. Liz Roman Gallese, "Moms and Pops Get Break as Employers Sponsor Day Care," *Wall Street Journal* (May 9, 1980): 17.

138. Ibid.

139. One hospital administrator, for example, concluded that it was less expensive to sponsor child care than to have to recruit nurses on an ongoing basis. "Why should I

spend $150,000 advertising throughout the country for nurses, when I can spend $50,000 underwriting the center to take care of their kids?" asked Joe DiLorenzo, administrator of the Park View Hospital in Nashville. Paul B. Brown, "Band-Aids by the Boxcar," *Forbes* 128 (August 31, 1981): 88.

140. Lorimer, "For Companies with Day Care," 1-L. One Boston bank was not so fortunate: in 1982 it lost eight female vice-presidents who had become pregnant, after failing to reach an accommodation with them about working part time. This bank's experience prompted other banks in the city to quickly reassess their policy regarding hours. See Diane Casselberry Manuel, "Business Responds to Family Concerns," *Christian Science Monitor* (May 10, 1982): 17.

141. Dana E. Friedman, "Company, Community Forces Shape Response to Family," *World of Work Report* (February 1983): 13.

142. Jacquelyn McCroskey, "Work and Families: What Is the Employer's Responsibility?" *Personnel Journal* 61, no. 1 (January 1982): 32–33.

143. McCroskey, "Work and Families," 30.

144. See Clifford Baden and Dana E. Friedman, eds., *New Management Initiatives: Reports from an April 1981 Conference* (Boston: Wheelock College, 1981).

145. "Employers offering even limited child-care assistance" often received complaints and heard expressions of resentment from nonparents, Joann S. Lublin reported; see "The New Interest in Corporate Day Care," *Wall Street Journal* (April 20, 1981): 18.

146. The 1981 Boston conference devoted an entire workshop to this subject; see Baden and Friedman, *New Management Initiatives,* 99–103.

147. Judy Foreman, "Working Parents Do Better in Boston," *Boston Globe* (April 8, 1981): 63.

148. These included Con Agra Refrigerated Foods, which operates plants on round-the-clock shifts, many of them located in rural areas where quality child care is hard to find, and Levi Strauss, with a largely female, low-wage workforce. Both started programs for low- to moderate-income families in the early 1990s. See Anne Mitchell, Louise Stoney, and Harriet Dichter, *Financing Child Care in the United States: An Illustrative Catalogue of Current Strategies* (Kansas City, Missouri, and Philadelphia: Ewing Marion Kauffman Foundation and the Pew Charitable Trusts, 1997), 68–71.

149. Ibid., 72–73.

150. Ibid., 74–75. Similar strategies have been used by Corporate Champions in Charlotte, North Carolina; Seattle; Fort Worth; Denver; Rochester; and other cities.

151. T. Berry Brazelton, M.D., *Working and Caring* (Reading, Mass.: Addison-Wesley, 1985).

152. Statement by Bettye Caldwell, *Comprehensive Preschool Education Hearings,* 331–44.

153. See Bettye M. Caldwell, "A Comprehensive Model for Integrating Child Care and Early Childhood Education," *Teachers College Record* 90 (1989): 404–14; and Caldwell, "Early Childhood Programs at Home and Abroad," *Journal of Clinical Psychology* 20 (1991): 94–101.

154. See, for example, Phyllis Schlafly, ed., *Who Will Rock the Cradle? The Battle for Control of Child Care in America* (Dallas: Word Publishing, 1989).

155. Alexa Klimas, "Why Did We Believe the Children? A Closer Look at Allegations of Sexual Abuse in Day Care Centers in the 1980s," B.A. thesis, Princeton University, 1995, chap. 2.

156. For a devastating exposé of the dubious allegations and shoddy investigatory methods that gave rise to mass hysteria, see Debbie Nathan and Michael Snedeker, *Satan's Silence: Ritual Abuse and the Making of a Modern American Witch Hunt* (New York: Basic Books, 1995). See also Klimas, "Why Did We Believe?" and David Finkelhor and Linda Meyer Williams, with Nanci Burns, *Nursery Crimes: Sexual Abuse in Day Care* (Newbury Park, Calif.: Sage, 1988).

157. Victoria Pope, "Children's Hour," *U.S. News and World Report* 123, no. 12 (September 29, 1997): 4.

158. Although family providers did not generally disapprove of their own daughters or daughters-in-law working outside the home and leaving their children to be cared for by their grandmothers, they did tend to disapprove of the *other* (nonrelative) mothers who were their clients. On the tensions inherent in a relationship between caregivers who believe strongly in the importance of having children cared for by either their mothers or other close relatives, and parents (especially mothers) who choose to place their children in care with nonrelatives outside the home, see Zinsser, *Raised in East Urban;* Margaret K. Nelson, "Providing Family Care: An Analysis of Home-Based Work," *Social Problems* 35, no. 1 (1988): 78–94; Margaret K. Nelson, "A Study of Turnover among Family Day Care Providers," *Children Today* (March–April, 1990): 8–12; and Margaret K. Nelson, *Negotiated Care: The Experience of Family Day Care Providers* (Philadelphia: Temple University Press, 1990).

159. See Wrigley, *Other People's Children.*

160. In this sense the legislative situation was similar to that of 1971, when Congress was simultaneously considering the Family Assistance Plan and the Comprehensive Child Development Act.

161. Historically and typically, child allowances are offered by governments as a pronatalist measure; this has been the case, for example, in France and Germany, particularly during postwar periods. From the 1960s through the 1990s, left-wing Swedish feminists repeatedly opposed efforts on the part of the bourgeois parties to institute care allowances on the grounds that not all women (i.e., nonmothers) would be able to take advantage of them. See Celia Winkler, "The Canary in the Coal Mine: Single Mothers and the Welfare State, the Swedish Experience," Ph.D. dissertation, University of Oregon, 1996, 205–14. The rationale for Bush's proposal seemed simply to be an effort to counter the demand for child care and demonstrate that he upheld family values. There was little opposition to this proposal from U.S. feminists, and in any case it did not go very far.

162. Mary Frances Berry, *The Politics of Parenthood: Child Care, Women's Rights, and the Myth of the Good Mother* (New York: Viking, 1993), 193–94.

163. Some states and localities were more effective in gaining public support for child care during this period. Among the measures put in place were local property taxes, state and local sales taxes, fees, and lotteries. Some were devoted exclusively to child care, whereas others included child care as part of a bundle of services and provisions for children; for a detailed overview of these new sources of public revenue, see Mitchell et al., *Financing Child Care,* 7–45.

164. It is ironic that this same group of mothers had only recently been denounced for their alleged parental irresponsibility.

165. Galinsky et al., *Children in Family Child Care*, 6. This is not the first time that child care has been promoted as a form of workfare; the WIN program of the late 1960s and early 1970s also attempted to channel welfare mothers into this occupation. In her 1977 bestseller *Every Child's Birthright: In Defense of Mothering* (New York: Basic Books), child psychoanalyst Selma Fraiberg criticized this practice on both psychological and economic grounds (chap. 4). Unfortunately, Fraiberg's critique was embedded in a blanket rejection of child care in general as "impersonal" and far inferior to mothers' care.

166. See, for example, laudatory articles such as "Child-Care Solutions in a New World of Welfare," *New York Times* (June 1, 1997): A1, A15.

167. Middle-class women have, however, formed several national organizations, including "Mothers at Home" and "Stay-at-Home Mothers," to defend their decision to leave the workforce to care for their own children. See the "S.A.M. [Stay-At-Home Mothers] Newsletter" on the World-Wide Web: http://members.aol.com/Samnewsltr/samnews.htm.

168. See Gøsta Esping-Andersen, *The Three Worlds of Welfare Capitalism* (Princeton: Princeton University Press, 1990), chap. 1. For definitions of these terms, see the introduction to this book.

169. For the importance of similar ideals in other societies, see Jan Windebank, "To What Extent Can Social Policy Challenge the Dominant Ideology of Mothering? A Cross-National Comparison of Sweden, France and Britain," *Journal of European Social Policy* 6 (1996): 160.

170. NOW's interest in child care flagged when the chair of its child care committee, Joan Israel, stepped down to take a paid social service position in Detroit in 1971. See Joan Israel papers, Wayne State University Archives of Labor and Urban Affairs, boxes 2 and 3.

171. There is evidence that, as in the 1970s, low-wage working mothers are being pitted against those just moving from welfare to work in the competition for scarce subsidized public child care resources; see Sara Rimer, "Children of Working Poor Are Day Care's Forgotten," *New York Times* (November 25, 1997): 1, 13. The solution, according to a Florida welfare official, is to "base child care subsidies on income, not welfare status" (13). As a first step, a few states, including Illinois, Washington, and Rhode Island, have merged child care and other services for low-income families into one agency.

172. See Nancy Folbre, "Children as Public Goods," *American Economic Review* 84, no. 2 (May 1994): 86–90; see also Peter Baldwin, *The Politics of Social Solidarity* (New York: Cambridge University Press, 1990).

173. The Family and Medical Leave Act, signed into law by President Clinton in 1993, offers up to twelve weeks of leave for childbirth (among other things), but because it is unpaid, many new parents cannot afford to take advantage of it.

EPILOGUE

1. The report, published in New York in 1989 by the French-American Foundation, was written by Gail Richardson and Elisabeth Marx and based on the research of the

foundation's Child Care Study Panel, whose members included Hillary Rodham (later Clinton) and Bettye Caldwell.

2. This narrower approach is still useful in analyzing specific policy outcomes; see Yasmine Ergas, "Child-Care Policies in Comparative Perspective: An Introductory Discussion," in Organization for Economic Cooperation and Development (OECD), *Lone-Parent Families: The Economic Challenge,* (Paris: OECD, 1990): 173–99.

3. Gøsta Esping-Andersen, *The Three Worlds of Welfare Capitalism* (Princeton: Princeton University Press, 1990), chap. 1. Other terms include "social policy environment" (see Jan Windebank, "To What Extent Can Social Policy Challenge the Dominant Ideology of Mothering? A Cross-National Comparison of Sweden, France and Britain," *Journal of European Social Policy* 6 [1996]: 151) and "national policy-making style" (Vicky Randall, "The Irresponsible State? The Politics of Child Daycare Provision in Britain," *British Journal of Political Science* 25 [1995]: 333, following Jeremy Richardson, Gunnel Gustafsson, and Grant Jordan, "The Concept of Policy Style," in *Policy Styles in Western Europe,* ed. Jeremy Richardson [London: Allen and Unwin, 1982], 1–16). These terms, though useful, strike me as less historically dynamic and thoroughly political than Esping-Andersen's.

4. As Esping-Andersen puts it, "there is no single pure case"; elements from the other two types may become admixed in any given regime at one time or another; *Three Worlds,* 28–29. This is particularly true, I would add, because as democracies, these regimes are subject to periodic political shifts.

5. Vicky Randall argues that Britain, despite the expansion of its welfare state under postwar Labour governments (the National Health system being the most visible remaining vestige of that period), also falls into the liberal category; see "The Irresponsible State?" 344–45. For a historical account of this pattern, see David Marquand, *The Unprincipled Society* (London: Jonathan Cape, 1988), chap. 1.

6. Esping-Andersen, *Three Worlds,* 26–27.

7. Ibid., 27.

8. Ibid., 3.

9. See Orloff, "Gender and the Social Rights of Citizenship: The Comparative Analysis of Gender Relations and Welfare States," *American Sociological Review* 58 (1993): 303–28; and O'Connor, "Gender, Class and Citizenship in the Comparative Analysis of Welfare State Regimes: Theoretical and Methodological Issues," *British Journal of Sociology* 44 (1993): 501–18. For an excellent example of what such an index might look like in practice, see Janet C. Gornick, Marcia K. Meyers, and Katherin E. Ross, "Supporting the Employment of Mothers: Policy Variation across Fourteen Welfare States," *Journal of European Social Policy* 7 (1997): 45–70.

10. The use of feminist criteria may not entail a total realignment of Esping-Andersen's clusters (because states may take similar approaches toward policy making with regard to both women and men), but they are likely to reveal inconsistencies between degrees of decommodification and autonomy enhancement that require further explanation. By measuring the gap between these two indices in a given welfare-state regime, we can ascertain how much its policies favor one gender over the other.

11. Windebank, "Social Policy and the Ideology of Mothering."

12. Siv Gustafsson, "Childcare and Types of Welfare States," in *Gendering Welfare States,* ed. Diane Sainsbury (London: Sage, 1994), 60–61.

13. Patterns vary; in some societies, public child care has been eliminated entirely, while in others, efforts have been made to retain provisions. The new states of eastern Germany, for example, continue to offer highly subsidized state provisions; see William T. Gormley, Jr., "Kinderpolitik in Eastern Germany," manuscript, Department of Government and Public Policy Program, Georgetown University, Washington, D.C. [1995?]. For changes in other formerly Communist societies, see Nanette Funk and Magda Mueller, eds., *Gender Politics and Post-Communism: Reflections from Eastern Europe and the Former Soviet Union* (New York: Routledge, 1993).

14. Urie Bronfenbrenner refers to this as the "Anglo-Saxon mode"; see his "Child Care in the Anglo-Saxon Mode," in *Child Care in Context: Cross-Cultural Perspectives* ed. M. E. Lamb, K. J. Sternberg, C. P. Hwang, and A. G. Bromberg (Hillsdale, N.J.: Lawrence Erlbaum Associates, 1992). In Britain, current child care provisions, both public and private, are even scarcer than in the United States; see Randall, "Irresponsible State?"

15. See Barbara Hobson, "Feminist Strategies and Gendered Discourses in Welfare States: Married Women's Right to Work in the United States and Sweden," in *Mothers of a New World: Maternalist Politics and the Origins of Welfare States,* ed. Seth Koven and Sonya Michel (New York: Routledge, 1993), 396–430; also Barbara Hobson and Marika Lindholm, "Collective Identities, Women's Power Resources, and the Making of Welfare States," *Theory and Society* 26 (1997): 475–508.

16. For a detailed account of these debates, see Celia Winkler, "The Canary in the Coal Mine: Single Mother and the Welfare State, the Swedish Experience," Ph.D. diss., University of Oregon, 1996, chap. 5. See also Barbara Hobson, Stina Johansson, Livia Olah, and Caroline Sutton, "Gender and the Swedish Welfare State," in *Swedish Welfare: Policy and Provision,* ed. Edward Brunsdon and Margaret May (Stockholm: Social Policy Association, 1995), 3. Winkler notes that left-wing feminists also opposed child care provisions that targeted single mothers or low-income families; these feminists seem to have been acutely cognizant of the dangers of targeted programs and continually insisted on universal policies for reasons of equity as well as quality. The contrast between this and the typical American approach to social policy is striking.

17. Unlike the United States, Sweden did not experience a sharp split between early childhood education and charitable day nurseries in its pre-public child care phase; conversation with Katrin Hatje (Sweden's foremost historian of child care), Stockholm, July 15, 1994. Sweden's effort to use public child care to achieve social integration paralleled simultaneous efforts by American liberals to use early childhood programs to achieve racial integration; American efforts were, however, stymied when President Nixon vetoed the Comprehensive Child Development Act in 1971. See chapter 7 of this book.

18. Rianne Mahon, "Child Care in Canada and Sweden: Policy and Politics," *Social Politics* 4, no. 3 (Fall 1997): 390.

19. See Arnlaug Leira, *Welfare States and Working Mothers: The Scandinavian Experience* (Cambridge: Cambridge University Press, 1992). In 1993 the Swedish parliament passed a law mandating that the final month of a year's parental leave be taken by the father, but this has not resolved the problem completely; see Leira, "Caring and Social

Rights: What Does 'Daddy Leave' Entail?" paper presented at a conference on Gender, Citizenship and the Work of Caring, University of Illinois at Urbana-Champaign, November 14, 1997.

20. Mahon, "Child Care in Canada and Sweden," 392–418.

21. When the centrist parties came to power in 1991, they rescinded *Lex Pysslingen,* a law passed by the Social Democrats that banned commercial child care (Pysslingen, a famous character in Swedish children's literature, was the name taken by the child care company); the centrists also passed the care allowance that Social Democratic women had opposed since the 1960s. When the Social Democrats returned to power in 1994, they promptly restored *Lex Pysslingen* and rescinded the care allowance; ibid., 17. It should also be noted that commercial child care made little headway with Swedish parents.

22. For a detailed description of the French system, see Richardson and Marx, *A Welcome for Every Child.*

23. See Rachel Fuchs, *Abandoned Children: Foundlings and Child Welfare in Nineteenth-Century France* (Albany: State University of New York Press, 1984), 100.

24. "Report on Crèches," July 8, 1904, Public Control Committee, London County Council, Greater London Record Office; my thanks to Seth Koven for providing me with a copy of this document.

25. Laura Lee Downs, *Manufacturing Inequality: Gender Division in the French and British Metalworking Industries, 1914–1939* (Ithaca: Cornell University Press, 1995), 169–74. Note that it was this practice to which American maternalists Julia Lathrop and Josephine Dodge took great exception; see chapter 2 of this book.

26. For an overview of the politics of child care during this period, see Sian Reynolds, "Who Wanted the Crèches? Working Mothers and the Birth-Rate in France, 1900–1950," *Continuity and Change* 5, no. 2 (1990): 173–97. For a general discussion of the gender politics of family policy, see Herrick Chapman, "French Democracy and the Welfare State," in *The Social Construction of Democracy, 1870–1990,* ed. George Reid Andrews and Herrick Chapman (New York: New York University Press, 1995), 305–9.

27. Chapman, "French Democracy," passim.

28. These complicating developments were not mentioned in the seamless narrative of Richardson and Marx, *A Welcome for Every Child.*

29. Jane Jenson, "Childcare Policy in France: A Plurality of Provisions," paper prepared for the Workshop on Comparative Child Care Policy, Princeton University, July 1996.

30. I am suggesting not that this is optimal but simply that it does guarantee mothers a modicum of recognition as well as a secure income that is not, as in the case of AFDC in the United States, stigmatized. Swedish women, it should be noted, are counted as workers while they are on maternity leave, because their benefits are predicated on previous employment records and it is assumed that they will return to their positions.

31. A. Phillips and P. Moss, *Who Cares for Europe's Children? The Short Report of the European Childcare Network* (Luxembourg: Commission of the European Communities, 1989), 20–21.

32. See chapter 7 of this book.

33. Japan, though not included in Esping-Andersen's comparative mix of welfare-state

regimes, which is heavily weighted toward the West, would fit most readily into the category of corporatist conservative.

34. Sheldon Garon, "Child Care Policy in Japan," case study prepared for the Workshop on Comparative Child Care Policy, Princeton University, July 1996. Garon notes, "Although the Japanese government increasingly trumpeted the ideal of the 'good wife and wise mother' for aristocratic and middle-class women after 1899, the state expected most other women to work" (5).

35. See Thomas R. H. Havens, "Women and War in Japan, 1937–45," *American Historical Review* 80 (1975): 913–34.

36. Economic recovery was, of course, a priority for most other industrial societies during this period, but they addressed the need for labor in different ways. West Germany, for example, brought in *Gastarbeiter* (foreign workers) to fill unskilled and semi-skilled positions in industry and construction. The United States, with the most highly developed industrial infrastructure, reserved higher-level jobs for men, especially veterans, while women, including mothers, quietly (and with little governmental help in terms of child care) filled the growing demand for clerical and service workers (see chapters 5 and 6 of this book). Sweden later followed Japan's policy of opting to mobilize workers from its own female population, but this was not part of postwar economic recovery.

37. See Janet C. Gornick, Marcia K. Meyers, and Katherin E. Ross, "Public Policies and the Employment of Mothers: A Cross-National Study," Luxembourg Income Study (LIS), Working Paper 140 (July 1, 1996). On trends toward part-time work in many European countries in the 1980s, see Jane Jenson, Elisabeth Hagen, and Ceallaigh Reddy, eds., *Feminization of the Labor Force: Paradoxes and Promises* (New York: Oxford, 1988).

38. Garon, "Child Care Policy," 3.

39. See Joy Hendry, "The Role of the Professional Housewife," in *Japanese Women Working*, ed. Janet Hunter (London and New York: Routledge, 1993), 224–55. Given the nature of the political system, it is not surprising, as Barbara Molony points out, that Japanese women have been most successful in pressing their demands for both increased civil rights and improved work and family policies when those demands have been couched in maternalist and social eugenicist terms; see "Equality versus Difference: The Japanese Debate over 'Motherhood Protection,' 1915–50," in Hunter, *Japanese Women Working*, 122–48.

40. Deborah Brennan, *The Politics of Australian Child Care: From Philanthropy to Feminism* (Cambridge: Cambridge University Press, 1994).

41. Ibid., chap. 1. The development of Australian philanthropy was, on the whole, somewhat delayed in comparison to that in the other Anglo-American cases because of the specific history of Australian colonization and state formation.

42. Ibid., chap. 2.

43. For other aspects of the Whitlam government's impact on women, see Patricia Grimshaw, Marilyn Lake, Ann McGrath, and Marian Quartly, *Creating a Nation, 1788–1990* (Ringwood, Victoria, Australia: McPhee Gribble, 1994), chap. 13.

44. Brennan, *Australian Child Care*, 71. As Kimberly Morgan has pointed out (personal communication to the author, April 22, 1997), the negative role of children's and family professionals and bureaucrats in Australia contrasts with the positive role they played in

other societies such as Japan and Canada. As this book has shown, they also played a largely negative role in the United States.

45. On the turn to the private sector, see Brennan, *Australian Child Care,* chap. 9. Despite this shift, corporate child care still accounts for only a small percentage of Australia's provisions.

46. Ibid., 10.

47. See Deborah Brennan, *The Politics of Australian Child Care: Philanthropy to Feminism and Beyond,* rev. ed. (Cambridge: Cambridge University Press, 1998), chap. 10; information about reactions to the Howard government cuts is from a personal communication from Brennan, June 20, 1998.

48. Larry Prochner, "A Brief History of Daycare in Canada: The Early Years," *Canadian Children* 19, no. 2 (1994): 10–15.

49. Susan Prentice, "Struggles for and over Childcare Services in Postwar World War II Toronto," paper presented at the Ninth Berkshire Conference on the History of Women, Vassar College, 1993; see also Susan Prentice, "Militant Mothers in Domestic Times: Toronto's Postwar Child Care Struggle," Ph.d. diss., York University, 1993.

50. Prentice points out that in 1950 the Toronto Welfare Council engaged a team of American social workers to advise them on how to design a system of voluntary welfare services; see "Struggles for and over Childcare," 16–17. For the American discourse, see chapter 4 of this book.

51. Sue Colley, "Day Care and the Trade Union Movement in Ontario," *Resources for Feminist Research* 10, no. 2 (July 1981), 29–31; see also Mahon, "'Both Wage Earner *and* Mother,'" 33.

52. Damaris Rose, "'Collective Consumption' Revisited: Analysing Modes of Provision and Access to Childcare Services in Montreal, Quebec," *Political Geography Quarterly* (1990): 365–66.

53. Mahon, "'Both Wage Earner *and* Mother,'" 29.

54. Ibid., 34–35.

55. One exception is in Quebec, where feminist demands for public, parent-controlled child care have found a warm reception in the Parti québecois, which is concerned with addressing poverty issues, encouraging maternal employment, and preparing children for school; see Jane Jenson, "Two Models, Two Results: A Neo-Institutionalist Analysis of Child Care Reforms in France and Quebec," paper presented at a conference on Gender, Citizenship and the Work of Caring, University of Illinois at Urbana-Champaign, November 15, 1997.

56. This is being done through the Child Care Stimulation Act of 1990; Gustafsson, "Childcare," 55–56. The outcome of this effort is still unclear and currently under study; conversation with Trudie Knijn, Madison, Wisconsin, February 1, 1997.

57. Gornick et al. note that conservative-corporatist Italy and Belgium also have substantial child care provisions; "Supporting Employment," 60.

58. Jane Jenson, "Gender and the State: Making Sure That Where You Come Down Is Not Simply the Result of Where You Stand," paper presented at the conference on Comparative Research on Welfare States and Gender, University of Wisconsin-Madison, January 31, 1997.

59. Although feminist analysts such as Mahon, Orloff, and O'Connor would criticize such policies for limiting women's labor force participation, there may be another interpretation. Women's labor historian Dorothy Sue Cobble points out that American working-class feminists in the postwar period sought to achieve a balance between work and family responsibilities by limiting their hours of work (while maintaining pay levels by increasing productivity); "Rosies, Flight Girls and Waitress Moms: Working Women and Economic Justice in Post-War America," Seventh Annual Milton Derber Lecture, Institute of Labor and Industrial Relations, University of Illinois at Urbana-Champaign, April 2, 1997. Cobble's findings suggest that the same may be true for *some* women in Sweden, France, and other countries whose policies are designed to allow women to combine part-time employment and child rearing; we need more data to determine if this is so. Attitudes would probably vary according to class and to the demands and especially the rewards of specific occupations.

60. In Finland, for example, a policy of extended child home-care leave (until children reach age three) has been used to draw mothers out of the labor force; as a result, "more women in their twenties are now defined as housewives"; *Bulletin on Women and Employment in the EU* (October 1996): 5.

61. On the United States, see Kimberly Morgan, "Race and the Politics of American Child Care," paper presented at conference on Comparative Research on Welfare States and Gender," University of Wisconsin-Madison, February 2, 1997. On Australia, see Brennan, *Australian Child Care,* 5–6; on Canada, see Mahon, "'Both Wage-Earner *and* Mother.'"

62. On parallels between the United States and Britain, see Paul Pierson, *Dismantling the Welfare State? Reagan, Thatcher, and the Politics of Retrenchment* (New York: Cambridge University Press, 1994). Pierson argues that to a surprising extent both countries resisted pressures to dismantle their welfare states, and he attributes this to "the political supports that have developed around mature social programs." While concurring with him in general, I think he overestimated the protections surrounding AFDC and particularly child care (181) and thus failed to anticipate the severity of the cuts made in 1996.

63. The case of the Netherlands, by contrast, reveals the vulnerability of a conservative-corporatist regime not inoculated by pronatalism or labor shortages (if anything, over-crowding and unemployment were perceived as longstanding problems) but instead hobbled by a strong male breadwinner ideal, which made it all the more susceptible to the pressures of global competition.

64. This misuse of child care, which almost inevitably leads to stigmatization of recipients and low-quality care, is precisely what Swedish feminists sought to prevent in their debates with the bourgeois parties. See n. 16 above.

Acknowledgments

This book has been in the making for a long time, and I have incurred many debts of gratitude during the course of its gestation. The idea for studying child care originated in a seminar of James T. Patterson's at Brown University, where I first learned that social policy had a history. My interest in the field developed into a dissertation under the direction of Mari Jo Buhle, with Jim Patterson and Frances Kobrin Goldscheider as members of my committee. As I narrowed in on the topic of child care, a Hoopes Prize from Harvard University, a National Endowment for the Humanities Travel to Collections Grant, and a Summer Fellowship from the Library Company of Philadelphia/Historical Society of Pennsylvania enabled me to gather material from archives in Minneapolis and Philadelphia. With the support of a Spencer Foundation Fellowship, I spent the year 1989–90 at the Bunting Institute, Radcliffe College, where I completed a first draft.

Grants from the Research Board of the University of Illinois at Urbana-Champaign provided research assistance and release time to aid in the writing. A Fulbright Fellowship to Sweden in the spring and summer of 1994 gave me an opportunity to study the justly celebrated child care system of that country as well as others in Scandinavia, and I had the benefit of a fellowship at the Shelby Cullom Davis Center at Princeton University in 1995–96. The topic of that year's seminar, "Business, Enterprise and Culture," drew my attention to the significance of employer-supported child care in the United States. Portions of the final chapters were written as part of a consultancy to the Pew Charitable Trusts in the summer of 1996. I am grateful to my colleagues in the Department of History at the University of Illinois at Urbana-Champaign for releasing me from teaching and other responsibilities so that I could devote uninterrupted time to this project.

Portions of chapter 2 previously appeared in Sonya Michel, "The Limits of Maternalism: Policies toward American Wage-Earning Women in the Progressive Era," in *Mothers of a New World: Maternalist Politics and the Origins of Welfare States,* ed. Seth Koven and Sonya Michel (New York: Routledge, 1993), 277–320. Portions of chapter 7 appeared in Sonya Michel, "A Tale of Two States: Race, Gender, and Public/Private Welfare Provision in Postwar America," *Yale Journal of Law and Feminism* 9, no. 1 (Fall 1997): 123–56; in Sonya Michel, "The Politics of Child Care in America's Public/Private Welfare State," in *Families in the U.S.: Kinship and Domestic Politics,* ed. Karen V. Hansen and Anita Ilta Garey (Philadelphia: Temple University Press, 1998), 837–48; and in Sonya Michel, "Childcare and Welfare (In)Justice," *Feminist Studies* 24, no. 1 (Spring 1998): 44–54.

My research would not have been possible without the resources of many libraries and archives and the guidance of their archivists. It began, as has so much U.S. women's history, at the Schlesinger Library, Radcliffe College, where Barbara Haber and Eva Moseley provided invaluable assistance. David Klaassen, the curator of the Social Welfare History Archives at the University of Minnesota, and the late David Miller, curator of the Urban Archives at Temple University, pointed me toward numerous sources that proved to be important elements of my story. The staffs of the Historical Society of Pennsylvania and the Library Company of Philadelphia were unfailingly helpful, and the Interlibrary Loan offices at the University of Illinois and Princeton University Libraries put essential but obscure sources at my fingertips.

Throughout my research, friends and family helped make the life of this itinerant scholar more comfortable. I thank Frances Gouda and Gary Price, Ian and Margo Michel, Seth and Joan Koven, Sara Evans, and Barbara Hobson for their hospitality.

Several colleagues have read all or parts of the manuscript, in some instances more than once. I have benefited greatly from the suggestions of fellow historians Barbara Bergmann, Eileen Boris, Frances Gouda, Dirk Hartog, Barbara Hobson, Olwen Hufton, Felicia Kornbluh, Seth Koven, Mark Leff, Robyn Muncy, Susan Porter, Leslie Reagan, Emilie Stolzfus, and Lynn Weiner. The conceptualization of this study gained from conversations with colleagues in other disciplines, including Cynthia Daniels, Nancy Fraser, Margaret Higonnet, Janet Lyon, Barbara Mooney, Kimberly Morgan, Carol Neely, Ann Orloff, Sonya Rose, Susan Suleiman, and Lucie White. Jet Bussemaker, Sheldon Garon, Jane Jenson, Rianne Mahon, and George Ross offered important comparative insights based on their work on child care in other societies. Victoria Pope helped me to see contemporary child care from a journalist's perspective.

I wish to thank Elisa Miller for her able research assistance, Regina Felix for imaginative suggestions about the jacket design, Katherine Bullard for assistance in indexing, and the staff of the Women's Studies Program at the University of Illinois for bearing with me as the manuscript went through the final hectic stages of preparation.

Charles Grench, editor in chief at Yale University Press, has supported me throughout this long process; I am grateful for his patience and for his faith in this project. My manuscript editor, Jenya Weinreb, has improved the manuscript with her firm yet thoughtful editing.

Special appreciation is reserved for Frances Gouda and Seth Koven, whose warm friendship, good humor, intellectual stimulation, and unfailing support over the years have meant a great deal to me.

I would also like to acknowledge the skilled and warm attention devoted to my daughter, Nadja, by various care providers: Anne Allison; the staff of the Peabody Terrace Children's Center in Cambridge, Massachusetts; and the After-School Program at the Leal School in Urbana, Illinois. Knowing that she was being nurtured so well made it possible for me to go about my work during her early childhood years. These people and programs have been in the back of my mind as I conducted my research, and in many ways they serve as models for the kinds of child care I would like to see made available to every mother and child in the United States.

Finally, my thanks go to my family, immediate and extended, for standing by me throughout the writing of this book. Nadja has long since left child care and become a skilled babysitter (among her many other talents). My son Colin has assumed responsibility for apprising me of the latest cultural developments and generally keeping me in touch with the real world (New York). My son Joshua and his wife, Claire, have produced (without my even asking) two wonderful grandchildren, Sydney and Caleb, who present a welcome distraction from my research while reminding me of why it is so important. Jeffrey Herf, my husband, has, I think, finally come to accept the fact that I must work in my own way and at my own pace. His love and faith are precious to me, all the more so because I know I haven't always made it easy.

Index